1500
FASCINATING
FACTS

1500
FASCINATING
FACTS

Simon Goodenough
with additional text by
Tim Dowley
Michael March
Janet Sachs
Suzie Siddons

DEAN

First published in Great Britain in 1983 by
Octopus Books Limited

This edition first published in 1992 by
Dean,
part of Reed International Books Ltd.,
Michelin House, 81 Fulham Road,
London SW3 6RB

ISBN 0 603 55074 6

Printed in Czechoslovakia

50426/11

CONTENTS

Space

Mercury is the smallest of the planets and the nearest to the Sun.

Mercury has a diameter of 4880 kilometres (3032 miles) and circles the Sun in a highly elliptical orbit. The orbit ranges from about 46 million kilometres (29 million miles) to more than 69 million kilometres (43 million miles). Mercury takes 87.97 Earth days to circle the Sun but it revolves on its own axis so that a 'day' on Mercury lasts more than 58 Earth days.

Venus is about twice as far from the Sun as Mercury and more than twice as large.

Venus is 108 million kilometres (67 million miles) from the Sun. With a diameter of a little more than 12,000 kilometres (7456 miles) it is only slightly smaller than the Earth. It takes 243 Earth days to spin on its axis and nearly 225 Earth days to circle the Sun, so that a 'day' on Venus is longer than an Earth year. Venus can often be seen as a bright 'star' in the night sky.

Mars is the last of what are known as the 'inner' planets.

Mars is sometimes called the 'red planet'. It has a diameter of nearly 6790 kilometres (4219 miles) and is 228 million kilometres (141 million miles) from the Sun. Mars circles the Sun once every 687 Earth days and has a 'day' only a few minutes longer than an Earth day – 24 hours, 37 minutes and 23 seconds. There are seasons on Mars, as we can see by the advancing and receding ice caps.

Mercury

Venus

Earth

Mars

Jupiter

Saturn is 1,427 million kilometres (886 million miles) from the Sun, almost twice as far again as Jupiter.

Saturn has a diameter of approximately 119,000 kilometres (74,000 miles). It takes 29.5 Earth years to complete one orbit of the Sun, although it appears to rotate almost as fast as Jupiter. It is the farthest planet visible to the naked eye and the last one that was known to the ancient astronomers.

Pluto was discovered in 1930.

Pluto has a diameter of approximately 6000 kilometres (3728 miles), about half that of the Earth. Its orbit averages 5900 million kilometres (3666 million miles) from the Sun but varies to such an extent that at one point it comes closer to the Sun than Neptune. It is so far away that it is still difficult to observe Pluto accurately.

Jupiter is the first of the 'outer' planets.

Jupiter is 778 million kilometres (483 million miles) from the Sun, almost three times the distance from the Sun as Mars. With a diameter of approximately 143,000 kilometres (89,000 miles) it is more than eleven times bigger than Earth. Its surface layers spin round once in every nine hours and 50 minutes but it takes 11.9 years to orbit the Sun.

Neptune is only slightly smaller than Uranus and nearly 4500 million kilometres (2796 million miles) from the Sun.

Neptune rotates once every 15 hours or so, and takes nearly 165 Earth years to orbit the Sun, almost twice as long as Uranus. Neptune was discovered in 1846. It will not return to the position in which it was first discovered until the year 2011.

Uranus was discovered by William Herschel with a telescope in 1781.

Uranus is 2870 million kilometres (1783 million miles) from the Sun, twice as far again as Saturn It revolves on its axis in just under eleven hours and takes just over 84 Earth years to orbit the Sun. The tilt of the 'equator' is such that each 'pole' has in turn a 42-year winter followed by a 42-year summer. Uranus has a diameter of approximately 52,000 kilometres (32,000 miles), about four times the size of Earth.

The diameter of Earth is approximately 12,750 kilometres (7922 miles).

The Earth is 150 million kilometres (93 million miles) from the Sun. Its own planet, the Moon, has a diameter of 3476 kilometres (2160 miles) which makes it about three-quarters the size of Mercury.

This diagram shows the planets of our system and their relative sizes. As you can see, Jupiter is the largest of all the planets, followed by Saturn, Uranus, Neptune, the Earth, Venus, Mars, Pluto and Mercury the smallest. Many of the planets have their own small moons revolving around them, just like the Earth's moon. Two of Jupiter's moons, called Ganymede and Callisto are larger than Mercury. Jupiter has at least eleven other moons or satellites and more may yet be discovered.
Saturn has ten satellites but is more famous for the beautiful rings that surround it. These rings are only a few kilometres thick and are made up of small chunks of ice and rocky material. Scientists used to think that only Jupiter had rings but it was recently discovered that Uranus, too, had a system of rings. Our knowledge of the planets has greatly increased, and as space probes become more sophisticated, we will probably find out more about the planets in years to come.

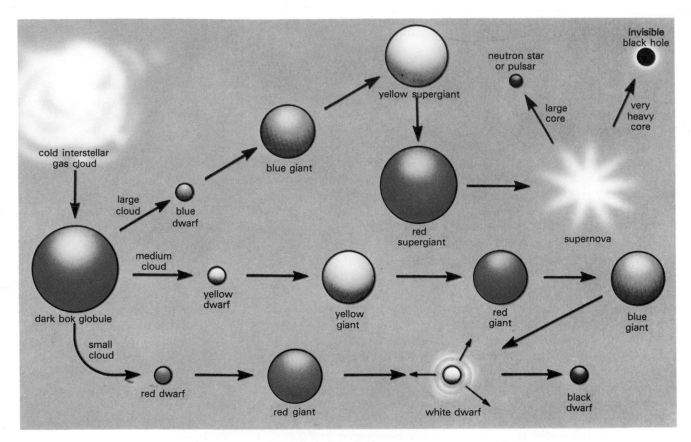

The colours of the stars depend mainly on the age and mass of the star. Many stars in the sky look white to us, but they are not.

The stars give out light of different colours

There are many different types of star and all the stars are at many different stages of development. Their colour tells us a great deal about them. This chart shows how certain types of stars have probably developed from clouds of interstellar gas. Ordinary small stars are red, larger ones are yellow and still larger ones are blue. Sometimes they start to give off more light than apparently they should and they grow into red, yellow and blue giants. Sometimes these grow even larger and may change colour and become supergiants, 10,000 times as bright as the Sun. White dwarfs are caused by shrinking after their nuclear activity has ceased; in time they may become cold, black dwarfs. Supernovae are exploded stars which may condense to black holes or become neutron stars or pulsars.

Longitude and latitude in space are used to fix a star's position

The Greeks worked out a system to describe a star's position in the sky which is very much like the system of longitude and latitude used on Earth. The latitude, or 'angle of declination' as it is known, is the number of degrees the star is north or south of the celestial equator. The longitude, or 'right ascension' as it is known, is the number of degrees the star is to one side of an imaginary north-south line in the sky, rather like the Greenwich Meridian of 0° on Earth. Lines of longitude or right ascension are drawn at 24 'hourly' intervals, or in 24 lots of 15°, from this line to match the Earth's 24-hour rotation. Because the Earth wobbles on its axis the equinoxes are not at the same time every year. When an astronomer refers to a star's position he must give the year of the celestial co-ordinates.

The 'first point of Aries' has moved to Pisces

The most important imaginary line of longitude in the sky is the prime meridian, from which the angle of right ascension is taken. This line was fixed at the point at which the path of the Sun crosses the celestial equator at the beginning of spring in the northern hemisphere. This is the time when day and night are the same length and so it is called the spring or 'vernal' equinox (equinox means 'equal night'). The prime meridian is the line drawn north and south from this point. When the Greeks established this system 2000 years ago, the spring equinox lay in the constellation of Aries and so the meridian is still sometimes known as the 'first point of Aries'. However, because of the slight wobble of the Earth's axis, the spring equinox is at a slightly different time each year and moves, or 'precesses', in a complete circle once in 26,000 years. The spring equinox (and therefore the prime meridian) is now in the constellation of Pisces.

There is no South Pole star, as there is a North Pole star

Polaris, or the North Pole star, is almost exactly over the North Pole and provides an important guide for navigators. But in the southern hemisphere the best reference point is Crux, the Southern Cross, which can be seen to point towards the South Pole, from a distance. The Milky Way appears in the southern hemisphere, just as it does in the northern hemisphere. Two objects outside our galaxy are visible with the naked eye in the southern hemisphere. These are the Larger and Smaller Magellanic Clouds, which are both irregular galaxies.

Below: *The diagram on the right shows the position of the sun at the vernal equinox as fixed by the Greeks. Because of the Earth's wobble, the equinox has changed as shown on the diagram at the left to the constellation Pisces.*

The last supernova in our galaxy occurred in 1604

When a supernova occurs, it flings into space all the chemical elements it once possessed in a desperate bid to keep shining. Carbon, oxygen, nitrogen, neon, silicon, magnesium, iron and even heavier elements created in the holocaust itself drift and swirl among the gases destined to give birth to young stars and their planets. Among them are the chemicals which are the seed of life itself. We owe our existence, not to water, nor oxygen, nor to our ideal place in the solar system, but to the fact that millions of years ago an exploding star impregnated gas atmosphere and spread life-producing minerals and water. We do not know how many times supernovae have occurred but scientists believe that another spectacular star death will happen in our lifetime. When it does happen, it will be quite spectacular as the gas that a supernova ejects travels at up to 10,000 km (6,000 miles) per second. They are reckoned to occur once or twice each century.

The Earth is in the Milky Way galaxy

A galaxy is a collection of millions of stars which is held together by gravity. The galaxy in which the Earth, all the planets and the sun belong is called the Milky Way. Astronomers believe that there are 100,000 million stars in the Milky Way.

Distance in space is measured by light years

Because the universe is so large and distances are so great, measurements in miles would be meaningless. Scientists measure distances between the stars in light years. A light year is the distance a beam of light travels in one year and is equivalent to 9,460,000 million kilometres (5,912,500 million miles). The Milky Way is estimated to be 100,000 light years in diameter. If we had to write that out it would be 946,000,000,000,000,000 kilometres. So it is easier to say 100,000 light years than to try to say the actual distance.

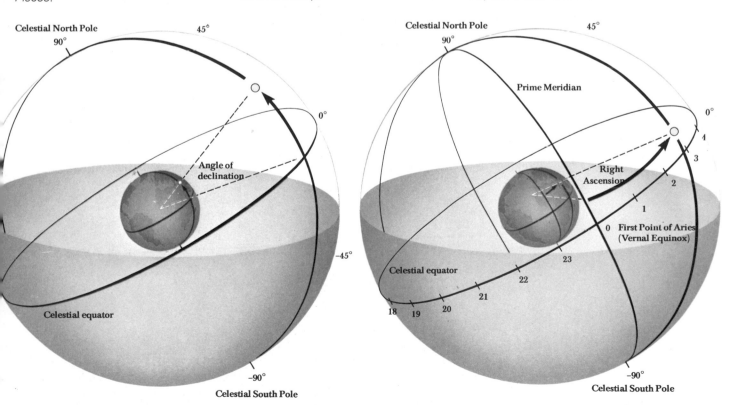

After the first Moon landing, the astronauts were put in quarantine

The three astronauts from *Apollo II* (Armstrong, Aldrin and Collins) returned from the first landing on the Moon in July 1969. They were put in quarantine for 17 days, together with all the Moon rocks that they had brought back with them, for fear of 'Moon germs'. Since no germs were found, material from subsequent Moon landings has been released to waiting scientists immediately it has been brought down.

Below: *This diagram shows the path that the space rocket carrying Neil Armstrong, Aldrin and Collins took in their successful moon landing in Apollo II in 1969.*

Future space programmes include the setting up of space colonies

Longer visits to the Moon will be made by the end of this century and there will probably be landings on Mars shortly after the year 2000. More ambitious projects include solar power satellites which will beam the Sun's energy down to Earth from outside the blanket of the atmosphere. There is also a vast space telescope planned which would be free of the restrictive and distorting effects of the Earth's gravity. This telescope might be able to pick out individual planets around nearby stars. The greatest project of all is to create space colonies, vast spaceships where as many as 10,000 people might live. The colonies would largely be made of materials from the Moon.

Strange experiments are carried out to discover what goes on inside the Sun

We still do not know exactly what goes on inside the Sun. The illustration *(right)* shows the core, from which radiation leaks out until it is blocked by the surrounding convective gases. These circulate like boiling oil, releasing the star's heat to the surface. To discover more about the Sun, scientists have been trying to study more carefully the neutrinos (neutral particles with zero mass) that fly out through the surrounding gas into space. One and a half kilometres down in a disused goldmine in South Dakota, shielded from all normal cosmic radiation, there is a huge tank. This contains several hundred thousand litres of dry-cleaning fluid which has been

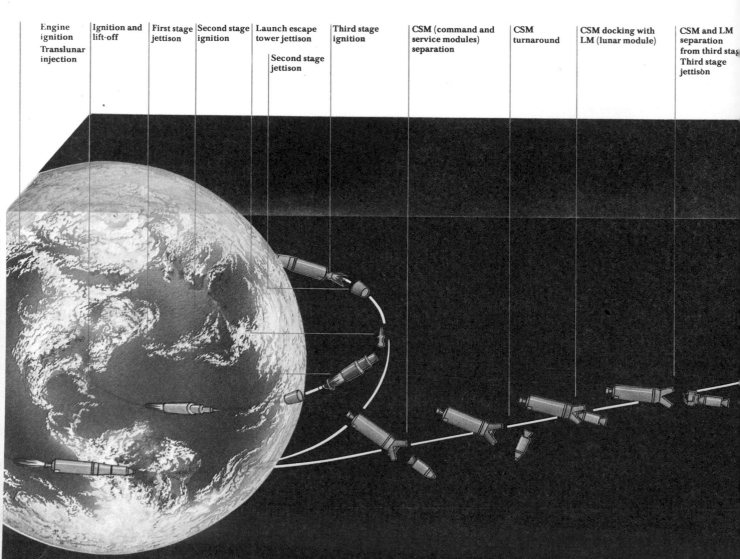

| Engine ignition Translunar injection | Ignition and lift-off | First stage jettison | Second stage ignition | Launch escape tower jettison Second stage jettison | Third stage ignition | CSM (command and service modules) separation | CSM turnaround | CSM docking with LM (lunar module) | CSM and LM separation from third stage Third stage jettison |

used to trap neutrinos. Chlorine in the fluid reacts with the neutrinos and produces the gas argon, so that it is possible to identify the number of neutrinos emitted by the Sun. From this, scientists hope to be able to discover more about the Sun.

Right: *A cut-away diagram of the inside of the sun showing the layers of gases. In the core, hydrogen fuses into helium at huge temperatures. The heat radiates through the radioactive zone and is then carried by convection to the surface where the temperature is 5500°c.*

The sun has a diameter of 1,392,000 kilometres (865,000 miles). Our sun is an average star — some stars have surface temperatures of up to 40,000° C while others are as cool as 3,000° C.

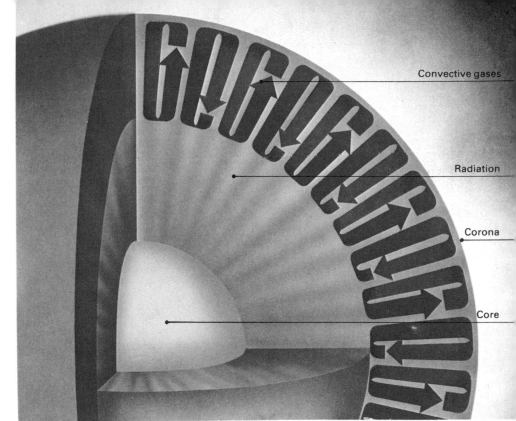

Convective gases

Radiation

Corona

Core

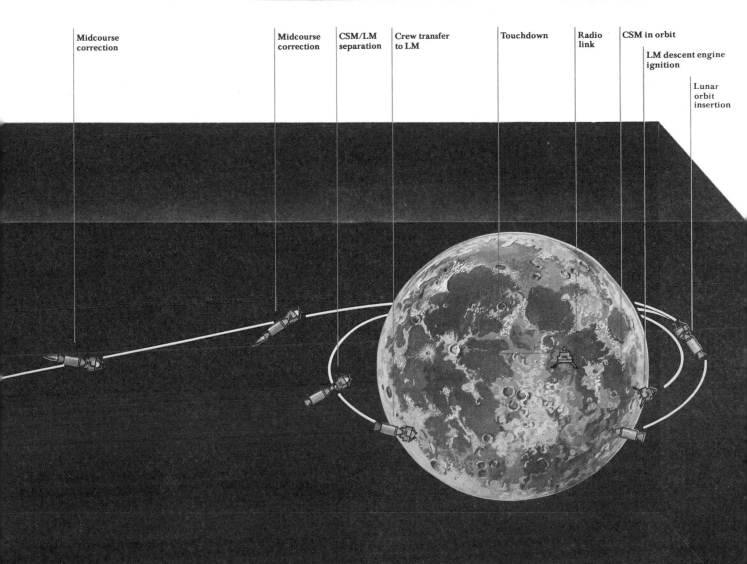

Midcourse correction

Midcourse correction

CSM/LM separation

Crew transfer to LM

Touchdown

Radio link

CSM in orbit

LM descent engine ignition

Lunar orbit insertion

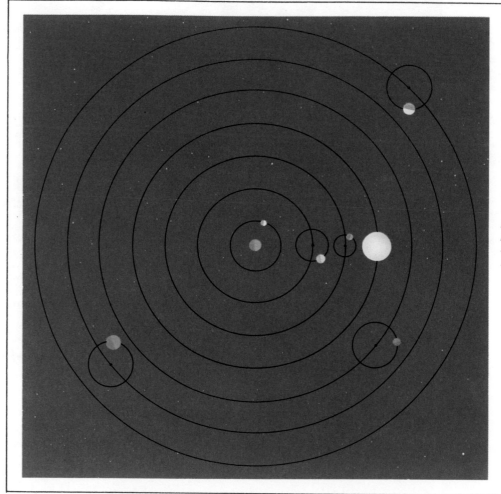

Until the 16th century models of the universe always showed the Earth at the centre, with the sun and the other planets revolving around it. In 1543, Nicolaus Copernicus, published his theory that the sun was at the centre and the planets revolved around it in perfect circles. The Roman Church refused to accept this, even when it was confirmed by Galileo. Later, Johannes Kepler suggested that the planets did not move in perfect circles, but in ellipses, and this is what we know to be true today.

There was a time when people believed that the Earth was the centre of the Universe

Some early Greek philosophers and astronomers suggested that the Earth might circle the Sun but their ideas were largely ignored. Throughout the Middle Ages the Church encouraged the view that everything in the Universe went round the Earth. Astronomical charts showed the Earth at the centre, then the Moon, then Venus, Mercury, the Sun, Mars, Jupiter and Saturn, which were the only planets visible to the naked eye. It was not until 1543 that Nicolaus Copernicus once again suggested that the Earth went round the Sun. His book on the subject was condemned and banned by the Church. A century later, Galileo started using the telescope to look more closely at the stars and planets. He confirmed what Copernicus had said, but the Church still refused to accept his theory.

Sputnik was the first artificial satellite in space

In Russian, the word *sputnik* literally means 'a travelling companion'. The Soviet Union launched the first artificial Earth satellite on 4 October, 1957, and they called it *Sputnik 1*. In November 1957, *Sputnik 2* had a real, live 'companion' – the dog Laika.

Galileo borrowed the idea of the telescope from a Dutchman

It has often been thought that the great astronomer Galileo invented the telescope but this is now believed to be wrong. A Dutch spectacle-maker called Hans Lippershey made the discovery accidentally in 1608 when he held up two lenses to the light, one behind the other. Galileo, in Italy, heard of the invention and improved it. He was the first astronomer to use the telescope to make observations of the Moon, the planets and the stars.

Aerosol sprays may be destroying our atmosphere

Some scientists believe that the increasing use of aerosol sprays, such as deodorants, glue, and many others used every day all around the world, may be slowly destroying the atmosphere. This is because the tiny particles do not dissolve in the air but rise up and up into the atmosphere where they may be acting like a greenhouse, allowing heat from the sun to enter, but not escape when it gets too hot.

Manned space flights in stay orbit

The only space flights by humans operating today are orbiting the Earth. The American Space Shuttle leads the way, putting more missions into space each year than any other craft. Some of these launches carry out experiments which can only be conducted properly in zero gravity. Other journeys by the Space Shuttle are to launch or repair satellites. Satellites have many uses. They may help scientists predict the weather, or be used to beam television programmes from a transmitter to thousands of homes. Several satellites are owned by the military and are used to spy on the forces of other nations.

Future manned space flights will move beyond orbit

Spacecraft large enough to carry humans are very expensive. However, American space scientists are planning a journey to Mars. The flight will take many weeks to complete. Because of the technical problems which need to be solved, the flight may not take place for several years.

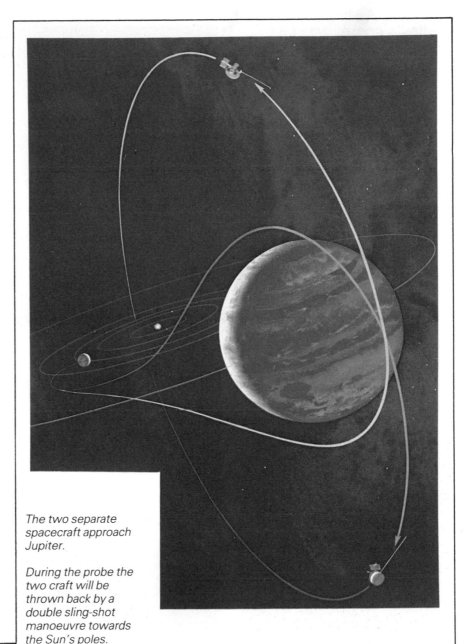

The two separate spacecraft approach Jupiter.

During the probe the two craft will be thrown back by a double sling-shot manoeuvre towards the Sun's poles.

Space probes investigate the planets and the sun

Small uncrewed space probes packed with scientific instruments are currently investigating the furthest reaches of the Solar System. One mission which began in 1988 is made up of two probes which will circuit Jupiter before heading for the Sun to investigate the super-hot solar poles. When their missions are finished, probes continue beyond the Solar System into deep space.

Halley's comet was last seen in 1986

Halley's Comet has a 76-year cycle and was last sighted passing the Sun in 1986. It provided a useful opportunity to study what comets are made of and possibly to find out more about origins of the Solar System. Scientists have suggested various devices for getting an even closer look at it from deep in space. The vast sail of the 'Yankee Clipper' would use the pressure of sunlight to sail in formation with the comet. The Heliogyro would have 12 enormously long sails, extending more than seven kilometres (4 miles), and would look rather like a giant asterisk. This, too, would use the pressure of sunlight. Scoop-shaped panels could catch sunlight to power an ion-drive rocket to keep the space probe in line.

Above: 'Yankee Clipper'. Below and below left: *The Heliogyro.*

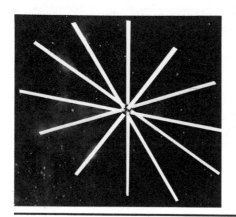

Some of the stars you can see in the sky may have disappeared centuries ago

The nearest star is called Proxima Centauri and it is in the southern hemisphere. It is about 42 billion kilometres (26 billion miles) away. Such a distance is almost impossible to imagine. Light from the nearest star takes more than 4.25 years to reach us, with light travelling at 299,000 kilometres (186,000 miles) a second. We say that the star is 4.25 light years away. This means that when you look at the star you are seeing it as it was 4.25 years ago, when the light left it. The nearest star in the northern hemisphere, Sirius, is eight light years away. Even the light from the Sun takes eight minutes to reach Earth. The light from some of the stars that can be seen through powerful telescopes has been travelling for thousands of millions of years. Probably some of those stars have already ceased to exist.

When you look at the night sky some stars appear much brighter than others. This is often because they are larger and hotter stars. However some stars, such as Sirius, only appear bright because they are so close.

Stars also appear to form patterns in the sky. Ancient astronomers knew some of these groups and gave them names, such as Orion's Belt and Gemini, the twins. By learning the shapes of the constellations you will be able to find your way about the map of the sky at night. Astronomers still use the ancient names when discussing distant stars and galaxies. The Greek astronomer Ptolemy knew of about 48 constellations in the 2nd century AD and we have named about 40 more since then. One of the best-known in the northern hemisphere is the Plough, also known as the Big Dipper or the Great Bear (Ursa Major). Two of its stars point in a direct line towards the Pole Star.

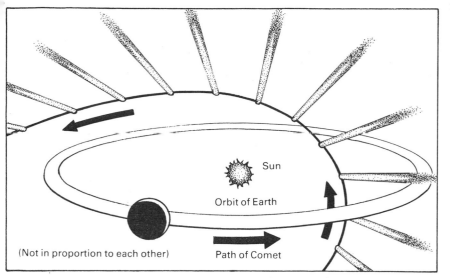

Sun

Orbit of Earth

(Not in proportion to each other)   Path of Comet

Comets fly in orbits

Comets can sometimes be seen at night with the naked eye. They usually appear as a bright head, consisting of gases, rock particles and dust, with a long, spectacular tail. This gaseous tail is only formed as the comet nears the Sun and the gases are blown back by the Sun's radiation. As the comet passes the Sun and starts to move away, the tail moves round and flies ahead of the comet, blown forward this time instead of back. There are probably thousands of millions of comets in orbit round the Sun beyond the planet Pluto. We see only the few whose elliptical orbits bring them near the Sun. Encke, for example, appears every 3.5 years in its orbit. Halley's Comet appears every 76 years and is next due in about 2062. It was named after Edmund Halley in 1682, but was recorded in the Bayeux Tapestry in the 11th century and first noted more than 2200 years ago as an omen of ill fortune.

Space shots are looking for life in the stars

Earth seems to be the only planet with life on it in our system, but some people believe that as there are so many stars in the universe life must exist on some of them. The American Pioneer space probes each carry a plaque giving information about the Earth, and voyager probes carry gramophone records of human speech, as well as photographs. We also send radio messages into space, and if another civilisation was trying to contact us by radio, astronomers are always listening for them with radio telescopes. If any of our messages were picked up, an instant reply from the nearest stars would take nine years to reach us. Space is so big that messages received and replied to could take 600 years to reach the Earth. Despite this, many people sincerely believe that beings from other planets have visited Earth. They must have very advanced technologies to have done this.

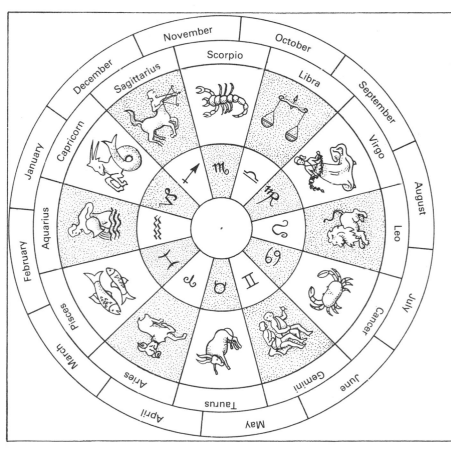

There are 12 signs of the Zodiac

The zodiac is an imaginary band in the sky – the path of the Sun against the background of the stars as the Earth circles the Sun during the course of the year. The constellations of stars that lie along this band are known as the constellations of the zodiac. Ever since Babylonian times many people have believed that their lives are influenced by the particular constellation through which the Sun moved at the time of their birth. The word 'zodiac' comes from an old Greek word for 'animals', because many of the constellation signs are animals. The constellations are Capricorn (goat), Aquarius (water-carrier), Pisces (fish), Aries (ram), Taurus (bull), Gemini (twins), Cancer (crab), Leo (lion), Virgo (virgin), Libra (balance), Scorpio (scorpion) and Sagittarius (archer).

Prehistoric Times

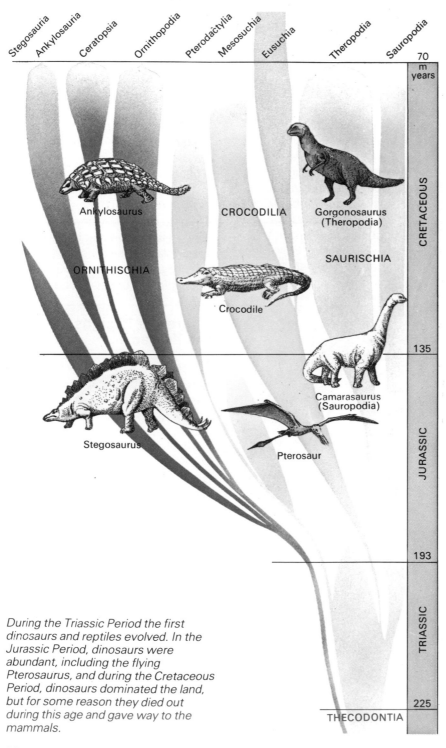

Stegosauria · Ankylosauria · Ceratopsia · Ornithopodia · Pterodactylia · Mesosuchia · Eusuchia · Theropodia · Sauropodia

70 m years

CRETACEOUS

135

JURASSIC

193

TRIASSIC

225

Ankylosaurus

CROCODILIA

Gorgonosaurus (Theropodia)

SAURISCHIA

ORNITHISCHIA

Crocodile

Camarasaurus (Sauropodia)

Stegosaurus

Pterosaur

THECODONTIA

During the Triassic Period the first dinosaurs and reptiles evolved. In the Jurassic Period, dinosaurs were abundant, including the flying Pterosaurus, and during the Cretaceous Period, dinosaurs dominated the land, but for some reason they died out during this age and gave way to the mammals.

Animal life on land evolved through various stages

The first land plants appeared more than 400 million years ago. No insects or animals could have lived on the land until the plants were there to provide food and shelter. Amphibians and insects appeared next. They increased greatly during the Carboniferous period, when there were great forests of plants over much of the land. Many of these plants are preserved as coal. By about 300 million years ago, the reptiles had developed from the amphibians. The great age of the reptiles and dinosaurs was between 250 and 80 million years ago. Small mammals existed during much of this time but did not begin to develop properly until after

When plants and animals began to live on land they had to change in several ways

The very first plants and animals lived in water. Both plants and animals had to change in certain ways to survive on land. The plants developed strong, woody stems to support themselves without the help of water, and the animals developed legs. Both developed a tough outer skin to stop their bodies drying out on land. Plants and animals also had to find new ways to reproduce. Many plants adopted various ways of pollination

Two great dinosaurs – Tyrannosaurus rex (meaning King Giant Lizard) was 5½ metres (18 feet) high, and Triceratops with its bony shield to cover its vulnerable neck.

and many animals developed internal fertilisation. Animals also needed internal lungs, instead of gills, for breathing air.

The dinosaurs disappeared from Earth mysteriously

Dinosaurs of many different kinds lived successfully for about 140 million years and then, within a relatively short period of time, they disappeared completely from the Earth. There have been various theories as to why this happened. The most likely reason is a change of climate. Cold weather replaced the warm, moist weather to which the dinosaurs were accustomed. They had no fur or feathers to protect them from the cold and many of the plants they fed on also died out. The dinosaurs died out about 60-65 million years ago.

Brachiosaurus and *Diplodocus* were the greatest of the dinosaurs

Brachiosaurus was the largest of all the dinosaurs. Its name means 'arm lizard' and it refers to the huge forelegs of *Brachiosaurus*, which were even bigger than its back legs. *Brachiosaurus* stood about 12 metres (39 feet) tall and was about 24 metres (79 feet) long. *Diplodocus* was about 27 metres (88 feet) long, but not so large, and its front legs were smaller than its back legs. It was called *Diplodocus*, or 'double beam', because its neck and tail stretched out like two long beams, or poles, at either end of its body. Both these giants grazed on plants and trees.

There is a reptile with a third 'eye'

The tuatara is a reptile that looks like a lizard and lives in New Zealand. It is covered in scales and has a scaly crest down its neck and back. Its name, in Maori, means 'spiny'. The tuatara is very rare, the last survivor of a prehistoric order of creatures with beak-like heads, the Rhynchocephalia. The strangest feature of the tuatara appears in the young during the first six months of their life. It is the remains of what looks like a third eye, now covered by skin. Scientists are not sure whether this really was an eye, nor do they know exactly how it might have been used.

Corythosaurus – a duck-billed dinosaur.

Life may have begun in a chemical 'soup'

One theory about the beginning of life on Earth suggests that it may have begun spontaneously, without outside interference. Ultra-violet rays bombarding the methane and ammonia in the atmosphere broke these down into hydrogen, nitrogen and carbon atoms. Much of the hydrogen escaped, leaving nitrogen and carbon dioxide. Plants used the carbon to build their tissues and gave out oxygen as waste matter. This oxygen enabled animal life to develop. In 1953, Dr Stanley Miller of Chicago simulated the original conditions. He passed water vapour through a mixture of methane, ammonia and hydrogen. Then he passed an electric current through the mixture until it condensed into a liquid. In the liquid he found the basic elements of life: the amino-acids out of which protein molecules are formed. He imagined that these proteins would eventually form living cells.

The Earth was a molten mass 4,600 million years ago

Some people believe the Earth was formed from a mass of dust and hot solar gases. Some believe that it condensed from a cloud of solid particles. In either case, it went through an immensely hot phase about 4,600 million years ago, when it became a molten mass with temperatures of about 4000°C (7232°F). As this boiling mass swirled round in space, the heaviest elements such as iron and nickel sank to the centre. A mantle or solid crust of islands began to form as the Earth cooled to about 1000°C (1832°F). Clouds of gases formed in the atmosphere, consisting of methane, ammonia and water vapour, until they, too, cooled and the water vapour condensed into rain. This rain fell for thousands of years. It formed seas together with water that was trapped in the rocks and released as vapour through volcanoes.

Life may have come from outer space

An alternative theory about the origin of life suggests that tiny cellular structures of simple, single-celled plants were brought to Earth on meteorites from outer space. These cells then populated the Earth. There is some evidence for this theory. Signs of primitive fossilised 'sponges', with short spines like algae, have been found embedded in meteorites.

Below: *An artist's impression of what life looked like millions of years ago. The land was bare rock, weathered by rain and heat. The sea was less salty than today and contained amino-acids which began all life on earth.*

Four facts about the Earth's atmosphere

The Earth's atmosphere protects us from harmful radiation

The Earth's atmosphere is like a blanket that protects the surface from much of the harmful radiation from space. The atmosphere may be divided into four main zones, of which the highest is the exosphere. This rises from about 640 kilometres (398 miles) above the surface of the earth and merges the ionosphere with interplanetary space. Helium and hydrogen are the main elements.

The ionosphere reflects radio waves

The ionosphere has an enormous range, from 80 to 640km (50-398 miles) above the Earth's surface. The few molecules of gas in the ionosphere are widely spread out. Solar radiation ionizes particles in the ionosphere (hence the name). This causes those layers in which the particles are more densely clustered to act as reflectors of radio waves. There are two such layers, at approximately 110 and 240 kilometres (68 and 149 miles) above the Earth. The temperature increases with altitude in this zone and therefore it is sometimes known as the thermosphere.

The stratosphere lies between the ionosphere and the troposphere

The stratosphere absorbs much of the harmful ultra-violet radiation from the Sun. The ultra-violet radiation changes oxygen into ozone, which provides a form of 'lid' to the weather system below and gives its name to the 'ozone layer' at about 35-40 kilometres (22-25 miles) above the Earth. The stratosphere itself ranges from about 18-80 kilometres (11-50 miles) above the Earth, although the area from between 50 and 80 kilometres (31-50 miles) is often known as the mesosphere. The air is still quite thin in the stratosphere and atmospheric pressure at 30

kilometres (18 miles) above the Earth is only one per cent of what it is at sea level. Airliners, or 'strato-cruisers', take advantage of the relatively low resistance and the steady winds which sometimes blow at about 300km/h (186 mph).

The troposphere is the zone which helps to create the Earth's weather

The troposphere ranges from the surface of the Earth to about 18 kilometres (11 miles). It is a very unstable layer and responds to the temperature and moisture content of the Earth's surface, creating our weather. Pressure and temperature decrease towards the top of the troposphere. Atmospheric pressure at the top of Everest, nearly nine kilometres (five miles) above sea level, is less than a third of what it is at the bottom. Only radio waves, visible light and some ultra-violet rays penetrate through the troposphere.

The top layer is the exosphere which extends upwards from about 640 km. (400 miles) merging with the interplanetary medium. It consists largely of diffuse hydrogen and helium.

The next layer is the ionosphere, which spans the region from 80 km. (50 miles) to 640 km. (400 miles), is an electrically conducting region. Here the atoms and molecules have had their electrons removed by solar radiation.

In the stratosphere (second bottom layer) ultraviolet radiation from the Sun converts oxygen into ozone, thus absorbing harmful radiation. This reaction raises the temperature of the stratosphere to about 0°C., acting as a 'lid' on the weather systems of the troposphere below.

The troposphere (bottom layer) extends from the surface up to about 16 km. (10 miles). This unstable region, subject as it is to the differences in temperature and moisture content of the Earth's surface, is responsible for almost all the Earth's weather. Only radio waves, visible light and a few ultraviolet rays penetrate to this level.

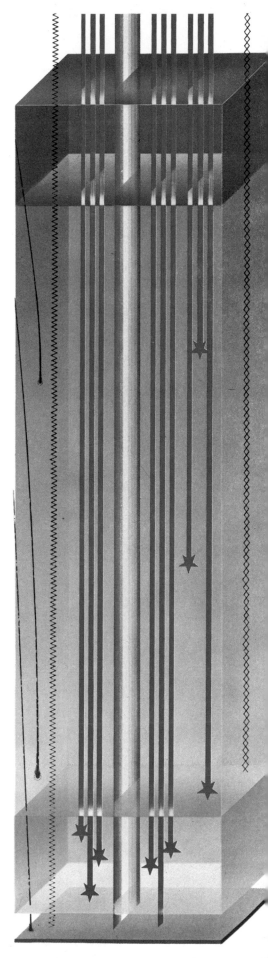

There was life in the ocean before the first fish evolved

Life in the ocean developed greatly during the 200 million years between the Cambrian and the Silurian periods (400-600 million years ago). Jellyfish, tubular sponges, bivalve molluscs and sea lilies, or crinoids, were already present in Cambrian times and are still found today. Trilobites were very common and many of their fossils can be found quite easily. They died out about 300 million years ago. Hard-shelled ancestors of the squid and octopus existed during the Ordovician period, about 500 million years ago, by which time there were many corals and brachiopods with hinged shells. There were also giant sea-scorpions. The first great armoured fish had appeared by the beginning of the Silurian period, about 440 million years ago.

The first animals on the land came from the sea

The illustration on these pages shows a scene from the Carboniferous period which began 345 million years ago. The habitat came about because great earthquakes created mountains out of what had previously been sea-bed. Many animals which had lived in the sea were found to adapt to this new, half-water, half-land environment. Before this, large invertebrates like the huge dragonfly were in possession of the land. The dragonflies had a wingspan of up to 70 centimetres (27.5 inches). The animal shown half-in and half-out of the water is a Crossopterygcan which is similar to the ancestors of today's land quadrupeds. All the trees are primitive ferns, club mosses and horsetails. We know quite a lot about prehistoric times because of the evidence that fossils give us. Fossils are the remains or impressions of animal or plant life preserved in the Earth's crust. People who study fossils are called palaeontologists.

The names of many dinosaurs can tell us what they looked like

Just as Tyrannosaurus rex means 'king of the tyrant lizards' and gives us some idea what it looked like, so the names of other dinosaurs tell us something about them. For example, Ornithischian means 'bird-hipped', Pterosaur means 'winged lizard', Sauropad means 'reptile foot', Stegosaurus 'roof lizard', Triceratops 'three-horned face', and so on. Using fossilized bones and other evidence, many museums have reconstructed models of dinosaurs which give us a good idea of how awesomely large many of them must have been.

Most of the Earth's area is covered by water

The five oceans of the world - the Pacific, Atlantic, Antarctic, Arctic and Indian - between them cover more than 71 per cent of the Earth's surface. The largest, the Pacific, has an area of 181,000,000 square kilometres (70,000,000 square miles).

Ocean tides are caused by the Moon

As the moon moves around the Earth, its gravitational pull attracts the water of the oceans. When the Moon is above a certain point of the ocean it tends to pull the water at that point away from the Earth and this causes a high tide. The moon also pulls the Earth away from the water at the other side of the Earth and this also causes a high tide. In between the two tides are low tides where the water has been pulled away. The amount that the tides rise and fall varies from place to place. The greatest tidal range is about 15 metres (50 feet) which occurs at the Bay of Fundy, in Eastern Canada. In France there is a large tidal range at the mouth of the River Rance and scientists have designed a special power station which harnesses the power of the tides. This is one way in which scientists are trying to tap new resources of power to help the world after fossil fuels run out.

The trees in this artist's impression of the Carboniferous period are all primitive ferns, horsetails and club mosses. The tall ones (right) are cordaits. Club mosses are seen at the left of the picture. The marshy habitat of this time was the result of geological upheavals which created folded mountain ranges in areas that had been under the sea previously. Some aquatic animals were stranded in this new habitat and gradually evolved into new species. The fish shown half in and half out of the water is similar to the one that gradually became the ancestor of the land quadrupeds. The amphibian is an early forefather of crocodiles and alligators. Even as long ago as this, there were ants living in the forests – perhaps after man has gone from the earth, the ants will still be there.

The World

Rocks built up in layers provide a record of past geological events

Many rocks consist of layers which were laid down over a vast period of time. Most of these rocks were formed in river deltas, particularly during the Carboniferous Period. By studying these rocks we can trace the events which gave rise to each layer. A layer of shale is formed first from mud brought down by the river. Then comes a layer of sandstone formed from coarser material that overlays the mud. Plants grow beside the delta and fall into the mud to form a layer of coal. Slowly the delta advances and more mud is brought down by the river and the cycle starts over again. Sometimes the sea flows back up the delta, leaving a layer of limestone full of marine fossils.

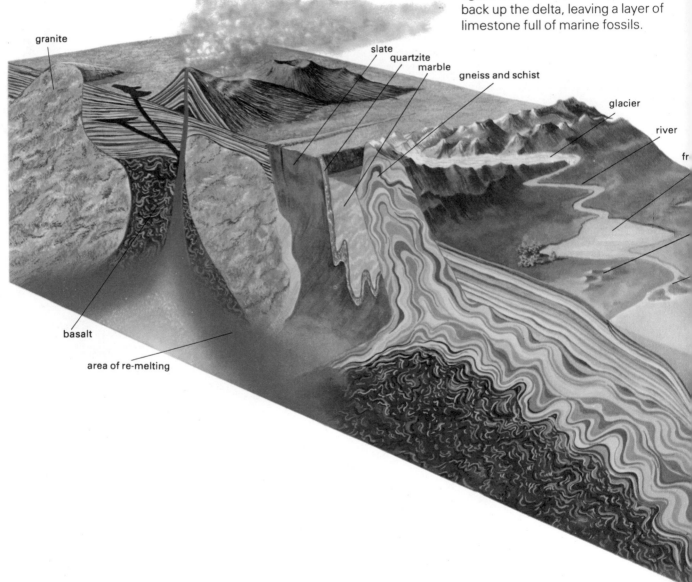

granite

slate
quartzite
marble

gneiss and schist

glacier

river

fr

basalt

area of re-melting

Sedimentary rocks are made up of various bits and pieces, from the 'sediment' of rocks, chemicals and skeletons

Examples of sedimentary rocks are, sandstone that comes from particles of rocks that have been eroded; gypsum that comes from particles of chemicals in sea water; and chalk that comes from the skeletons of once-living creatures and plants. The sediments are buried and compressed by later deposits; they are also bound together by minerals from the water that seeps through them. Sedimentary rocks are usually formed in layers, or beds, and often contain fossils.

Below: *A cut away diagram showing the various kinds of rocks and where they are found in the earth's crust.*

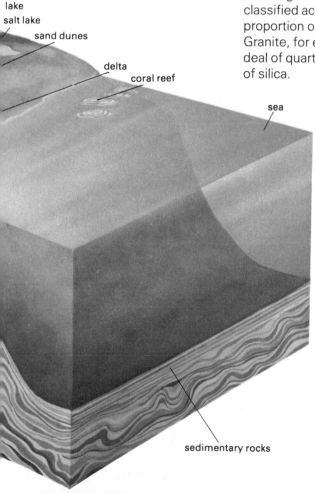

lake
salt lake
sand dunes
delta
coral reef
sea
sedimentary rocks

Metamorphic rocks are igneous or sedimentary rocks that have been changed by heat or pressure

Rocks that have been changed by pressure are more common than those that have been changed by heat. Metamorphic rocks are often found in mountain ranges, where the original rock has been forced upward and contorted. Slate is a metamorphic rock. Marble is a metamorphic rock that comes from limestone, a sedimentary rock.

The most important types of rock are igneous rocks

These have formed from molten material (magma) that has come up from within the Earth and cooled on the surface. Different kinds of rock may be formed from the same magma, either by absorbing different minerals or by cooling at different speeds, producing varieties of coarse or fine-grained rocks. Igneous rocks are often classified according to the proportion of silica within them. Granite, for example, with a great deal of quartz, has a high proportion of silica.

Rocks can tell us much about lakes and rivers of the distant past

Sedimentary rocks often contain ripple patterns formed by the motion of waves in what were once shallow lakes. Areas that were muddy millions of years ago may also have left permanent cracks as the mud turned to rock. Ancient river beds may reveal themselves in sedimentary rocks that still show the S-bends formed by the river currents. These are all clues to the geography of the past.

Mountains are formed in several ways

Some mountains are built up as volcanoes. Molten rock is pushed up through a weak point in the earth's crust and cools on the surface as lava. Many islands in the Atlantic and Pacific Oceans are the tops of extinct underwater volcanoes. Other mountains are built up when a section of the earth's crust folds. This means that underground forces push areas of land together and cause mountains to rise. Such mountains are called fold mountains. Another way is when great blocks of the earth's surfaces move. Some blocks are lifted up, others are sunk. These movements cause flat-topped mountains and flat bottomed valleys. A fourth way is due to pressure beneath forcing the surface up in blister-like mounds. These are called dome mountains.

Mercury is a liquid metal

Mercury, or quicksilver, is a metal that is liquid at normal temperatures. It must be cooled to −39°C (−38°F) before it becomes solid. Mercury is found in combination with other substances in the ground which have to be refined before the mercury can be extracted. Mercury has some useful and peculiar characteristics. In its liquid form, it can be poured out of a jug and yet leave the inside of the jug completely dry. It expands when it is heated, which is why it is used in thermometers.

Above: *An early mercury thermometer.* Right: *Early thermometers were cumbersome.*

The biggest gold nugget in the world weighed as much as a grown man

Gold has been considered the most precious metal for the last four or five thousand years. It glitters, can be easily shaped and never perishes or tarnishes. It is quite difficult to extract, even though it exists in great quantities in rocks and as tiny grains in river beds and the sea. In a goldmine, about 28 grams (1 ounce) of gold is obtained from every five tonnes of rock. Sometimes an enormous nugget of gold is found. The biggest pure gold nugget was found in Australia in 1869. It weighed more than 68 kilograms (150 pounds). Most gold now comes from South Africa but some of the greatest gold rushes have been in California (1848-49), in Australia (1851), in South Africa (1886) and in the Yukon (1896).

Nickel was named after a goblin

Nickel is a whitish-coloured, very hard metal. It is obtained from rock and is used mainly for mixing with steel to strengthen the steel for industrial use. Cupronickel is a mixture between copper and nickel. It does not rust easily and is used for coins and, with zinc added, for nickel or 'silver' plating. The name nickel comes from the German *Kupfernickel*, which means 'Nickel's copper'. Nickel was supposed to be a goblin who lived in German copper mines. He was responsible for mischievously creating the metal (nickel) that looked like copper but was not really copper.

Precious stones can stand for passion, faithfulness and freedom

Since ancient times, certain precious stones have always been connected with certain months of the year, although there are one or two different versions of which stone is connected with which month. A person born in a particular month, therefore, has a particular birthstone, just as they have their own sign of the zodiac. The stones are also connected with certain characteristics, so you benefit from the characteristics of your birthstone. For example, garnet of January gives faithfulness; the topaz of November also gives faithfulness and friendship; the amethyst of February stops violent passions and the emerald of May promises that your love will be true.

Chemists of the past tried to change lead into gold

Chemistry began with the Greeks and Egyptians at Alexandria in the 3rd and 4th centuries AD. Just like modern chemists, they were interested in combining chemicals and recording their effects on certain minerals. But their main purpose was to win everlasting riches by changing 'base' metals, such as lead, into silver and gold. The search for this source of wealth was taken up by alchemists in the Middle Ages. Many pretended that they had found the secret. No one ever did.

Water can be used to crack rocks in half

When water freezes, it expands. This is because ice is less dense than water and therefore the same weight of ice takes up more room than a similar weight of water. Expanding ice has such great strength that it can burst water-pipes in the home, and car radiators as well. It can also cause cracks in rocks and, over the centuries, split off whole boulders. In ancient times, this strength was sometimes used in stone quarries to break off boulders.

Hardness scale	Mineral	Test
10	Diamond	will scratch glass
9	Corundum	
8	Topaz, Beryl, Zircon	
7	Quartz, Garnet, Tourmaline	
6	Feldspar, Turquoise, Rutile, Celsian	can be scratched with steel knife
5	Apatite, Bornite	
4	Fluorite, Malachite, Azurite	can be powdered by scratching with coin
3	Calcite, Argonite, Barytes	
2	Gypsum, Salt,	can be scratched with fingernail
1	Talc, Aluminite	

Minerals can be identified in three different ways

Rocks are made up of minerals in different proportions. A mineral within a rock can be identified by three different tests: by its hardness, by the colour of the mark left when it is scratched against a hard white surface, and by the way it splits or breaks up. The diagram on the left shows the comparative hardness of some minerals on a scale of 10, with diamond as the hardest. The middle diagram shows how different minerals make different-coloured marks. The right-hand diagram shows one way in which a mineral splits into layers. The comparative hardness scale was formulated by Möhl and is named after him. It is used to test the hardness of new compounds.

Amber is not a stone, but is formed from pine resin

Most precious stones are minerals. But there are some, such as pearl, amber, coral and jet, that come from animals or plants. Amber comes from pine trees that lived millions of years ago, mostly around the Baltic. It is formed by drops of resin from the pine that have hardened and turned to transparent golden 'stones'. Many prehistoric insects that were caught in drops of the resin have been preserved intact inside lumps of amber. The Romans valued amber for jewellery. They also believed that its powers could cure and used it as a charm against witches. The Greeks found that amber would attract certain objects to itself if it were rubbed. They called it *elektron*, from which we get our word 'electricity'.

Centuries ago, a fly became trapped in some sticky resin and was unable to escape. As the resin hardened into amber, the fly was surrounded by it for ever.

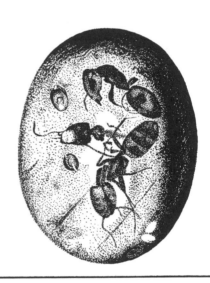

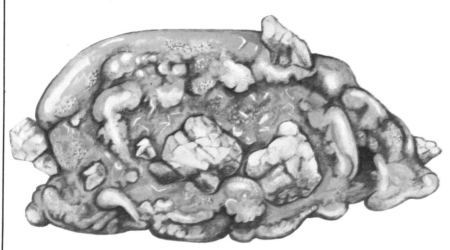

Above: *Quartz crystals surrounded by gold.*

Gem stones are formed from slowly cooling igneous rock

There are many different forms of igneous rock, from heavy basalt to light pumice. Whether the rock has cooled quickly or slowly, above or below ground, helps to shape these differences. When igneous rock has cooled slowly, some of the mineral forms regularly shaped crystals. These are gem stones such as diamond, sapphire, emerald, ruby, garnet, jade, opal, quartz, topaz, turquoise, zircon and many others. Igneous rock also contains metallic ores, such as gold, silver and tin.

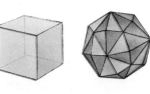

Cubic: minimum symmetry four 3-fold axes. Examples are fluorite, garnet and diamond.

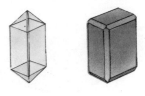

Tetragonal: minimum symmetry one 4-fold axis. Examples are zircon, calomel and wulfenite.

Orthorhombic: minimum symmetry three 2-fold axes. Examples are barytes, alexandrite and olivine.

Monoclinic: minimum symmetry one 2-fold axis. Examples are malachite, orthoclase and moonstone.

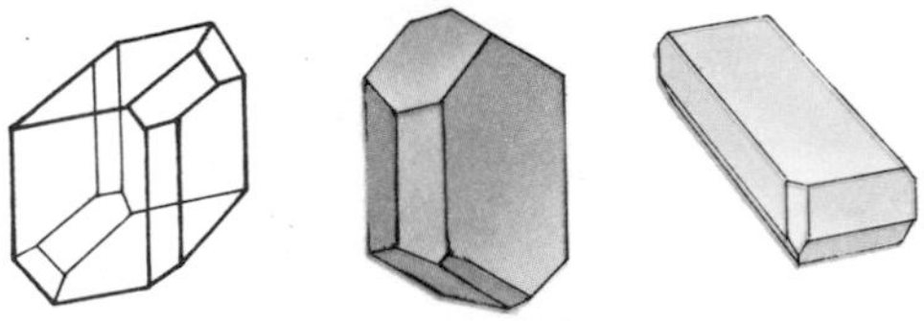

Triclinic: minimum symmetry none. Examples are sunstone, turquoise and chalcanthite.

Hexagonal: minimum symmetry one 6-fold axis. Examples are emerald, zincite and apalite.

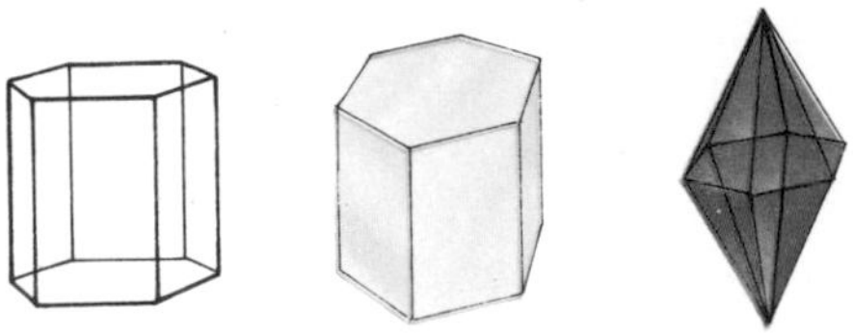

Trigonal: minimum symmetry one 3-fold axis. Examples are calcite, rose, quartz and tourmaline.

Minerals split in remarkable and beautiful shapes

The marvellous shapes shown in the diagram are produced by certain minerals when they split. There are seven basic groups of shape shown here. In each group, we give the mathematically descriptive name of the shape and some examples of the minerals in that group. The groups range from the cubic structure of garnet and diamond to the trigonal structure of calcite.

The most common metal in the world has been in use for only 100 years

There is more aluminium than any other metal in the Earth's crust. In fact, nearly eight per cent of the Earth's crust is made of aluminium. However, aluminium is found only in combination with other substances in the rocks. About 100 years ago a cheap way was at last found to separate the metal from these substances by using a powerful electric current. Aluminium is extremely useful because it is strong and light (about one-third the weight of iron) and it does not rust. It is also a good conductor of heat. We use it for cooking equipment as well as aircraft and motor car engines.

Copper turns green as a means of self-protection

Copper is very pink when it is first mined. It turns red when it is exposed to air and then, gradually, it turns green. This change on the surface protects the copper beneath from further corrosion. The green colour can sometimes be seen on the copper domes of churches. Copper was probably the first metal to be known and mined by man, after gold. It not only had an attractive shine but it could be shaped into a variety of useful and attractive objects. One of the earliest places in which copper was found was Cyprus. The Greek word for Cyprus is Kypros, and hence copper got its name.

Asbestos is a fire-resistant mineral

Asbestos is the general name for a group of minerals found in rocks. These minerals consist of soft fibres that can be spun and woven into a cloth-like felt. Its most important characteristic is that it can stand very high temperatures without burning. In ancient times, lamp wicks made of asbestos were probably used in temples, so that they kept burning for a long time. Now, asbestos is used for fire-fighting protection and to shield machine parts that might cause fires by their friction or heat. Asbestos dust can be dangerous to the health of workers, so they must wear masks when handling the material.

The ruby is the most precious of all precious stones

The old saying goes that 'diamonds are a girl's best friend' and it is certainly true that diamonds are often sold at auctions for huge sums of money, but the most valuable uncut stone is the ruby. This is because most rubies are from Sri Lanka and Burma and supplies dwindled after 1955. Diamonds, however, are found in South Africa and are not as uncommon there, as rubies.

Gold was used for coins as early as the 7th century BC

Gold has always played an important part in history. Throughout the ages the very thought of gold created visions of riches and power. As we have already seen, early scientists tried to change base metals into gold. Gold was one of the first metals that man discovered and the oldest surviving gold decorative objects come from the early Stone Age and we know that gold coins were in circulation in the 7th century BC. Gold was one of the gifts that were given to the infant Christ by the three kings and right up until the early part of the twentieth century most countries measured their currencies against their reserves of gold. Until recently more than half of the world's gold was mined in South Africa's Transvaal and there are also vast deposits in Russia.

A famous diamond is cursed

In the Smithsonean Institute in Washington there is a diamond called the Hope Diamond. Many who have owned it have died mysteriously. 500 years ago a Hindu priest stole it from the forehead of an Indian temple idol. He was put to death for this crime. It fell into the possession of a Frenchman, Jean Baptiste Talfernier, who was eventually torn to death by a pack of wild dogs. The diamond then fell into the hands of the French royal family. The Princess de Lamballe was beaten to death by a mob. Marie Antoinette went to the guillotine. The next owner, Jacques Celot, went insane and killed himself. Its Russian owner, Prince Kanitovski gave it to his mistress, then murdered her. It was later bought by Henry Thomas Hope,

Metals are often mixed with others to produce harder alloys

When silver and copper are found in igneous rocks, they sometimes have the appearance of fronds of seaweed or leaves. Gold is found with quartz crystals in lumps. Gold is a soft metal and can be shaped easily. The Aztec sacrificial knife shown here would not have been very sharp. Copper is also soft and is usually mixed with zinc to form brass, or with tin to form bronze. Silver is sometimes mixed with copper to form an alloy that is harder and stronger than pure silver.

A new ice age could be caused by man's carelessness

There have been several Ice Ages in the world's history, caused by the ice of the Arctic spreading south and the ice of the Antarctic spreading north. The last Ice Age finished about 11,000 years ago, but it is quite possible that we might have another Ice Age in the future. No one knows exactly why the ice caps begin to expand. It may be that cycles of volcanic activity throw off layers of dust into the atmosphere. This blocks off the sun's warmth and causes a drop in the world's temperature. Some people believe that the dust particles produced by man-made industry could have the same result. They say that the world is already getting colder. Others say that the dust would in fact stop the sun's heat from being reflected back out of the atmosphere and that this would cause the ice to melt and to flood the world!

If all the glaciers melted, London, New York and Paris would be drowned

Glaciers are formed when excess snow in the mountains does not melt in the summer. As more snow falls on top of it, the old snow turns into a solid mass whose sheer weight causes it to flow slowly down to the sea, like a great river, carving out valleys as it goes. Some of the most spectacular glaciers in the world are in Alaska. Russia also has a vast amount of glaciers. Some are about three kilometres (two miles) thick and most move at about five centimetres (two inches) a day. The glacier in the Yukon was once seen moving about half a metre (two feet) an hour. There is so much frozen water caught up in the glaciers that if they all melted at the same time they would raise the level of all the oceans in the world by about 61 metres (200 feet), drowning many coastal and low-lying cities.

Snow is sometimes red or green

Snowflakes are made up of ice crystals formed from frozen water vapour in the atmosphere. The snow appears white because of the light reflected from the tiny faces of each beautifully shaped crystal. But sometimes the snowflakes pass through layers of coloured dust or fungi floating in the air. The snow collects these particles and brings them down to earth. Dust and fungi can colour the snow red, green, black and many other colours. In the same way, rain clouds can often collect dust in the atmosphere and carry it thousands of kilometres to drop it in a coloured rainshower over a different continent.

Rain nowadays contains elements that can cause death

Men and women could not exist on this planet if it was not for rain. Rain fills up our streams and reservoirs and helps flowers and plants to grow. These flowers and plants produce oxygen which is essential for all life. However, in recent years, chemical pollutants are becoming more and more common. These are sucked up into the atmosphere and fall back down to earth as acid contained in raindrops and other forms of precipitation. Northern Sweden is particularly exposed to acid rain. This is because the prevailing winds blow the chemicals north, from the industrialised parts of Europe. By the time it has moisturized, the deadly rain is over northern Sweden.

There was once human hailstones

In 1930 a German glider pilot who baled out of his 'plane, was carried upwards into a region of super-cooled vapour where he became the nucleus of a huge hailstone. As he fell, he unfroze, his parachute opened and he survived.

The North and South Poles have almost no clouds

Clouds are formed by evaporation of surface water into the atmosphere and by condensation of that water in the atmosphere. The sun draws this water into the air, from the land, from vegetation and from seas, but because the sun is weaker at the Poles than anywhere else on Earth, the little heat that does reach the Poles is reflected directly back again by the white surface. This means that the land never gets hot enough to cause much evaporation and with little evaporation there can be few clouds.

Sea breezes change direction morning and evening

During the day the air above the earth warms up more quickly than the air above the sea. The cold air above the sea is heavier and is drawn towards the warm air which causes a wind to blow from the sea towards the land. In the evening the wind changes direction and goes from the land to the sea. This is because the land cools more quickly than the sea, and the air above it becomes cooler than the air above the sea, causing a movement of air from the land outwards. This is one reason why fishermen in sail boats fish at night. The evening breeze blows them out to sea and the morning breeze blows them safely back home.

Italian farmers use rockets to prevent hailstorms

In Italy, hailstorms can be so severe that whole crops can be damaged and in some cases completely ruined. When the farmers see the clouds of a hailstorm approaching they fire rockets into the clouds to try to shatter the hailstones before they fall down to earth; in one case 50,000 rockets were fired into a potential storm. They had the desired effect.

No two snowflakes are ever the same

Despite the countless numbers of snowstorms that must have occurred since man first appeared on earth, and the countless millions of snowflakes that fall each time, no two snowflakes that fall are ever identical. Snowflakes are formed by the crystalisation of water vapour in the atmosphere into beautiful geometric forms, and the shape depends on the temperature of the air. In the cold high atmosphere where water vapour is scarce, simple needle and rod shapes are formed, and in the lower altitudes where the air temperature is warmer, much more complex and beautiful, hexagonally-shaped crystals are formed. The snowflakes form when the crystals fall into warm, low atmospheres, where they melt together into the beautiful snowflakes that we see falling during a snowstorm. Because of all the elements of chance involved, it is unlikely that two identical snowflakes have ever fallen.

Snow can speak

The sound that snow makes when it is trampled underfoot, tells a listener what the temperature is. If a footstep makes a deep crunch in the snow, then the temperature of the snow is slightly less than 0°C (32°F). If the sound is unpleasantly high like a badly played violin, then the snow's temperature is –5°C (5°F). As it gets even colder, the sound increases in pitch.

Icebergs from Antarctica are usually larger than those from the Arctic

Icebergs are huge chunks of ice that break off, or calve, from glaciers or from the ice shelf in spring and early summer. Icebergs from the Arctic drift south and meet the warmer waters of the Pacific or the North Atlantic and the Gulf Stream. They may be anything up to 1600 metres (one mile) long and about 61 metres (200 feet) high on the surface. They can be up to nine times that bulk below the water. Despite this vast size, the warm waters make them melt and break up. In the south, icebergs may be much larger, and melt much more slowly because of the cold currents that prevail in the oceans that surround Antarctica.

Below top: *Antarctic icebergs are larger and flatter than Arctic icebergs (left).* Bottom: *Icebergs are formed when huge chunks of ice break off from the glaciers. As you can see, the part seen above water is only a small fraction of what is underneath.*

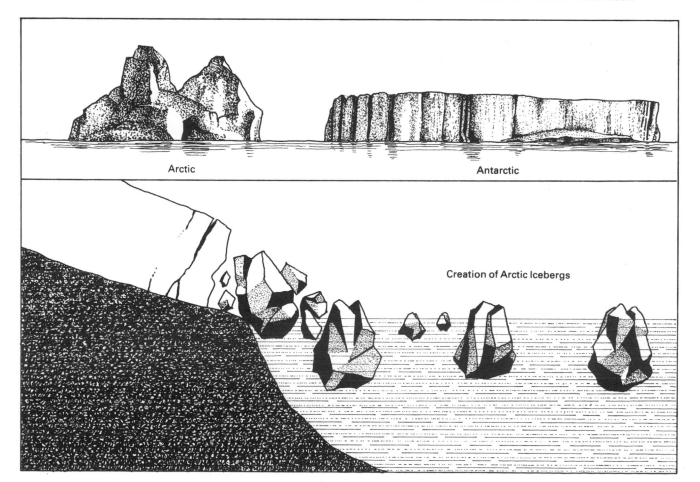

Arctic

Antarctic

Creation of Arctic Icebergs

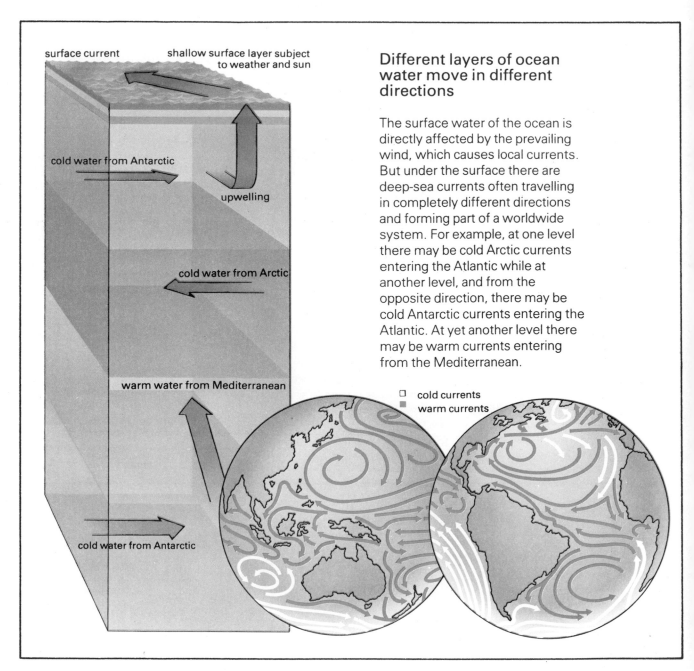

surface current

shallow surface layer subject to weather and sun

cold water from Antarctic

upwelling

cold water from Arctic

warm water from Mediterranean

cold water from Antarctic

Different layers of ocean water move in different directions

The surface water of the ocean is directly affected by the prevailing wind, which causes local currents. But under the surface there are deep-sea currents often travelling in completely different directions and forming part of a worldwide system. For example, at one level there may be cold Arctic currents entering the Atlantic while at another level, and from the opposite direction, there may be cold Antarctic currents entering the Atlantic. At yet another level there may be warm currents entering from the Mediterranean.

☐ cold currents
■ warm currents

The continents we live on are slowly moving

In about 1912 a German scientist, Alfred Wegener, suggested that the continents had once fitted together in a single great land mass. By looking at a map of the world it is still possible to see how the continents might fit together like giant jigsaw pieces. Later scientific exploration confirmed that this was probably true. The continental land masses, as well as the ocean floors, rest on a few great plates of rock, up to 96 kilometres (60 miles) thick, that float on a sea of molten rock

beneath. These plates are still moving at a rate of about 1.3 to 15 centimetres (0.5-6 inches) each year.

The longest mountain range in the world is under water

The Mid-Atlantic Ridge is a mountain range that curves down between Europe and Africa on one side and the Americas on the other side. It has a total length of about 16,093 kilometres (10,000 miles), making it the longest mountain range in the world. The average

height of its mountains is about 3048 metres (10,000 feet), although most of the peaks are about 1.6 kilometres (1 mile) below the surface.

Sailors once believed that ships could become stuck fast in the Sargasso Sea

In the middle of the North Atlantic currents there is an area of calm, the Sargasso Sea. Large amounts of sargassum weed float in these waters and sailors used to believe that their ships would be trapped by the weed.

Nature furnishes man's vital needs by recycling water

The hydrologic, or water cycle circulates the waters in nature, continuously changing them from one state to another. The path of this complex cycle, which has no beginning and no end, may stretch to a height of 15 kilometres (9 miles) above the Earth's surface, or reach to a depth of 1 kilometre (0.62 miles) beneath the Earth's crust. In simple terms, what happens is that water in the oceans and on land evaporates, rises into the atmosphere and is finally returned to Earth as snow or rainfall. The latter part of the cycle is known as the precipitation process. Water that percolates down through the soil is stored naturally underground and will eventually return to the sea, by way of streams, to be evaporated once more. Worldwide, the total amount of water in the hydrological cycle remains the same, but the distribution of the water will vary with time of year and climate. Since water is vital to man's survival attempts have been made to harness the hydrological cycle, including the storage of water in reservoirs behind dams. This is particularly important for countries where a rainy season may be followed by a prolonged drought.

Tides on Earth are affected by the Sun and Moon

Ocean tides are caused largely by the effects of gravitational forces exerted by the Sun and Moon acting on the Earth. The force will vary in relation to the distance between any point on the Earth and the centre of the attracting body, in this case the Sun or Moon. Thus the closer together they are the greater will be the attractive force, the further apart the weaker it will be. This is all according to Newton's laws. Obviously, the distance between any point on the Earth and the centre of, say, the Moon will be changing all the time. Also, at any one time some points will be closer to the Moon, and so more influenced by gravitation, than others. It is the variation in the gravitational forces acting upon the oceans, rather than the direct force itself, that produce tides. In general, the effect of the Moon on our tides is the greater because it is very much closer to us - 390 times nearer than the Sun, in fact. This is despite the Sun's far greater mass. Tides thus tend to follow the 'lunar day' of 24 hours and 50 minutes, with high tide occurring regularly twice a day. In some places, the difference in height between high and low tide may be less than half a metre (or as little as a foot) or, in the Bay of Fundy in Canada, as much as 15 metres (50 feet). Port Adelaide in Australia is one of the few places in the world where the solar tide is dominant and high waters occur at 12-hourly intervals. Today, scientists are trying to harness tide power to supply electricity.

Ocean water contains many elements

Strangely enough, ocean water is one of the purest natural substances. It consists of approximately 96.5 per cent water. Nearly 2.9 per cent of the remainder consists of sodium and chlorine, which together form salt. This is washed down into the oceans from the rivers. Since the salt always remains dissolved in the water and never disappears, the oceans are steadily becoming saltier. There is also approximately 0.3 per cent sulphate and 0.1 per cent magnesium in ocean water. In the remaining fraction of a percentage, almost every other element is present in some proportion or other, including such metals as gold, silver, lead, mercury, copper and uranium.

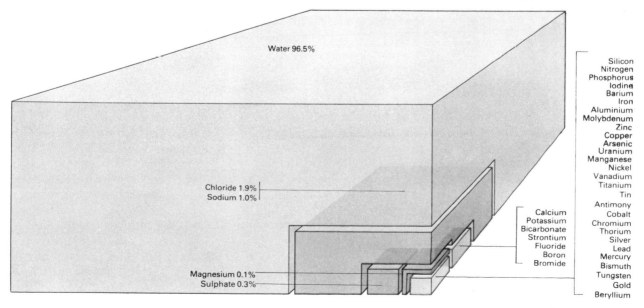

Water 96.5%

Chloride 1.9%
Sodium 1.0%

Magnesium 0.1%
Sulphate 0.3%

Calcium
Potassium
Bicarbonate
Strontium
Fluoride
Boron
Bromide

Silicon
Nitrogen
Phosphorus
Iodine
Barium
Iron
Aluminium
Molybdenum
Zinc
Copper
Arsenic
Uranium
Manganese
Nickel
Vanadium
Titanium
Tin
Antimony
Cobalt
Chromium
Thorium
Silver
Lead
Mercury
Bismuth
Tungsten
Gold
Beryllium

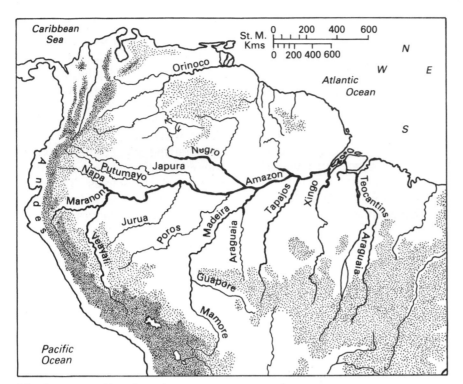

The Amazon and its tributaries.

There is fresh water in the Atlantic, out of sight of land

Spaniards sailing across the Atlantic, in the early days of the explorers, discovered a flow of fresh water when there was still no land in sight. They followed the flow back to its source and found themselves at the mouth of the River Amazon. The Amazon is the largest river in the world by volume and by the area of its drainage basin. The waters of the Amazon can be detected flowing more than 161 kilometres (100 miles) out to sea. The Amazon carries one-fifth of all the fresh water that drains down the rivers of the world, and it drains two-fifths of South America. It runs more than 6437 kilometres (4000 miles) from its source in the Peruvian mountains to the Atlantic, drawing in countless tributaries.

Rainwater may have a spectacular effect on limestone

Rain collects carbon dioxide as it falls through the air. This forms a weak solution of carbonic acid. This acid will gradually dissolve the mineral called calcite, of which limestone is largely made up. The acid gets into the cracks of the rock and hollows out caverns underground. As more water drips into the caverns it evaporates, leaving behind crystals of calcite. These accumulate to form stalactites hanging from the roof, or drip down to the floor to form stalagmites.

The world's most spectacular stalactites and stalagmites are found in the Carlsbad Caverns in New Mexico; the deepest caves, 1.6 kilometres (1 mile) in depth, are at Gouffre de la Pierre St Martin on the border of France and Spain. The Blue Grotto, on the Isle of Capri, is a sea cave that fills with sapphire-blue light when the sun shines through its waters. Waitomo Cave in New Zealand contains thousands of tiny glow worms.

The Niagara Falls are not the highest waterfall in the world

The Angel Falls, named after the man who discovered them, are hidden amongst the thick jungle of southeast Venezuela. The waterfall drops a sheer 810 metres (2650 feet) over a precipice, with a total drop in just two stages, of 980 metres (3215 feet). No other falls are as high as the Angel, and no other has such a long single drop. The Yosemite Falls in the Sierra Nevada mountains of California is the second waterfall in the world, but is 240 metres (800 feet) lower than Angel, and falls in several stages. The falls having the second longest drop is also in Venezuela, near the border with Guyana. This is Cuquenan, which plunges 610 metres (2000 feet) straight down. In comparison, the American section of the Niagara Falls drops only 51 metres (167 feet) and the Canadian Horshoe only 48 metres (157 feet). But the Niagara is still a mighty spectacle measuring 792 metres (2600 feet) across at its widest point.

The Volga is the longest river in Europe

The River Volga flows for nearly 3850 kilometres (2400 miles) from the hills to the northwest of Moscow down to the Caspian Sea. For three months of the year most of the river is frozen over. Canals link the river to Moscow itself and to the River Don, which flows into the Black Sea. There are also waterway links from the Volga to the Baltic, creating a passageway from north to south of western Russia. These are important in connecting the Volga Valley with the Russian borders. The river valley is a very fertile wheat-growing region and the centre of a large petroleum industry. The great Volga Delta, at the mouth of the Caspian Sea, is about 110 kilometres (70 miles) wide, and with the Caspian Sea makes up one of the world's great fishing grounds. Loading wharves along the Volga often need to be moved up higher because the river is constantly eating away at its banks. The Volga lies entirely within the Russian Republic.

If you sailed directly south from Iceland, you would sail for thousands of kilometres before hitting land

The Atlantic Ocean stretches all the way from within the Arctic Circle in the north down to within the Antarctic Circle in the south. If you sailed directly south from Reykjavik, the capital of Iceland which is just south of the Arctic Circle, you would pass just east of the Azores and Cape Verde Islands and just west of the Canary Islands and you would travel more than 14,400 kilometres (9000 miles) without meeting any land until you reached the Antarctic, a little to the east of the Weddell Sea.

You can read a book while floating on your back in the Dead Sea

The so-called Dead Sea is the lowest lake in the world, about 397 metres (1300 feet) below sea level. It contains the saltiest water in the world. This is because several mineral-carrying rivers and streams flow into the lake but no streams flow out of it. The surface water evaporates but all the minerals, including the salt, remain behind. The salt makes it easy for swimmers to float and because the lake contains six times more salt than ordinary sea water, a swimmer's body is buoyed up six times better than usual. The lake lies between Jordan and Israel. It has a maximum length of 82 kilometres (51 miles) and ranges between 5 kilometres (3 miles) and 18 kilometres (11 miles) in width.

The Gulf Stream is a river that flows across an ocean

The Gulf Stream is a remarkable river, at one point 80 kilometres (50 miles) wide, travelling at 8 kilometres (5 miles) an hour, with a depth of more than 450 metres (147 feet). It is created by currents which cross the Atlantic from east to west. The Gulf Stream breaks out past the southern tip of Florida and flows into the Atlantic, up the south-east coast of the United States. As it turns away from the coast, it collides with the Labrador Current from the Arctic and is deflected eastwards. It brings its warmth to the seas around western Europe and then swings south to return across the Atlantic to America in the form of the North Equatorial Current. The Gulf Stream also carries the warm northwesterly winds that help to make the climates of Great Britain and Northern Europe warmer than other places equally far north. This has important commercial consequences. Fishing ports such as Hammerfest in Norway can remain free of ice throughout the winter, while Riga, further south, is icebound in winter.

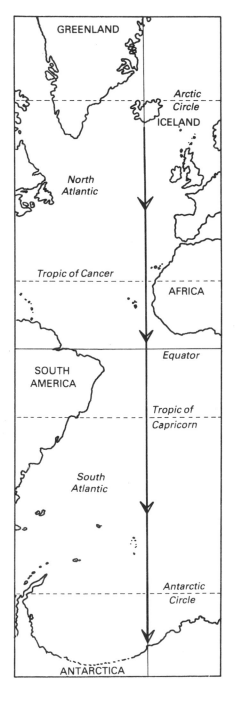

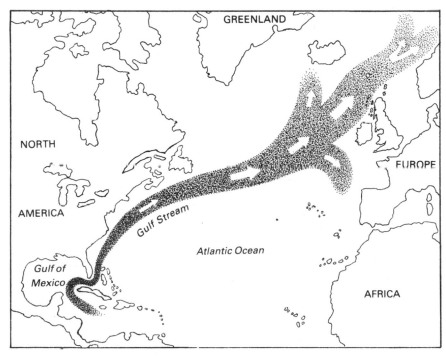

The course of the Gulf Stream.

Oil comes from the remains of living creatures

Millions of years ago, even more of the world was covered by sea than today. When sea-creatures died, they sank to the bottom, and over the centuries their bodies became covered with sandy sediment.

Over millions of years, their remains decomposed and were changed into oil and gas trapped beneath layers of rock. As the seas began to recede, the bottom of the sea gradually became dry land and that is why much of the oil we drill for today is beneath the land, and some is still beneath the ocean bed.

The Mediterranean may once have been a dry desert

Recent discoveries suggest that about six million years ago the Straits of Gibraltar became blocked, thus cutting off the Mediterranean from the Atlantic Ocean. It is thought that after this event the Mediterranean dried out. This is possible because the Sun would have evaporated the water in the Mediterranean faster than the rivers could have filled it again. Today, the Straits of Gibraltar are open to the Atlantic and the Mediterranean is constantly being topped up by water from the ocean. It is believed that the natural dam created by the blocking of the Straits held back the Atlantic for about one and a half million years. This theory arose from research carried out on the US ship *Glomar Challenger* in 1970. Scientists found rock layers beneath the Mediterranean that are only associated with dry land. The theory was given greater strength when deep river gorges were also discovered beneath the present level of the Mediterranean. This suggests that rivers had once run across the bed of the Mediterranean. How the Straits became blocked and, later, unblocked, no one knows.

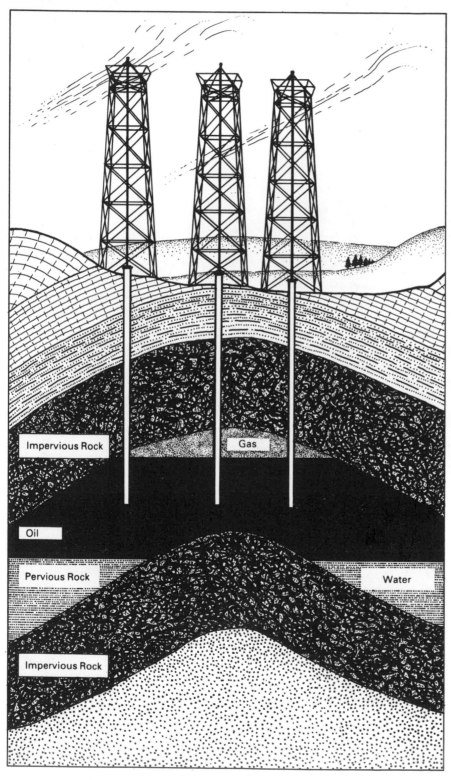

Left: *Oil drilling is one of the major industries of the twentieth century. Oil is found in many countries of the world and comes from the remains of tiny creatures who died many millions of years ago. Today, as oil becomes more and more scarce, we have had to drill deeper and deeper for it, even drilling the ocean floor to reach the oil there. The first oil-well was drilled in 1859 by an American, Willard Drake, at Titusville in Pennsylvania and his discovery led to a tremendous upsurge in drilling there. Before an oil-well is drilled, the owners must be very sure that there is oil there, as it is a tremendously costly business. The owners will spend a great deal of money on geologists' reports to confirm the presence of oil. But once it has been established that oil is there, it is a tremendously profitable undertaking.*

Labels in illustration: Impervious Rock · Gas · Oil · Pervious Rock · Water · Impervious Rock

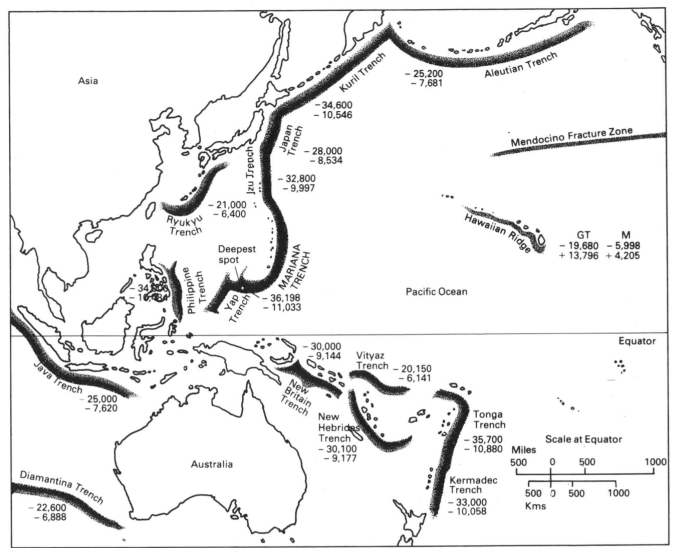

Asia

Kuril Trench
− 25,200
− 7,681

Aleutian Trench

Mendocino Fracture Zone

− 34,600
− 10,546

Japan Trench
− 28,000
− 8,534

Izu Trench
− 32,800
− 9,997

Ryukyu Trench
− 21,000
− 6,400

Hawaiian Ridge

GT   M
− 19,680 − 5,998
+ 13,796 + 4,205

Deepest spot

Philippine Trench

MARIANA TRENCH

Pacific Ocean

− 34,800
− 10,684

Yap Trench
− 36,198
− 11,033

Equator

− 30,000
− 9,144

Vityaz Trench
− 20,150
− 6,141

Java Trench
− 25,000
− 7,620

New Britain Trench

New Hebrides Trench
− 30,100
− 9,177

Tonga Trench
− 35,700
− 10,880

Australia

Scale at Equator

Miles
500   0   500   1000

500   0   500   1000
Kms

Kermadec Trench
− 33,000
− 10,058

Diamantina Trench
− 22,600
− 6,888

There are trenches under the sea which are deep enough to contain the world's highest mountains

Mount Everest, in the Himalayas, is 8848 metres (29,000 feet) above sea level. The Challenger Deep, off the Marianas Islands in the western Pacific, is more than 11,000 metres (36,089 feet) deep. Everest would disappear without a trace in this huge trench. There are several other large trenches near the Marianas, including the Japan Trench and the Kuril Trench. Others occur at points between New Zealand and Samoa along the Kermadec and Tonga Trenches. If you took a measurement from the bottom of the ocean, the tallest mountain in the world is probably Mauna Kea in Hawaii. It rises more than 4800 metres (15,748 feet) under the sea and another 4200 metres (13,779 feet) above it more than 9000 metres (29,527 feet).

Coastlines are constantly being changed by the action of seas and rivers

It is easy to see the effect of huge waves crashing day after day, year after year, on the rocks of the seashore. Headlands are worn away, while river deltas and estuaries are built up by fresh deposits. Gradually the rough edges of the coastline are worn smooth and straight. One of the most dramatic effects of the waves occurs when they attack a headland from either side and cut it off from the mainland to form a stack. Sometimes the waves eat into joints in the cliff and form caves. Blowholes are formed when the pressure of the waves builds up in a cave and blasts a hole through the roof. When the tide comes in the results are spectacular.

The Mediterranean was once a desert

Six million years ago the Mediterranean was a lake that extended from present-day Israel to Gibraltar. Six million years ago, it dried up leaving a vast desert, but then the ocean burst through the piece of land that connected Europe and Africa and the Mediterranean was created.

Not all volcanoes form high cones

Volcanoes are caused by molten magma forcing its way up through a weak spot in the Earth's crust. The magma rises through a vent and comes out as lava which builds up a cone around the vent. Lava with a little silica in it is runny and forms low, wide cones, as in Iceland. Lava with more silica in it causes more violent eruptions and forms steeper cones. The vent may become blocked by the solidifying lava. Then it either forms a neck or blows suddenly under pressure from within. When a vent is empty, the cone sometimes collapses inwards, forming a broad crater known as a caldera. Subsequent eruptions may cause a new cone to rise in the middle of the caldera. Hot springs and geysers may also form in volcanic regions.

In 1963 a new island rose out of the sea

In 1963, an underwater volcano erupted off the coast of Iceland. The water boiled, steam hissed up in great clouds and volcanic ash showered down as a new volcanic cone formed an island where before there had been only sea. The volcano continued erupting for several days. When it stopped, there was an island more than 1.6 kilometres (1 mile) long and nearly 183 metres (600 feet) high. It was named Surtsey, after a legendary Norse giant. Scientists have watched the island carefully and protected it from man's interference. Birds carried seeds to Surtsey and nested there. Within a few years the first flowers grew. But Surtsey may not last. Its lava rock is already being worn away by the beating of the sea.

There are still about 500 active volcanoes in the world

Most active volcanoes are in a great belt around the Pacific Ocean and around the Solomon Islands, New Guinea and Indonesia. There is also a group in the Mediterranean that includes Etna and Vesuvius, and there is a chain running from Tristan da Cunha through the Azores to Iceland. These are some of the weak spots in the Earth's crust, through which molten rock, or magma, occasionally bursts. In Indonesia alone, there are nearly 30 volcanoes still giving off gases. Many eruptions occur without causing much damage to mankind but in the last 100 years there have been at least two catastrophic eruptions. In 1883, at Krakatoa, in the Sundra Straits between Java and Sumatra, 36,000 people were killed. Nearly 20 years later, 30,000 people were killed when Mount Pelée in Martinique erupted.

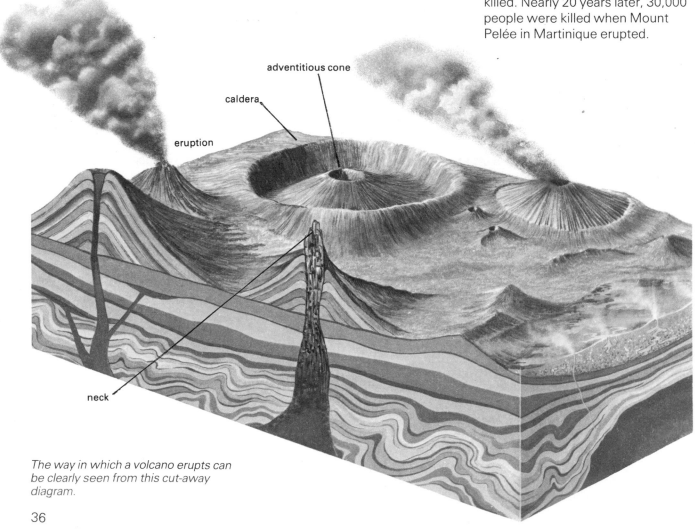

The way in which a volcano erupts can be clearly seen from this cut-away diagram.

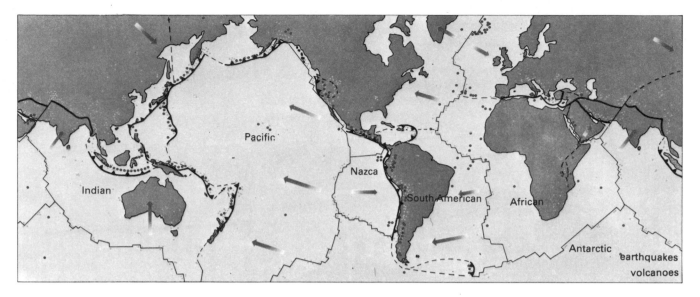

Indian · Pacific · Nazca · South American · African · Antarctic

earthquakes
volcanoes

Earthquakes produce three different kinds of shock waves

The Earth's crust is not solid but consists of several large plates which move gradually over time. Between the plates are weak spots known as fault lines, where stress may build up between two plates. An earthquake itself is the sudden breaking of that stress and a slight movement of the two plates. Shock waves travel out from the focus of the earthquake which is deep down in the Earth, below the epicentre where most of the damage is done. The first or primary wave is a form of compression wave. The secondary wave produces long-distance tremors. Both types of wave travel through the Earth at a known rate and enable scientists with seismographs to pinpoint the position of the epicentre. It is the third wave that travels on the surface which causes the greatest damage.

The plates on which the world sits are constantly moving. Where the plates are near to each other, are the fault lines along which earthquakes often occur. Many happen under the ocean's surface and are recorded on instruments called seismometers. One of the most famous faults is the San Andreas Fault that runs down the west coast of the United States. Some people believe that a catastrophic earthquake will occur along the fault line very shortly – even more devastating than the earthquake that almost destroyed San Francisco in 1906.

Volcanic eruptions can affect the climate

In 1816 North America and Western Europe experienced a very cold summer. In New England most of the corn crop was lost and Geneva recorded the lowest July temperature for 200 years. At the time there was much speculation as to why the weather machine was misbehaving so. Nowadays, scientists believe that it may have been connected with volcanic dust. The year before the cold summer there was an eruption of the Tambora Volcano, on the island of Subara in the Java Sea, believed by some to have been the greatest ever witnessed by man. In such volcanic explosions, dust particles are flung high into the atmosphere. This can have a screening effect on incoming solar radiation.

At the Earth's core the temperature is believed to be 6000°C (11,000°F)

The temperature of the Earth increases with depth. For every kilometre deeper you go the temperature rises, on average, by 30°C (or 140°F for every mile). The heat is thought to be caused by radioactivity within the Earth's core, and possibly by rock movements and chemical changes taking place under extreme pressure. The Earth's crust acts as an insulating layer between the surface and the interior. In places the crust is fractured or stretched and the hot underlying materials move closer to the surface, raising the temperature beneath. This naturally occurring heat energy is often emitted as hot water or steam.

How glaciers are formed

Very simply, glaciers form when more snow falls during the winter than melts and evaporates in summer. This extra snow begins to build up in layers, gradually getting heavier, and presses upon the snow crystals beneath the surface. Eventually, at depths of 15 metres (50 feet) or more, the crystals are compressed into crystals of ice, which combine to form glacial ice. Over time, this ice becomes so thick that it begins to move under the pressure of its own weight. Most glaciers become slightly larger in winter on account of the snow that falls on them. Away from the poles, they may decrease in size in the warmer weather of summer. When glaciers reach the sea, huge chunks of ice break off into the water to form icebergs.

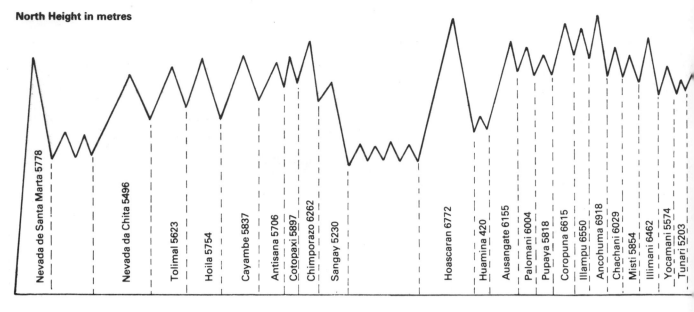

Nevada de Santa Marta 5778
Nevada da Chita 5496
Tolimal 5623
Hoila 5754
Cayambe 5837
Antisana 5706
Cotopaxi 5897
Chimporazo 6262
Sangay 5230
Hoascaran 6772
Huamina 420
Ausangate 6155
Palomani 6004
Pupaya 5818
Coropuna 6615
Illampu 6550
Ancohuma 6918
Chachani 6029
Misti 5854
Illimani 6462
Yocamani 5574
Tunari 5203

The Andes are the longest range of mountains in the world

The Andes stretch for almost 9000 kilometres (5590 miles) down the length of South America, from the Caribbean, through Colombia, Venezuela, Ecuador, Peru, Bolivia, and along the borders of Chile and Argentina. The tallest peak is Acongua, at 6960 metres (22,834

Ocean waves can travel as fast as a jet plane

Earthquakes deep in the Pacific cause some of the most terrifying waves in the world. These are called *tsunami*. They spread out from the centre of the earthquake, travelling very fast. At first they rise only a little above the surface of the water but they grow more powerful as they near the shore and rise 9-12 metres (30-40 feet) in the air before crashing down on coastal villages. Although Japan suffers more than most countries from these tsunami, one of the worst tsunami disasters occurred in Hawaii in 1946. Then a wave travelled 3600 kilometres (2250 miles) in 4 hours at an average speed of 800 kilometres (500 miles) per hour and reached a height of 13.71 metres (45 feet) before hitting the town of Hilo and killing 173 people. Warning stations which use seismographic equipment that monitors and records earthquakes have now been set up to forecast possible tsunami. Scientists are working on methods to make such warnings more accurate.

Much of North Europe is like a see-saw

North and west England, together with Scotland and Wales, are gradually rising up out of the sea at a rate of about thirteen centimetres (five inches) every 100 years. In the 700 years since Harlech castle was built in 1286 on the shoreline of mid-Wales, that adds up to about one metre (three feet). In contrast, the south and east of England is sinking at about the same speed, so are parts of the west coasts of Denmark and Holland, whereas northern Scandinavia is rising. This movement is the result of the Ice Age when the sheer weight of ice that crept down over northern Europe and northern Britain, tens and hundreds of thousands of years ago, pressed the land down. Along the coast of Denmark the weight of ice was so great that it eroded valley floors far below sea-level before floating away into the sea. After this ice melted, seawater flooded the valleys and formed fjords. They are long narrow arms of the sea extending far inland. Sogne-fjord in Norway is 1,234 metres (4,078 feet) deep.

Winds are caused by the sun

Winds are large masses of air moving over the Earth's surface. The motion results from the sun's rays heating the land and seas unevenly, and varies according to place and time of year. Air coming into contact with the warmer parts of the Earth's surface is heated, rises and is replaced by cooler air. The direction and speed of air motion is affected by the Earth's rotation as well as by local climate and physical geography.

When winds act upon the oceans they cause waves

The Tradewinds that occur in the tropics are strong and steady, moving at speeds of between 18 and 22 kilometres (11-15 miles) per hour. They are thought to have been given their name by the crews of the sailing ships who depended on them for their livelihoods. The Tradewinds blow evenly across oceans, where the weather is more uniform than over continents.

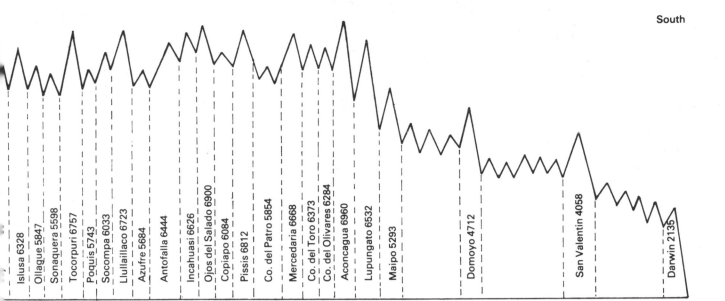

Islusa 6328
Ollague 5847
Sonaquera 5598
Tocorpuri 6757
Poquis 5743
Socompa 6033
Llullaillaco 6723
Azufre 5684
Antofalla 6444
Incahuasi 6626
Ojos del Salado 6900
Copiapo 6084
Pissis 6812
Co. del Patro 5854
Mercedaria 6668
Co. del Toro 6373
Co. del Olivares 6284
Aconcagua 6960
Lupungato 6532
Maipo 5293
Domoyo 4712
San Valentin 4058
Darwin 2135

feet), not far from Santiago in Chile. For almost half their length the mountains rise to peaks of more than 3500 metres (11,483 feet). In the north of the Andes there are tropical valleys with forests, strange plants, jaguars, all kinds of monkeys and condor vultures.

All the major peaks in the Andes and their heights are shown in this artist's representation.

Tornadoes may cause great damage as they travel over the land

Like the hurricane, the tornado is shaped by violent winds around a centre of low pressure. But, unlike the hurricane, the tornado travels over land and is short-lived. It moves at about 45-50 kilometres (28-31 miles) per hour and may last less than ten minutes. It may also be only about 300-400 metres (984-1312 feet) in diameter, or as little as 30-40 metres (98-131 feet). However, the winds themselves reach an incredible 300-600 kilometres (186-373 miles) per hour, sucking everything in their path into their upward spiral. Tornadoes are sometimes known as 'twisters' or 'whirlwinds'. They occur frequently in the Mississippi and Missouri basin of the United States. In 1965, 47 tornadoes hit six states in two days, causing more than 250 deaths. A tornado that occurs over water is known as a waterspout and is much less violent.

There are basically only three main types of clouds

There may seem to be a mass of different shaped clouds in the sky, all with complex scientific names, but there are, in fact, only three main types and all the others are variations on those three. 'Cirrus' clouds generally have a feathery shape and are made of ice crystals. These are the highest clouds. 'Cumulus' are much lower and are generally heaped up in thick piles above a flat base. 'Stratus' clouds are the lowest, spread out in layers of dark or grey streaks. Combinations of these occur all the time. For example, 'strato-cumulus' clouds are heaped up clouds that are spread across the whole sky. Clouds refered to as 'nimbus', as in 'cumulo-nimbus'.

The weather sculptures the surface of the land

Rock folds and faults caused by pressures within the Earth are only the first part of the shaping process.

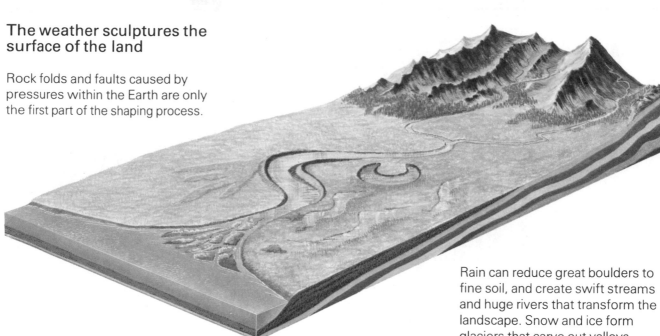

Above: *This landscape is the result of many millions of years of the weather's influence which has caused it to be what it is today.*

Afterwards the weather does its work to fill in the hollows and wear away the prominences.

Rain can reduce great boulders to fine soil, and create swift streams and huge rivers that transform the landscape. Snow and ice form glaciers that carve out valleys. Frost breaks down the soil and can crack giant boulders. Wind may sandblast the surface of a rock to produce strange shapes.

Rock faults are caused by stresses and strains inside the Earth

Sedimentary rocks may form in neat layers but they rarely stay that way. Most layers are contorted or displaced by faults. A fault occurs when one block of rock shifts in relation to another. There are several kinds of fault, all caused by stresses within the Earth. Lateral faults are caused by blocks moving sideways in relation to each other. Dip-slip faults occur when blocks move up or down in relation to each other. A central block that drops down between two others is known as a 'graben'. One that goes up between two others is a 'horst'. If the slip is at angle, then the fault is either a 'normal', a 'reverse' or a 'thrust' fault.

One meandering stream resembles another

A meander is a U-bend in a stream that normally occurs in a series. The name derives from a river in Asia Minor known to the Greeks as the Maender (and to modern Turks as the Menderes). Meanders are most often found in alluvial materials (sediment deposited by the stream) and adjust their shape and flow to the slope of the alluvial valley. A meandering channel is usually about one and a half times as long as the valley. Often the width of the channel is kept fairly constant by deposits on the inside curve offsetting the erosion of the bank on the outside curve. Meandering streams are also found cut deep into bedrock. A meander wavelength, that is two consecutive U-bends measured across at their widest point, will normally be 8-12 times the width of the channel. Thus one meandering stream will look like a scale model of another. Nature has done her job well. If the bends were very tight or much more open there would be far more resistance to the flow around them. All streams are rich with wildlife. As well as fish and other water creatures, it is possible to find plants, birds and insects around streams, making them a superb place to study nature at her most beautiful.

Folds of rock reveal the forces within the Earth

Rocks do not always split sharply along a fault line when they are under stress. Instead, they often fold up or down. Sometimes these folds are visible as hills on the surface, but sometimes the dips have been filled in and the rises have been eroded. Upward folds are called anticlines and downward folds are called synclines. A recumbent fold is one that is leaning completely over on its side. When the folds start falling on top of each other and begin to break up, slip and become eroded, it is difficult to see how the original layers of rock were arranged.

It is possible that the north of Scotland was once an island

The Great Glen Fault runs from the east to west of Scotland along the line of Loch Ness, Loch Lochy and Loch Linnhe. About 400 million years ago this fault was probably responsible for joining the northern part of Scotland to the mainland. Before this time it is likely that the north was an island more than 100 kilometres (62 miles) to the east. This is an example of a lateral fault.

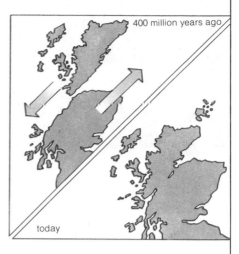

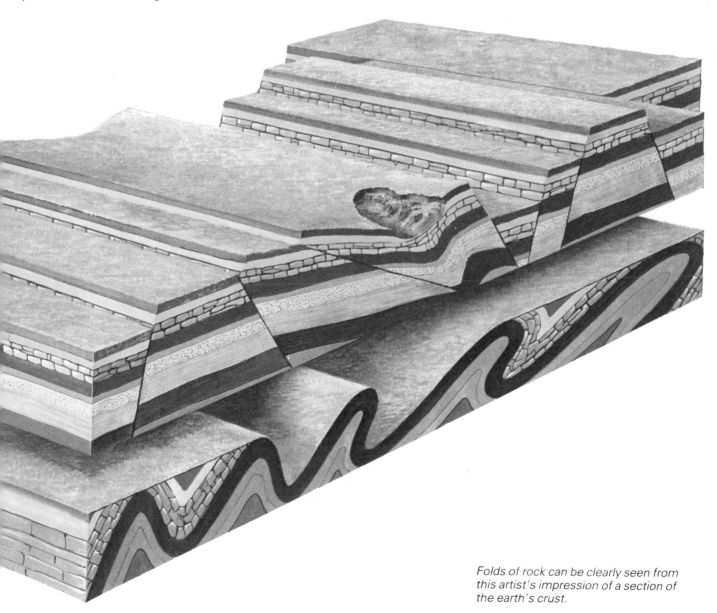

Folds of rock can be clearly seen from this artist's impression of a section of the earth's crust.

Africa and the Middle East

The Moors came from Mauritania

The name 'Moor' comes from the Mauri, the people of Mauritania in north-west Africa. Mauritania was an old name for the modern countries of Morocco and Algeria. The Arabs conquered the Mauri in the 7th century AD and converted them to Islam. These Moorish Arabs then conquered southern Spain and set up their own kingdom in Spain. They developed a rich civilisation which introduced many Arab influences and skills into Europe. They were not driven out of Spain until the end of the 15th century. The Barbary Pirates who sailed out from Algiers and other ports to prey on ships in the Mediterranean during the 17th and 18th centuries were also Moors.

The Dutch settlers called native South Africans stammerers

The Dutch were surprised by the strange language of the people around the Cape of Good Hope when they first landed there in 1632. They called them the 'stammerers', or Hottentots. These Hottentots and other bushmen were the original inhabitants of South Africa. There are ancient coloured drawings on the rocks in places from which the bushmen and Hottentots have been driven away. The Hottentots still exist in some dry areas. They are gentle people who work as herdsmen and labourers. The bushmen are smaller and live by hunting with bows and arrows.

Zimbabwe was a mighty empire in the Middle Ages

In Zimbabwe there are the remains of a powerful empire that flourished in the Middle Ages and existed until the 17th century. There are stone walls 2.5 metres (8 feet) high and a building that looks like a temple, with walls 5 metres (16 feet) thick and 10 metres (33 feet) high. There is also a strange stone tower that appears to be solid, and more stone ruins and stone-carved birds on an acropolis, or hill-fort, nearby.

The Phoenicians sailed round Africa 2000 years before Bartholomew Diaz

In AD 1487 Bartholomew Diaz, the Portuguese explorer, sailed round the Cape of Storms (now called the Cape of Good Hope) and opened the way for Europe to start trading with India and the Far East. But the trip around the southern tip of Africa had been made in the opposite direction in about 600 BC by Phoenician sailors. The Phoenicians claimed to have sailed from the Red Sea around Africa and back to the Mediterranean through the Straits of Gibraltar. The historian, Herodotus, recorded their story 150 years later. He did not really believe it, despite the proof put forward by the Phoenicians that they had seen the sun to the north of them at midday. This would only be possible if they had passed the equator into the southern hemisphere. (North of the equator, the sun is always to the south at midday.)

Pygmies are short people under 1.5 metres (4 feet 11 inches) tall

There are pygmy peoples throughout the world: in New Guinea, the Philippines, the Andaman Islands, the Kalahari Desert and the Congo. True pygmies are not more than 1.5 metres (4 feet 11 inches) tall. They usually live in small groups. Most are nomadic hunters who live in temporary huts. Many still use poison arrows to kill their prey.

Left: *A map of Africa showing all the countries and their capitals. The dotted line around its eastern coast stretching from Portugal to Angloa Bay, in present-day South Africa, shows the route taken by Bartholomew Diaz when he rounded the Cape of Good Hope in 1487. Many explorers played important parts in opening up the dark continent. David Livingstone, a Scottish Missionary, spent much of his life in Africa and discovered the Victoria Falls. When another explorer, Henry Stanley, went in search of Livingstone and found him, he is reported to have said, 'Doctor Livingstone I presume,' and these words have become almost as famous as Livingstone and Stanley themselves.*

Sagres

Tunis

Algiers
TUNISIA
Rabat
MOROCCO
Tripoli
Mediterranean Sea

Dakar
ALGERIA
LIBYA
Cairo

El Aouin
EGYPT

Western
Sahara
R.Nile

MAURITANIA
MALI

Nouakchott
R. Niger

SENEGAL
NIGER
CHAD
Al Khurtum
DJIBOUTI

Bamako
Niamey
SUDAN

GUINEA
Najamena
Addis Ababa

IVORY
COAST
GHANA
Benin
NIGERIA
CENTRAL AFRICAN
EMPIRE
UGANDA
ETHIOPIA
Somalia

LIBERIA
Abidjan
Accra
Lagos
CAMEROON
Bangui
KENYA
Mojadisho

Monrovia
Lomé
Porto-Novo
Yaoundé
R. Congo

SIERRA LEONE
Equatorial Guinea
Kampala

Freetown
Sao Tome
Bata
CONGO
Nairobi

Conakry
Libreuille
GABON
Equator

GUINEA-BISSAU
ZAIRE
ZANZIBAR
Dar es Salaam

GAMBIA
Brazauille

Bissau
Kinshasa
TANZANIA

Banjel

Luanda

Atlantic Ocean
ANGOLA
ZAMBIA
Tombae

Lusaka
MADAGASCAR

Salisbury

NAMIBIA
ZIMBABWE
Antananarivo

BOTSWANA

Windhoek
MOZAMBIQUE

Tropic of Capricorn

Gabarone
Mapoto

Pretoria
Mbabane
SWAZILAND

REPUBLIC
OF SOUTH
AFRICA
Maseru

LESOTHO

+ – + – + Route of Bartholomew Diaz

Algoa Bay
Indian Ocean

Miles
200 0 200 400 600 800 1000

200 0 200   600   1000
Kms

43

The Queen of Sheba's land is now the modern state of Yemen

The Old Testament of the Bible tells us very little about the Queen of Sheba, except that she went to visit King Solomon in Jerusalem because she had heard of his wealth and wisdom. The Queen was also rich and powerful and arrived with spices, gold and precious stones. The land of Sheba, or Saba, lay along the Red Sea route into the Indian Ocean, and far to the south of Jerusalem. This area is now the modern Yemen, in the south-west corner of Arabia. Legend has made much of a romance between the Queen and Solomon, but the signing of a commercial treaty seems far more likely, for Sheba was once a rich trading centre between India and Arabia. Today only a few ruins remain of the Queen's kingdom.

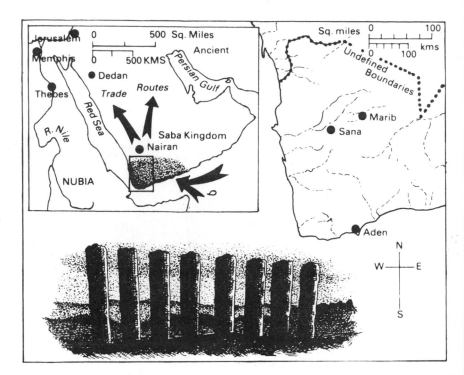

The pillars of the Sabaean moon-god temple near Marib are all that remains of Sheba's capital, Marib. The shaded area in the left-hand map shows where Sheba used to be. The right-hand map shows Sheba in greater detail, with modern day Aden pinpointed to give the reader an idea of where Sheba was.

The churches of Lalibela are underground wonders

Lalibela is an insignificant village in Ethiopia. It is named after the king who lived there more than 750 years ago and who made it his capital. In Lalibela is the amazing Church of St George which is cut out of the ground. Its top is flush with the surface, as if it had been dropped into a hole. The church is in the shape of a cross, with a trench all around it. There are several other equally strange little churches, either sunk into the ground or tunnelled into the side of a hill, all carved out of solid rock. It is said that King Lalibela spent all his wealth on cutting out these churches, but some of them appear to date from an older period.

Assassins were drug addicts

An 'assassin' is one who kills by treacherous and violent means. The word is usually used for people who murder politicians or statesmen. There was once a whole group of people known as 'Assassins' or 'Hashishin', because they made their attacks under the influence of the 'hashish' or any other drugs which they took to give themselves courage. The Assassins were a Moslem sect of religious fanatics founded in about 1090 by Hassan ben Sabbah, known as the Old Man of the Mountain. They lived in southern Persia, or Iran, and fought against the Seljuk Turks, who occupied part of their territory. They were not broken up until about 1273, when the Mongols and the Sultan Bibars drove them out of their hideouts.

The bleak Sahara desert was once rich with plants and wild animals

The Sahara desert is spreading south, threatening more land with drought and starvation year by year. Low rainfall, a change in wind patterns, and man's misuse of the soil and water resources are all to blame. But cave paintings from nearly 10,000 years ago tell a different story. In caves at Tassili, in southern Algeria, there are scenes of tribesmen hunting antelope, buffalo, lions and even elephants. Other paintings from 6000 years ago show tribesmen grazing domestic cattle on rich pastureland. These farmers were able to find food and water for their herds until about 2000 BC. Then the desert took over and the herds disappeared.

The Jericho that Joshua destroyed was falling down already

Jericho was an important city in Biblical times and long before. It lay a short distance north of the Dead Sea and west of the River Jordan. The city stood in the way of the Israelites as they made their way into the Promised Land after their wanderings in the Wilderness. Joshua made his people march round Jericho for seven days and on the seventh day he made them shout and blow their trumpets until the walls fell down. The sudden vibrations from such a tremendous noise could certainly have shaken the walls, but only if they were already weakened. Some historians now believe that the city had already been seriously damaged by attacks more than 100 years before the Israelites arrived there.

One city gave its name to a type of steel, a type of cloth and an ornament

Damascus is the capital of Syria. It has been ruled in turn by Egyptians, Assyrians, Persians, Romans, Byzantines, Arabs, Mongols and Turks. In the Middle Ages, it was a famous centre for sword-making, using a strong and flexible type of metal which became known as Damascus steel. It consisted of iron and steel welded together and then hammered out. It was characterised by a wavy pattern. Similar steel was used to make Damascus barrels for guns. The Damascans made beautiful ornaments by inlaying gold and silver into another metal. This process came to be known as 'damascening'. 'Damask' was a form of woven cloth that came from the city, which also became famous for handmade glass.

Baghdad was once the centre of a huge empire stretching from North Africa to China

Around 4000 BC the area that is now Baghdad, and the capital of Iraq, formed part of ancient Babylonia. Later, from 500s BC to AD 600s, the region was controlled, in turn, by Persians, Greeks and Romans. When Abu Jafru al-Masru became leader of the Arab empire in 752, Baghdad was still a small village. But within 50 years Baghdad had a population of more than a million and was a world centre of education.

Coffee may have been discovered by goats

'Coffee' comes from the Arabic word 'qahweh'. According to legend, Kaldi, an Arab goatherd in Ethiopia, first discovered coffee in about 850 AD, after noticing the strange effects the plant had on some of his flock who had been feeding on it. But it was not until the thirteenth century that coffee reached Arabia, and 200 years later, Turkey. From there it was introduced into Europe. Before its use as a beverage, coffee was a food, then a wine and later a medicine. Because of its stimulating effects it was denounced by the Islamic church as an intoxicant, and prohibited by the Qur'an. Yet despite the threat of severe penalties coffee drinking spread rapidly among the Arabs and their neighbours, and had established its popularity in Europe and North America by the end of the seventeenth century.

Three of the world's great religions all come from the same part of the world

Of the major religions practised in the world today Judaism is believed to be the oldest, originating with Abraham in 1700 BC, and Islam the most recent. Islam was founded by Muhammad in Arabia less than 1400 years ago. With Christianity, these religions share in common their place of origin - the area of the world around the Red Sea - and their monotheism, that is the belief in one, all-powerful god. This is quite unlike Hinduism, for example, the religion with the biggest following after Christianity and Islam, which is polytheistic - has many gods - and derives from India. Hinduism, which began about 1500 BC is said by some to be older than Judaism as a practising religion, for the Jews may not have been converted to monotheism until 600 years or more after Moses.

The Wailing Wall was once part of a sacred temple

For many centuries the Wailing Wall in the Old City of Jerusalem has been a place of prayer and pilgrimage for Jewish people. It is the sole remains of a temple that was held to be uniquely holy by the ancient Jews, and destroyed by the Romans in AD 70. Originally the 'Western Wall', it was given the name 'Wailing Wall' by Europeans who witnessed the mournful prayers of pious Jews before the relic of the sacred temple. There they lament its destruction and pray for its restoration. The oldest part of the wall dates from about 200 BC, but it now forms part of a larger wall that surrounds a mosque. For this reason Jews and Arabs have long fought over its control. Today, the wall measures about 50 metres (160 feet) long and about 20 metres (60 feet) high.

There are three Tripolis

Tripoli is the capital of Libya, and an important seaport on the Mediterranean coast. It is also the name of the second largest city in Lebanon, another Mediterranean seaport, and of a substance, composed of fine grains of silica, that is sometimes used in paper making. This substance is believed to take its name from Tripoli, Libya, where it was supposedly first used as a powder for polishing glass, marble and metals. In ancient times both cities were closely associated with neighbouring cities. The name 'Tripoli', deriving from the Latin or Greek form, implies 'three cities' or 'one of three cities'. Between about 150 BC and the 5th century AD the two Tripolis came under Roman rule, and later, in the 7th century fell to Muhammad and came under Arab domination. The Arabs distinguished between the cities by calling them, in Arabic, Eastern Tripoli (in Lebanon) and Western Tripoli (Libya).

Europe

Lapland is part of four different countries

The people called Lapps have a language and culture of their own but the land they live in, Lapland, is not a separate country by itself. It is an area made up of the northern parts of Norway, Sweden, Finland and the north-west corner of the Russian Republic. Most Lapps live very far north, above the Arctic Circle, and keep herds of reindeer, from which they get milk and meat. They also use reindeer skins for clothes and coverings and they use the reindeer to tow sledges.

Democracy was banned in Eastern Europe for over 40 years.

From the end of the Second World War in 1945 until the early 1990s democracy was banned in the nations of Eastern Europe, such as Poland, Hungary, Romania, Czechoslovakia and Bulgaria. These nations were ruled by the Communist Party, largely under the control of the Soviet Union. In 1989 Soviet control was lifted and the Communist regimes collapsed, to be replaced by democracies.

There are 11 republics in the Commonwealth of Independent States

When central Communist power collapsed in the USSR in 1991 four of the republics left the Union to become independent. These are: Latvia, Estonia, Lithuania and Georgia. The remaining 11 republics formed a loose confederation called the Commonwealth of Independent States. The individual states are largely in control of their own affairs and only co-operate on major issues. The 11 republics are: Russia, the largest, Ukraine, Belorussia, Armenia, Azerbaijan, Kazakhstan, Kirghizia, Moldavia, Tadjikistan, Turkmenistan and Uzbekistan.

Finland is a land of lakes and islands

Finland, an independent republic is bounded by Sweden and Norway in the West and by the Russian Republic in the east. It used to run between the Baltic and the Arctic Seas, but since the Second World War the Russian Republic has cut off its access to the Arctic. The capital, Helsinki, is in the south of the country and most of the five million population live in the south. The population is very small for a land of nearly 340,000 square kilometres (130,000 square miles) but as much as 70 per cent of the country is covered by forests and the southern half is pitted with tens of thousands of lakes. The long coast line along the Gulfs of Bothnia and Finland is broken into almost as many islands as there are lakes inland.

Above: *Finland, Russian Republic, Sweden and Norway are in relation to each other. The black box in the smaller map shows how*

Lapland's 'boundaries' intrude into all four countries. The Lapps are the only people who can cross all the borders without being questioned.

Moscow is in Europe, not Asia

The western end of the Commonwealth of Independent States, including the capital, Moscow, and the great city of St Petersburg, lies in Europe. The dividing line between Europe and Asia is along the steeper, eastern slopes of the Ural Mountains, which run from the Kara Sea in the north to the Aral Sea in the south.

Low-lying Holland is protected from the sea by dykes

Almost one-third of Holland lies below sea level. That is why Holland is also called the Netherlands or Low Countries. Large areas of new land are steadily being reclaimed from the sea and shut off by long dykes, or protective walls. These dykes were traditionally built to form three lines of defence. The nearest line to the sea was called the 'waker'; next came the 'dreamer' and then the 'sleeper'. There have been many severe floods in Holland's history. One of the worst was in this century when in many places both the waker and the dreamer were smashed and many people were drowned and made homeless.

Bismarck's old capital was controlled by four countries

It is well known that Berlin was once divided between East and West. In fact the notorious Berlin Wall completely surrounded West Berlin. What is perhaps less often realised is that West Berlin was over 100 kilometres (40 miles) inside the East German border, and was not constitutionally part of West Germany. East Berlin was the capital of East Germany (German Democratic Republic) but the status of West Berlin was a major source of disagreement between the Western and Soviet powers right up until 1971. Berlin had been the capital of Germany from the time of Bismarck, but fell to the invading allied armies in 1945, at the end of World War II. Although the city lay deep inside the new Soviet zone of Germany, it was agreed to divide it into four sections, each to be controlled by one of the four allies – United States, England, France and the USSR. It remained so until 1989. The Berlin Wall was built by the Russians in 1961, after a series of political crises between the West and the Soviet Union. It was eventually breached in 1989 with much jubilation.

The Danube flows through six different European countries

The Danube is the second largest river in Europe, next to the Volga, and it carries the most water. The river runs for more than 2800 kilometres (1740 miles) from the Black Forest in south-west Germany to the Black Sea. It flows past such famous old cities as Ulm, Vienna, Budapest and Belgrade. The Danube passes through West Germany, Austria, Hungary, Yugoslavia, Bulgaria and Romania, and it is joined by tributaries from Switzerland and Czechoslovakia. A canal link with the River Main, which in turn links with the Rhine, will eventually create a waterway right across Europe.

When the waterway is completed it will enable goods to be carried from the North Sea to the Black Sea.

Below: *The course of the Danube from its source at Black Forest in Western Germany to the Black Sea. The Danube has inspired many writers and composers. Perhaps the most famous is Johann Strauss who called one of his most famous waltzes after the river.*

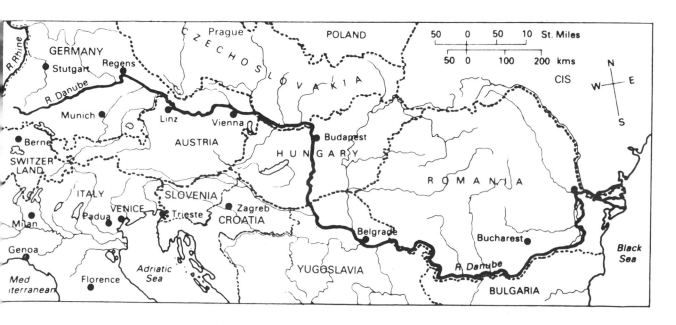

San Marino is the oldest republic in the world

The tiny republic of San Marino lies on the slopes of Mount Titano not far from Rimini on the Adriatic coast of Italy. A settlement was founded there by a Roman fleeing from persecution. In the 9th century a monastery was founded, and a republic was set up in the 10th century. San Marino remained independent when Italy became a united kingdom in 1871. However, police and judges were brought in from Italy to keep peace and order in the republic.

The arrow on the smaller map points towards San Marino and shows that, in area, the country is smaller than Rome, Florence, Venice and other major cities of Italy.

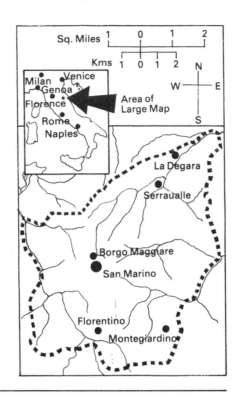

The Vatican is the smallest independent state in the world

Vatican City covers 0.45 square kilometres (0.17 square miles) in the heart of Rome. In 1929 it was recognised by the Italian government as an independent and sovereign state, all that was left to the popes of the vast power they had once wielded in the Papal States of central Italy. Within the city is the great church of St Peter's and the Vatican Palace, the spiritual centre of the Roman Catholic Church and the home of the Pope. Like any other government, Vatican City sends diplomatic representatives to foreign governments, as well as permanent representatives to Catholics in other countries. Vatican City has its own flag, its own post office, its own telephone and radio stations.

Italy was civilised long before the Romans

The Romans were not the first people to live a cultured and civilised life in Italy. They learnt a great deal from the 'Etruscans', who settled inland from the coast between the Rivers Arno and Tiber in about 1000 BC. They lived in isolated cities that never successfully united against the Romans who came later. The Etruscans were warriors and traders and they were also brilliant sculptors and engineers. They probably came originally from the eastern end of the Mediterranean.

Venice is sinking into the sea

The city of Venice rests on more than 100 small islands in a great lagoon. It is connected to the mainland of Italy by a causeway about four kilometres (2.5 miles) long. People travel between the beautiful buildings, churches and plazas along the canals, ferried by motor boats or gondolas. Tragically, the foundations of the buildings are slowly sinking into the sand of the islands. The buildings themselves are deteriorating and further damage is being done by floods and by the wash created by fast-moving motor boats. Although the problems are being carefully looked at Venice is in great danger.

Gibraltar is commonly known as 'The Rock'

The British Colony of Gibraltar lies at the tip of Spain's southern Mediterranean coast. It consists of a limestone and shale ridge known as the Rock and has a total area of only 5.8 square kilometres (2.25 square miles). The ancient Greeks called the rocks on either side of the Strait of Gibraltar the 'Pillars of Hercules'. In AD 711 Moors from North Africa invaded Gibraltar and stayed for nearly 600 years. The Spaniards conquered Gibraltar in 1309, lost it back to the Moors 24 years later, but finally regained it in 1462. In 1704 Gibraltar was captured by a British naval force and it has remained a British dependency every since. The strategic importance of Gibraltar as a naval port was greatly increased after the opening of the Suez Canal.

'Albania' means 'land of the eagle'

Albania is a tiny Balkan republic with a fertile, mountain-rimmed coastal strip on the Adriatic Sea. To the north Albania borders Yugoslavia, and Greece to the south. From the evidence of place names the people of Albania are thought to be descendants of the ancient Illyrians, and of Indo-European stock. They speak two main languages, representing different cultures, and use the Arabic, Cyrillic and Latin scripts. Surprisingly, Albanian history suggests that rivers have been a greater barrier between cultures than mountains. The attempts made after the First World War to create a unified language were only partly successful. The country's capital, Tiranë, was chosen in 1920, and Italian architects employed to re-plan the city with the focus on Skanderbeg Square. Skanderbeg was a 15th century Albanian prince who repulsed 13 Turkish invasions and became a hero throughout the whole of Europe.

A Mediterranean island stood against a three-year siege

The island of Malta has always been of great importance in the Mediterranean because it stands between Sicily and the North African coast. Phoenicians, Romans, Arabs, Crusader knights, the French and the British have all conquered Malta at one time or another. During the Second World War the Germans tried for three years to drive the British out of Malta. They wanted to use it as a base for supplying Rommel in North Africa, and for controlling the Mediterranean. The brave islanders held out against German air raids night after night, despite terrible damage and many deaths. Afterwards, the island was awarded the George Cross for the bravery of its citizens. Malta is now an independent republic.

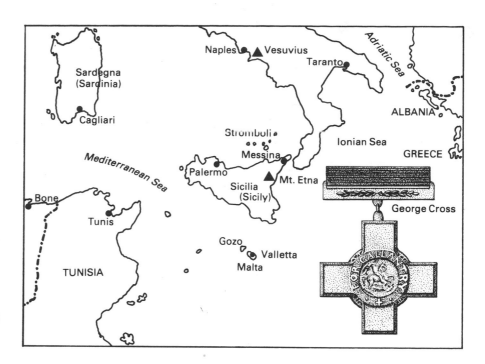

After they had successfully withstood the three-year German siege, the people of Malta were awarded the George Cross, shown here, by King George VI of Great Britain. The George Cross is the highest award that a civilian can be awarded for courage by the British monarch and showed his appreciation of the Maltese efforts during the War.

St Petersburg was built on a swamp

The former capital of Russia lies on a marshy lowland where the River Neva empties into the Gulf of Finland. Because of its far northern location, St Petersburg experiences only very short periods of daylight during the winter and 'white nights' in June when the sky is never completely dark. The city was built by Tsar Peter the Great in 1703, under the supervision of western architects. Its construction cost an estimated 30,000 lives, from undernourishment, disease and drowning.

Peter called the city his 'window on the west' and named it after his patron saint. In 1712 he moved the capital of the Tsarist court from Moscow to St Petersburg, symbolising a cultural and economic shift towards Western Europe. Nobles in government were required to take up residence there, and soon the new capital became the intellectual and social centre of the Russian Empire. In 1914 the city changed its name to Petrograd, the Russian form of the German name St Petersburg. In 1918 the capital was moved back to Moscow and in 1924 the name of the city changed again to Leningrad in honour of the famous Communist leader Lenin. In 1991 the city returned to calling itself St Petersburg.

Budapest is the union of three cities

The modern city of Budapest, the capital and largest city of Hungary, stands astride the River Danube, commanding the western approaches to the Great Hungarian Plain. The city has a history dating back to the second century when the Romans founded Aquincum, a town partly occupying the site of what is now Budapest. But it was not until the late 800s that Hungarians began to settle in the middle Danube valley. These settlements grew into the cities of Buda, Pest and O'buda, which, with Margaret Island, combined in 1873 to form Budapest. Today about three-quarters of the capital's inhabitants live on the east bank, in the former city of Pest. In the 19th century Pest was a great centre of national culture and Hungarian patriotism. On the west bank, what used to be Buda, there are beautiful renaissance buildings and scenic wooded hills.

Roman catacombs contain third and fourth century frescoes

Catacombs are underground passages and rooms which were used as Christian burial places. The most famous are found on the outskirts of Rome. There, the early Christians built a network of connecting rooms and corridors on a number of levels which covered a total area of 240 hectares (600 acres). These catacombs were used for funeral and memorial services.

The Americas

The capital of the USA is not in any one of the 50 states

When the original 13 states formed a Union after the American Revolution (1775-1783), each representative wanted to have the new capital in his own state. George Washington and Congress eventually decided to create an entirely separate area for the capital, on the banks of the River Potomac. They called this area the District of Columbia, which is why the capital, Washington, is known as Washington D.C. All the central government buildings are in the capital, including the White House, the Capitol, the Pentagon and the Supreme Court.

The United States banned all alcohol for thirteen years

Because of a campaign against alcohol by evangelical ministers the United States government banned the production and sale of all alcohol throughout the United States between 1920 and 1933. The ban was known as Prohibition. Millions of litres of wine and spirits were thrown away, but the ban did not work very well. The law was frequently broken by gangsters and bootleggers, who made and sold drink illegally and became rich in the process. After America had been hit by the Depression with a widespread loss of jobs in the early 1930s, alcohol was once again permitted in the hope that its manufacture would provide much-needed jobs.

The territories of the United States and the Russian Republic are only a few kilometres apart

The boundary between the United States and the Russian Republic passes through the Bering Strait which at its narrowest is only 90 kilometres (56 miles) wide. The International Date Line passes through the Diomede Islands in the strait. Little Diomede belongs to the United States and Big Diomede only a few kilometres away belongs to Russia. Therefore the two greatest nations on Earth are only separated by water between the two small islands.

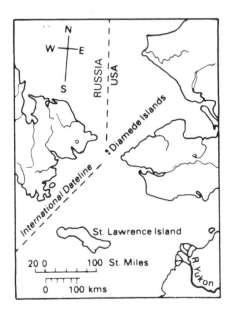

Travellers crossing the International Date Line which intersects the small space between Russia and the USA have to change dates. Going from east to west means moving forward one day and moving west to east means moving back one day.

Texas was the largest state in the USA until 1959

Texans have always prided themselves on having the biggest and the best of just about everything. Their own state was the largest in America. But in 1959 Alaska joined the Union as the 49th state and moved Texas out of the top spot. Alaska covers an area of 1.5 million square kilometres (586,400 square miles), about three times the size of France. Hawaii became the 50th and most recent state in the same year.

The great Alaska Highway was built in six months

During the Second World War, the Americans feared that the Japanese might invade North America from the Aleutian Islands and threaten sea communications between the United States and US bases in Alaska. An overland road link was planned and begun in the spring of 1942, to go through Canada to Fairbanks in Alaska. Ten thousand engineers from the US Army, as well as 4000 civilians, built more than 12 kilometres (7 miles) of road a day through forests and marshes and over rivers. They finished the road in November of the same year. By the following spring, many of the temporary bridges had been washed away but they were replaced by permanent ones. The Alaska Highway finally linked up with the Pan American Highway from North to South America.

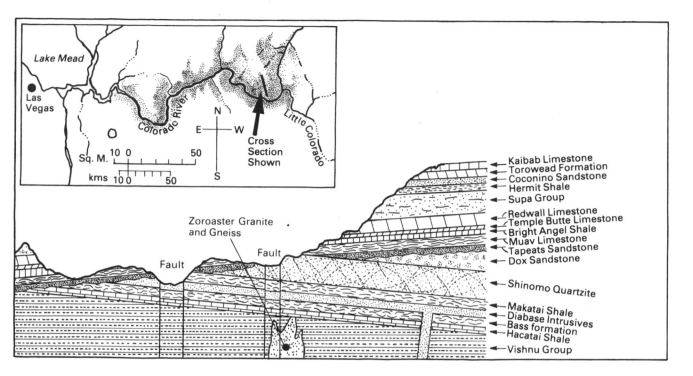

Labels on cross-section diagram:
- Lake Mead
- Las Vegas
- Colorado River
- Little Colorado
- Cross Section Shown
- Sq. M. 10 0 50
- kms 10 0 50
- Kaibab Limestone
- Torowead Formation
- Coconino Sandstone
- Hermit Shale
- Supa Group
- Redwall Limestone
- Temple Butte Limestone
- Bright Angel Shale
- Muav Limestone
- Tapeats Sandstone
- Dox Sandstone
- Shinomo Quartzite
- Makatai Shale
- Diabase Intrusives
- Bass formation
- Hacatai Shale
- Vishnu Group
- Zoroaster Granite and Gneiss
- Fault
- Fault

The Grand Canyon is a unique record of 2000 million years of geological history

The Grand Canyon is one of the greatest natural wonders on Earth. The Colorado River has cut a vast gorge through the high plateaus of north Arizona. The canyon is between 6 and 28 kilometres (3-17 miles) wide at the top. Its most dramatic section is about 90 kilometres (56 miles) long. The gorge narrows down to the river, which is between 1200 and 1500 metres (3937-4921 feet) below the top of the canyon. The rock layers exposed on the sides of the canyon are a unique record of geological history going back 2000 million years. The layers are rich in fossils of all kinds.

Christopher Columbus was not the first European to discover America

Columbus crossed the Atlantic in 1492 and sighted the Bahamas and several Caribbean islands. But other voyagers had crossed the Atlantic before him. Nearly 500 years earlier, the Norwegian Viking, Leif Ericsson, had set out from Greenland and discovered what he called Vinland, or 'Wine Land'. Vinland was probably northern Newfoundland. Ericsson established a colony there, which lasted only a short time, but remains of other Viking-type settlements have also been found there. It is also possible that there were even earlier voyages to North America. Many people believe that more than 400 years earlier, in the 6th century, the Irish monk, St Brendan, sailed across the ocean in a flimsy, hide-covered craft, in search of the 'Promised Land of Saints', later identified as the Canary Islands.

The United States of America originally had only 13 states

The American flag has 50 stars to represent the 50 modern states of the Union. It also has 13 stripes representing Connecticut, Delaware, Georgia, Maryland, Massachusetts, New Hampshire, New Jersey, New York, North Carolina, Pennsylvania, Rhode Island, South Carolina and Virginia – the original 13 states, after the War of Independence finished in 1783. The most recent of the states is Hawaii (1959).

The first people to live in America came from Siberia.

There were Indians in America long before the Vikings or Columbus or anyone else crossed the Atlantic. These Indians came from Siberia. About 20,000 or 25,000 years ago Siberia and Alaska were joined together by a land bridge (or rather an ice bridge). Hunters following herds of caribou and elk crossed this 'bridge' from Asia. As the great ice barriers across Canada began to melt at the end of the Ice Age, the hunters moved south. They began to filter down to the Caribbean about 10,000 or 11,000 years ago. Then they crossed over into South America and are the forefathers of all the tribes of North, South and Central America. The Indians did not refer to themselves generally by that name. Almost every group had its own name which reflected the pride the tribes took in themselves and their way of life. For instance, the Delaware Indians of eastern North America used a name which meant 'genuine men' The terms 'redskins' or 'redmen' used by white Americans probably arose from the Indians' custom of daubing their bodies with red paint on ceremonial occasions.

There are seven countries in Central America

Central America is the isthmus between North and South America. It consists of seven countries or states lying between Mexico in the north and Colombia in the south. These are Guatemala, El Salvador, Belize, Honduras, Nicaragua, Costa Rica and Panama. The isthmus is about 1900 kilometres (3000 miles) long and only about 48 kilometres (30 miles) wide at its narrowest point in Panama. A mountain chain, which still contains some active volcanoes, runs down one side of the isthmus.

Chile is 24 times as long as it is wide

Chile must be one of the most curiously shaped countries in the world. It is a long, narrow strip of land stretching more than 4260 kilometres (2647 miles) from north to south, between the Andes mountains and the Pacific Ocean. It has an average width of 177 kilometres (110 miles) and at no point is it wider than 400 kilometres (248 miles). Most of the people live in a long central plain, stretching for about 1000 kilometres (621 miles). Santiago is about half way up the coast.

Chile and its strange shape in relation to the rest of South America can be clearly seen from these two maps.

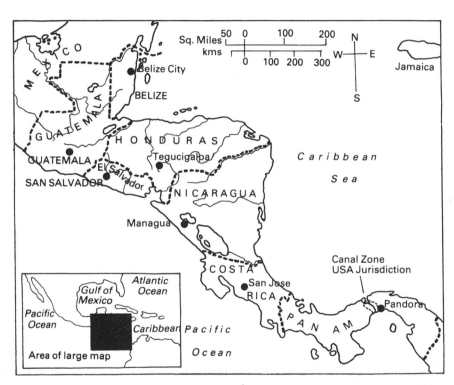

The construction of the Panama Canal, shown in the larger map, made it possible for ships to pass from the Atlantic to the Pacific Oceans without having to round Cape Horn at the tip of South America.

The Bahamas consist of 700 islands and 2000 rocks and cays

It was on the island of San Salvador, in the Bahamas, that Columbus first landed when he crossed the Atlantic in 1492. The islands are spread across the northern entrance to the Caribbean and the Gulf of Mexico, and have a superb climate. Only 30 of the islands are inhabited. Their main industry is tourism. The soil is poor and there are virtually no mineral resources. More than half the people live in the town of Nassau on New Providence Island. The 'cays' found among the rocks and islands are spits of sand and small reefs. Long ago, the islands were a home for buccaneers, the pirates of the Caribbean, and today they are popular with tourists.

The Mayan city of Chichen-Itza was abandoned even before Columbus discovered America

In its heyday, Chichen-Itza, in Central America, must have been one of the most impressive cities in the world. It was probably founded in the 6th or 7th century AD. It was abandoned, rebuilt, conquered and rebuilt again in the 13th and 14th centuries. The ruins of its greatest buildings still remain – the temple-crowned pyramid of El Castillo 30.5 metres (100 feet) high; the temple and hall of a Thousand Columns, which covers about two hectares (five acres); the vast ball court, nearly 137 metres (450 feet) long and 36.5 metres (120 feet) wide; crouching figures, carvings, columns and terraces. The city was suddenly abandoned in the 15th century.

The modern city of Brasilia was built in a wilderness

Rio de Janeiro was until recently the capital of Brazil. As long ago as 1822 there were plans to move the capital inland, to open up some of the vast area of Brazil that was still undeveloped. A site was selected in 1956. The new site was officially declared the capital of Brazil in 1960 and given the name Brasilia. It stands on a plateau more than 1000 metres (3300 feet) above sea level and more than 900 kilometres (560 miles) inland from Rio de Janeiro. Many of the materials for construction had to be flown in because of the remoteness of the area, until road and rail links were made with Sao Paulo and Rio. The first government buildings were not completed until 1968. Now there are many buildings, including a presidential palace, congress buildings, a cathedral, blocks of flats, churches, shops and hotels. There is a population of nearly half a million in this great city created out of nothing.

The natives of Peru built landing strips many centuries before there were aircraft

Not far from the coast of southern Peru, there are some extraordinary marks carved in the plain. More than 1000 years ago, the Nazca Indians drew out a series of lines, some parallel, some crossing, some extending for six to eight kilometres (four to five miles), some in geometrical shapes and patterns like vast spiders 46 metres (150 feet long) or humming birds several times longer still. The shape and extent of these signs can only be appreciated from the air. Since many of the lines look exactly like landing strips, some people think that they are proof that they were made for visitors from outer space. It is more likely that they were religious symbols made to please the gods. Some

people now believe that the Indians used hot-air balloons, made of animal skin, to rise above the plain and direct operations.

Mexico City is the largest city in the Western Hemisphere

Hundreds of years ago Mexico belonged to the Indians. They built large cities, developed a calendar, invented a counting system, and used a form of writing. The last Indian empire was that of the Aztecs, which was conquered by Spanish invaders in 1521. Mexico thus became a Spanish colony for about 300 years. During this time the Spaniards introduced changes in farming, government, industry and religion. As a result of intermarriage, a third group of people developed, the 'mestizos', who had both Indian and white ancestors. Today, they form the majority of the population. Mexicans take great pride in their Indian ancestry. In 1949 the Government made Cuauhteémoc, the last Aztec emperor, the symbol of Mexican nationality. His bravery under Spanish torture made him a hero.

Trinidad is the home of calypso and the limbo dance

The West Indian islands of Trinidad and Tobago are situated in the Caribbean Sea off the north east coast of South America. Together they cover an area of 5128 square kilometres (1980 square miles) and have a population of just over a million. The people are very musical. Many play native musical instruments called 'pans', which are made from empty oil drums, and sing calypsos. Calypso is a type of folk music which originated in the songs of slaves brought to Trinidad from Africa. Nowadays,

calypso competitions attract many visitors to the island. Champion calypso singers are selected for the wit of their lyrics and their rhymes rather than the music.

Haiti is the second oldest free nation in the Western Hemisphere

After the United States, Haiti was the first country in the Western Hemisphere to gain independence. The former slaves of the island rebelled against French colonial rule and in 1804 established the republic of Haiti. The name comes from the Indian, meaning 'high ground', as much of the country is covered with rugged mountains. Haiti covers the western third of the West Indian island Hispaniola, which lies between Cuba and Puerto Rico in the Caribbean Sea. It was the first Spanish colony to be established in the New World. Later the French developed Haiti into the richest colony in the Caribbean. To this day many Haitians still follow the customs their ancestors brought with them from Africa. Some practise a religion called voodoo.

The Amazon River carries more water than any other river in the world

Beginning high in the Andes mountains in Peru, the Amazon, the second largest river in the world, flows for a distance of 6437 kilometres (4000 miles) eastwards across Brazil, and finally into the Atlantic Ocean. More than 200 tributaries flow into the Amazon, and the river carries more water than the Nile, Mississippi and Yangtse put together. At many points the Amazon is too wide to see across to the opposite bank. Its width ranges from 2.4 to 10 kilometres (1½ to 6 miles) to 140 kilometres (90 miles) at its widest. The depth of the Amazon averages about 12 metres (40 feet), but in some places is as much as 91 metres (300 feet).

The Far East

India was once ruled by a private company

After western explorers had opened up the way around the Cape of Good Hope from Europe to India and the East Indies, European nations competed with each other for the rich trade to be won. The competition was not so much between the governments of these European countries as between the private trading companies that were set up to organise the trade. The British East India Company was established in 1600. It competed first with the Portuguese and then with the Dutch and the French. The Company had its own well-armed ships, known as East Indiamen, and its own soldiers. The French were eventually thrown out of India in 1757 and the East India Company continued to represent British power in India until the Indian Mutiny of 1857. After that, India was ruled directly by the British government.

The Ganges is a sacred river

The Hindus believe the Ganges to be a sacred river and they bathe in its waters to wash away their sins and also to cure disease. At the holy city of Benares, or Varanasi, there are temples along the bank with stairs, known as ghats, which lead down to the river. Pilgrims crowd on to these steps at dawn to wash themselves. The Ganges is one of India's most important rivers. It provides water for crops

and when it floods it leaves a coating of mud that makes the soil richer and more fertile. The Ganges flows from the Himalayas to the Bay of Bengal, a distance of 2500 kilometres (1553 miles), and is joined by the great rivers Jumna and Brahmaputra. The delta formed by these rivers is about 300 kilometres (186 miles) wide.

The Hindus of India belong to four main groups, or castes

Hindus have traditionally been divided into castes, or groups, of different levels of importance. Each caste has its own customs, keeps separate from the others and marries within itself. There are hundreds of subtle variations of caste but there are four main groups. These are the Brahmans (priests), the Kshatriyas (warriors), the Vaishyas (traders) and the Shudras (servants). The most humble of the Shudras were known as the 'Untouchables' because they cleaned the sewers, dug the graves and did other 'unclean' tasks. The Untouchables had no rights at all in Hindu society until Mahatma Gandhi gave them political rights when India became independent in 1947. He called them the 'Harijans' or 'Children of God'.

Thugs sometimes pretended to be ordinary merchants

A modern 'thug' is a tough, rough person who commits violent acts. The name originally came from

gangs of robbers and murderers in India. These thugs, or 'stranglers', as they were sometimes known, worshipped Kali, the goddess of destruction. They would often join a group of merchants and travel with them peacefully for days, pretending to be merchants themselves. Then they would suddenly attack the merchants, rob them, kill them and bury their bodies so that no one would know what had happened. Lord William Bentinck, the governor-general of India, started to take action against the thugs in 1828 but it took several decades to rid India of thugs.

At Ajanta there are Buddhist cave shrines carved inside a hill

The village of Ajanta is in the Aurangabad district of India, in the western central part of the country, inland from Bombay. Near the village there are 30 caves cut into the steep side of a ravine. Some are like monasteries, with little cells for the monks. Others are meeting places with shrines. The most elaborate goes more than 20 metres (65 feet) into the hill and has a three-dimensional domed shrine, or stupa, at its heart. The columns of stone that hold up the roof are cut to look like tree trunks, in memory of much older shrines that were built in the jungle. In some of the caves there are wonderful fresco paintings. Some of the rock-cut sanctuaries date from the 1st or 2nd century AD but most of them are from about the 6th or 7th century.

The Taj Mahal was based on a dream

It is widely agreed that the Taj Mahal is one of the most beautiful buildings in the world. It stands at Agra, in northern India, and was built in the 17th century by the Emperor Shah Jehan as a tomb for his wife, Mumtaz Mahal. It is said that the building appeared to Shah Jehan in a dream. An architect was engaged to draw plans for the building. He was given a drug so that he, too, would experience a vision of the building before he began work. Four slender pillars stand at the corners of the terrace on which the eight-sided, dome-capped tomb is built. There is a carved marble screen inside, around the tombs of Mumtaz and Shah Jehan. The bodies themselves are buried in a simple chamber beneath the floor.

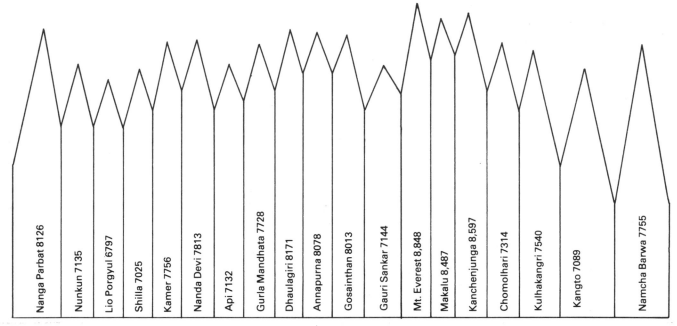

Nanga Parbat 8126
Nunkun 7135
Lio Porgyul 6797
Shilla 7025
Kamer 7756
Nanda Devi 7813
Api 7132
Gurla Mandhata 7728
Dhaulagiri 8171
Annapurna 8078
Gosainthan 8013
Gauri Sankar 7144
Mt. Everest 8,848
Makalu 8,487
Kanchenjunga 8,597
Chomolhari 7314
Kulhakangri 7540
Kangto 7089
Namcha Barwa 7755

This chart shows the sizes of the peaks in the Himalayan range which separates the Indian sub-continent from the rest of Asia. Because the weather can be so bad, there is a climbing season in the Himalayas when the weather is suitable. During this season, it is not unusual to find several expeditions climbing the same peak.

Kailasanatha is a vast temple cut into the side of a mountain

Kailasanaha is near Elora, in west Central India, not far north of the Ajanta caves. In about the 8th century AD, a great Buddhist temple was cut out of the sloping side of a mountain. Open space surrounds the building on all four sides and its spires and towers reach towards the sky. The outside as well as the inside of the temple is intricately carved. There are doorways, great halls and shrines within, and yet all the stone is still part of the mountainside.

A hundred different languages are spoken in Assam

Assam is a small state in north-east India, with a population of about 16 million people. The people belong to tribes with very different origins and so they have many languages. Each language is quite distinct from the others, although many words can be mutually understood. Assam is a vast valley running down on either side of the Brahmaputra river. Rice fields on the floor of the valley lead up to tea and timber plantations on the surrounding hillslopes and mountains.

Calcutta is named after the goddess of destruction

Calcutta, once the capital of the British Raj in India, and fourth largest city in the world today, is named after the Hindu goddess, Kali. She is often depicted with devilish eyes, tongue dripping blood, and snakes or garlands of skulls entwined about her neck. Her image strikes fear into the devout, and to this day sacrifices and flowers are laid daily before her. Indian mythology tells how Siva the Destroyer, her husband, was inconsolable on his wife's death. With her corpse draped around his shoulders he began a violent dance of mourning that became so furious that the other gods feared that the world would be destroyed in his rage. So Vishnu the Preserver, who with Siva and Brahma stand at the head of the Hindu religion, hurled his knife at Kali's corpse, splitting it into 52 pieces that were strewn throughout the world. The little toe of the right foot is said to have landed by a great river in Bengal, where a temple was erected and a village grew up, Kalikata, named after the goddess. Kalikata was the beginning of what is today the great city of Calcutta.

Thugs were religious fanatics

For 300 years 'thugs' travelled throughout India and robbed and killed in the name of religion. The name derives from the Hindustani 'thag' which means 'cheat' or 'rascal'. Thugs strangled their victims with a handkerchief or noose and consecrated them to Kali. They chose this method of killing because it was against their principles to spill blood. They believed, according to legend, that Kali disposed of the bodies by devouring them. In the 1830s the British in India, supported by the Indian princes, launched a drive to stamp out the practice of 'thuggery' once and for all. Over

3000 thugs were arrested within a 6-year period, many of whom were hanged, transported or imprisoned for life. Today - mercifully - the practice has become almost extinct.

The Indian Climate is governed by winds

Winds, called monsoons, blow across India for months at a time. In the cool season (October to February), they blow from the north-east and only the south-eastern tip gets any rain. From March to June the sun is directly overhead and the land becomes baked. The moist air over the ocean is sucked in over the land and from June to November the monsoon brings a hot, wet season.

Delhi consists of two cities

There have been many cities on the site of Delhi but two major cities still stand there. One is Old Delhi, which was the capital of the Mogul Emperor Shah Jehan in the 17th Century. This great walled city contained many beautiful palaces and mosques, some of which are still standing. After many attacks and lootings, the capital was moved to Calcutta but in 1912 it was moved back to Delhi. A new city, known as New Delhi, was planned and built there. The city remained the capital of India when the country became independent.

Below: *A map of China showing the Great Wall, the only man-made construction in the world that is visible from spacecraft above the Earth.*

The Great Wall of China can be seen from space

The Great Wall of China is probably our greatest building enterprise. It stretches for more than 2540 kilometres (1600 miles) from the Gulf of Chihli on the Yellow Sea westwards to the Jade Gate to Central Asia, where the ancient silk route once passed. It was built by the emperor Shih Huang Ti, about 200 years before the birth of Christ, to keep out the Hsiung-nu, the Hun horsemen of the north who were raiding his land and cities. The emperor did not in fact have to start from scratch. He joined up sections of walls that already existed and although he died soon after the wall was begun his successors carried on constructing for several hundred years.

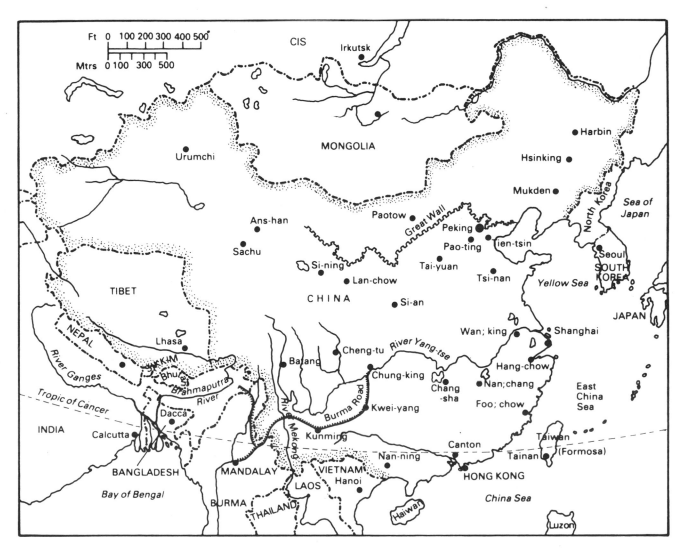

Indonesia is a country made up of thousands of islands

Indonesia is a string of islands between the Malay Peninsula and Australia that have formed themselves into an independent republic. There are several thousand islands in the group, including many very small ones, and there are more than 120 million people in Indonesia. The capital is at Djakarta, on Java. Other important islands in the group include Sumatra, the Celebes, Timor, Bali, Kalimantan (the name given to the southern part of Borneo) and Irian Jaya (the name given to the western half of New Guinea). Many of the islands were colonised by the Dutch in the 17th century. After the Second World War and a struggle with the Dutch, Indonesia won independence in 1949.

Bangkok is a city of canals

Bangkok is the capital of Thailand. Although it is 40 kilometres (25 miles) up the River Menam Chao Phya, it is also the chief port of Thailand. There are roads now running through the city, but until recently many of the houses were built over the river on platforms and the people used a maze of canals to move themselves and their goods about the city. There is still a lot of boat traffic and there are markets set up on rafts in the water. Modern buildings now mix with the marvellous pagodas, the temples, the bell-shaped towers and the stone carvings, as well as the great palace of old Bangkok.

The city of Angkor Thom was 'lost' for 500 years

Many men have looked for legendary lost cities but few ever find one. In 1861, a Frenchman, Henri Mouhot, stumbled across the most splendid of all Asian temple cities in the jungle of northern Cambodia. This was Angkor Thom, the capital of the once-powerful Khmer Empire. It was founded in the 9th century AD and is surrounded by a moat, 3.2 kilometres (2 miles) square. Vast gateways lead into the city over causeways. Towers, terraces, squares, tombs and sandstone carvings of gods, strange creatures, kings, lions and elephants fill the city. A mile outside the city is the marvellous shrine of Angkor Wat which has ornate fairytale-like towers. The city and shrine were sacked by enemies and finally abandoned in the 15th century when the vital irrigation system was destroyed by enemies.

The city that is 'the indestructible heart of Burma'

Mandalay is the second largest city in Burma, after the capital Rangoon, and the chief inland river port. The city was originally founded as the capital in 1857 by King Mindon Min, and as an important religious centre. It is still the home of many Buddhist monks and contains the ruins of numerous temples, monasteries and

Malaysia is a federation of countries

There are two main parts of Malaysia. East Malaysia includes Sarawak and Sabah, on the northern coast of the island of Borneo. (The rest of the island, known as Kalimantan, is part of Indonesia.)

West Malaysia lies at the southern end of the Malay Peninsula. The capital of the federation is Kuala Lumpur, in western Malaysia. There had been an ancient Malay kingdom on the peninsula long before the Portuguese arrived there in the 16th century. Later, the Dutch and British became rivals in the area.

The Japanese conquered Malaya during the Second World War and after the war Malaya became independent. The Federation of Malaysia was founded in 1963 and at first there was great rivalry with Indonesia, the other main influence in the area. Malaysia is a member of the British Commonwealth.

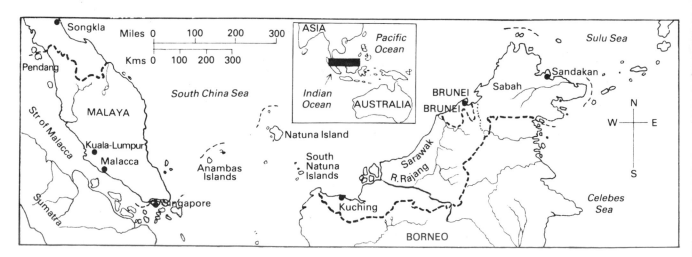

pagodas. At the foot of Mandalay
Hill there are 730 pagodas formed
into a square and housing sacred
white marble tablets on which the
Buddhist scriptures are recorded.
Mandalay's most famous pagoda,
the Mya Muni, stands to the south
of the city and contains a 5.7-metre
(12-foot) high brass Buddha that is
believed to be very old. The famous
Zegyo bazaar of Mandalay still
attracts traders from all over the
country.

The Gobi desert is twice the size of Texas

Lying on a plateau in Central Asia,
about 800 metres (half a mile)
above sea level, is the Gobi Desert.
It is a vast, sandswept, treeless
area shaped like an arc and
covering 1.3 million kilometres
(50,000 square miles). Nowadays
the only inhabitants of the desert
are a few nomadic tribesmen,
moving their sheep or cattle from
one poor grazing ground to
another. But archaeologists have
found evidence of very old
civilizations in the Gobi.

Their are more than 700 languages spoken in New Guinea

New Guinea, in the western Pacific
Ocean, is the second largest island
in the world after Greenland,
occupying an area of 807,400
square kilometres (311,740 square
miles). Politically New Guinea is
divided, the western half since
1949 belonging to Indonesia, the
eastern half obtaining
independence from Australia in
1975 as Papua New Guinea. The
geography and climate of the island
are varied. Much of the interior is
covered in rugged, snow-capped
mountains, while the lowlands
along the northern and southern
coasts are hot steamy jungles and
swamplands. Altogether, more
than 700 languages are spoken on
the island and this sometimes
leads to problems in
communication.

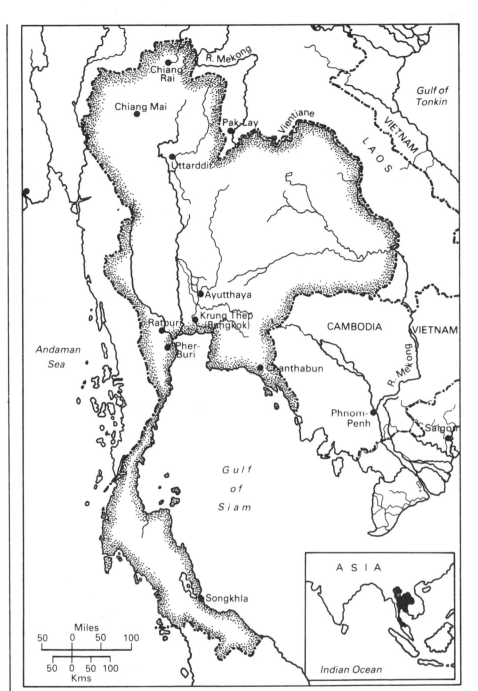

The map of Thailand is shaped like an elephant's head

The elephant has always been an
important part of life in Thailand. It
has been used to drag timber from
the forests and to act as a beast of
burden for warriors and princes. It
is not surprising that the Thai
people see it as a symbol of their
country, and see their country in
the shape of an elephant's head.
The long trunk stretches down the
peninsula towards Malaysia and
Singapore. The ear hangs down

*The elephant-like shape of Thailand can
be clearly seen from this map. Thailand
is an independent kingdom, but has
recently been threatened by forces
from neighbouring Cambodia and
Vietnam.*

towards Laos and Kampuchea
(Cambodia). The top of the head
lies north towards Burma. It is quite
easy to see this shape when you
look at a map.

Time

The world is divided into 24 time zones

Each of these time zones is either one hour ahead of or one hour behind the next-door zone and all are connected to Greenwich Mean Time (GMT). Time in each zone follows the rising sun. Thus the zones to the west of Greenwich are behind GMT and zones to the east are ahead of GMT. An imaginary line in the Pacific, called the International Date Line, enables you to gain or lose a day, depending on which way you are going. Each zone covers approximately 15 degrees of longitude but the lines are often bent to include whole countries within the same zone. In America there are five different time zones: Atlantic, Eastern, Central, Mountain and Pacific.

St Valentine's Day has little to do with St Valentine

St Valentine's Day, the 14th February, is the traditional day when lovers send each other anonymous 'Valentine' cards. In earlier times girls chose their lovers or husbands on this day. It is also the feast day of two different saints, both called Valentine and both martyred in the 3rd century AD. But neither of them had much to do with the traditions of the date. It was, however, the date on which the birds were believed to choose their mate for the spring and it was also close to the date of the ancient Roman feast of Lupercalia, which celebrated the time when the wolf suckled Romulus and Remus.

'Egg-timers' can run from four minutes to four hours

The traditional egg-timer is a form of hour-glass made of two bulbs of glass joined together by a narrow neck. Sand inside the bulbs runs from one to the other through the neck in an exactly measured amount of time. In the case of an egg-timer, the sand takes about four minutes to run through. But even before glasses were used to time eggs, preachers often had an hour-glass on their pulpits, which

A sixteenth-century hour glass.

ran for a full hour, so that everyone could see how long the sermon had still to last. Ships had four-hour-glasses, which told the length of the watches and were turned over at the end of each watch. Another 'hour-glass' on board lasted only 28 seconds and was used to time a length of line thrown overboard with a log at the end – the number of knots on that rope that ran out during the 28 seconds gave the speed of the ship.

Many countries and people do not celebrate their New Year on 1st January

Because different countries and religions have different ways of calculating the year, their New Year does not begin on 1st January, and, indeed, the actual date of New Year can vary from year to year. The Chinese New Year falls at some point, between January and February. The Buddhist New Year varies between March and April. The Jewish New Year is in September or October. In ancient Egypt and Persia, New Year began on 21st September, at the autumnal equinox, when day and night were of equal length. The Greeks celebrated the New Year on 21st December, at the winter solstice, when the day was at its shortest. Julius Caesar altered the Roman New Year to 1st January but in various European countries, including Britain, it continued to vary between a number of dates until Pope Gregory altered the calendar and settled New Year's Day as 1st January.

Clock faces once had their own special symbol for the number 4

Have you ever looked closely at the numbers on the face of an old clock, or even on some modern ones as well? They are usually in Roman numerals, such as I, V and X. Most people write the number '4' as 'IV' and that is how you will normally see it written on tombstones and memorial stones. But on clock faces it is almost always written 'IIII' instead. This custom lasted for hundreds of years.

An English clock dating from the seventeenth century.

Many clocks depend on the law of gravity

If a string with one end fixed, and a weight hanging on the other, is pulled back and released, it will swing to and fro in a regular motion. This is a simple example of a pendulum, and the uniform motion is due to gravity. The laws of the pendulum were discovered by Galileo in the 16th century, and it was he who realised that it could be used to regulate the movements of a clock. The pendulum commonly used in clocks has an 'escapement' device which gives small regular pushes to the pendulum to keep it swinging. Each time the pendulum swings aside, one tooth of a tooth wheel turns past the escapement, so producing the familiar 'tick tock'.

April Fool's Day has a long history

The real name of this special day for practical jokes is 'All Fools' Day' and it is observed in many parts of the world. It is probably a leftover from the time when the New Year began on 25th March and 1st April marked the end of the week's festivities. It was always important that the week ended with a flourish! In France, someone who has been tricked is known as *un poisson d'avril*, or 'an April fish'. In Scotland, the expression is a 'gowk' or 'cuckoo'.

Some of our months have the wrong names

The names of the twelve months date from Roman times. In early Roman times, the year began in March and so *September*, *October*, *November* and *December* were the 'seventh', 'eighth', 'ninth' and 'tenth' months of the year. Although they no longer are, the names stuck. The rest of the names are a mixture, mostly made up when the calendar was changed by Julius Caesar. January was named after Janus, the double-faced Roman god of entrances and doorways, looking back to the old

year and forward to the new year. February was named after 'februa', the Roman festival of purification. March stood for Mars, the Roman god of war. April came from the Latin word for 'opening buds'. May was Maia, the goddess of growth. June came from Juno, the goddess of heaven, or from the well-known Roman family of Junius. July was named after Julius Caesar himself. August was named after August Caesar, the first Roman emperor.

Biological clocks are mysterious timing systems

What controls the patterns of our sleeping and waking hours, or the bodily rhythms necessary to health and life? Some scientists believe that all living things have built-in timing systems. Others are of the opinion that 'biological clocks' are set by the natural rhythms of the Earth's electromagnetic or gravitational forces. Still others consider that both internal and external forces are responsible. Plants manifest rhythmic changes in their 'sleep movements'; they raise their leaves during the day and lower them at night. Interestingly, this rhythm is maintained even where light and temperature are kept constant.

Stonehenge may have been an astronomical calendar

Stonehenge is a circular ancient monument, composed of huge, roughly cut stones, standing on Salisbury Plain in Wiltshire. It is believed to have been built during the Late Neolithic Period and Early Bronze Age, around 1800-1400 BC. Although the monument is no longer intact, it has proved possible to envisage how it once looked from what remains. Scientists have shown that, correctly read, the monument was capable of accurately predicting the eclipses of the sun and moon.

Some clocks are accurate to a few seconds in 100,000 years

An atomic clock is a device for measuring time by measuring the frequency of electromagnetic waves which are given off or absorbed by atoms or molecules. This method is extremely reliable because the clock is not subject to change in temperature or wear.

Fossils

There are some strange beliefs about fossils

Fossils of sea creatures, deposited originally on the sea bed, are often found on dry land where the rocks that were under water have subsequently been forced upwards. Some people used to believe that these creatures had been washed up on land by the biblical Flood. Others believed that the fossils were unsuccessful attempts at the creation of life. There were theories that they were the tricks of the Devil, especially placed in the rocks to deceive humans. Some people even believed that they were created by thunderbolts.

Fossils are formed from the remains of dead animals and plants

Sometimes dead plants and animals become buried beneath sediment and do not decay. Their remains are preserved as fossils. Water seeps through the sediment that lies over the body and brings with it particles of dissolved chemicals such as silica, iron pyrites and calcite. These chemicals may build up in the body. In time the chemicals harden and form a perfect copy of the animal. Fossils may also be formed in a different way. Sometimes the original body dissolves, leaving a hollow in the sediment. A fossil cast is formed when this hollow is filled by minerals seeping through the sediment.

Evidence of past life on Earth is preserved in many ways. One of the most beautiful is an insect, trapped forever in amber.

A crinoid, an early life form has left its cast form in limestone. Fossil hunting is rewarding, and can be a financially profitable hobby. Within a few days of searching in an area known for its fossils, even a beginner should be able to find evidence of early life.

Ammonites are probably the most commonly found fossils in Jurassic shales. They are the the fossils of shells of soft-bodied molluscs related to squids and can be found made of many minerals and occur in many sizes.

Mammals such as this woolly mammoth have been fossilized since they died over a million years ago.

Mammoths have been found with their last meals still in their stomachs

Fossil remains only rarely include the whole original animal or plant. Tree resin has preserved insects 100 or 200 million years old and the bodies of Ice Age creatures have sometimes been preserved perfectly in the ice. Woolly mammoths about 25,000 years old have been found in Alaska and Siberia, the hair of their bodies intact and their last meal still inside them. Mammoth steaks have even been fed to modern dogs; they proved tough and inedible for man. Fossil mammoth ivory has been used by modern man for a variety of purposes and has attained some economic importance. Mammoths were hunted by primitive man and figured significantly in his art. European cave dwellers realistically depicted herds of the animals with humps on their backs. There is no trace of these humps in fossil remains, but they were probably a means of storing energy.

The evolution of the horse is well recorded

The ancestor of today's horses was a little mammal called eohippus which first appeared in the world 54 million years ago. It browsed on soft leaves and vegetation and as the centuries and millenia passed it gradually grew larger as its legs become longer and longer. This change is associated with a running mode of life. It also changed its eating habits and became a grazing, rather than a browsing animal. It also developed a strange, high-crowned tooth structure to enable it to grind its food efficiently. We know all this because horses lived in America and there are fossils of them there ranging from Eocene to recent times. Ironically, the horses crossed the narrow land bridge that used to connect Asia with America millions of years ago. By the time man developed there were no horses in America and they were introduced into the American continent by Spanish conquerors.

Dinosaurs were not giant lizards

Dinosaurs were reptiles that inhabited the Earth from about 225 million to about 65 million years ago. They varied in size, appearance and habits and different species existed on the Earth at different times. The celebrated tyrannosaurus rex that lived between 130 and 65 million years ago was 12 metres (40 feet) long and a fierce carnivore; the brontosaurus, which first appeared 180 million years ago, was twice as big, and a plant-eater. Some dinosaurs were no bigger than a large chicken. The word 'dinosaur' comes from two Greek words meaning 'terrible lizard'. For many years dinosaurs were believed to have been clumsy, slow-moving creatures living much like reptiles seen today. But evidence from fossils suggests that some were far more active. In their leg and foot structure and upright posture many bore a closer resemblance to birds than to present-day reptiles.

Nature

Chewing gum was invented a long time ago

The ancient Maya and other Central American Indians used to chew chicle, which is the thick, rubbery, milky juice of the sapodilla tree. Some North American Indians chewed spruce gum resin. European settlers in America began to market this in the 1800s and then moved on to the chicle based chewing gums. These had a better chewing quality and also held the flavours that were added to them. Chicle is still used as part of the basis for modern gums.

The Maya Indians played with rubber balls 900 years ago

The bouncing quality of rubber has been known for a long time. The Maya Indians of Central America tapped latex from the rubber tree and made it into simple rubber balls for their children to play with long before the Spaniards arrived. So did the Aztecs. The Indians also used a type of rubber bottle for holding liquid, and used rubber for the soles of some shoes to keep the water out. Today, most rubber comes from the Far East.

The banyan tree grows 100 trunks

The sacred banyan tree of eastern India and Malaysia grows so large that it must support and feed itself by sending down new roots from its massive branches. These roots become new trunks from which more branches spread, so that the banyan grows wider and wider until a single tree looks like a whole grove of trees with 100 or even 200 trunks. The tree may eventually cover an area more than 300 metres (984 feet) in diameter. Some trees are used as market places. People set up their stalls between the trunks and buy and sell their goods beneath the natural shelter of the branches. In fact, Hindu merchants were once called 'banians'.

Scientists cut down the oldest tree in the world

Methuselah (see page 65) only became the oldest tree in 1964, for in that year, scientists cut down an even older bristlecone for study. When it was studied it gave the scientists an amazing picture of its life, because trees are a 'computer record' of the weather of their lifetime. By looking closely at the rings of the tree, the scientists were able to tell that in one summer in the 15th century (1453) and again in 1601, there were freak cold spells. The research also helped scientists to rethink certain aspects of prehistoric times. Scientists date prehistoric times by a system called radio-carbon. This dating system involved measuring the amount of Carbon 14 that remains in a fossil, and by estimating the rate of loss of this substance, scientists thought they could date things very accurately, but this depended on the amount of carbon in the atmosphere caused by bombardment having remained constant. Examination of the bristlecone showed that this was not so, but showed fluctuations. This proved that the old system was slightly inaccurate. Bristlecones have also been used to investigate fluctuations in the earth's magnetism; the effect that a nuclear bomb test has on the atmosphere; and air pollution and the effects of lead chemicals that are pumped out into the atmosphere from car exhausts. Perhaps thousands of years from now, tomorrow's scientists will be able to carry out similar investigations on trees planted today, and claim with reasonable authority, that the amount of lead in the air has decreased as oil became less common a fuel.

The olive branch is a symbol of peace

Olives have been cultivated since prehistoric times, and are still vitally important to the daily life of the Mediterranean countries who grow them. Olive oil provides their main source of edible oil, besides being a valuable commodity for export. At one time it was used for lighting as well as for cooking, and even for anointing the body in religious ceremonies. There are frequent references to the olive in Greek and Roman writings and in the Bible. The crop has changed little since those times, perhaps because these hardy shrubs have been known to live for 1500 years. They are the oldest European tree.

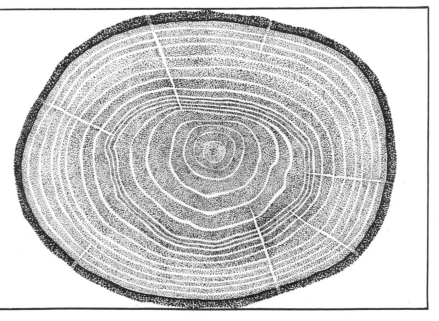

In some parts of the world clocks run on salad oil

The Horseradish Tree, native to northeast Africa and India, is widely grown in villages throughout the tropics. The roots of the tree, like true horseradish, are an aid to digestion. The seeds are rich in an oil, called Ben Oil, which can be used for cooking or for lubricating watches and clocks. Ben Oil has no smell, does not go rancid and makes an excellent salad oil. It is also used for making high-quality soap because it can absorb and retain fragrance.

Cashew nuts might be considered to come from apples

The kidney-shaped cashew nut is the fruit of a tree that first grew in the West Indies, but is now cultivated throughout the tropics. As it grows, the nut protrudes from its fleshy receptacle, known as the cashew apple. This is red and yellow and juicy when it is ripe, and resembles a normal apple. The shell of the nut contains a pungent oil, and the nuts are heated before the kernel is extracted so as to reduce its effect. The cashew apple is used in local beverages, jams and jellies.

Plane trees shed their bark to stay healthy

Plane trees survive better than most other trees in cities. When their outer bark has become damaged by the polluted air, the bark flakes off leaving fresh bark beneath in the same way that the human body sheds skin.

In California there is a tree which is over 4,000 years old

The oldest living thing in the world grows on poor soil 2,743 metres (9,000 feet) up in the White Mountains in California. It is a bristlecone pine, nicknamed Methuselah, which is about 4600 years old. The age of the tree was estimated by counting the number of its growth rings. Within the ancient rings of the tree, scientists have found seeds that tell them much about vegetation in past times.

Herbs were once the most important part of any garden

Herbs were grown in ancient times and throughout the Middle Ages not only for their scents and colours. They were grown for their flavouring qualities and, above all, for their medicinal qualities. They were also used in magic potions, for love or to thwart the devil for example. The Greek, Theophrastus, wrote a history of plants and herbs in the third century BC and the Roman, Dioscorides, wrote out a selection of herbal remedies in the second century AD. Every monastery had a herb garden and the idea for the modern flower garden probably developed from the more colourful herbs. One of the best-known books on herbs was written by Nicholas Culpepper in the seventeenth century. It is called *The Complete Herbal.*

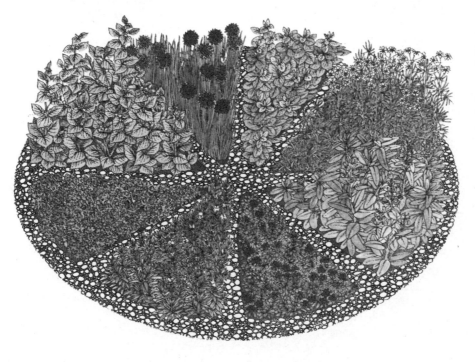

Herbs have been used throughout the ages

Balm was once exactly what its name implies, a 'balm' or cure-all for sick people in general. A drink made from it was believed to be soothing to the nerves, comforting to the heart and cheering to the spirit.

Chives were used by the Chinese more than 2000 years ago as an antidote to poison and as a means to stop bleeding.

Camomile is a herb to drink, to walk on and to cure a fever with

Camomile was one of the most popular herbs in ancient times. Garden paths were often made of camomile because it was said that the more the plant was crushed underfoot the better it grew and the sweeter it smelled. It was also used to reduce fever and soothe a headache. People with blonde hair used a solution of it as a hair rinse and it is still used for making a kind of tea or tisane, a refreshing drink. Many people believed that if camomile was planted next to a sick plant then the plant would revive.

The Ancient Greeks and Romans believed that the bay tree had many virtues

The bay leaf became a symbol of success for a variety of professions. The doctor wore a wreath of bay leaves because the bay tree was important for good health. The scholar wore one because it was the tree of Apollo, the god of poetry. The athlete wore one because Apollo was also the god of archery and the bay tree was also a symbol of courage. Soldiers wore one for the same reason and because the bay tree was believed to give protection against lightning, symbolic of the gods of war.

The Romans spread marjoram through Europe and it became known as a charm against witchcraft. Its delicate scent was thought to be unbearable for anyone who had sold their soul to the Devil.

Coriander was once used for flavouring both gin and bread. A popular sweet called a 'comfit' was made by coating the seed with a hard sugary covering.

It was considered a compliment in Ancient Greece to tell someone that they smelled of thyme. Also bees are particularly fond of the smell of thyme.

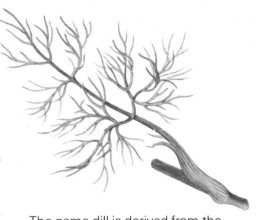

The name dill is derived from the Saxon word 'dilla' meaning 'to lull'. Gripe water, which is made from dill seeds, is used to quieten colicky babies and induce sleep.

Sage was thought to be good for the memory, which is perhaps how it got its 'wise' or 'sage' name. There was also an old superstition that a sage plant will droop if its owner is unwell and thrive if he is fit.

The Romans believed that a garland of parsley worn round the head would prevent drunkenness at a dinner party. They also believed that the horses of the gods and heroes ate parsley to give them strength.

The Greeks believed that fennel induced courage, strength and longevity. The Chinese and Hindus used it as a remedy against snake bites. Today it is still considered an aid to expelling poisons from the blood.

Winter savory is stronger than summer savory. It is often known as the 'bean herb' because it adds excellent flavour to beans. The Romans used it as a general medicine and it is still thought good to rub savory on a bee sting.

Rosemary is a versatile plant with a clinging pinetree fragrance. A little rosemary sprinkled over hot coals while barbecueing meat will show why Greeks and Romans valued it as incense and why it has always been used as a meat seasoner. Rosemary tea is reputed to ensure a good night's sleep; and is particularly effective against headaches.

One of the oldest herbs known to man, basil is considered sacred in India where Hindus place it in the hands of the dead to ensure a troublefree passage to paradise.

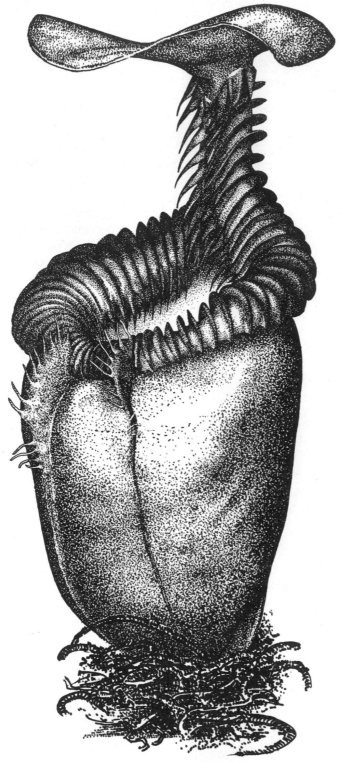

Pinks are flowers which are not always coloured pink

Pinks are not called 'pinks' because of their colour – they may be white or purple, or a variety of other shades. The name 'pink' refers to the edges of the petals, which are ornamented with little notches, or 'pinked'. In the same way, scissors that are used for cutting the edge of cloth in a notched pattern, to stop it fraying, are called 'pinking' sheers.

Buttercups are not all as innocent as they might appear

Aconite, or monkshood, belongs to the buttercup family. It grows in damp woods and hedgerows and has bluish-purple flowers. In the past its poisonous root was used to smear bait to catch wolves. For this reason it was often known as wolf's bane. Whalers also used it on the tips of their harpoons.

The bathroom loofah is really a pumpkin

A loofah is a long, rough kind of sponge that is often used in the bath. It is in fact a vegetable that belongs to the same family as pumpkins and gourds. The climbing tendrils produce a long fruit with a tough outside and a fibre-like inside which is dried before being used as a bathroom loofah.

Some plants live off each other

Just as some animals co-exist in symbiotic relationships, so some plants do the same with animals. The roots of clover and other members of the pea family have little swellings called root nodules. These nodules contain bacteria which can convert nitrogen into nitrates. These are very important plant foods. The bacteria get shelter and some food materials from the plant and the plant derives benefit from the bacteria.

Some plants feed on insects

The Pitcher plant *(above)* and Venus flytrap like richer food than most other species of plant. They feed on insects. The Pitcher plant is found mainly in tropical Asia. Its leaves are shaped like vases, or pitchers, and contain a sweet juice called nectar. Insects enter the pitchers to drink the juice. Once inside, they are caught by hairs and fall down into the digestive acid at the bottom of the pitchers. The Venus flytrap is found in the United States. It has leaves fringed with little teeth. When an insect lands on one of the leaves, the leaf closes in half and the insect is trapped inside. Juices inside the leaf digest the insect within about ten days.

The bitter sloe is the ancestor of the sweetest plums

The sloe is sometimes known as the blackthorn. It is a very thick, wild shrub with sharp thorns and small, purple-blue fruits. This is the ancestor of all the cultivated plums of today. The sloe itself is extremely bitter and is normally never eaten raw. The small fruit can be used in jellies and for making sloe gin and wine. We know that Stone Age people used sloes because piles of sloe stones have been found on Neolithic sites.

Cotton was used to make cloth 3000 years before Christ was born

When Europeans first came across the cotton plant in comparatively recent times they thought that the fibres were, literally, a form of wool. But in fact the fibres had been spun into yarn as long as 3000 years before Christ and remains have been found at Mohenjo-Daro in Pakistan, one of the most ancient cities in the world. Cotton is a light cloth that is pleasant and cool to wear. It is woven from yarns that are spun from cotton fibre or 'bolls'. These are white balls of fibre that grow from the seeds of the plant. The process of separating the fibres from the unwanted seeds was slow and laborious until Eli Whitney invented a special machine to do the work in 1793. He used the machine on the cotton plantations of the southern states of North America. As the demand for cotton increased, the southern cotton industry expanded, and created the need for extra labour. This need was met by the slave traders who shipped in blacks from Africa. Cotton thus became a source of enormous wealth to the plantation owners of the Old South, and earned the name 'King Cotton'. The move by the North American states to abolish slavery was one of the causes of the American Civil War.

People once thought a vegetable could scream

The mandrake is related to the potato but it is poisonous. Its large roots are forked and can sometimes resemble a human figure, with legs and arms and even a head. Many legends have grown up around the root. In the Middle Ages people believed that it screamed if it was pulled out of the ground, causing the person who pulled it to die shortly afterwards. Sometimes figures were cut from the root and used as charms. The root grows mainly around the Mediterranean area.

Plants may have emotions

An American lie detector expert once attached a machine to the leaves of a philodendron and was surprised to find that it produced a reading similar to that of a human being who has been subjected to emotional stimulation. He decided to experiment further by burning the leaf of the plant. While he was thinking about doing this the tracing pattern began to sweep upwards dramatically. He had apparently frightened the plant with his thoughts. He concluded not only that plants have emotions, but that they are capable of some form of telepathy!

The beautiful rhododendron in our gardens may be deadly

Laurel, azalea and rosebay are all members of the rhododendron family. The name comes from the Greek, meaning 'treerose'. These flowering shrubs vary considerably in size. One species originating in California can grow as tall as 6 metres (20 feet) and has huge purple flowers. But large or small, these plants are poisonous. They can cause headache, giddiness, and even paralysis and death. The rhododendron is a common flower found throughout the world. It is bitter to the taste.

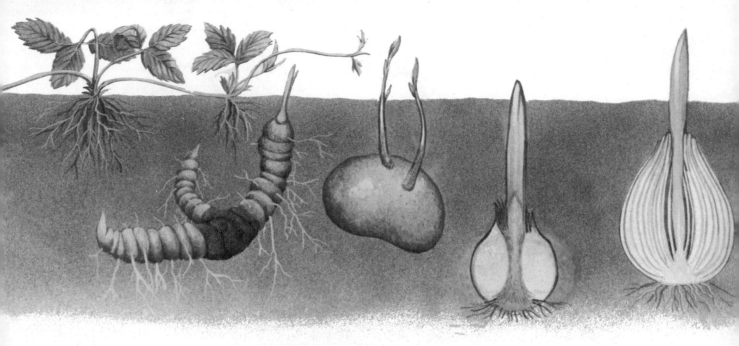

Some plants reproduce asexually

In asexual reproduction, plants do not produce flowers with male and female parts. There are several ways of reproducing asexually. Simple plants such as algae and fungi produce spores, which are blown to new areas. Strawberries produce surface runners with a new plant on the end. Iris rhizomes extend underground and send up new shoots. Potato tubers are forms of underground storage units for new growth. Gladioli and crocus corms are swollen underground stems that also store food. Tulip, daffodil and lily bulbs are underground buds that send down new roots each year for further growth.

Above left to right: *A strawberry plant with a new plant at the end of its runner. Iris rhizomes. Potato tubers pushing new growth above the ground. The swollen underground stem of a crocus corm. A tulip bulb sends down new roots each year.*

Most flowering plants need help to transfer the pollen to the stigma

Some plants pollinate themselves by their own pollen falling on their own stigma, but most plants depend on the pollen from one plant being taken to the stigma of another plant. The wind is one form of transport. Wind-pollinated plants tend to be fairly colourless and they are specially designed for both pollen and stigma to catch the slightest breeze. Plants that are pollinated by insects tend to be brightly coloured. They often attract the insects with sweet scents and nectar. The pollen is transferred to the stigma of another flower when the insect moves on to feed on nectar elsewhere. Pollination and the ways in which different plants pollinate have been studied by botanists for many years.

Flowering plants are only a very small proportion of the total plant world

There are anything between 250,000 and 500,000 species of plants, of which flowering plants form only a very small group. Among the many other kinds of plants, there are the simple algae, which reproduce by splitting in two. There are seaweeds, lichens and fungi, which reproduce by means of spores. Liverworts and mosses use both spores and sexual reproduction. Clubmosses, horsetails and ferns have stems and leaves but no seeds. Gymnosperms, such as conifers, are seed-bearing plants with naked seeds not enclosed in an ovary. Angiosperms, or flowering plants, have ovary-covered seeds. These and all other plants have adapted to their environments as successfully as animals have.

All animals rely on plants for food

All food is produced by plants. Even the carnivore, which eats the flesh of other animals, relies on the energy stored in its victims from the plants that they themselves have eaten. Plants make their own food. They do this through the green chlorophyll cells in their leaves. Chlorophyll combines water from the soil and carbon dioxide from the air to form sugars. It does this with the help of energy from sunlight. These sugars are used immediately to help the plant grow, or they are stored in the form of seeds or tubers. This process is called 'photosynthesis', from the Greek words *photo* (light) and *synthesis* (putting together). This process is complicated and man has never managed to duplicate it although scientists have tried.

Suction draws water from the roots of a tree to its crown

Like all plants, trees need water to carry food around their branches and stems. Water also keeps the leaves firm and stops them from wilting. But no plant has a 'heart' to pump the life-giving water round its system. Instead, it relies on suction. The surface cells of the leaves have tiny pores called stomata. Water evaporates into the air through the stomata. As the water escapes, more water is sucked up from the soil through the roots. It passes up narrow tubes within the trunk. We call this process 'transpiration'.

How plants collect and store water in areas of little rainfall

Plants that grow in very dry climates develop special methods for collecting and storing water. Some cacti, for instance, grow roots over large areas just below the surface of the ground. This enables them to absorb water quickly, which is vital where rainfall can be light or torrential, as in deserts. The water is stored in the cacti's fleshy stems. Cacti also grow spines, rather than leaves, which prevent excessive loss of water through transpiration. They carry out photosynthesis through their stems using the stored water.

Seed dispersal plays an important role in the distribution of plants

People help to spread seeds by taking food crops and other plants to wherever they settle. Wind, too, scatters seeds far and wide. The wing-like seeds of the maple tree and the fluffy dandelion and milkweed plants are all dispersed in this way. Coconut seeds can float on water from one land area to another. A few species of plants distribute their own seeds independently of wind or water.

Flowering plants reproduce sexually

There are four main parts to a flower. These are the calyx, or outer cover; the corolla, or petals; the stamen, or male part; and the carpel, or female part. The calyx is usually divided into sections or sepals. The stamens consist of stalk-like filaments with anthers, or pollen sacs, on their ends which produce the pollen. The carpels are usually in the centre of the flower.

They consist of a style, or stalk, with a stigma at the top and an ovary, containing ovules, at the bottom. The stigma and the style together are known as the pistil. Pollen rubs off on the stigma and travels down the style to the ovules, where the pollen and ovule cells join up, enabling the ovules to become fertile seeds.

Below: *The sexual parts of flowers are the same in all plants that reproduce sexually.*

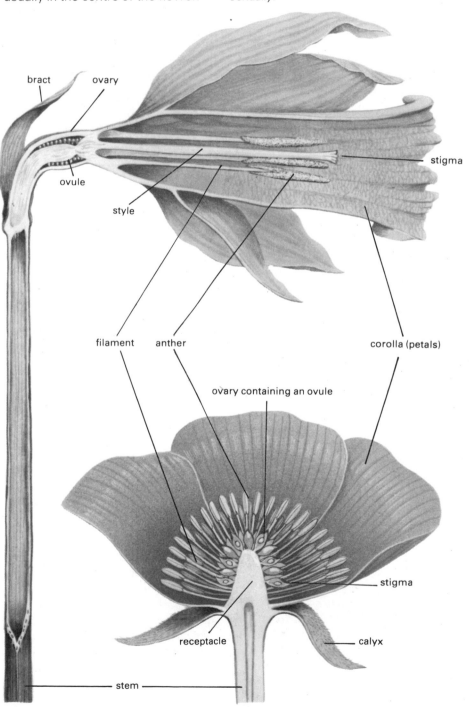

The mistletoe under which you kiss at Christmas was once linked with human sacrifice

The mistletoe is a parasite that is normally found growing on apple trees, sometimes on oak trees and also on some other trees. It is evergreen and it has white berries. The ancient Druids of Celtic Britain used it in their sacrifices. They also prepared it as a drink for curing sterility and as a protection against poison. Although the Christians forbade it to be hung in their churches because of its connection with the Druids, it eventually became a popular decoration in the home at Christmas time. A kiss under the mistletoe was believed to lead to marriage.

Some almonds contain poison

There are two kinds of almond: the sweet almond and the bitter almond. Both kinds grow around the Mediterranean and in California on trees about six metres (19 feet) high. They have a soft fruit on the outside, with a hard shell containing the nut inside. The sweet almond, with its pink blossoms, is eaten raw or used for marzipan and as an oil in cosmetics. The bitter almond has a white blossom and contains a highly poisonous prussic acid, which gives the bitter taste. However, the prussic acid can be removed. The almond can then be used for flavouring and for its oil. There are also several types of ornamental almond trees.

The pink damask rose provides the essence of the most expensive perfumes

'Attar' sometimes written as 'Otto' of roses is the essence or oil of certain roses. The essence is used in making the most expensive perfumes and also in some liqueurs. The rose that is most often used is the pink damask rose, grown in the valleys of Bulgaria. Centifolia roses are grown for the same purpose in the south of France and in Morocco, south of the Mediterranean. It takes more than 100 kilograms (220 lbs) of rose petals to produce less than 30 grams (1oz) of the precious essence.

A roadside weed grew into a variety of vegetables

The original wild cabbage can still be found growing in the countryside. It has a scraggy head of yellow flowers, a stalky stem and a few broad leaves at the base. From this simple plant has come a wide range of everyday vegetables: cabbages, cauliflowers, brussels sprouts, broccoli and kale. Less well-known types include kohlrabi. These vegetables have been developed over many years by careful seed selection.

The bark of trees can be used to make clothes

There are people in the Pacific Islands who make cloth from the inner bark, or bast, of certain trees. This was once quite usual in Sri Lanka, the Malay Peninsula, the Philippines, Polynesia, Central America and parts of Africa. It was also customary in ancient China, India and Peru. In Polynesia, mulberry, breadfruit and fig trees are used for their bark. The inner part is stripped off, soaked and beaten, then dyed and painted and shaped into clothes and covers.

Cork is obtained from the bark of an oak tree

Human kind has used cork from as early as 400 BC. It has the advantages of being light, springy and non-absorbent. The Romans wore cork sandals and used cork to float their fishing nets. Bottle stoppers have been made from cork since the 1600s. Nowadays, cork is also used in the manufacture of linoleum, cork tiles and insulating materials. Cork comes from two species of evergreen oak tree, popularly known as the cork oak and the live oak. The one is native to the Mediterranean, and the other is found in parts of North America and in Cuba and Mexico. The live oak once provided the Americans with their heaviest timbers for shipbuilding. To gather cork, the dead bark is stripped from the tree about once every 10 years. This does not harm the tree. A tree has to be 20 years old before the first bark is thick enough for stripping. Cork trees live from 300 to 400 years, but seldom grow higher than 15 metres (50 feet).

South American Indians were taking snuff long before King Charles

The powerful drug Yopo is made from a bean that grows in the Orinoco, the frontier region between Colombia and Venezuela, in South America. The drug which is inhaled like snuff, is used by some South American tribes according to a custom that dates back many centuries. The effects of the drug and the methods of preparing it have been recorded by explorers over the ages. According to one account, the pods of the plant are broken, moistened and left to ferment. Later the softened beans are made into cakes, mixed with snail's lime and powdered, to produce the snuff. When inhaled, this is said to induce a state like drunkenness, followed by wild excitement and hallucinations.

The oldest dyestuff known comes from a Turkish oak

It is likely that the 'scarlet' mentioned in Genesis and other places in the Bible, was a dye produced from a Mediterranean shrub of the oak family. The red juice from which the dye is made was squeezed from bugs - at first thought to be berries - found on the plant's leaves. It was then treated with alum, according to a process discovered in India over 4000 years ago, to give it its colour-fixing property. Once applied to cloth, the dye would withstand both washing and intense sunlight. A different dyestuff, obtained from the Aleppo oak that is found in Cyprus and western Asia, also has a long history of use. The Roman historian Pliny mentions it, in the first century AD, as a dye for keeping the hair black.

The ancient Chinese considered soya beans their most important crop

Soya beans are one of the oldest crops raised by human beings. It is believed that the plant first grew in Eastern Asia and was cultivated about 5000 years ago. To the Chinese it was one of the five sacred grains necessary for life. Soya beans were introduced into Europe in the AD 1700s but were not widely cultivated until early this century. Since then, and up until fairly recently, they were used in the west mainly as animal feed or in the manufacture of fertilizer. Soya beans have only lately been recognized as a valuable source of protein, and a possible aid to easing world food-shortages. Soya beans grown on 0.4 hectares (1 acre) of land can provide up to 10 times as much protein as beef cattle raised on the same land.

The breadfruit tastes like potatoes and is baked like bread

One of the more important foods of the people of the Pacific Islands is the breadfruit. The tree grows to about 12 to 18 metres (38-58 feet) tall and has large, shiny leaves. The male flower is rather like a small banana and the female flower grows into a round fruit which has a rough rind and a soft, pulpy inside. It is usually baked when eaten but it may also be ground up, like flour, after it has been sliced and put out to dry. The inside bark of the tree is sometimes used for making cloth and the wood can be used for making furniture or even canoes. In the 18th century breadfruit was introduced to the New World, and nowadays is grown in the West Indies and in tropical America.

The loganberry is named after an American judge

Judge J. H. Logan, who lived in California towards the end of the nineteenth century, was interested in fruitgrowing. He carefully planned a cross between the wild blackberry and the cultivated raspberry. The result was the Loganberry, a large soft fruit with a slightly bitter taste but a delicious flavour when bottled and sweetened. Loganberries are now grown in America, Tasmania and the United Kingdom.

Stinging nettles make a tasty meal

It is possible to eat stinging nettles without being stung. The process of cooking the nettles destroys the formic acid which is responsible for the sting. Young nettle shoots have been used as food for a long time, either cooked like spinach and kale or made into a purée. Nettles have also been used as dyes and their stems have been used for weaving into a form of cloth.

'Jumping beans' have an animal inside them

Certain shrubs in Mexico have seeds that look very much like round beans. These particular beans are used as homes by the larvae or caterpillars of certain species of moth. If the beans are put in a warm place or held between the hands for a while, the larvae become active and start to twitch. If the bean is then put on the ground or laid in the palm of the hand, the bean will move in a series of jumps. This is the secret of the famous 'jumping bean'.

'Lion's teeth' are grown as vegetables, and to make wine and coffee

The common weed called the dandelion gets its name from the Norman-French *dent de lion*, or 'lion's tooth'. This is because of the ragged edge to the leaves that look a little like the teeth of a lion. The dandelion is a very useful plant. The Japanese use the cooked root as a vegetable. The fresh leaves make an excellent salad. When dried, the roots can be ground up to make a kind of coffee. The flowers are used to make a home-made wine. The yellow head actually consists of a cluster of flowers which open in the morning and close in the evening. Dandelions have smooth, hollow stems containing white milky juice. Their roots are long and thick, with hairlike roots branching off them.

The bean family enriches the soil with nitrogen

The bean family (Leguminosae) is an important group of plants which includes clovers *(below)*, lucerne, peas, beans, soya beans, ground nuts, lentils, sweet peas and lupins *(far right)*. The seeds are rich in protein and the plants also enrich the soil with nitrogen. On the roots of leguminous plants are tiny modules which contain bacteria. The bacteria take nitrogen from the air and make it into compounds which the plants use. When the plants die, the nitrogen remains in the soil.

There are about 2000 species of trees, shrubs and herbs in the rose family

The rose family, or Rosaceae, includes many wild fruits, such as brambles, hawthorns and blackthorns, as well as raspberries, strawberries, loganberries, apples, plums, pears, peaches, cherries, apricots and almonds. Garden roses have all been bred from wild roses.

Lupins (legume)

Raspberry (rose family)

Blackthorn (rose family)

White clover (legume)

Rose hips contain four times as much Vitamin C as blackcurrants

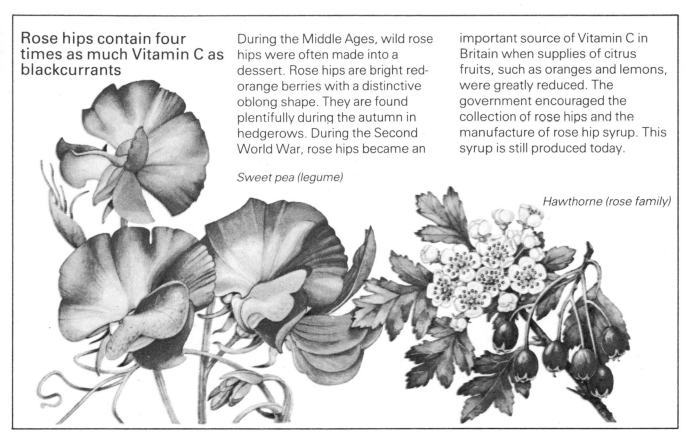

Sweet pea (legume)

Hawthorne (rose family)

During the Middle Ages, wild rose hips were often made into a dessert. Rose hips are bright red-orange berries with a distinctive oblong shape. They are found plentifully during the autumn in hedgerows. During the Second World War, rose hips became an important source of Vitamin C in Britain when supplies of citrus fruits, such as oranges and lemons, were greatly reduced. The government encouraged the collection of rose hips and the manufacture of rose hip syrup. This syrup is still produced today.

Farmers once protected their fruit crops from birds by planting decoys

It is difficult for fruit farmers to net all their currant bushes to protect them from the birds. It was an old custom to plant a single white currant bush along with every line of black currant bushes, so that the birds would eat the sweeter white currant instead.

There are more than 15,000 known species of orchid

Orchids are found as far apart as the humid tropics and the Arctic regions of Alaska, Greenland and Siberia. Most obtain their nourishment from the air, soil moisture, rain and light, and carry on photosynthesis like other green plants. Some in the tropics grow on the bark or outstretched limbs of giant trees. A few, including a species called coral-roots, found north of the Equator, depend upon absorbing organic compounds released from rotting vegetation.

Besides being beautiful flowers, orchids have attracted the interest of scientists because of their pollination habits. Some orchids can limit the insects that transfer their pollen to just the one sex of a single species. Charles Darwin, the great 19th century biologist, was so fascinated by this that he wrote a book on the subject.

The coconut palm has been described as the 'tropical jewel' among other plants

Probably originating in south east Asia and the Pacific Islands, the coconut palm is now found throughout the tropical and sub-tropical world. It stands 12 to 30 metres (40 to 100 feet) high and has large featherlike leaves spreading from the top of its branchless trunk. These leaves are often used for thatching roofs and for making hats, mats and baskets. The sap from the tree's blossom is the main ingredient in several soft and alcoholic drinks, and is also used in making sugar, vinegar and soap. A well-tended coconut palm will yield about 100 coconuts a year. They take nearly a year to ripen, and if left will fall from the tree naturally.

Mustard plants were called 'swastika plants' by the Hindus

Mustard flowers have four petals, arranged symetrically like the arms of a cross. For this reason the plants are known as crucifers, from the Latin for 'cross'. In both of the commonest varieties, black mustard and white mustard, the flowers are a yellowish colour and measure about 2 centimetres (¾ inch) across. They cluster loosely around the ends of branches from the coarse, leafy stem, which rises 1.8 to 3.0 metres (6 to 10 feet) above the ground. Most of the mustard consumed in Europe is made from the black mustard seed, except in the British Isles where the hotter flavour of the white mustard variety is generally preferred.

There are more than 3600 different kinds of grass in the world

If you look carefully at any field or meadow, or even at a lawn, it doesn't take long to discover that it is made up of many different kinds of grasses. Cereal crops such as wheat, barley, maize, oats, rye and millet are all forms of grass. So are rice, sugar cane and bamboo. They all have certain common features in their roots and the structure of their leaves that make them part of one large family of plants.

Bent grass

Meadow fescue   *Rye Grass*   *Timothy Grass*   *Marram Grass*

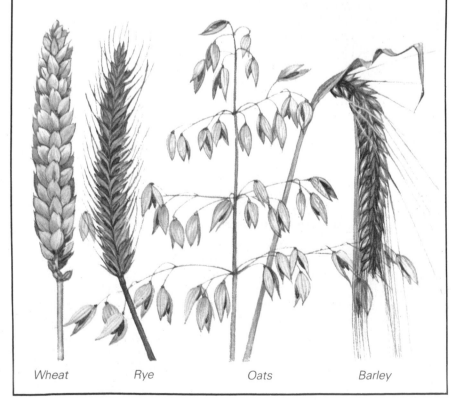

Wheat   *Rye*   *Oats*   *Barley*

The Aztecs used cocoa beans as money

Our word 'cocoa' derives from a misspelling of 'cacao', the tree from which cocoa beans are obtained. The tree was given its name by the Mayan Indians of Central America. It is supposed to mean 'bitter juice'. Cocoa beans were cultivated by both the Mayans and the Aztecs long before Columbus arrived in the New World. To the Aztecs cocoa was sacred, and eating the fruit was believed to be a way of acquiring wisdom. But cocoa also had more mundane uses, and was drunk as a beverage then, much as it is today. The cacao tree grows to about 7.6 metres (25 feet) high and produces leaves, flowers and fruit all the year round. The ripe fruit, or pod, is usually red and yellow in colour and contains between 20 and 40 seeds, or beans. It is these beans that are ground down and processed to produce cocoa or chocolate.

An African legend says that the creator planted the baobab tree upside down

Starting as a graceful sapling the baobab tree rapidly enlarges its trunk to a diameter of as much as 9.1 metres (30 feet). This looks totally out of proportion to its twisted branches at the top, which take on the appearance of roots rather than branches. But the baobab lives in the dry savannas of East Africa, and the huge trunk is actually a reservoir of water that is protected by a fibrous outer bark. This bark is sometimes used for making rope and cloth. When the centre of an old baobab dries out, there is enough room inside to provide shelter for a whole family. There is a baobab in Mozambique that bears the initials of Dr Livingstone on its inner wall and is also mentioned in his diary. In periods of drought baobabs are often attacked by elephants who want the moisture inside.

Mosses existed as long as 225 million years ago

Common mosses are soft green plants growing so close together that they form pads, or cushions. Sometimes they resemble very tiny groves of ferns or trees. The plants reproduce by type either sexually or asexually, producing spores that are dispersed by the wind. Altogether in the moss family there are about 15,000 species distributed throughout the world, except in salt water. These vary in size from microscopic to plants more than 1 metre (40 inches) long. Moss grows in shallow fresh water and on banks, rocks and trees, and can live at many different heights and temperatures. Mosses, together with lichens and liverworts, which belong to the same family, may have been the first plants to live on land. In fact, they help to control land erosion by providing a surface cover and absorbing water.

Sugar cane is an ancient crop

Sugar cane growing began in India as early as 3000 BC and only spread to the New World in the 15th and 16th centuries. The three major sugar cane producers today are India, Brazil and Cuba. Sugar cane is a tall plant with sturdy stalks of 2 to 5 metres (7 to 15 feet) high, and about 5 centimetres (2 inches) in diameter. These contain the sugary juice from which sugar and syrup are made. The plant requires a fertile soil that can hold large quantities of water. The colour of cane varies from whitish, through yellow, green and red, to deep purple. Even cane striped in different colours is known. The fibre remaining, after the juice has been extracted from the cane, is known as 'bagasse'. This has many uses, including serving as a wood-substitute in paper making, and as a source of cellulose for manufacturing animal feeds.

Bamboo can grow at the rate of 40 centimetres (15 inches) per day

Bamboo is a form of giant, woody grass. It grows in tight clumps and the roots spread rapidly, sending up clusters of new shoots. The hollow segments of the stem are used for sticks, for buckets, for building houses, for water pipes, for flutes, for boat masts and even for paper. Some bamboos give nut-like fruits and some have fleshy fruits. The Chinese eat the tender young shoots of bamboo. One Indian bamboo flowers every 32 years; another flowers every 60 years. One type flowers in times of drought, thus providing food for people when their rice cannot grow.

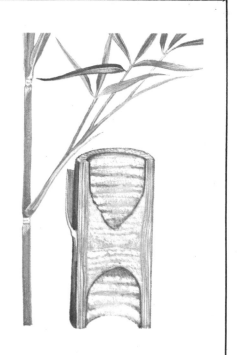

Different kinds of mushrooms lead different kinds of lives

The 'lifestyles' of fungi vary greatly. Some can be found thriving in a wide variety of habitats; others may require very special conditions for their existence, such as one type of tree, or burnt ground. Whichever is the case, all mushrooms are dependent on a preformed source of organic food. This is because they lack the green pigment chlorophyll, and must exist, directly or indirectly, at the expense of green plants. They may differ, however, in the way they extract their food. The majority, including most of the smaller mushrooms found in fields and woodlands, live on the dead remains, or waste, of plants and animals. Others are parasites that grow on living organisms, often causing serious damage to plants and trees. It is the microscopic relatives of these fungi that attack animals and humans and cause athlete's foot and ringworm. Some fungi, although living off trees, have a 'give and take' relationship with certain trees which is to their mutual benefit. This is known as symbiosis.

Jute is one of the cheapest natural fibres

Jute is a relative of the basswood trees that are found in Europe, Asia and North America. They include amongst their number the beautiful lime tree. For many years basswoods have been exploited for their fibre. At one time the fibrous tissues stripped from the inner bark (the bast, hence 'basswood') were made into bandages. Nowadays the fibre is often used in the manufacture of paper and cloth. But none of the basswood fibres have been as successful as jute, which is second only to cotton in its versatility and the quantity produced. Jute is used for making everything from coarse sacking to the finest imitation silk. The plant, which reaches a height of 2.4 to 3.7 metres (8 to 12 feet), grows best in warm humid climates, and is a rainy season crop. Harvesting begins about four months after planting. This involves cutting the stalks, soaking them and stripping the fibres. These are then washed and dried and tied into bundles. Jute has been cultivated in Bengal for many centuries. India and Bangladesh are the main producers.

Termites build giant towering nests

Termites live in North America, North Africa and temperate Eurasia. They live on grass, leaves and wood and can do terrible damage to buildings and forests. Some build their nests underground but others construct great cathedral-like spires of mud that may be as much as 6 metres (20 feet) high. A colony of termites may take as long as eight years to build a nest as big as this. In time, they abandon it and fly off to start a new colony. The most impressive colonies are in Africa and near Darwin, Australia, where many of them can be seen together in one area.

Tree ants produce their own glue

The tree ants of south-east Asia create a nest out of leaves that they glue together with special 'tubes' of gum. One group of ants holds the edges of two leaves close together. Another group, on the inside of the leaves, hold up young grubs, or larvae, from which they squeeze a sticky substance that gums the edges of the leaves together. Only the young can produce this sticky glue.

The leaf-cutting ants of South America grow their own food

The leaf-cutting ants of South America are mushroom farmers who cultivate their crops with care. They go in large parties to tear up leaves and plants into portions small enough to carry home. Then they chew the bits up into a form of compost which they spread on the floors of their underground chambers. After some time fungus grows on the compost. The ants then eat the fungus.

The dazzling dragonfly lives most of its life underwater

The dragonfly, with its brilliant colours and rapid movement, goes through several stages of development before it appears in the air. These are called 'larval' stages and they occur underwater. The larvae, or 'nymphs' as they are known, live in the mud where they catch other insects with their sharp claws. The nymph changes its skin several times before climbing up a grass or reed stem and emerging as a dragonfly. It may live for several months. Some stay on the wing almost all day, and can fly at up to 64 kmh (40 mph). Dragonfly fossils have been found from 260 million years ago. Some of these look almost identical to today's dragonflies.

Spiders spin webs to catch their prey but some have different methods

The majority of spiders spin webs from spinnerets at the rear of their bodies, making a variety of intricate and marvellously strong nets in which to trap their victims. But some do not use this 'netting' technique. The wolf spider runs very fast to catch its prey on the ground. The crab spider waits motionless and pounces on its prey as it passes. The trap-door spider makes a hole for itself with a lid and pops out unexpectedly to drag its victim down into its lair. The average house spider is harmless to humans but some are dangerous. The tarantula for example can cause considerable pain with its bite; and the most dangerous spider of all is the American black widow spider.

Ants have herds of 'cows' which they farm for their milk

Human beings are not the only creatures to keep herds of domestic animals. Ants keep herds of aphids, tiny insects about 6 milimetres (0.24 inches) long which produce a juicy 'honeydew' milk. The ants gather many of these insects into their nests, where they care for them and feed them. When the ants want a drink, they stroke the aphids with their feelers and suck the juice as it oozes out.

Beetles are probably the most successful of all insects

Beetles have two characteristics which combine to distinguish them from other insects. These are strong biting jaws and a protective sheath for their wings. This sheath is in fact the front pair of wings that have become hardened and lie back over the delicate rear wings to protect them and the rest of the body. The sheath is called the *elytra*.

Spiders are not insects

All creatures are divided up by scientists into families and sub-families, each with their own special name. Insects belong to the Insecta family, but spiders, along with scorpions and mites and others, belong to the family Arachnida, which is the Greek word for spider. The Greeks say that a girl called Arachne was so good at weaving that she challenged the goddess Athene to a competition and won. Athene was so furious that she changed Arachne into a spider and condemned her to weave a web spun out of her own body for the rest of time.

The caddis fly makes its own house of shells

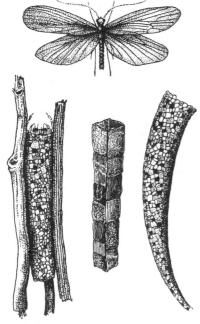

The caddis fly lays its eggs near fresh water and the caddis larvae live in the water until they mature. In order to protect themselves, they build around their body a house of pebbles and bits of shell. They glue it together with a silky liquid from their body. Some carry this house around with them. Others fix it to a stone and weave a net over the entrance, in which they catch their prey.

Ladybirds are distinguished by the number and colour of their spots

Ladybirds are useful to gardeners because they feed on greenfly and other creatures harmful to plants. Different kinds of ladybird have different numbers of spots. Some have two spots (one on each wing case), some have three, four, six, seven, ten and even 22 spots. Common ladybirds have red wing cases with black spots. Some have black wing cases with red spots. The variety with 22 spots has yellow wing cases with black spots.

The sacred beetle lays its eggs in a ball of dung

The scarab or dung-beetle was sacred to the ancient Egyptians as a symbol of creation and rebirth. They wore amulets in the shape of a scarab as good luck charms and they placed similar scarabs in their tombs. What impressed them about the beetle was the way in which it apparently laid its eggs in a ball of dung and rolled the dung along the ground to a safe hiding place, from which the young beetles eventually emerged. In fact, the scarab generally rolls dung into a hollow place and then lays its eggs in the dung so that the young have something to eat when they hatch.

Fireflies and glow-worms produce light more efficiently than people do

Electric light wastes a lot of energy in the form of heat, which is not required. You only have to put your hand near a light-bulb to feel that. Fireflies and glow-worms produce light without wasting any of their energy on heat. The lights are produced by the action of certain chemicals within the creatures' bodies. Both flashing and steady lights can be produced from patches on the sides or undersides of the beetles. They use the lights to attract each other. Fireflies usually glow with a greenish light.

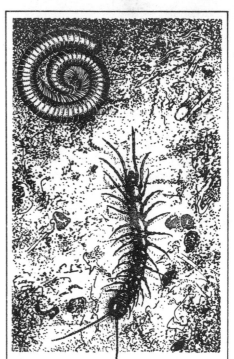

Centipedes rarely have 100 legs and millipedes never have 1000 legs

A centipede has a body made up of segments. Each segment has one pair of legs growing from it. The front segment usually has a pair of pincers for injecting poison into its prey. Sometimes centipedes have more than 100 legs but generally they have less, sometimes as few as 28. Millipedes also have segments to their bodies but each segment has two pairs of legs. They never have as many as 1000 legs, despite their name, which means 'thousand-footed'. Millipedes can grow up to 30 centimetres (one foot) long, whereas the longest centipedes are between 20 and 25 centimetres (8-10 inches) long.

The bombardier beetle sprays its enemies

The green-winged bombardier beetle earns its name from the burst of spray that explodes with a little bang from the glands at its rear when it is startled. The repellant spray stops the enemy in its tracks for long enough for the bombardier to escape.

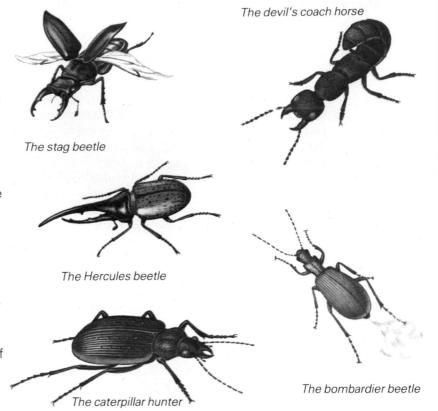

The stag, the hercules and the goliath are fearsome-looking giant beetles

The great antler-like jaws of the stag beetle may look frightening to its enemies but are not as dangerous as they seem. They are mainly used in fighting with other beetles for a mate. The one-up, one-down pincer-jaws of the hercules beetle are also used more for sparring than for killing. The goliath beetle from West Africa grows as large as a human fist and there is a beetle in the Amazon forest which grows to fifteen centimetres (six inches) long. The sharp jaws of the caterpillar-hunter are probably much more effective than the outsize jaws of its giant cousins and so, too, are the jaws of the black, scorpion-like, devil's coach horse when it rears up to fight.

The devil's coach horse

The stag beetle

The Hercules beetle

The caterpillar hunter

The bombardier beetle

The young of the caddis fly make their own houses of shells

The caddis fly lays its eggs near fresh water. When they hatch, the young caddis larvae live in the water until they mature. In order to protect themselves, they build around their body a house of pebbles and bits of shell, glued together with a silky liquid from their glands. Some carry this house around with them. Others fix it to a stone and weave a sieve-like net over the entrance, in which to catch their prey. After some time, each larva turns into a pupa within its house. Later it cuts its way out with its strong jaws.

The praying mantis does not really pray

The male praying mantis has to approach the female cautiously. If she can catch him before he mates with her, she will probably kill him. He creeps up from behind in a lethal game of grandmother's footsteps, freezing in his tracks every time she turns round, for she will only attack when she sees something move. He waits until her attention is distracted and then quickly moves in to mate. Even then, he is not safe. There is a good chance that she will kill him and eat him afterwards, instead. There are about 800 species of praying mantis. They get their name from their long front legs, which they hold out in front of them, as if they were praying. Don't be deceived. They are waiting to seize their victim.

There are 850,000 different kinds of insects in the world

This figure is about three times as many as all the other different kinds of animals added together. All fully grown insects have certain similar characteristics. The most important of these is that their body is made up of three parts, or segments. These are the head, the thorax (chest) and the abdomen (stomach). In some insects the thorax and abdomen seem to be joined together into one segment, but if you look very carefully underneath you can usually see the separation. Insects are the most adaptable of all animals and are found in every corner of the world from the Arctic to the jungle.

Insects breathe through their bellies

Humans and animals breathe through their nostrils and through their mouths. Fish breathe through their gills, which are just behind their heads. Insects need to breathe also but they do so through spiracles, little openings along the chest and belly (known as the thorax and abdomen). One insect, the water scorpion, has a breathing tube at the end of its abdomen, which it can push up to the surface of the water, rather like the snorkel of an underwater swimmer.

The dance of the bees tells its own story

Bees don't talk but they need to tell each other where they have found nectar. Those that have been successful return to the hive and perform a little dance. The dance tells the others exactly where to go. The pattern and speed of the dance indicate whether the flowers are near or far, towards the sun or away from the sun. The particular smell of the flower on the returning bee also tells the others exactly what kind of flower they are looking for.

Some common British beetles:
1. *Cockchafer.*
2. *Comb-headed cardinal.*
3. *Rhagium bafiscatum.*
4. *Seven-spotted ladybird.*
5. *Lined click beetle.*
6. *Nettle phyllobius.*
7. *Christolina polita.*
8. *Stenus bimaculatus.*
9. *Hoplia philanthus.*
10. *Green tortoise beetle.*
12. *Leaf beetle.*
13. *Christolina polita.*
14. *Great diving beetle.*
15. *Whirligig beetle.*
16. *Great diving beetle.*
17. *Comb-headed cardinal.*

A man who could leap like a flea would be able to jump 100 metres (328 feet) in the air

Fleas are extremely small. They vary between one millimetre and one centimetre (0.039-0.39 inches) in length. They are parasites that live by sucking the blood from other living creatures. Fleas have no wings but they have three pairs of remarkably strong legs. Depending on its size, an average flea can leap about 20-25 centimetres (8-10 inches) upwards or about 30-35 centimetres (12-14 inches) along. It can usually manage any distance between 50 and 100 times its own length. If an average man could leap rather more than 50 times his own height, then he would be able to clear 100 metres (328 feet). The strength and skill of fleas used to be demonstrated in special flea circuses. They were made to race.

Sheep still live in the wild

The mouflon was probably the ancestor of most domestic sheep. It still lives in the wild in Corsica and Sardinia. The mouflon is brown, with woolly underfur beneath rougher outside hair. Other wild sheep include the bighorns and Dall's sheep of North America, the Barbary sheep of North Africa and the massively horned wild sheep of Central Asia.

Mouflon

Dall

Bighorn

Goats and sheep are closely related

Although goats and sheep are closely related and some wild sheep look very goat-like, they differ in several obvious ways. Goats tend to have curved-back, scimitar-shaped horns, instead of outward-curling ones. (The horns of some goats, such as the Himalaya markhor, are spiral or corkscrew.) Male and female goats have horns, whereas only male sheep, or rams, have horns. Most kinds of goat have beards but sheep do not. Goats have short, upturned tails instead of the long, hanging tails of sheep.

The goat is one of the most useful of all domestic animals

The goat can survive in poor conditions and does not need high-quality food to survive. Its body can also be used for a great variety of things useful to man. It produces milk which is sometimes considered better for babies and invalids than cow's milk. It provides meat from its flesh, leather from its hide and wool from its back. Short wool is obtained from the eastern goat with long floppy ears. Angora and cashmere goats are used for their much longer wool.

A goat can leap across a chasm 12 metres (42 feet) wide

The ibex is one of the most astonishing mountaineers in the animal kingdom. It can scale what appears to be an almost vertical cliff, jumping from outcrop to outcrop, finding footholds where none seem to exist and leaping across gaps of more than 12 metres (42 feet) with dizzying drops below. The ibex is usually about one metre (3 feet) at the shoulder and has long, curved-back horns with ridges on one side that tell its age. The Alpine ibex is now quite rare. The Asiatic ibex is larger and may have horns as long as 1½ metres (5 feet).

Chamois leather is mostly made from sheepskin

Chamois leather, pronounced 'shammy', comes from the chamois, an antelope that once lived on the plains of central and southern Europe and has now taken to the mountains. It is a nimble climber, very nervous, quite short, with strangely hooked-back horns. The special leather made from its skin is particularly soft and has many domestic uses. It is often used for drying down a car before polishing it. Unfortunately, the chamois has now become quite rare, because it has been hunted so much. A similar sort of leather is produced instead from a special fine grade of sheepskin. This leather is often falsely called 'chamois' by many people.

A mule is a cross between a male ass and a female horse

Mules look like asses, or donkeys, but they are quite often almost as large as a horse. They have the strength of a horse and the stubborn determination of an ass, and are particularly useful for dragging heavy loads in rough country. Mules very rarely give birth to young. A male horse and a female ass produce a 'hinny'.

An alpaca is a mixture of sheep and camel

The alpaca is related to the llama and both creatures belong to the camel family. Although it has no hump, the alpaca can go for several days without food or drink. It is used for carrying loads up and down the slopes of the Andes in Peru, Chile and Bolivia. It has been used as a domestic animal since the days of the ancient Incas. As well as a long, camel-like neck, the alpaca has woolly hair all over its body. This is sheared every two years and used for making cloth.

Antelopes are the world's highest jumpers

The Klipspringer, a tiny antelope from Africa, is said to be able to jump up to seven and a half metres (about twice the height of a London bus) and land exactly where it intended to. This is an amazing feat when you consider that the Klipspringer is only as tall as a six month old baby. Even more amazing is the fact that the Impala, another African antelope, can jump horizontally more than three metres further than the Klipspringer jumps vertically. The Springbok is another record-breaking animal athlete.

The original horse was the size of a dog and had four toes

The ancestor of the modern horse lived about 60 million years ago. We call it *eohippus*. It was about the size of a spaniel or a terrier and it had four toes instead of a single hoof. Gradually, the four toes evolved into the single hoof. Mesohippus, who lived about 40 million years ago, had three toes. In Pliohippus, about 15 million years ago, the two side toes had withdrawn a little, leaving the central toe larger. The proper hoof appeared by about one million years ago. The change came about as the horse needed to run faster and had to rise on its toes to gain greater leg length and extra speed to escape its enemies.

The Gnu is the oddest antelope in Africa

The Gnu has a tail like a horse, a pony's hindquarters and a goat's beard. Its head and shoulders look like a buffalo's and its muzzle is as flat as a moose's. It may look incredibly odd but it is as active and agile as all the other antelopes in Africa. The Gnu is also known as the Wildebeest and its Latin name is *Connochaetes taurinus*.

The African buffalo is one of the most dangerous wild animals in the world

The largest buffalo live in East Africa and may sometimes grow to more than 1.5 metres (5 feet) high at the shoulder. A wild buffalo may weigh a tonne and could easily trample a man to death. It has a short temper and will often charge unexpectedly from a hiding place in the bushes, particularly when it is already wounded. Because of the broad-based horns that protect its head, it is very difficult to stop a charging buffalo with a rifle bullet.

The ancient Egyptians trained baboons to pick fruit for them

The baboon is a type of monkey. One of the most colourful baboons is the Arabian baboon. It has a lion-like mane and a bright red behind which it turns towards its enemies to frighten them. The Egyptians used to train baboons for climbing trees and picking fruit. There are many illustrations of baboons on ancient Egyptian wall paintings.

There are four different kinds of apes

Apes are generally bigger than monkeys and they do not have tails. They are more related to human beings than any other creatures. The four types of ape are the gorilla and the chimpanzee from Africa, the orang-utan from Borneo and Sumatra and the gibbon from South-east Asia. Their skeletons are very much like ours and they mostly live in family groups. Even the gorilla is not the wild savage it is generally held to be. Gorillas are gentle and loving creatures that spend a great deal of their time playing together.

Some monkeys can use their tails as a fifth 'hand'

Monkeys often use their tails for balancing and for extra support but the spider monkey can do almost anything with its tail that it can do with its hands or feet. It can swing by its tail only, leaving all four limbs for picking food. It can pick up, carry and even throw objects with its tail while it swings from its arms or legs. The baby spider monkey uses its tail to keep a firm hold while it rides around on its mother's back.

The Romans called monkeys 'small men'

Although the origin of the word monkey is not certain, it is possibly derived from the Latin word 'homunculus' which means 'a little man'. There are two main groups of monkeys - the first are found in the tropics of Africa and Asia and are called Catarrhini and the second are found in the tropics of the American continent and are called the Platyrrhini. Monkeys and apes belong to the highest order of primates and are probably man's closest animal relatives. Although they are essentially wild animals they live in families and take as much care of their young as do humans. Naturalists used to think that one of the main differences between man and monkey was that only man had the intelligence to use tools, however apes have been observed in the Serengeti, using twigs to fish for termites in much the same way as an angler uses a fishing rod. Monkeys also communicate with each other, mainly by grunts, whistles and facial expressions. The first true apes appeared late in the Miocene Period along with whales and grazing animals. These forest-dwelling apes gave rise to man's immediate ancestors.

Some of the primates of today's world:
1 The red-spider monkey.
2 The ring-tailed lemur.
3 Hamodrye Baboon.
4 The Gorilla.
5 Rhesus Macaque.
6 The chimpanzee.
7 Tarsi.
8 The Loris.

The Howler Monkey is the loudest of all the monkeys

When a Howler Monkey screams it can sometimes be heard five kilometres away, and a family of Howlers travelling through the treetops make an awesome sound which has been mistaken for a thunderstorm. These monkeys have enormous voice-boxes and their throats have large pouches which act as amplifiers for their voices.

can teach apes to communicate in this way. The apes learned words and could use them properly. For example, if an ape wanted milk, he knew which sign to make to tell the researcher of his needs. What the apes cannot do, however, is to string the words together to make sentences. Like all other monkeys, the apes make sound signals and research has shown that these are used to tell each other about their environment and whether danger threatens the adults or the children.

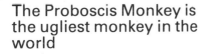

Marmosets have a secret language

Marmosets which live in Central and South America are the smallest of all monkeys. One of them, the Pigmy Marmoset is only 15.2 cm long. All marmosets talk in sounds that are similar to a bird's song. They also make ultrasonic sounds which human beings cannot hear. So next time you see a marmoset in a zoo and they appear to be sitting silently, they may, in fact, be talking to each other.

The Proboscis Monkey is the ugliest monkey in the world

The male proboscis monkey which lives in Borneo has a very long, flabby nose which hangs three or four inches over his mouth, and as the monkey ages, grows longer and longer. There are records of proboscis monkeys with noses hanging seven inches below the mouth.

Apes can be taught to talk

Apes cannot use their voices to make human language sounds in the way that humans do, but an amazing series of experiments carried out in the United States has shown that humans who are fluent in 'deaf and dumb' sign language

Apes can solve puzzles

Apes are intelligent enough to identify shapes and associate the shape with a colour. They can also differentiate between colours themselves. Laboratory experiments with captive apes showed that they readily selected an 'odd' shape from a series of similar shapes, particularly when the 'oddness' of the shape suggested that the difference would lead to a food reward. Apes also solved several problems using tools (boxes and sticks) which they arranged in a manner that allowed them to reach a food source that was otherwise inaccessible. This learning can be transmitted between the apes themselves, the mothers passing the advantageous behaviour patterns on to the tiny ape babies.

Hares and rabbits are different

The ears of a hare are longer than those of a rabbit and its hind legs are much bigger than the fore legs. The hare is a bigger creature altogether and leaps farther as it moves across the ground. The two animals live in completely different ways. Rabbits like to live in groups underground but hares prefer to live above ground and do not usually live in groups. Their nests are called 'forms'. They are made of beds of grass hidden from view.

Hare

Rabbit

Armadillos can roll themselves into a ball

There are ten different kinds of armadillo, or 'little armoured one'. They live in Central and South America and range in size from the dwarf armadillo of 15 centimetres (6 inches) to the giant armadillo of 1.5 metres (5 feet). Armadillos have bony plates in flexible bands around their middle, so that they can curl themselves up for protection. Nine is the most common number of bands but there are variations on this. The armadillo also has powerful legs for digging up termites, insects and roots.

There are more than 70 different kinds of opossum

There are more than 70 different kinds of American opossum. The opossum is a small pouched mammal, or marsupial. It has a peculiar method of defending itself. If attacked, the opossum will roll over on its side and pretend to be dead. You might think that this would only encourage the attacker to seize on an easy meal, but perhaps the idea is to put the attacker off by making it believe the corpse is a trap or has been dead too long to eat. When a person pretends to be dead in the same way, we call it 'playing possum'.

Lemmings march to their death every four years

The lemming is a bit like a mouse, about 13 centimetres (5 inches) long, tawny-yellow and reddish-brown. It lives mainly in the mountain chain between Norway and Sweden, although there is an American variety that migrates to the Arctic. About every four years, the Scandinavian lemmings go on a mass march, usually when there are too many of them for the available food. Millions of lemmings follow ancient migration paths, destroying whatever stands in their way, until they reach the coast, where they sometimes plunge over the cliffs to their deaths. Many may also drown trying to cross rivers to reach new feeding grounds.

Two mammals lay eggs

Birds, fishes and most reptiles lay eggs but most mammals, including whales, give birth to live young. There are only two mammals who lay eggs. These are the platypus, who lays them in a burrow, and the spiny ant-eater, or echidna. The echidna can twist its body round and lay its eggs directly into a pouch in its skin, where they are kept safe until they hatch.

A giraffe has the same number of bones in its neck as a human being

A male giraffe may stand 3.6 metres (12 feet) at the shoulder and 5.8 metres (19 feet) from head to toe. Like all other mammals, including humans, it has only seven bones in its long neck. A full-grown giraffe weighs between 1 and 2 tonnes and can travel at about 45 kilometres (28 miles) an hour. Its tongue can stretch out about 45 centimetres (18 inches) to pick leaves off the trees.

The fox catches a hedgehog by rolling it into water

Hedgehogs are insect-eaters but they will also eat mice, eggs, frogs, fruit, plants and even snakes. The young are born almost naked and their spines grow soft and white at first. Then they become hard and sharp. When alarmed, the hedgehog rolls into a ball, exposing its spines in all directions. It is difficult for an enemy to attack the hedgehog without pricking itself on the spines. A fox may sometimes roll a hedgehog into some water so that the hedgehog will have to unroll in order to swim. That is the moment when the fox can seize the hedgehog by its soft belly.

A squirrel can fall more than 30 metres (98 feet) without hurting itself

A squirrel can use its tail for balancing as it leaps from branch to branch. It can also use its tail as a blanket to wrap around itself in cold weather, as a protection when fighting and as a form of parachute if it falls from a high tree. It can fall more than 30 metres (98 feet) and run off immediately along the ground quite unharmed. The common grey squirrel is probably the best-known but there are many other varieties throughout the world, including the red squirrel, the flying squirrel and the ground squirrel. Squirrels may bury thousands of nuts in many different underground holes for the winter. They can find them without any trouble, even when the ground is covered with snow.

The Etruscan shrew is probably the smallest mammal in the world

Shrews usually eat insects and worms. They have long noses and they are very active, feeding almost all the time. Some shrews may consume their own body weight within three or four hours. There are many different kinds of shrew. The common shrew and the pygmy shrew live on land. There are also water shrews and tree shrews. The largest tree shrew lives in Borneo. The smallest shrew is the Etruscan shrew, which weighs only about 2 grams (0.07 ounces). Shrews are fierce and will turn and bite creatures much larger than themselves. The word shrew is also used to describe a woman who is fierce and hot tempered.

Sponges may look like plants but they are the remains of animals

Sponges are one of the simplest forms of animal life. They live in the sea. Sponges have a horny skeleton and little threads called flagella. The flagella suck in bacteria from the water through tiny holes, or pores, and push out waste matter. This action of sucking in food and pushing out waste shows that the sponge is an animal rather than a plant. There are many different colours of sponges, ranging from green to scarlet. They also have many shapes, from fan-shaped and cup-shaped to elegant tracery shapes. When sponges are fished, the animals inside the skeleton have to be killed and cleaned out.

There is a mole with a flower-like nose

Moles live underground in burrows and feed on small animals, insects and worms. If they have a surplus of worms, they will store them in 'larders'. A mole's fur stands up straight on end so that it can lie down either way when the mole is going backwards and forwards in its tunnel. The American star-nosed mole has a ring of 22 flower-like feelers on the end of its nose. These are sensitive and probably help the mole to find its food.

The tiny hyrax is related to the elephant

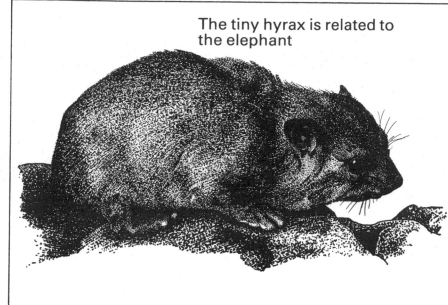

Rock rabbits and tree bears are both different forms of hyrax. They are nothing to do with rabbits or bears. In fact, they are more closely related to primitive elephants and creatures with hooves. Hyraxes look a bit like overgrown, hairy rats. They have fat heads, pointed noses, short necks and no tails, and are between 35 and 45 centimetres (14-18 inches) long. Some rock rabbits live in desert areas, in holes in the ground or cracks in the rock. The tree bears live in trees and cling to the trunk and branches with soft, rubber-like pads on their feet. They live in Central and West Africa.

Some people believe that elephants have their own graveyards

Elephants are sociable animals who usually live together in herds. These herds may consist of up to 40 elephants, usually led by a mature cow elephant. She decides the direction in which the herd shall move. Healthy elephants will often stay with a sick or injured elephant, protecting it and even trying to support it on its feet for a time. Some people believe that old or sick elephants go to special places to die. There is some evidence for this because piles of elephant bones have been found in particular places.

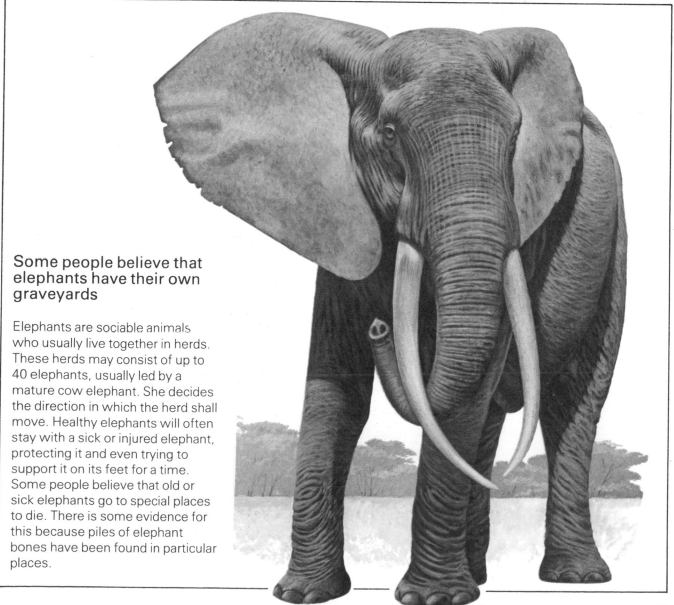

The sloth is so slothful that algae grow in its hair

The sloth quite rightly gets its name from its slothful habits. It is probably one of the laziest creatures on Earth. It spends its life hanging upside down from tree branches, hooked on by its curved claws. It eats leaves, bark and fruit at night and sleeps during the day.

The sloth moves slowly and carefully and rarely bothers to clean the algae that grow in its hair. Sloths live in South and Central America. There are two kinds, one with two toes on the front feet and three on the back, and one with three toes on both front and back.

The mongoose and the snake are deadly enemies

The mongoose has short legs, rough fur, a long nose and a long tail. It looks a bit like a large ferret and it is related to the cat family. Mongooses normally live on rats, mice, lizards and similar small creatures. The Indian mongoose has a reputation for fighting — and killing — snakes. Its success depends on the speed with which it can move, dodging the snake as it strikes and seizing it by the head or neck. Mongooses have been introduced in a number of islands especially to get rid of the snakes and also rats. They have sometimes proved to be more of a problem than a help, as they are quick to realise that it is easier to kill the local chickens, instead of tackling the snakes.

The 'horn' of the rhinoceros is made of hair

The horn of the rhinoceros is made of hairs that are tightly bound together, so tightly that the creature can charge into a solid object and remain undamaged. Cars have been knocked over and trains derailed by bad-tempered charging rhinos. The Indian rhino has a single horn but most others have two horns, one in front of the other. The longest horns may measure as much as 130-150 centimetres (51-59 inches). Although rhinos appear to be fierce, they are protective and caring towards their young.

Beavers have built a dam 600 metres (1968 feet) across

Fossils have been found of beavers that were two metres (6.5 feet) long but the average beaver today is only about 75 centimetres (30 inches) long and weighs about 22 kilograms (48 pounds). Even so, these hardworking creatures can build large dams and lodges from trees that they cut down and drag great distances. Some lodges are large enough for a man to lie down in, at full stretch. One dam in Montana, USA, was as much as 600 metres (1968 feet) long, creating a vast pond for the beaver

lodge. In constructing these lodges, beavers can stay under water for as long as 15 minutes. The North American beaver is the best-known but there is also a European beaver which still exists in parts of Scandinavia and northern Europe.

Some animals sleep throughout the winter

Hibernation is very deep sleep. Animals that live in cold climates often hibernate throughout the winter when food is scarce. Hibernating animals such as dormice, hedgehogs, frogs, toads, bats and snakes, store up food in the form of body fat before the winter begins. They then find a warm place to hide, usually underground. Their breathing and heartbeat become very slow and faint, and the temperature of their bodies drops so that little energy is being used. Some animals, such as bears, do not hibernate properly but they do sleep more than usual and come out of their dens to feed only occasionally during the winter. No one knows exactly what it is that tells them to wake in spring.

The guinea-pig is not a pig and does not come from Guinea

Guinea-pigs are common pets. They are about 25 centimetres (10 inches) long, with short, round ears and no tails. Their soft coats are sometimes long and sometimes short. They are related to certain rodents that live in burrows and rock holes in the Andes Mountains in South America. The Indians of South America used to eat them.

An animal is the first proper word in a dictionary

Most dictionaries start with the word aardvark, in fact the word is not English but is an Afrikaans word which means 'earth-pig' which is a very appropriate name

for this mammal. It is about the size of a farmyard pig, and it has an oddly shaped mouth and a very long tongue which can grow to 45.7 cm long. The aardvark has a very thick tail which it uses when it sits up on its hindquarters like a kangaroo. They are great diggers and can make themselves a burrow which is large enough for a man to crawl into, and when the aardvark is threatened it digs deeper into the burrow at a tremendous rate.

The warthog walks on its knees

When the warthog, one of nature's ugliest creations, is rooting for food, it shuffles along on its knees, which allows its flat, sensitive nose to smell out the underground morsels it so enjoys.

Some of the biggest whales have no teeth

There are several whales, including the humpback whale, the blue whale and the mink whale, which do not have any teeth. Instead, these whales have hundreds of hanging plates attached to their upper jaw. This dense mesh is made of whale-bone, or baleen, and it acts like a sieve. The tiny krill on which the whales feed are sucked in with great mouthfuls of water. They are then strained against the feathery inside edge of the baleen, by the pressing action of the whale's tongue.

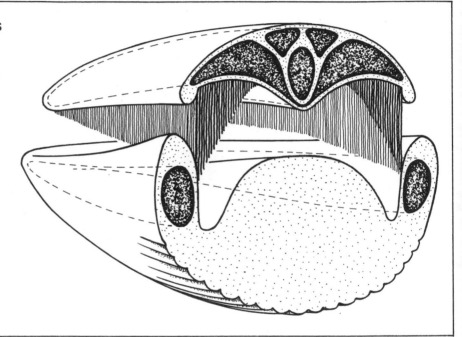

The indigestion of the whale can make a beautiful perfume

Sperm whales are valued for their oil. They are also valued for soft, smelly, black lumps of matter that they regurgitate from their insides. This is called ambergris. When ambergris is exposed to sun, air and sea water it becomes harder, changes to a light grey colour and smells pleasant. It is blended with perfumes to make them keep their fragrance longer. It is sometimes found inside whales that have been caught but more often it is found floating in lumps in the sea. Ambergris is produced because of irritation in the whale's stomach caused by the horny beaks of squid

and cuttlefish on which it feeds. It usually occurs in small lumps but lumps of 45 kilograms (100 lbs) or more are sometimes found.

The whale lives all its life in the sea, but it is not a fish

The ancestors of the whale once lived on land but they gradually adapted themselves to living in the sea. Whales are still mammals and give birth to live young which they feed on their own milk. Fish can breathe under water through their gills but the whale must come to the surface to breathe air, like a mammal. Fish are cold-blooded but the whale is warm-blooded and is protected by layers of fat, or blubber.

Whales are mammals and need to breathe air, but some can stay underwater for over an hour

Some types of whale can stay beneath the surface of the water without breathing for as much as 70 or 80 minutes. Others easily manage half this time. Whales can hold their breath this long because their muscles contain large amounts of a substance called myoglobin. Myoglobin enables them to store oxygen. When a whale does come up for air, it first breathes out stale air through its blowhole. It may breathe out up to 90 per cent of the air in its lungs. People usually breathe out less than one quarter of this percentage.

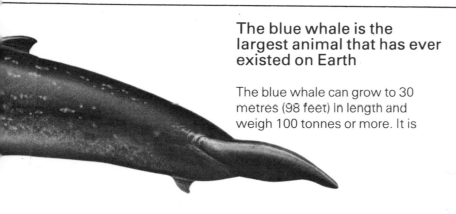

The blue whale is the largest animal that has ever existed on Earth

The blue whale can grow to 30 metres (98 feet) in length and weigh 100 tonnes or more. It is longer and heavier than *Diplodocus*, the biggest of the dinosaurs. The largest living land animal is the elephant. Although it weighs about 10 tonnes and stands 4 metres (13 feet) high at the shoulders, the elephant is small by comparison with the blue whale. Despite its great size the blue whale feeds entirely on krill — tiny sea creatures which are only five centimetres (2 inches) long.

A dolphin can hear sound underwater 24 kilometres (15 miles) away

In recent years we have begun to realise how intelligent and sensitive dolphins are. These water mammals have a brain almost as large as ours and a 'language' of more than 30 sounds for communicating with each other. They live together in schools of several hundred and always help any dolphins who may be in distress. For example, they have been known to support a sick or injured dolphin so that it can breathe at the surface, for days on end. They use echo-location to find objects underwater. Sound carries well in water.

Sharks cannot float – they have to keep swimming or they will sink

Bony fish have swim bladders of gas that help them to keep afloat and rest at any level in the water without effort. But the shark, with its body of cartilage instead of bone, has no swim bladder. If it stopped moving for a moment, it would drop to the bottom of the sea. One species has given up the endless struggle to keep afloat. The rays save their energy and live on the sea bed, eating molluscs and various crustaceans. Manta rays, however, skim along just beneath the surface, supporting themselves on their enormous 'wings', which can be several metres across.

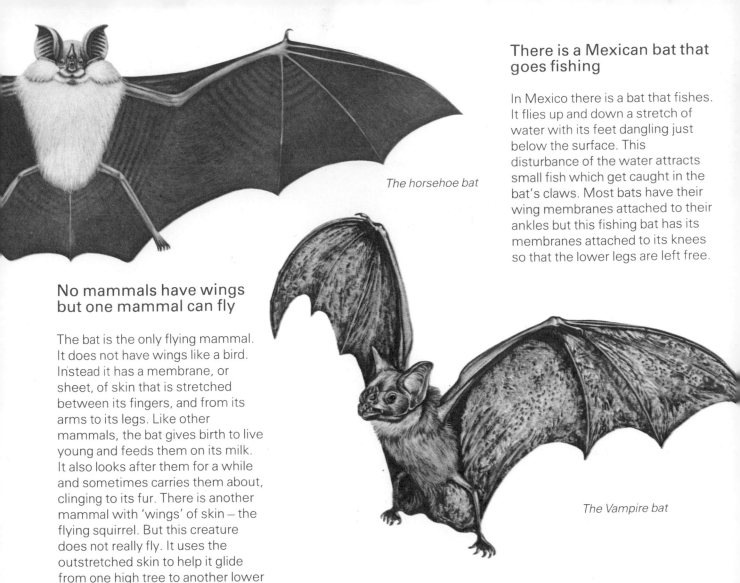

There is a Mexican bat that goes fishing

In Mexico there is a bat that fishes. It flies up and down a stretch of water with its feet dangling just below the surface. This disturbance of the water attracts small fish which get caught in the bat's claws. Most bats have their wing membranes attached to their ankles but this fishing bat has its membranes attached to its knees so that the lower legs are left free.

The horsehoe bat

The Vampire bat

No mammals have wings but one mammal can fly

The bat is the only flying mammal. It does not have wings like a bird. Instead it has a membrane, or sheet, of skin that is stretched between its fingers, and from its arms to its legs. Like other mammals, the bat gives birth to live young and feeds them on its milk. It also looks after them for a while and sometimes carries them about, clinging to its fur. There is another mammal with 'wings' of skin – the flying squirrel. But this creature does not really fly. It uses the outstretched skin to help it glide from one high tree to another lower down.

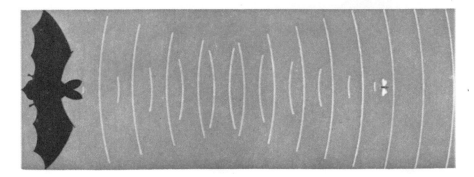

Left: *The high-frequency sound waves emitted by the bat are reflected back by anything in its way. Because the echoes received by the two ears are slightly different, the bat can calculate exactly where his prey is.*

Vampires were said to change into bats and live off human blood

The story of the vampire has its roots in Eastern Europe, in Transylvania and Wallachia, the Carpathian Mountains and the Balkans. Stories about vampires have been circulating for centuries. It was said that vampires were evil spirits who took over the corpses of others for evil purposes and that the soul of a person who was too wicked to find eternal peace could live on in the corpse as one of the undead. Transylvanian vampires were said to be very pale and thin, with compelling eyes. They had dreadful breath and were amazingly strong. There were many superstitions about vampires; they had the power to change themselves into bats or wolves; they could only be killed by driving a stake through their hearts before the sun set; they made no

Ultrasonic sound guides bats with complete accuracy

The flight of the bat is almost soundless, it flies in complete darkness at times and yet has the uncanny ability to fly through winding tunnels, miss tiny objects and hunt for insects almost too small to be seen. Bats do not use their eyes to navigate in the dark, for one thing their eyes are not powerful enough and in the dark they are useless anyway. It has been known since the eighteenth century that blind bats lose none of their manoeuvrability. The first man man to experiment with bats and to try to discover how they managed what at that time seemed a fantastic feat, was Lazaro Spallanzani. In partnership with Louis Jurine of Switzerland, he covered bats' ears but left their eyes uncovered. To his surprise he found that the bats became completely disorientated, bumping into large objects that they could perfectly well see and even into each other. From this he deduced that the bats were using sound to direct their flight, and yet the only sounds audible to the human ear was the rustle of their wings. For several years the answer remained a mystery. In 1920 an explanation was offered by an English scientist, H. Hartridge. He suggested that the bats were using ultrasonic sound to orientate themselves. Ultrasonic sound is at too high a frequency for human ears to hear and can only be detected by sophisticated apparatus. Many animals can distinguish ultrasonic sound, (dog

sound, (dog whistles often make a sound unrecognisable by humans but easily heard by a dog). Cats, guineapigs and rats can all distinguish sounds up to 30,000 cycles per second whereas the human ear cannot hear anything above 20,000 cycles. Further experiments carried out between 1938 and 1941 confirmed Hartridge's original theory. G. W. Pierce and Donald R. Griffin studied the behaviour of the small brown bat Myotis I. lucifugus. These bats are smaller than house mice. The two scientists tested the bats' ability to avoid obstacles by making them fly through an obstacle course of hanging wires. They found that the tiny creatures could avoid wires as small as three sixteenths of an inch across. When wires one twentieth of an inch in diameter were used, their "score" went down to 70 per cent, and became worse when the bats' ears or mouths were covered. While bats have for many years been of interest to scientists because of their natural ability to navigate by sonar, they are probably better known for their roles in fictional horror stories and films. In reality, though they have few natural enemies, bats are shy creatures. Often they live in groups in secluded places such as abandoned mine workings and buildings, and only venture from their nesting places at dusk, when they begin hunting for food. Probably the most famous colony of bats is at Carlsbad, New Mexico, near the border of the United States and Mexico. Here, great clouds of bats can be seen each evening, as thousands of these tiny

winged creatures leave the famed Carlsbad Caverns - a national monument and famed tourist spot - for their nightly foraging.
While many bats are in fact carnivorous, only the vampire bat of subtropical and tropical America will feed upon other mammals. So skilful is the vampire in taking its meal, however, that the victim is seldom aware that it has been attacked. The biggest problem posed by the vampire bat is not that it kills cattle, but rather that the small bite wound will become infected by smaller but more dangerous animals. Like many other animals, however, bats can become infected with rabies. This disease affects the brain and causes such distress that the animal is unable to control the way it acts; worse, the disease can be passed on to other animals, or humans, that the infected animal bites. Stories about bats infected with rabies probably inspired the writers of horror stories to make these relatively harmless creatures the 'stars' of fictional stories about witchcraft and the occult. Different species of bats may have widely differing eating habits. Many species eat insects, catching them on the wing with echo-locating sonar; some, like the large fruit bats, are strictly vegetarian; others prey on small animals such as birds, frogs and lizards; the long-nosed bat has a delicate diet of nectar and pollen. Species of bats are to be found all over the world with the exception of the arctic and antarctic regions. In the cooler regions, a number of bat species hibernate during the long, cold winter months.

reflections in mirrors; they terrorised villages and demanded that maidens be sacrificed to them; if a pregnant woman looked at them, then her child would be born a vampire; and many more. Many authors wrote about them, including Alexandre Dumas, but perhaps the most famous book

about them is *Dracula* by Bram Stoker. Stoker was an Irishman who was business manager to the great actor, Sir Henry Irving. He created a wonderful story. His hero was one of the undead who came to England, in a coffin filled with the earth of his grave, and landed near a lunatic asylum in Northern

England. There he took possession of a beautiful girl and threatened to gain control of others but he was foiled by a vampire expert. It is from *Dracula* that many of our popular beliefs about vampires come and it is still as exciting to read now as it was when it was written more than 80 years ago.

Hunting dogs have been bred for different purposes

Dogs have been domesticated and used for hunting by man for a very long time. Their natural instincts have been developed and different breeds have been used for a variety of sports. Foxhounds, deerhounds and wolfhounds are named after the animals they hunt. The German dachshund was a 'badger' hound. Beagles and bassets were bred for hunting rabbits and hares as well as otters. Spaniels and poodles were bred for chasing birds out of the water. Terriers catch rats and dig out foxes. Pointers and setters show their masters where the birds are and retrievers bring them back when they are shot. Bloodhounds were once used for hunting down criminals.

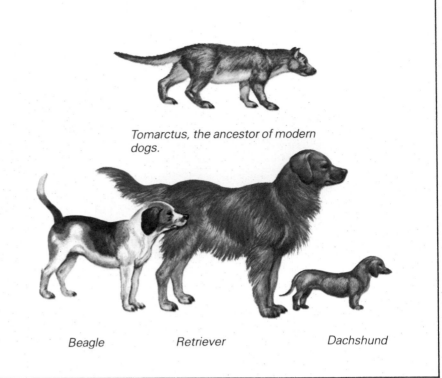

Tomarctus, the ancestor of modern dogs.

Beagle   *Retriever*   *Dachshund*

Pigs and poodles have a good nose for truffles

The truffle is an edible fungus that grows about seven centimetres (three inches) below the ground. The best truffles come from Perigord, in France, and usually grow under oak trees. In England, truffles are usually found under beech trees. The truffle itself is round, dark and knobbly but it has been much prized as a delicacy since Roman times and is used to bring out the flavour of the food with which it is served. Pigs were often used to sniff out the truffles but Spanish poodles were also used as truffle hounds in the past. Once the pig or poodle had located the truffle, its master could dig it out before the creature ate it.

Dogs are one of man's hardest working friends

Dogs were originally domesticated as hunting animals but today they work for us in many other ways, as well. Many big dogs such as Labradors are used as guide dogs for the blind. Bulldogs and mastiffs are used as guard dogs. Alsatians do police work. Huskies are the sledge dogs of North America, the Arctic and the Antarctic. Old English sheepdogs and Scottish collies work the sheep farms. Welsh corgies herd the cattle, too. St Bernards are used for rescue work in the Alps. Pyrenean mountain dogs do their share of herding and so do Newfoundland sheepdogs, which were also once used to rescue drowning people.

There are two animals found only in Tasmania

The Tasmanian devil looks rather like a fierce dog with a long, sharp nose. It is a marsupial (a pouched animal like a kangaroo or an opossum) and it feeds on lizards, small animals and birds. Once it existed all over Australia but now it can only be found in the island of Tasmania. Another creature that is unique to Tasmania, and which was once thought to be entirely extinct, is the Tasmanian wolf, or thylacine. The wolf is larger than the devil and was killed widely by farmers because it ate their sheep. Now a few are believed to have survived.

The Wolverine is one of the most savage animals living

The Wolverine, the largest member of the weasel family, has an unrivalled record for savagery. Although this creature is only a metre long and weighs less than 17 kilos it has been known to kill animals as big as deer. It is completely fearless and very cunning. Trappers in the Canadian Forests, where wolverines are found, detest them, since they will raid camps and cabins and rob traps that have been set for other animals. Wolverines themselves are rarely taken in traps. These creatures are also known as Gluttons, probably because of their voracious appetites. Their fur is highly prized since it sheds moisture very efficiently and makes an excellent edging for collars and hoods where condensed breath would form a rim of ice. They are also found in the northern parts of Europe and Asia. Wolverines, like most animals will not attack humans unless they are threatened, but if they do, they can cause great injuries and can even kill attackers.

The American bison nearly became extinct during the 19th century

The North American bison, weighing up to 800 kilograms (1764 pounds) and standing up to two metres (six feet) high, with its great shaggy shoulders and beard, used to roam the prairies in millions. The Indians who hunted it for its meat and skin made little impression on its vast numbers. It was European settlers with their rifles, in the 18th century, who began to slaughter them faster than they could reproduce. By the end of the 18th century, nearly all the bison east of the Mississippi had gone. The demand for their meat increased during the 19th century, as thousands of hungry men laboured at the building of the railroads across the continent. The last herd in Texas was destroyed in 1888 and by the end of the decade it was reckoned that only about 1000 were left in Canada and the northern States. Since then, the bison has been protected and some herds have slowly regrown.

The wild ancestor of domestic cattle survived until the 17th century

All domestic cattle, both beef and dairy, are thought to come originally from the wild, and now extinct, 'auroch'. It was known to the Romans and may have survived in the forests of Poland until the 17th century. It was a huge creature, mostly black, about two metres (six-and-a-half feet) high at the shoulder and with great forward curving horns. There are illustrations of the auroch in ancient pictures. Other primitive wild cattle were the Bronze Age shorthorn and the long-horned white cattle of which there is still a herd at Chillingham in England.

Cows have different digestive systems from human beings

Human beings rely on gastric juices to break down, or digest their food. Most of the useful materials are absorbed as they pass down the small and the large intestine. We have a single stomach which acts largely as a storage area where food is kept before being processed. Cows rely on micro-organisms in their stomach to break down food. They have more than one stomach and, like other grazing animals, they return their food to their mouths to be rechewed before it passes from one stomach to another. This is sometimes known as 'chewing the cud'. The inside of the cow's stomach is often washed and cooked and eaten as tripe. It is considered to make excellent food for invalids because it is so easily digested by them.

Some of the cattle found around the world today.

Highland

Hereford

Longhorn

Friesian

Zebu

Domestic cattle have special names to distinguish between the sexes and their ages

A bull is a fully grown male that is used for breeding. A bullock (or a steer) is a young male that has been operated on so that it cannot breed and is fattened up for beef instead. A cow is a fully grown female that is used for breeding and for milk and a heifer is an immature female that has not yet bred.

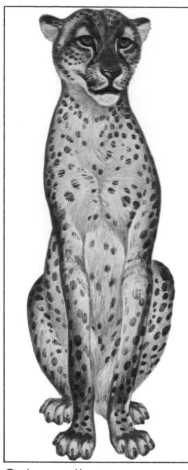

The cheetah can break the speed limit on the motorway

The cheetah is a member of the cat family. It is the fastest animal in the world. In a short burst of speed it can top 96-112 kilometres (60-70 miles) an hour, when hunting down its prey. Cheetahs weigh about 100 lbs, stand about 0.76 metres (2.5 feet) at the shoulder and are about 0.91-1.21 metres (3-4 feet) long, with an extra 0.76 metres (2.5 feet) of tail. They live on the plains, in southern Africa to India. There was a time in Asia when cheetahs were domesticated and used for hunting by man. Strangely enough they were usually captured and disciplined when adult, rather than being bred in captivity from young. The cheetah differs from all other cats in that it has no sheaths for its claws, it cannot therefore completely retract its claws which may be a great help when running.

Only small cats purr

It is only the small cats who can purr. These are the bobcats, lynxes, ocelots, pumas, jaguarandas, panthers and domestic cats - although they can purr they cannot roar. The large cats, such as lions and tigers cannot purr, but as anyone knows who has seen them in the wild, they can certainly roar.

The Egyptians worshipped the cat

The cat was sacred to the ancient Egyptians. Many mummies of cats have been found, not only in the tombs of their masters but also in special cemeteries that seem to have been created solely for cats. Bast, one of the Egyptian deities, is almost always represented as having a cat's head. The Abyssinian cat of today probably most resembles the sacred cats of ancient Egypt.

Cats brought fear to Europe

The great witch hunts of the Middle Ages were responsible for the slaughter of hundreds of thousands of cats. Since cats were associated with witches, they were thought to be 'pets of the Devil' and were burned alive alongside their masters and mistresses. On Saints' Days in France, sack-loads of cats were ritually burned in bonfires up to the end of the reign of Louis XIV.

A cat always lands on its feet

A cat is so supple and has such a good sense of direction that even when it is falling, it automatically turns in mid-air so that it will land on its feet. The hip and shoulder joints of cats are so springy that they can take the strain of a fall from a considerable height. Perhaps this ability has given rise to the legend that cats have nine lives.

The leopard and the jaguar have different kinds of spots

It would be difficult to confuse a jaguar with a leopard, except in a zoo, because jaguars live in South America and leopards live in Africa and Asia. They both tend to hide their prey in trees to protect it from scavengers and they both have spots, usually in the form of rough-edged rosettes. However, the rosettes of the jaguar generally have an additional small spot in the centre, whereas the rosettes of the leopard do not.

The male lion very rarely hunts

Lions spend a great deal more time resting in the shade than they spend hunting. They usually hunt only once every few days and then it is usually the females who do most of the work. They stalk their prey, usually zebra, antelope or wildebeest, in teams, often laying clever ambushes and once the kill has been made it is the male who eats first.

The secretions of one 'cat' are used to make perfume

The civet cat is not really a cat at all, although it looks a bit like one. It has short legs and a thick, furry tail, with a long black ridge of colouring going down the back of its half-spotted, half-stripey body. Around the base of its tail, the civet has a large pouch filled with a smelly substance with which it marks its territory and signals to the opposite sex. The Chinese sometimes used this substance as a form of medicine and, since very ancient times, it has been used as the basis for certain perfumes. It is still used in this way and in some places civets are kept in captivity specifically to provide the substance.

Catgut is not made from cat gut!

Catgut is a form of very strong thread used for stitching wounds and openings in surgery. It is also used for the strings of musical instruments and for some tennis rackets. But even in ancient times, catgut was probably never made from the guts of cats. It is usually made from the guts of sheep and sometimes from the guts of horses, cattle and pigs. It comes from the narrow end of the animal's intestine. This tube is cleaned and then cut into fine strips and twisted to make threads. It is then treated in order to preserve it and to make it hygienic.

Cats have always been valuable

In Ancient Egypt, the penalty for killing a cat was death, and the Egyptians so valued their cats that when, during the seige of Pelusium, the attacking Persian army, led by Cambyses, threatened to throw live cats over the walls of the city, the citizens of Pelusion surrendered rather than allow such a dreadful thing to happen to animals they revered so much.

Some cats were kept on leads

In Japan, cats were so precious that they were kept on leads until 1602, when by order of the Emperor they were released so that they could kill the vermin that were threatening the silk crop. In 1750, the first cat imported into Paraguay was sold for the enormous sum of one pound of solid gold.

The duties of a cat were once laid down

Hywel Dda, King of South Wales in 936, actually proclaimed the worth of a cat - he stated that should anyone kill or steal a cat they must pay the equivalent of grain that would completely cover the cat from nose to tail and a fine of 4 legal pence. The duties of the cat and her kittens were strictly laid down - she should kill mice, have a complete set of claws, rear her kittens well and not go caterwauling at the moon.

Tabby cats are the oldest breed in the world

The word tabby come from a district in Old Baghdad called "Attabia" where weavers of silk produced a beautiful material which was patterned rather like the coat of a tabby cat. Tomb painting from Ancient Egypt show cats with tabby markings and even pure bred kittens today often carry faint tabby markings which hint at their ancestry.

The first official cat show took place in 1871

This was held at Crystal Palace in London, six years later the National Cat Club was formed with Harrison Weir as its president.

Legends that tell of the origin of cats

The Mohammedans have a legend that states that the first cat appeared on the ark when a lion sneezed. The Chinese say that the common cat is the result of a lioness mating with a monkey.

The cat has many wild relations

The domestic cat has many of the characteristics of its wild relations: the whiskers, the sharp retractile claws, the agility, the ability to see at night among them. There are nearly forty species of cat. The five 'big' cats are the lion, the tiger, the leopard (or panther), the snow-leopard and the jaguar. Smaller cats include the puma (cougar or mountain lion), the cheetah (the only cat that cannot retract its claws), the European wild cat *(right)*, the North American bobcat, the serval and caracal of Africa, the lynx of Europe and North America, and the pampas cat from South America.

The wildcat

Seaweeds do not have roots

Seaweeds grip the rocks with 'holdfasts'. These are disc-like pads on the end of strong threads. The pads cling to rocks so tightly that they can withstand any amount of battering by the waves. Most seaweeds are very tough and leathery, so that they can slide easily over the surface of the rocks. Some, like bladder wrack, have bubbles of air which keep them floating in the water. Seaweeds do not have proper stems, leaves, flowers or fruits either.

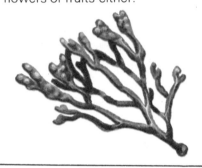

The sea anemone is an animal, not a plant

Anemones are flowers but the sea anemone is an animal which lives by the seashore. It was given its name because its tentacles, or feelers, look like flower petals. The sea anemone uses its tentacles to sting and paralyse tiny sea creatures. The tentacles then pull the victim into the sea anemone's mouth.

Limpets always return to the same home

Limpets cling to seashore rocks with a strong foot. At night they move across the rocks to feed on young seaweed plants, but they always return to the same spot. They gradually wear away a groove in the rock which fits the shape of their body. When they cling to the groove with their strong foot, it is very difficult for their enemies to pull them off.

Pearls can be found in ordinary mussels

Pearls are not only found in oysters. They may be found in several kinds of mollusc. Pearls are formed when a tiny piece of grit or other matter gets inside the mollusc's shell. The mollusc surrounds the grit with layers of a special substance. This builds up the pearl. Pearls found in mussels tend to be rather small, and no pearls are as good as those found in pearl oysters. The 'mother of pearl' which lines the inside of a mussel shell has in the past been used for making buttons.

Pearls are the oyster's answer to an uncomfortable irritation

When a bit of sand or some other hard object gets inside an oyster's shell, the oyster protects its soft body by coating the sand with layers of mother of pearl. These build up and harden into a fully formed pearl. 'Cultured' pearls are made on special oyster farms by deliberately inserting an irritating substance into oyster shells. These pearls are not as valuable as natural pearls. The Chinese first developed the skill of producing artificial pearls in the 13th century.

Giant clams are strong enough to drown a man

Clams are called clams because of the way in which their two shells 'clam' together very tightly. There are many different kinds of clams, including mussels, oysters, scallops and razor shells. The most famous is probably the giant clam of the East Indies. This monster can grow to more than one metre (three feet) across and it can weigh more than 200 kilograms (440 pounds). If a swimmer should get his foot caught in the mouth of a giant clam, he would not be able to pull it out again. He could end up being drowned.

Anthropods are superb adaptors

Anthropods, such as the sea slater below, have produced species suitable for life in almost every kind of habitat and diet. There are ten main classes of anthropods and within these classes there are almost 850 different species ranging from lobsters to ticks and mites.

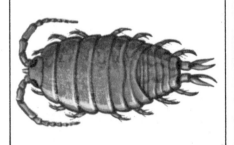

Many people once believed that barnacles turned into geese

Barnacles are small shellfish which fix themselves firmly to rocks, old piers or the bottoms of ships. There are several different kinds, including acorn barnacles, and gooseneck barnacles. Gooseneck barnacles have a long stalk with a shell and feathery legs on the end. These are shaped like the neck and head of a goose. Many people used to believe that these barnacles actually turned into geese. Scientists even tried to explain how the change took place. As a result of this myth, one type of goose is called a barnacle goose.

Not all starfish have five arms

Many starfish have five arms stretching out from a central point. Underneath these arms, there are tube feet with suckers that are strong enough to open the shells of molluscs. The sun-starfish, however, has 13 arms, and the feather-star (which is a relation of the starfish) has ten arms, all with tiny side branches that make the arms look like underwater feathers.

The squid moves by jet propulsion

The squid moves by a method of jet propulsion. It forces water through flaps along its body. In this way, it can move with equal speed backwards or forwards. When frightened, it can produce a cloud of inky liquid to hide itself from its enemies. There is a flying squid that can skim across the surface of the water, and a giant squid which lives deep in the North Atlantic waters. The giant squid may grow up to 20 metres (65 feet) long.

The seashore is an ever-changing world

Creatures that live by the seashore live in a world of great contrasts. Twice a day the tides cover and uncover the rocks. In hot weather, rock pools can partly dry out between high tides. The water that is left becomes excessively salty, but if it rains the pools are suddenly filled with fresh water and their normal saltiness is diluted. The depth and darkness of the water close by the shore changes constantly with the tides. Periods of calm are broken by storms that batter living creatures with crashing waves and showers of pebbles. These are only some of the natural problems to which shorelife is adapted. Each creature and plant has its particular level on the waterline.

There is a crab so large that it could wrap its claws round two or three men

The largest of all crabs is the Japanese spider crab. It measures about 30 centimetres (12 inches) across its shell and has a span of more than 3 metres (10 feet) from claw-tip to claw-tip. Another large crab is the robber crab, which goes ashore and climbs trees in search of coconuts. It can wrap its legs around the tree trunk as it climbs.

A mollusc shares its home with a flower

The periwinkles shown here are small marine molluscs, but there is also an evergreen plant with light blue, pink or white flowers called periwinkles. They are found mainly in Europe.

Cowrie shells are used as charms against evil and as money

There are more than 160 species of cowrie in the world. Each has a rounded, polished shell with a serrated slit underneath. The cowrie lives inside the shell. Part of its soft body emerges from this slit and folds back around the shell. The tiger cowrie is probably the best-known, with its patterned shell. Golden cowries are strung together and worn as a necklace by important people in Figi and Tonga. Some are worn as charms against evil or sterility. The small money cowrie was for a long time used as a form of money by African tribes.

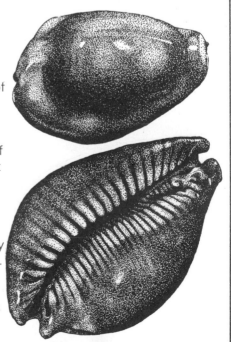

Tortoises, terrapins and turtles are all different

These are all horny-shelled, four-legged reptiles. The tortoise lives on land and has stubby legs. It ranges in size from the small tortoises that are kept as pets to the giant tortoises of the Galapagos Islands. Terrapins live in fresh water and tidal water and are usually found in the United States. They have slightly webbed feet. Turtles live in the sea and their legs are like flippers. The females crawl up the sandy shore to lay their eggs. The leatherback is the largest of the turtles.

The Galapagos giant tortoise

The female turtle deposits about 100 eggs in her nest.

The turtle

The soft-shelled Trionyx turtle

Tortoise-shell comes from a turtle, not a tortoise

Tortoise-shell is brittle and, when it is highly polished, it becomes a lovely mottled yellow-and-brown colour. It is used for the handles of combs and knives and for decorating boxes with inlaid veneer. The Romans valued tortoise-shell very highly and although there have been various modern imitations of the substance none of them have been as good as the real thing which comes not from a tortoise but from the shell of the hawksbill turtle. This is the smallest of the sea-going turtles and lives in the waters around the East and West Indies and off the coast of Brazil.

Seals use their hind legs to swim; sealions use their front flippers

Seals and sealions are almost certainly descended from different land-dwelling ancestors. True seals do not have external ears but sealions (and their relations, the fur-seals and the walrus) do have ears. The limbs are also different. Sealions can prop themselves up on their flippers and tuck their hind legs beneath them so that they can move about on land quite well. Seals cannot rear up and have little use for their hind legs on land. In the water, the seal propels itself largely by its hind legs, whereas the sealion uses its front flippers.

Seals are cruelly killed

Every year hunters kill young seals which herd together. The reason is to keep the numbers down and to sell their fur. But all over the world groups of men and women are protesting about the unnecessary cruelty of this.

The tender crocodile carries its young in its mouth

The Nile crocodile is only one of many kinds of crocodile. It lays its eggs well away from the river and buries them in sand or mud to keep them warm. When the time for hatching comes, the mother listens for the crying of the young crocodiles within the shell. She uncovers the eggs so that the young can break out. Then male and female carry the young gently in their mouths down to the river. They swim to special nursery areas where the baby crocodiles grow up and learn to fend for themselves.

Cone shells can kill

The beautiful cone shells of the Indo-pacific sea are one of the deadliest hazards to collectors. These exquisite shells can secrete a poison strong enough to lead to heart failure and death and the shell stings so deftly and quickly that the victim may not know he has been stung.

The turtle eats poison

Sea turtles have a remarkable ability to eat Portuguese Man of War Jellyfish without seeming to come to harm. They obviously enjoy the taste of these deadly creatures and are unaffected by the poison they digest internally even though the tentacles of the jellyfish usually inflict painful stings to the turtle's face and eyes.

Crocodiles allow birds to clean their teeth

The crocodile is one of the most vicious killers in the animals' world. Once it has its prey, including man, in the water there is no escape. Indeed, if a human being is caught between water and a crocodile on the land, the crocodile will force him into the water and kill him there. It pulls pieces off its prey by gripping parts of the prey's corpse in its huge jaws and then spins around on its own axis until the piece of flesh is free. But despite this, the crocodile will allow the little plover into its mouth and let it pick bits of decaying food from between its teeth. So the plover is really the crocodile's dentist. There are other examples of animals living like this. The hermit crab uses a disused whelk shell to protect its soft body, and although its diet is smaller water life, it often allows the ragworm to share its shell with it. The shark allows the remora to attach itself to it and live off the parasites that attack its skin. The cattle egret in Africa often travel around on the backs of buffaloes and antelopes. The oxpecker lives off the ticks that infest the buffalo's hide and often becomes so attached to its host, that it makes a permanent home on its back. Scientists call this behaviour "symbiosis" which comes from a Greek word that means living together.

Alligators eggs are hatched by the sun

Alligators lay their eggs in the mud and sand of the swamps where they live. The hot sun hatches them.

Alligators and crocodiles are quite different from each other

Alligators tend to be heavier and rather less active than crocodiles. Their heads are fairly broad and flat and their snout has a rounded shape. The head of a crocodile is more pointed and the snout sometimes turns up at the end. Crocodiles also have fewer teeth than alligators. They both have an enlarged fourth tooth on either side of the lower jaw. This cannot be seen in the alligator when it has its jaws closed, but in the crocodile the fourth lower tooth fits into a notch outside the snout and can be clearly seen. Alligators are found only in the Americas, except for the small Chinese alligator. Crocodiles live in America, Africa, Asia and Australia.

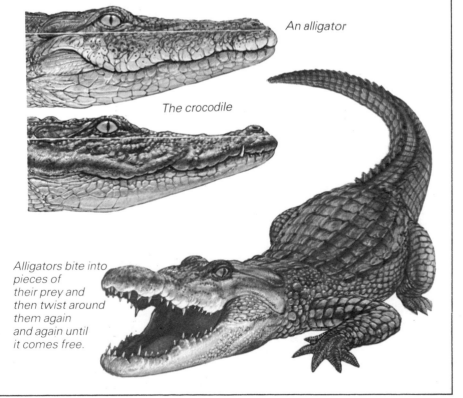

An alligator

The crocodile

Alligators bite into pieces of their prey and then twist around them again and again until it comes free.

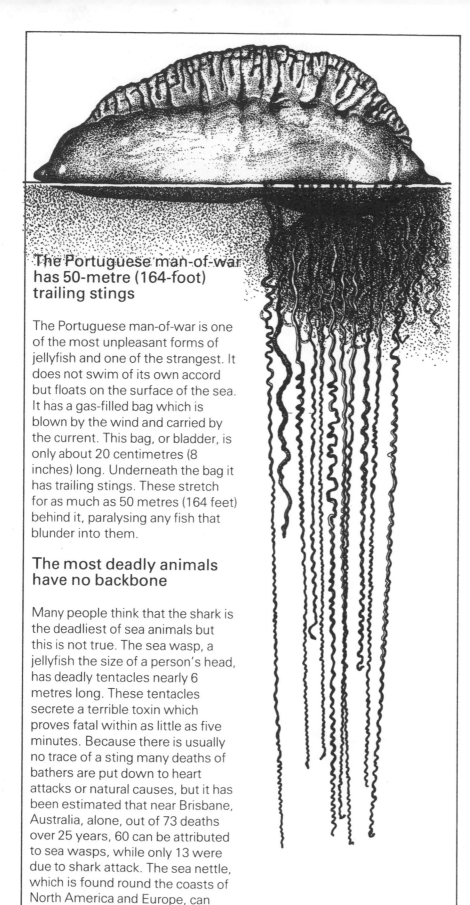

There is a fish with the head of a horse and the tail of a monkey

The seahorse is a real fish, not some mythical beast out of the past. It has an arched head and neck, just like that of a horse, with a sucking tube for a mouth. Its body is protected by bony rings and its long tail can cling, just like that of a monkey. It can also change colour to match its surroundings. The seahorse is usually about 15 centimetres (6 inches) long but can be double that length or less than a quarter of it. It swims upright by moving its dorsal fin, and it can move backwards, forwards, up and down. After the female has laid her eggs, the male keeps them in his own pouch until they hatch.

Deadly flowers of the sea

The Portuguese man-of-war has 50-metre (164-foot) trailing stings

The Portuguese man-of-war is one of the most unpleasant forms of jellyfish and one of the strangest. It does not swim of its own accord but floats on the surface of the sea. It has a gas-filled bag which is blown by the wind and carried by the current. This bag, or bladder, is only about 20 centimetres (8 inches) long. Underneath the bag it has trailing stings. These stretch for as much as 50 metres (164 feet) behind it, paralysing any fish that blunder into them.

The most deadly animals have no backbone

Many people think that the shark is the deadliest of sea animals but this is not true. The sea wasp, a jellyfish the size of a person's head, has deadly tentacles nearly 6 metres long. These tentacles secrete a terrible toxin which proves fatal within as little as five minutes. Because there is usually no trace of a sting many deaths of bathers are put down to heart attacks or natural causes, but it has been estimated that near Brisbane, Australia, alone, out of 73 deaths over 25 years, 60 can be attributed to sea wasps, while only 13 were due to shark attack. The sea nettle, which is found round the coasts of North America and Europe, can inflict a painful sting, the results of which can last for several days.

Sea Anemones secrete a poison which protects them from attack by hungry fish. Sponge fishermen are often badly affected by the stings of sea anemones. Even these deadly flowers are sometimes colonised by tiny fish who are either agile enough to avoid the stings or immune to the poison which is created by the deadly anemones which are strangely attractive to look at.

The Great Barrier Reef stretches for 2011 kilometres (1250 miles)

The Great Barrier Reef lies off the north-east coast of Australia. It has been built by millions and millions of tiny creatures called coral polyps. The polyps protect their soft bodies by building limestone shells, known as coral. When a polyp dies, its coral shell is left behind as part of the reef. There are many different kinds of polyp. They produce marvellous shapes and colours of coral, such as brain coral, staghorn coral, leaf coral and star coral. Many Pacific islands have coral reefs around them. Atolls are coral reefs that have formed a ring with a lagoon in the centre. The Great Barrier Reef of Australia is the largest animal building in the world. The only construction larger than it is the Great Wall of China.

As far down as 45 metres the coral is still alive, but below that depth dead coral skeletons may have been laid down for at least 10,000 years. During the day the coral animals stay hidden in the stony cups formed by the bones of their long-dead ancestors, but at night they put out their tentacles to feed and the coral looks truly alive. Some corals are really deadly, and secrete the venoms that can be dangerous to man. These are not only painful but can cause a serious inflammation of the skin. Particularly dangerous are the scratches and cuts that coral can cause. These heal really slowly and more often than not become infected, perhaps because the coral may produce a poison which causes wounds to fester. This is what is known as coral poisoning.

Fire coral is not true coral at all

So called "Fire coral" is not coral at all, but a relative of the Portuguese Man of War family. The tentacles of fire coral discharge a potent toxin when touched which can lead to temporary paralysis.

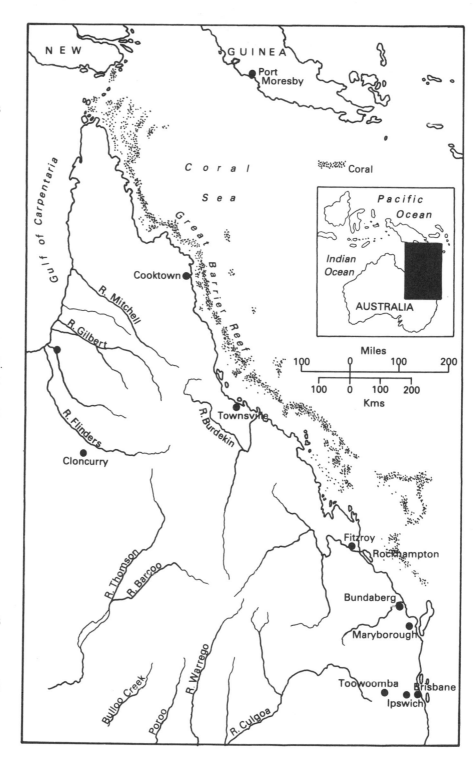

Above: *The Great Barrier Reef of Australia runs down the north-west coast of Australia and is made up of the remains of the polyp. One part of the Great Barrier Reef has been turned into a nature reserve. It is called the Heron Island Marine National Park, and although it is a tiny part of the reef it is one of the richest. Here fish of immense variety constantly amaze the visitor. There are beautiful coral formations, turtles and stunning seabirds as well. There are other national parks on the mainland including the sub-tropical Lammington Park where secretive and nocturnal creatures have become used to man's presence and behave naturally when he is there. Kangaroos are popular at the Wyperfield Park, and birds are the main attraction at the Arnhelmland Park along with Freshwater and Estuarine crocodiles. But for beauty and enchantment, none of them can compare with Heron Island which is a major Australian tourist spot.*

There are fish that fly

Flying fish have long pectoral fins, just behind their heads, which enable them to glide above the surface of the water. There are also 'four-winged' flying fish that have large pelvic fins beneath their bodies as well. They work up speed with their tails just below the surface, and leap clear of the water to avoid their enemies. They can reach speeds of more than 15 kilometres (9 miles) per hour and glide for nearly 200 metres (656 feet). By sculling rapidly with their tails as they come down to the water again, they can 'hop' still farther. Flying fish are generally found only in warm places.

The lungfish makes a cocoon for itself in dried-up mud

Lungfish live in the flood-plains of Africa. They also exist in Australia and South America. The flood-plains dry up for several months of the year and the lungfish are left without any water. If they were like ordinary fish, they would die at once. Each lungfish burrows into the mud and makes a cocoon for itself, with a thin tube for air to come down from outside. It exists in a sort of coma throughout the dry months. As soon as the rain comes, it wakes up and swims off.

Angler fish go fishing with rod, line and bait

Angler fish have their own special lines and baits for catching prey. There are several different types of Angler fish. Some live in shallow water but most live in deep seawater. One deep-sea type has a bony projection above its head. From this stretches a long, thin line. On the end of the line is a luminous point which acts as bait. Deep-sea shrimps are attracted by the light and the Angler fish snaps them up in its enormous jaws. In some types of Angler fish only the female has a light-lure. The much smaller male lives as a parasite, fixed to his mate, living off her catches.

The lumpsucker fish anchors itself to guard its eggs

The male lumpsucker is about half the size of the female and does all the work of guarding the eggs. Using a sucking disc beneath its body, the male anchors itself to the rocks where the eggs are laid. It fans the eggs with its fins so that they have plenty of oxygen. Sometimes, when the tide is very low, the male is left out of the water. It is able to take in oxygen from a special store of water kept in its stomach. But it cannot survive for very long in this fashion.

The most poisonous fish in the world is a delicacy in Japan

The most poisonous fish in the world does not attack or even slash with its spines. These Puffer fish have such a collection of toxins in their bodies that a few mouthfuls of their flesh are invariably poisonous. There is no known antidote for this poison and in Japan, where the puffer fish is a delicacy, special cooks are trained in the art of preparing them so that they are not poisonous. However there are occasions when customers eat fish that have not been properly treated, and they die.

Shoals of herring may be more than ten kilometres (six miles) long

The herring has been an important source of food for many centuries, particularly around the North Sea. Herrings are about 25 centimetres (10 inches) long and are dark blue and silvery in colour. They live on plankton and swim in vast shoals, sometimes two or three thousand million strong. A shoal may stretch for more than ten kilometres (six miles). Some herrings are eaten fresh but most are salted, smoked or canned. Kippers are herrings that have been split lengthways and smoked or dried.

The sawfish has its own saw-blade

The sawfish is related to the shark. It grows to about seven or eight metres (23-26 feet) long. Sticking forward from its head is a saw-like blade with sharp, tooth-shaped scales on either side of it. This blade can be up to two metres (6.5 feet) long. The sawfish swims into a shoal of smaller fish and lashes its saw from side to side to stun its victims. It also uses the saw to scrape along the sea bed for food.

The sawfish

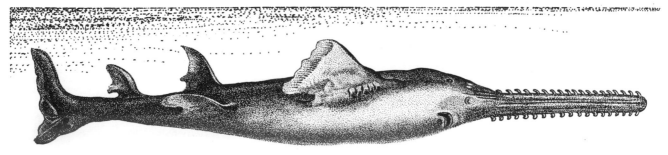

Flatfish have two eyes on one side of their head

When they are young, flatfish such as plaice or sole have eyes on both sides of their head, like ordinary fish. They swim near the surface of the water. When they are a few weeks old, one eye starts to shift across the top of the head to the other side. The fish then start to live at the bottom of the sea. They lie flat with both eyes on the upper side of their body. Flatfish can rapidly hide themselves on the sandy bottom by throwing sand all over their bodies, leaving only their eyes showing.

The sea hedgehog often swims upside down

The proper name for the sea hedgehog is the globefish. It gets its nickname from the sharp spines that stick up all over its body when it is frightened or angry. The globefish can blow itself up by filling an air bladder inside its body. This makes it look about three times larger than normal, and as round as a prickly ball. In this way the globefish frightens its enemies. It often floats upside down, with its air bladder towards the surface.

Needle fish are deadly by accident

The needlefish is a slender, elongated fish that has sharp bony jaws. It swims rapidly through the water and, like flying fish, can travel considerable distances over the surface. Because these fishes are attracted to light, there have been cases of fishermen, working late at night with side lights on their boats, being accidently wounded by these fish, serious wounds being inflicted by the needlelike bodies.

The barracuda is more dangerous than the shark

The barracuda with its torpedo shaped body and shearing teeth is bolder and more likely to attack than the shark. Most divers fear them. Large barracuda have been known to swim boldly into groups of bathers. The bite of the barracuda is clean edged and swift, usually directed at a splashing or glittering target. Even when barracuda have been hooked and landed they are still vicious enough to sever the fingers of anyone unwise enough to try to extract a hook from their mouth.

New evidence points to shark attack dangers

New evidence, compiled by the American Institute of Biological Sciences Shark Research Panel points to two important factors in shark attacks - most attacks happen when the weather is overcast and visibility is low and more often than not, the attacks take place on crowded beaches during the summer months.

Extinct sharks were the largest fish which ever lived

The largest shark which ever lived measured over thirty metres long with teeth of 10 centimetres.

Sharks may have up to one thousand teeth

A shark's teeth can be as sharp as razor blades with serrated edges. The shark is a fearsome eating machine, perhaps the most successful predator of the animal world. The teeth may be arranged in a dozen or more rows, with the teeth gradually moving forwards as the front row wears away.

Some fish have their own built-in electric batteries

Chemical reactions produce tiny electrical impulses in the nervous systems of almost all living creatures, including human beings. There are some fish, however, that generate considerable amounts of electricity for defence and attack. The Nile fish surrounds itself with an electrical field to sense the approach of enemies and possible prey. The electric eel of South America grows from 1.8 to 2.7 metres (6-9 feet) long. It can produce a discharge of 550 volts, enough to stun a small horse and quite enough to kill frogs and fish. The electric catfish of Africa is about half the size of the electric

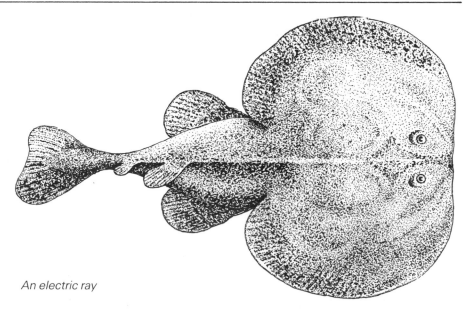

An electric ray

eel but it can produce about 300 volts. The North Atlantic electric ray uses only 50-60 volts. Sea water conducts electricity better than fresh water and therefore the ray does not need anything stronger.

The fins of fish have different uses

Fish fins are usually divided into those that are in pairs and those that are single. The pectoral and pelvic fins are in pairs. The pectoral fins are usually nearer to the front and on the fish's sides. They are normally used for moving and steering, though some grow into feelers, limbs, and even gliding wings. The pelvic fins are usually further back and beneath the fish. They are used to keep the fish balanced, though some also grow into feelers. The dorsal, or back, fin also helps to keep the fish steady. There is usually one dorsal fin, sometimes two, and sometimes one that extends along the entire back. On some fish the dorsal fin is spiny, on some it becomes a sucker, on some it is used for angling. The ventral, or anal, fin is beneath the fish towards the rear, and is another steadying fin. The tail fin is for propulsion.

There is a great variety of bony fish

There are more than 30,000 different species of fish. This is more than all the species of birds, mammals, reptiles and amphibians put together. More than 20,000 of these are bony fishes. These have a bony skeleton with skulls, backbones, ribs and spines to support their fins. They also have swim bladders. Bony fish are found in tropical and cold seas (marine fish) and in rivers and lakes (freshwater fish). The fish in the picture are listed here:

 1 American bowfin (fresh)
 2 Cod (marine)
 3 Grenadier (deep sea)
 4 Garfish (marine)
 5 Pipefish (marine)
 6 Herring (marine)
 7 Guppies (fresh)
 8 Sturgeon (marine/fresh)
 9 Butterfly fish (tropical reef)
10 Goby (fresh/marine)
11 Birchir (fresh)

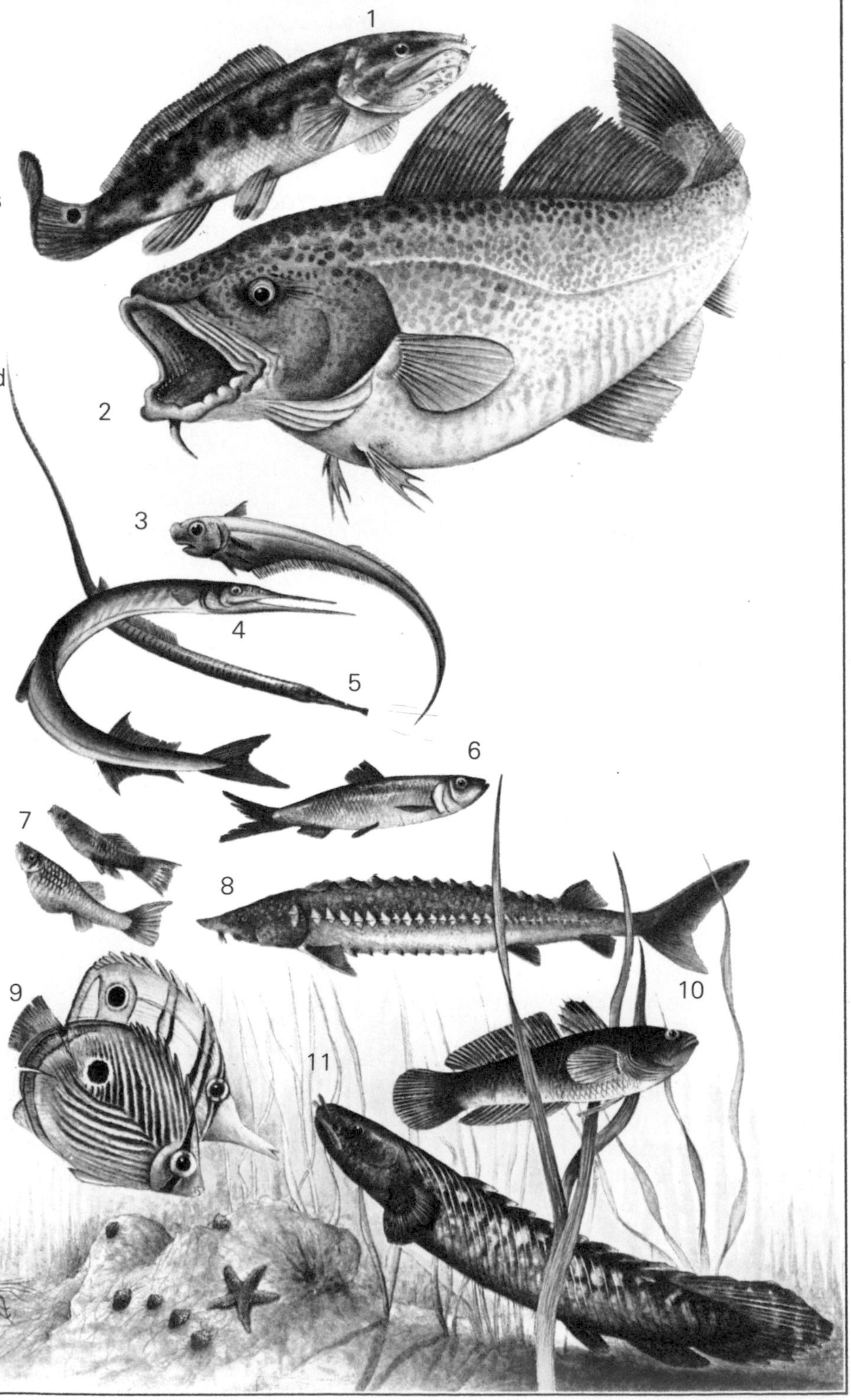

Sharks must swim all the time

Unless a shark is in constant motion, it will sink and drown. The water must pass constantly over the gills to allow the shark to take out the gases it needs for survival.

Frenzied sharks may eat themselves

The pain threshold of a shark, is so high that they feel very little pain. Indeed, sharks in a feeding frenzy have been seen to continue feeding even while other sharks have attacked and half eaten them. It can even devour parts of its own body which have become detached.

Sharks have no bones

Sharks, rays and ratfishes are the most primitive of the animals with backbones, even though they do not truly have bones at all, only cartilage (a supple, gristly framework). Because of the suppleness of the cartilage sharks can turn swiftly and because the cartilage is much lighter than bone, the fish can swim faster.

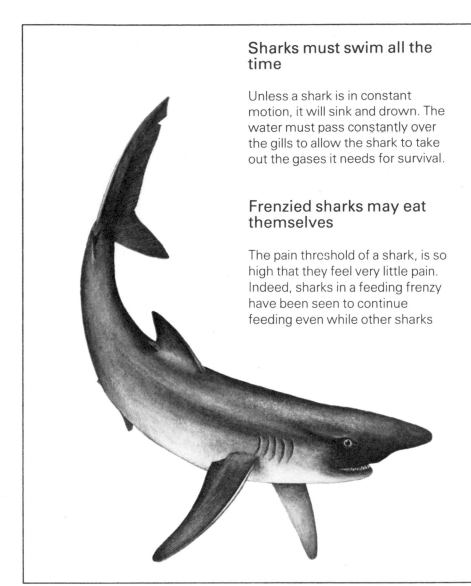

The blue shark (left) can grow up to 3½ metres (almost 12 feet long).

There are three ways to judge the age of a fish

There are three ways of finding the age of a fish. The easiest is by looking at its scales. Rings spreading out from the centre of each scale show the periods of growth. The rings are farther apart in summer, when the fish grows faster, and closer in winter. A wide ring and a narrow ring equal one year in the fish's life. Age can also be found by looking at the operculum, or gill-covering, through a microscope. For each year of life the operculum will show one dark and one light band of shading. Similar dark and light bands occur on the otoliths, the very small bones at the back of the fish's brain.

The grouper can swallow a man whole

The grouper, belonging to the family Serranidae, is among the largest bony fish to be found in warm seas. Some of these monsters weigh up to four and a half thousand kilogrammes. They are fearless and will attack anyone and anything that approaches their territory too closely. Accounts of divers who have been lost in waters populated by these huge fish suggest that they may be responsible for more than one human death. There are more than 400 species of Serranidae ranging in size from nearly 1000 pounds to diminutive ones that are almost weightless. It is the monsters that are the killers.

The spiny dogfish can be deadly

This fish is found in the cool waters of the Atlantic and Pacific Oceans. In front of its dorsal fins is a sharp, grooved spike. When the squirming fish is caught it attempts to slash at its captor with this spine. At the base is a poison sac which sends toxin down the groove in the spine into the wound.

Surgeonfish carry knives

These fish have a sharp spine which they usually keep hidden in a small groove near the base of the tail. When the fish become alarmed they raise the knife and inflict slashing wounds to other fish.

Some fishes are trained for fighting

The Siamese fighting fish is remarkable in several ways. The males have a habit of displaying their bright colours and battling with each other to the death. In Thailand and other places they are specially trained and bred to encourage their fighting characters Their owners place bets on contests, just as they would in a cock-fight. But the male fish has a gentler side to its nature. It builds the nest for the female's eggs by blowing bubbles which stick together on the surface of the water like a raft. It is the male, too, who guards the eggs until they hatch and looks after the young until they are old enough to fend for themselves.

The Coelacanth is a living fish which was thought to have died out 60 million years ago

Fossil remains of the Coelacanth have been found that range from 400 to 60 million years old. Since no fossils younger than 60 million years old have been found, scientists assumed that the fish had died out long ago. Then, in 1938, a fisherman in the Indian Ocean caught a living, 1.8-metre (6 feet) long specimen that was virtually identical to its fossil ancestors. Since then other Coelacanths have been caught. With their stubby, limb-like fins, they may well be a link with the first fish that crawled out of the water to begin the colonisation of the land.

Twenty thousand fish to a kilo

The Gobie, a tiny fish living in fresh water lakes in the Philippines, is the smallest fish in the world. It takes over twenty thousand of these to weigh a kilo; even when they are full grown they measure no more than 5 centimetres long. They are caught in fine meshed nets and sold to make fish-cakes. Gobies are the smallest animals with backbones.

The Ocean Sunfish has no body

The Ocean Sunfish, a huge fish weighing up to a ton, appears to be all head, since its body is so broad and its fins are set so far back. It is known as the Mola Mola.

The largest fresh water fish in the world weighs 500 kilos

There are reports from Russia of gigantic sturgeon weighing more than a ton. Sturgeon weighing up to 500 kilos were once caught in the western United States at Snake River, though catches of such a size are now rare.

The South American Catfish devours its home alive

The tiny South American Catfish is a parasite, living in the gills of larger fish. It chews at the gills of the host fish and lives on the blood that seeps out.

The Climbing Perch spends hours out of water

The strange Climbing Perch, found in Asia, clambers out of the water in search of food and spends hours on dry land, travelling considerable distances through mud flats and tangled roots. Even in water, it must surface every few minutes to take a gulp of air.

The Male Bluegill Sunfish acts as mother

The Male Bluegill Sunfish from North America makes the nest for the female to lay the eggs in and fertilises the eggs as they are laid. It is the male who watches over the nest until the tiny fish hatch and even then he stays around for a few days to protect his minute offspring.

Sea catfish carry their eggs in their mouths

The male sea catfish is a devoted father; he not only incubates the female's eggs in his mouth but also allows the young to hide there while they grow to a size suitable for solitary life. All this time he cannot eat since he would swallow not only his meal, but his children too.

Fish hardly ever die of old age

There are records of carp which have lived for over a hundred years, and of eels and catfish who have lasted almost as long. Fish as a rule are usually devoured by other predators before they can succumb to old age.

The King salmon swims two thousand miles to breed and then dies

The King salmon spend most of their life in the ocean, and then, when the breeding season approaches, they swim immense distances upstream to fertilise the female's eggs. This journey is so exhausting that few survive it. They usually die soon after the fertilisation.

The mystery of the eels is solved

For many years, no-one knew where eels went to breed. Now the truth has been discovered. Both American and European eels spawn at the edge of the Sargasso sea. The adults die and the young eels drift across the oceans for thousands of miles until they reach their "home". There they grow and mature until they are ready to begin the migration to the Sargasso sea where the cycle starts all over again.

Fishes of the deep

Some fishes live at such enormous depths that they are almost completely blind. The sea is so dark here that they have little need for eyes. The pressures at these great depths are great enough to crush the hulls of normal submarines and yet these fishes live here with no more protection than their scales. There are no plant foods available at these depths so the fish are of necessity carnivorous. They feed only on the dead creatures which float down to their deep kingdom or on smaller prey who, like them, live in the pitch dark.

Dolphins which live in rivers

Not all dolphins are sea creatures. The Amazon dolphin lives in the mainstream and tributaries of the Amazon River, often as far inland as the foothills of the Andes Mountains. In India, there are dolphins which live in the Ganges that have lost the use of their eyes because the Ganges and Indus are so muddy that their eyesight is of no use to them. They probe the thick mud of the river bed to find the crustaceans and fish that they need. They never leave their river habitat. These dolphins reach a considerable size. Like the dolphins of the Ganges, the Chinese River dolphins are also almost blind and never go back to the sea. Dolphins, as we have said (page 93), are not fish. They are mammals and give birth to live young, unlike fish who lay eggs which hatch outside the mother's body.

Game fishing is a sport over two thousand years old

One of the most famous flies used in trout fishing is the Red Hackle. This was first described in 200 BC. Of all the fishes sought by fishermen, the trout is perhaps the most highly prized. As a game fish it has few equals, since it is a brave fighter and requires much skill to catch.

The largest mammal on earth

The Blue Whale (Balaenoptera musculus) is the largest mammal on earth. This warmblooded creature can reach a length of 90 metres and weigh up to 115 tons. This magnificent creature is in danger of extinction as are many of the whale family.

The Goosefish can eat birds

The American Goosefish has a mouth so large that it can swallow fish as big as itself. It has been known to catch small geese and ducks. It has rows of backward curving teeth which make it impossible for its prey to wriggle free. The Goosefish has a strange 'lure' on its snout which attracts prey and leads it to within striking range. They can weigh up to 35 kilogrammes.

The mystery fish of the sea

The Albacore, a streamlined member of the Tuna fish family, has a most mysterious life. No one knows where they breed or where the young grow up. They can swim hundreds of miles in a single day and often appear suddenly in great shoals off Japan, the Hawaiian Islands and California. Their arrival is heralded by shoals of smaller fish. Their fins slip down into a slot in their backs when they are swimming at great speed so that there is no resistance to the water.

Basses can change sex

Members of the Serranid family such as Serranus subligarius can function as both a male and a female at the same time. Other species of bass begin life as females and five years later change into males.

Paddlefish provide caviar

There are two species of paddlefish; one lives in the Mississippi delta in the USA and the other in the Yangtze-Kiang River of China. They both have immensely long paddle-like growths on their snouts, sometimes reaching as much as a third of the entire length of the fish. They have a small patch of scales near the tail but are otherwise quite smooth. Their flesh is rich and tasty, and their eggs make excellent caviar.

Waterbugs make bread

In some areas of the world, waterbugs are farmed for food. These little insects, known in the west as water-boatmen, are either collected up and ground into highly nutritious flour or their eggs are farmed, dried and also ground up for flour. Since insects are high in protein, this is not so strange an idea as it sounds.

Grass snakes can swim out to sea

The grass-snake, one of the only water-loving snakes found in Europe, prefers a damp habitat and is not at all averse to a swim. There is a record of a fishing boat having spotted a grass snake swimming strongly several miles out to sea.

A river changes as it flows towards the sea

A single river provides many different forms of habitat, from its source in the hills to the estuary near the sea. At first it runs too fast to support much life but farther down the clear, cold, oxygen-full stream is perfect for trout, eels and young salmon. It becomes loaded with silt and begins to meander as it reaches the plains, creating pools suitable for fish such as barbel, grayling and perch. As the river nears the sea, it contains less oxygen and the water becomes murky and slower. There are bream and many forms of smaller river life. The estuary is affected by the tides, which in turn affect the creatures that live there. Some fish do move up and down the river but most forms of life stay within their special section.

Fresh waterways abound with wildlife as can be seen from this drawing:
1 *Coot.*
2 *Stonefly.*
3 *Forget-me-nots.*
4 *Mayfly.*
5 *Reed warbler.*
6 *Mallard.*
7 *Dragonfly.*
8 *Heron.*
9 *Water lilies.*
10 *Pike.*
11 *Dipper.*
12 *Roach.*
13 *Yellow Flag.*
14 *Eel.*
15 *Lesser reedmace.*
16 *Arrowhead.*
17 *Water Dock.*
18 *Otter.*

There are luminous pastures in the oceans

Vast pastures of tiny plants and animals drift about the oceans, just below the surface of the water. This 'plankton', as it is called, is the basis for most life in the sea. Even the giant Blue Whale feeds on plankton. Many of the creatures that make up the plankton are luminous, and when they rise to the surface at night time they glow with light.

A carp can live for 40 years

Large carp can live up to 40 years or more in captivity. Carp live in freshwater. They have two barbels, or fleshy whiskers, that droop down on either side of their mouths. Carp were once bred for food in monasteries. They can grow between 20 and 35 centimetres (8-14 inches) in a single year and usually weigh between 10 and 15 kilograms (22-33 pounds) when mature. Some have been known to weigh as much as 20 kilograms (44 pounds).

Rivers and streams support a great variety of life

The pike (10) is one of the most vicious freshwater fish. It can grow to about 1.4 metres (5 feet) and weigh more than 20 kilograms (44 pounds). It lives on fish mostly, such as roach (12) and eels (14). The pike also feeds on young coot (1) and ducklings such as the mallard (6). The otter (18) also feeds on fish and so does the heron (8). The reed warbler (5) and dragonfly (7) feed on insects. The dipper (11) walks along the bed of the stream, looking for food. Ducks also bob down to find underwater food. Plants and insects that are common by many streams are the lesser reedmace (15), water dock (17), yellow flag (13), stonefly (2) and mayfly (3).

Salmon always return to the river where they hatched to spawn

Salmon are probably the most prized freshwater fish. People spend large sums of money for the privilege of fishing in stretches of water where salmon are known to swim. Many sportsmen claim that the struggle between a salmon at the end of their lines and themselves is the most satisfactory form of hunting. When they hatch, salmon spend the first two years of their lives in the river. They then swim down to the sea where they spend another year. When they are ready to spawn, no matter where they are, they make there way back to the place where they were hatched in order to lay their eggs, struggling upstream against the currents making spectacular leaps on the way.

Salmon are called different names at different stages of their lives

For the first two years of their lives, when they are swimming the rivers of their births, young salmon are called parrs. For the third year of their lives when they swim in the waters off Greenland they are called grilse. Before they become grilse they are often called smolt as they make their way to Greenland.

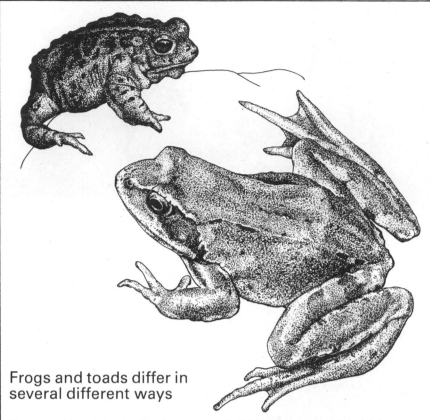

Frogs and toads differ in several different ways

Frogs and toads look alike from a distance but close up they are very different. Frogs usually have smooth, shiny bodies and long back legs for leaping. Toads have shorter back legs and cannot leap as far as frogs. They usually have a dry skin covered with warts. The frog lays its eggs, or spawn, in masses which often float on the surface of the water. Toad spawn is laid in long strands which are generally attached to underwater plants.

Top: *The toad with its warty skin and shorter legs.* Bottom: *The smoother frog with its more powerful back legs is a close relative but belongs to a different family.*

In Chile there is a frog which swallows its young

There is a very small frog in Chile that was originally found by the great naturalist Charles Darwin. Its proper name is Rhinoderma. The male waits by the eggs until they begin to show some sign of life. He then picks them up in his mouth and swallows them, as if he were eating them. They fall into the large vocal sac that hangs beneath his body and remain there until they have turned into tiny young frogs. Then they pop out of his mouth and face the dangers of the world on their own. If this does not happen the chances are the young would be eaten by predators.

The Pipa toad keeps its eggs in a pocket

Male and female Pipa toads mate in the water. As soon as the female has laid her eggs and they have been fertilised, the male pushes them gently on to the female's back. They stick there and the skin immediately grows up around them, making little pockets. The eggs sink into the pockets and are covered completely. Within two weeks, the movement of the little tadpoles can be seen beneath the skin. After another week they break out of the pockets and exist on their own, going through the various stages of growth until they become adult toads.

Toads without a tongue

In South America and Africa, but nowhere else in the world, there are tongueless toads who never leave the water. Because they feed entirely underwater they have no need for a tongue and their eyes are tiny and of little use to them. To feel their way through the murky water where they live they have sensitive bumps on the tips of their fingers. All the tongueless toads of Africa are called Clawed Toads because the top joint of their fingers has grown into a claw-like point.

Toads protect themselves with poison

The Marine Toad (Bufo marinus) secretes a deadly poison in its skin. The poison is held in warty lumps all over the toad's back and limbs. This poison is so deadly that dogs, snakes and even men have died from its effects. All toads produce an irritant substance in their skins which can be harmful if taken internally since it is absorbed through the sensitive skin in the mouth and stomach. It is not true that handling toads will cause warts. The superstition arises from the fact that toads are such warty creatures themselves. The poison that toads secrete is their only defence since they are so slow moving. The poison has been extracted by South American Indians and used to dip the tops of their darts into, making them extremely dangerous.

There is a frog that is as big as a dog

The Goliath Frog, found in the African Congo, is the largest of all the frogs found in the world today. It can reach the size of a small terrier and feeds on fresh-water crabs which it finds in the brackish pools of the Congo.

Frogs are edible

Many species of frogs can be eaten. They are popular in France where they are called *grenouilles*.

A frog can fly

The Flying Frog (Rhacophorus pardalis) has large webbed feet, much larger than any other member of the frog family. They are beautifully marked and very light in weight. When they leap they spread out their webbed fore and hind feet and sail for long distances. Some frogs of this family lay their eggs in trees although it is more usual to lay in water.

Fire Salamanders are not born in the fire

The belief that Fire Salamanders, a European species, were born out of fire was fostered by the fact that so many were seen crawling out of burning logs. The salamanders had not, in fact, hatched out in the fire but had been driven from their hiding places under the bark of the logs by the heat and flames. Fire salamanders are one of the few salamander species which give birth to live young, and can bear as many as fifty youngsters at once.

The largest living amphibian can grow to nearly two metres

The Giant Salamander from Japan is the largest amphibian alive today. This species can grow to a length of over one and a half metres and weigh more than a grown woman. Amphibians have never been the giants of the animal world, the largest amphibious fossils found only reached a length of two and a half metres and a weight of about 75 kilos.

Amphibians breathe in three different ways

Amphibians are the only aquatic animals who have no fur and breathe with lungs. They can breathe air in directly as humans do but since they spend so much of their time in water they also have the ability to take in oxygen through their skins and through the linings of their mouths. Amphibians must stay moist and damp or their skin dries out and they cannot breathe through it. Although amphibians are cold blooded, during very hot weather their temperatures can rise to the same levels as birds and other warm blooded creatures. If the temperatures fall to more than a few degrees below freezing all amphibians must hibernate in order to survive. They become completely dormant using very little oxygen and eating nothing at all, getting what little energy they need from the layers of fat stored under the skin. Amphibians will appear to hibernate in hot and dry weather as well. This hibernation is called estivation and they will remain motionless for weeks on end, conserving their body moisture.

Lung-fish make their own cocoons

The African Lung-fish, a distant relative of the salamander, toad and frog family, has been known to survive for nearly four years out of water, wrapped in a mud cocoon which it makes for itself. During dry spells, these fish build a protective coating out of mud with a small breathing tube to enable the fish to survive.

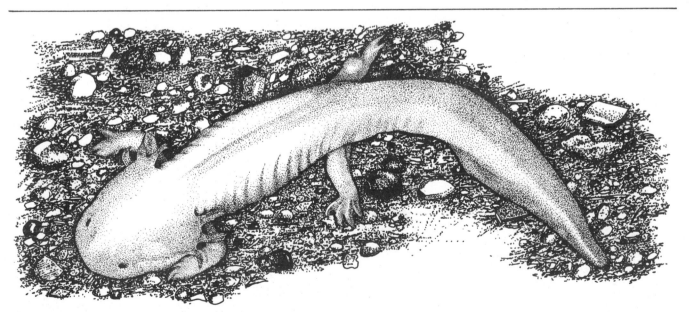

There is a salamander that never grows up

The axolotl lives in the lakes of Mexico. It looks like a salamander, except that it has feathery gills for breathing underwater. It is in fact a salamander newt, or 'larva', that has never developed into a fully grown salamander. However, the axolotl is sexually mature and can reproduce. It is black-speckled and dark brown.

The puffin can carry ten fish in its beak at once

Puffins do not have a pouch beneath their beaks like the pelican but they can still carry a large catch of fish. By arranging the fish crossways in their beaks, with the heads to one side and the tails all to the other, puffins can bring home as many as ten at a time. Their beaks are coloured bright red, yellow and blue at breeding time. During the rest of the year the colours fade and some of the beak is shed, leaving it considerably smaller.

Some pelicans fish in teams

There are several kinds of pelican, ranging in colour from white to brown. They all have the curiously large beak, in which they store their catch. This also becomes a feeding trough for their young, who thrust their entire heads in to take what they want when their parents return from fishing. The brown pelican makes its catch by diving at great speed from the air but other pelicans work in teams. They form a circle round a shoal of fish in deep water and all dip their beaks in at the same time so that the fish are kept within the circle and none escape. At other times they may form up in line abreast and drive the fish towards shallow water where they can be caught more easily.

King penguins make themselves into living nests

King penguins do not make nests for their young. There is not much to make nests out of in the Antarctic waste. When the female lays the egg, both parents take it in turn to keep it warm by resting it on their feet and covering it with the soft folds of their belly. When the egg hatches, the young penguin continues to be protected in the same way, peering out safely from between its parent's feet.

The albatross has a wing span nearly twice the height of the average man

The wandering albatross has the greatest wing span of any living bird. It can measure up to 3.5 metres (11 feet), with a body length of 112-135 centimetres (44-53 inches) and a weight of about 7-8 kilograms (15-18 pounds). It is found particularly in the southern oceans and can float almost motionless in the air, glide for vast distances, and reach speeds of 160 km/h (99 mph). Albatrosses have been known to fly more than 4830 kilometres (3000 miles) in 10 days, an average of 483 kilometres (300 miles) per day. Strangely enough, although they live on the sea, they are usually seasick when brought on board ships. They feed on fish and squid and lay only one egg at a time.

The Auk's eggs are designed for survival

The auk family contains Puffins, Razorbills, Guillemots and Little Auks. All these birds nest on high and narrow rock ledges in overcrowded colonies. There is a great danger of the eggs being dislodged and so rolling away to smash on the rocks far below the nests. The eggs of these birds are pear shaped, so that even if they roll out of the nest, they will roll in a circle and so be safer than an oval-shaped bird's egg. Since the auks do not build a nest, but lay their eggs on the bare rock this is a very necessary precaution. The Great Auk, the largest bird in this family, became extinct in 1844 when the last bird was killed in Iceland. Men had driven these great birds (most of them as big as geese) into pens and slaughtered them for their flesh and the rich oils in their skins.

Mother Cary's Chickens are sea birds

The Petrel, a sea bird about as big as a blackbird, flies along the wave crests with its feet skimming the waves. This is where their name comes from. It is a version of "Little Peter" after Saint Peter who walked on the water. Sailors also call these birds Mother Cary's Chickens (Mother Cary is a corruption of Virgin Mary). These little birds are so fearless that they will fly in all weather, seeming to be unaffected by even the most severe storms. The sailors believe that they must be protected by the Virgin Mary against the fury of the elements. Some petrels' feet are so weak they cannot walk on land.

Polar bears and penguins never meet in the wild

Polar bears live in the Arctic and penguins live only in the Antarctic. Penguins cannot fly but swim well. They have webbed feet and their wings are like flippers. They feed on fish and shellfish. Polar bears also swim well. They eat mostly seals and fish.

The mystery life of the Galapagos Penguin

The Galapagos Penguin lives further north than any other penguin species. It makes its home on the rocky Galapagos Islands near the equator. It is so shy and retiring that no one has ever seen its nest, eggs or chicks.

The Adelie penguin is an expert high-jumper

Adelie penguins live in Antarctica in crowds of more than 50,000. They travel more than 805 kilometres (500 miles) each year between their feeding grounds and nesting grounds. Adelies feed on krill and their main enemies are the skua gull that seizes eggs and young, and the leopard seal that eats the adults. Although they move awkwardly on land, Adelies swim well. When returning to land they jump out of the water straight up the vertical side of an ice floe, three or four times their own height.

Right: *Penguins are endearing and amusing birds. Their wings have gradually evolved into flippers which enable them to swim powerfully in their Antarctic homes. They are not very agile on land although many of them learn to toboggan through the snow and to slide into the sea with great ease. They spend most of their lives in the water and only come ashore to breed and to moult. They usually choose nesting sights that are close to the sea. Some birds nest in isolation and others in colonies of thousands of pairs. The nests can be simple burrows or well-constructed piles of stones. Some species build no nest at all. King and Emperor penguins lay only one egg each year which is incubated on top of the parents' feet covered by a fold of belly skin. Other species lay two eggs at a time, and some raise two clutches each year.*

Falconry and hawking were once highly organised sports

Hawks and falcons are birds of prey that hunt by day. Falcons are darker than hawks and have longer, pointed wings. They are also faster than hawks. The ancient Chinese trained these birds for hunting and the sport is still popular in the Near East and in parts of India. Falconry and hawking (the words used for hunting with the two types of bird) were common pursuits in the Middle Ages. There were supposed to be particular birds for particular ranks of society. In general a king used a gerfalcon, a noble used a peregrine falcon, a priest used a sparrowhawk, a lady used a merlin and a yeoman used a goshawk. Servants used kestrels.

Cormorants can be trained to catch and retrieve fish

The common cormorant is a sea bird about 90 centimetres (35 inches) long and its relation, the shag, is slightly smaller with a faint green tinge to its feathers. Cormorants normally fly low over

the water and dive to catch fish. One kind of cormorant from the Galapagos Islands has lost the use of its wings and dives directly from the surface. Cormorants swim strongly underwater and rise to swallow their catch head first, so that the scales of the fish do not stick in their throats. In China and elsewhere, cormorants have been trained to dive from fishermen's boats. A light chain is put around each bird's neck so that it does not swallow the fish.

Jackdaws are kept as pets

It is quite common to keep parrots and budgerigars as pets but there was a time when jackdaws were popular as well. They make good pets because they grow attached to their owners and will follow them around wherever they go, even when their wings have grown sufficiently for them to fly away. Jackdaws may even learn to repeat a few words. However, they have a habit of stealing trinkets and anything that glitters. This can become annoying to their owners.

A chicken may lay more than 1000 eggs in its lifetime

Chickens usually start to lay eggs when they are about 18 weeks old. They lay most during the first year. Each egg takes about one day to form inside the chicken but the birds do not lay continuously throughout their lives. Fewer eggs are produced in the second and third year but some chickens lay for five, six or even seven years, producing more than 1000 eggs in all. Although there are still free-range chickens on some farms, most are now kept in special batteries, where their food, light and temperature are carefully controlled to obtain maximum production.

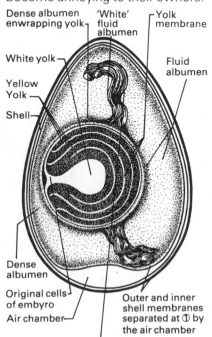

Dense albumen enwrapping yolk | 'White' fluid albumen | Yolk membrane
White yolk
Yellow Yolk
Shell
Fluid albumen
Dense albumen
Original cells of embyro
Air chamber
Outer and inner shell membranes separated at ① by the air chamber
Supporting yolk Membranes; ends are incorporated in dense albumen

The dodo has been extinct for 300 years

The dodo was a turkey-sized bird that was last found in Mauritius in the 1680s. It was clumsy and was unable to fly. It had a large hook-ended bill, a tuft of a tail, whitish breast and yellowish-white on the wings; the rest of its body was dark. There were, in fact, two forms of dodo but the Mauritius dodo was the better known and both are now extinct. Live specimens were sent to London but none survived for long. The island birds were killed by the settlers for food and the hogs that came with the settlers ate their eggs and young ones.

Only 40 whooping cranes are left alive

The whooping crane is only one of several different kinds of crane but it is one of the most beautiful. It is pure white with black wing tips and a carmine-coloured head. It is a large bird with a two-metre (six feet) wing span and its name comes from the curious whooping sound it makes. At the beginning of the 20th century it was quite common in North America but the species was nearly wiped out of existence by hunters, to the extent where it was believed there were only about 40 of the birds left alive in the world. Now their migration route between northern Alberta, Canada, and a special reserve in Texas is carefully protected and there is hope that the birds will slowly increase in numbers.

The lyrebird is named after a musical instrument

The lyrebird lives in Australia and gets its name from the extraordinary shape of the male bird's tail. The lyre was an ancient Greek instrument with a guitar-like body and two horn-shaped arms which support the strings. When the lyrebird displays to its mate, it raises its beautiful tail, rather like a peacock does. Several long feathers like the string of a lyre are spread between two large curved feathers that represent the horns of the lyre. Lyrebirds spend most of the time on the ground. They rarely fly and do not sing very well.

Humming birds squeak instead of humming

The song of the humming bird is a high, squeaky cadence of chirps. The humming noise is made by their wings which can beat so fast that they look blurred. The smallest bird in the world is the Bee Humming Bird.
Humming birds can only perch, they cannot walk or run and spend most of their waking hours in flight. They pollinate flowers in the same way that bees do.

The lyrebird is the largest member of the family known as passerines which also includes thrushes, larks and crows. It is usually about the size of a chicken. Until it displays its feathers it is a drab creature, but when it does display it fans its tail over its head with the two largest feathers spread out sideways and the more delicate ones are cast out in front in one of the most beautiful displays in nature.

Woodpeckers have exceptionally long tongues

Woodpeckers are very well adapted to their life of climbing and drilling on the trunks of trees. Most of them have two toes pointing forward and two pointing backward, to help them grip the bark. Their short, stiff tails also help them to cling to the tree when they are boring a hole or picking insects out of the wood. A woodpecker's tongue reaches right round the inside of their head and can reach into the smallest cranny for prey. The Californian woodpecker stores acorns by wedging them into the bark and one type of African and Asian woodpecker makes holes for its eggs in ants' nests that are suspended from the branches.

Swans do not sing when they are about to die

The old belief that swans sing on their deathbeds is not true but it has given rise to the phrase that someone's last action or performance is their 'swan song'. The idea that swans do sing when they die is very old and poets and storytellers have used it for many centuries. Perhaps the idea comes from the beautiful and mournful sound that some swans can produce.

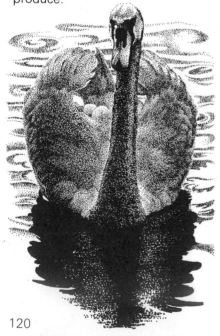

The kingfisher has many curious relatives

The European kingfisher is about the only one of its large family that does not usually live in a warm climate. Among its relatives are the todies of Central America and the West Indies, with their brilliant red chins; the mot-mots of Central and South America, with their marvellously long tail feathers; the bee eaters from Africa and elsewhere; the acrobatic rollers and the Australian kookaburra, which both eat snakes; the hoopoes of Africa, Asia and Europe, with their crests and long beaks; and the hornbills from India, with their strange head growths. The belted kingfisher is the only member of the family in North America.

The kingfisher's nest smells dreadful

The European kingfisher digs a tunnel with a small circular chamber at the end, in the river bank for nesting. Here it lays between six and eight eggs and when the young hatch, they are fed on fish. The nest soon becomes full of bits of decaying fish and regurgitated fish bones. Most birds remove their droppings from the nest but the kingfisher does not. The combination of droppings and fish on a hot day in a small space makes the nest one of the smelliest in the bird kingdom but the kingfisher does not mind at all.

Geese sometimes act as watchdogs

At different times in history people have kept geese as pets and watchdogs as much as for their eggs and meat. The ancient Egyptians, Greeks and Romans all valued geese very highly. There is a story from Roman times in which some geese warned of an attack by the Gauls and saved the city by their cackling.

Martha, the last of the passenger pigeons, died in a zoo in 1914

The passenger pigeon of North America was once one of the most common birds on earth. At the beginning of the 19th century, flocks of up to two thousand million were seen, stretching for more than 300 kilometres (188 miles). The birds were slaughtered systematically in their roosts and nesting sites by the ever-hungry settlers, who often cut or burnt down the nesting trees to get at the fledglings more quickly. By the end of the 19th century, the last few were confined to zoos and in 1914 the very last one, called Martha, died in Cincinnati Zoo, having survived alone since 1910. She was immediately preserved and is now in the Smithsonian Museum in Washington.

The kiwi lays an egg that is almost a quarter of its total body weight

The kiwi is a small, very rare bird, about the size of a domestic chicken, that lives in New Zealand. It has no tail and appears to have no wings. In fact, it has wings but they are too small to be seen among the almost fur-like feathers of this shy little creature. Its egg is relatively large and is hatched by the male. The nostrils of the kiwi are at the end of its fairly long bill. This enables it to smell out the worms it eats.

The bee-eater rides 'piggy-back'

The brilliantly-coloured bee-eater has long tail-feathers and a longish beak in which it catches bees, wasps and dragonflies on the wing. Before it eats the bees and wasps it rubs their bodies on a branch. This gets rid of substances that are poisonous to the bird. One type of bee-eater can sometimes be seen riding on the back of large birds such as storks or bustards as they walk along the ground, waiting for grasshoppers and other insects to be disturbed by the larger bird's feet.

The flightless kakapo is a cross between an owl and a parrot

The New Zealand kakapo, also called the owl-parrot or ground-parrot, gets its name from a Maori word. The face and beak look very much like those of an owl but the bird is a relation of the parrot. It is a greenish colour with brown and yellow markings. Although it does have wings, they are useless for flight and help it only to hop along the ground. It lives in burrows and climbs trees to feed on the fruit.

The shrike hangs its food on hooks

There are several species of shrike, or butcher bird, all over the world. Once they were prized as song birds. They are birds of prey, hunting mice and lizards and other, smaller birds, but they do not have the strong claws that other birds of prey have and so they find it necessary to impale their victims on sharp thorns while they eat them.

The extinct Great Auk still has living relatives

The Great Auk looked a little like a penguin when it stood up, with a large striped beak. It nested on rocky islands in the North Atlantic and was an excellent swimmer, but it could not fly, so seamen were able to catch the bird quite easily. It became extinct in 1844. The living relatives of the Great Auk can all fly. They include the puffin, the razorbill, the guillemot and the Little Auk, which is very different from its dead cousin. It is about one quarter of the size, with a small, sharp beak and a smart black and white front. It breeds in the Arctic.

The mot-mot uses its feathers to shape its tail.

The tody catches insects in its wings.

The hooper is one of the most beautiful of all birds.

The bower bird builds a bower to attract its mate

Bower birds come from New Guinea and Australia. The best-known is the smart, glossy, blue-black satin bower bird. The male makes a kind of dance floor out of twigs, surrounded by an upright arch of over-curving sticks. It places offerings of coloured feathers, stones, bits of bone and bright objects on the floor to lure the female. Later, the female builds its nest at a little distance from the bower. The brown gardener bower bird makes a thatched hut around a tree trunk, leaning stems of orchids against the trunk. It leaves an opening on one side, with a

threshold of moss covered with fresh flowers. It replaces the flowers whenever they begin to wilt.

The bird that mimics the songs of other birds

The best-known species of mocking bird lives in North America, although there are several other kinds in South America. 'Mocking' is another word for 'mimicking' or 'copying'. The songs of the bluebird and jay seem to be the favourites for the mocking bird but it can imitate others also. To look at, the mocking bird is fairly dull-coloured and about the size of a thrush. It builds a very rough nest of twigs.

The flamingo feeds with its beak upside down

The beautiful pink flamingo has a strangely shaped beak with a downward hook. When it feeds, it wades into the water on its long legs and lowers its neck so that its curved beak hangs upside down. Then it swings its beak from side to side, raking in the mud for plants and small living creatures. Its nest is also rather peculiar. It consists of a little mud tower with a hollow in the top for one or two eggs.

The pest out of the pages of Shakespeare caused havoc in the New World

At the end of the last century, an enthusiastic reader of Shakespeare decided to bring into America every single kind of bird mentioned in Shakespeare's plays. Among these were 40 pairs of starlings, the first starlings ever to reach the New World. They very soon became a national pest. A starling can have two or three broods a year and they are very aggressive in seizing the nests of other birds and throwing out their young. They destroyed crops and roosted among the warm, tall, cliff-like buildings of the cities. Schemes to destroy them or frighten them all failed. But new schemes such as recording and playing back of distress calls by the birds themselves which alarms others and warns them away are beginning to work.

The hornbill seals up its mate in the nest

Hornbills are curious-looking birds that live in Africa and parts of Asia. They have large bills with horny caps or domes at the base of the bill. The dome on top of the bill of

The hummingbird's wings beat 90 times per second

The wings of a hummingbird can beat so fast that they produce the 'hum' from which they get their name. They need to hover, upright, in mid-air, to probe into the flowers from which their long tongues take the nectar. The sword-bill hummingbird has a beak that is three or four times the length of its body, so that it can reach into the deepest flowers. The smallest hummingbird is the bee hummingbird from Cuba, which is 5 centimetres (two inches) long and weighs only 2 grams (0.07 ounces).

A hummingbird's hum is caused by the fast action of its wings.

the rhinoceros hornbill turns up strangely at the end, a bit like a rhinoceros's horn. Hornbills usually make their nests in hollow trees. The female sits on the eggs and the male seals up the entrance to the hole with wet mud so that predators can't get in. The male then feeds the female through a small hole. The entrance is unblocked when the young have hatched.

The Toucan's beak is hollow

The immense beak of the South American Toucan seems too large for the bird to carry, but in fact their beaks are made from a hard spongy material with large air spaces in it. This makes it strong enough to use, but very light and not as uncomfortable as it seems.

One hawk that fishes

The Osprey, a large hawk, is found in every continent. There is only one family. They are often called Fish Hawks because they have a habit of flying above lakes on the look-out for fish basking near the surface. When they see a fish close enough to the surface to catch they dive down at incredible speed and grasp the fish in their talons, the outer toe of which is reversible to allow the bird to grip more efficiently. The underside of the pads of their feet are rough and scaly which also helps the bird to grip its slippy prey. When the bird has finished eating it will fly along the surface of the water with its feet dangling below the surface to clean them. Ospreys feed only on fish and for this reason, and because ospreys will drive away any other predatory birds from its territory, American farmers used to build a platform with a wagon wheel on top of a tall pole to encourage ospreys to nest there. The birds would then keep other predators away from the hen houses. Ospreys have recently returned to nest in Britain.

Ostriches do not bury their heads in the sand

It is a fallacy that Ostriches bury their heads in the sand when frightened or alarmed. These birds (the largest of all the world's birds) in fact crouch down to the ground where their dusty colouring makes them almost invisible to predators. A male ostrich may weigh up to 170 kilos and stand higher than a tall man. They have survived because they can run at tremendous speeds - up to 40 miles per hour. They are fierce fighters, delivering tremendous kicking blows with their large, two toed feet. They can even defend themselves against lions and are fearless when attacked. They do not sing at all, but produce a loud sonorous roaring sound or at times a frightening hiss.

Birds are often more faithful than humans

In some species in the bird world a pair of birds that have chosen each other as mates will stay together for life. The Common Tern only chooses one mate and will never swap for another, often never mating again when the first partner dies. Geese are also faithful to their mates and there are cases of a gander pining away when his mate was killed.

One of the rarest birds in the world is a vulture

The image of a vulture is of a tattered, repulsive carrion eater, but the Californian Condor, now one of the rarest birds in the world (there are only about 50 left, and these are carefully protected) is a graceful bird which hunts swiftly and will catch its own prey. The Andean Condor is one of the largest flying birds and is represented on several South American Coins. It has a loud cry rather like the sound of an engine.

Some birds eat grit and stones to help them digest their food

Many birds cannot digest their food without grit and stones. Their problem is that they have no teeth and therefore cannot grind up the tough grain they often eat. The grit and stones pass down with the grain into the part of their stomach known as the gizzard. Together, the strong muscles of the gizzard and the grit and stones grind the bird's food so that it can be digested.

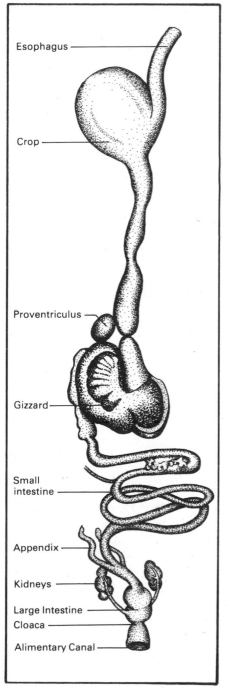

Esophagus

Crop

Proventriculus

Gizzard

Small intestine

Appendix

Kidneys

Large Intestine

Cloaca

Alimentary Canal

Above: *1. The Monarch. 2. The Large Copper. 3. The Camberwell Beauty. 4. The Swallowtail. Below each is shown the respective larvae.*
Below: *The beautiful Peacock butterfly.*

Caterpillars have two different kinds of legs

Caterpillars have several segments to their bodies. When it becomes a butterfly the first three segments become the thorax of the butterfly — that is the part that carries the wings and legs. The three pairs of legs on these three segments are tougher than the other legs of the caterpillar and will grow into the legs of the butterfly. The other pairs of legs (usually five pairs but sometimes less) are much softer and disappear completely.

Fragile butterflies can travel thousands of kilometres

To watch a butterfly flitting to and fro in a garden, you would not think it could fly as much as a kilometre in a straight line. But some species of butterfly migrate vast distances, just like birds. One of the most dauntless is the Monarch Butterfly of North America. It spends the winter in the Gulf of Mexico and when spring comes it starts on the long journey north to Canada, following the steady growth of the milkweed plant on which it feeds. On the way, it lays eggs, which hatch and produce young butterflies who carry on the journey. In autumn, the survivors fly south again in great clouds. In Europe, the Painted Lady migrates between North Africa and sometimes as far north as Iceland.

Moths and butterflies are different in several ways

One marked difference between butterflies and moths is their antennae. Those of the butterfly are club-shaped at the tips, whereas those of the moth are feathery-shaped. When at rest, butterflies usually close their wings together, sticking them straight up from their backs. Moths, on the other hand, spread their wings flat to either side of them or fold them along their back. It is not true that all moths fly at night and all butterflies fly during the day. There are some day-flying moths and some evening-flying butterflies.

One cocoon of the silk-moth caterpillar contains a thread of silk more than 500 metres long

The silk-moth caterpillar has been bred in captivity for thousands of years. Its caterpillar feeds on mulberry leaves and spins a silken cocoon for itself. The chrysalis inside the cocoon is killed before it becomes a moth and the silk is unwound. Strands are twisted together to make it stronger. The Chinese carefully guarded the secret of the silkworm for at least 2,000 years before it spread to Japan and India and then to Europe.

Camouflage is used by butterflies to deceive their enemies

Butterflies are experts at camouflage and deception. They need to be, because they have no other way to defend themselves. Although the upper surface of their wings may often be bright, the under surface is usually plain, so that when they close their wings it is difficult to see them. The Indian leaf butterfly looks exactly like the leaves on which it rests when its wings are closed. Some butterflies have bright spots, like eyes, on their wings. These deceive their enemies into snatching at the wrong parts of their bodies. Others are painted in bright colours to warn their enemies that they are unpleasant to eat. Some butterflies have a trick of shutting their wings suddenly in flight and dropping quickly to the ground to escape capture.

Caterpillars defend themselves in many curious ways

Caterpillars are very vulnerable to attacks from birds and from parasites and therefore must defend themselves to survive. Some, like the Magpie Moth, hide in webs; some can keep completely still and camouflage themselves to look like a stick or twig, some like the Woolly Bear, have irritating hairs and roll themselves into a ball for protection; some squirt formic acid at their attacker or, like the Swallowtail, extrude an evil smell; some rely on bluff, as with the large 'eyes' of the Elephant Hawk Moth; and some have developed bright colours to warn attackers that they have an unpleasant taste.

Some caterpillars trick their way into a feast

One species of caterpillar is able to trick ants into welcoming it into their nest. The ants enjoy the sweet substance that is secreted from the back of the caterpillar; at the same time the ants help to keep parasites off the caterpillar. Once in the nest, the caterpillar makes a fine meal of the ant larvae.

There are more insects than people

Of all the animals in the world, more than 80 per cent of them are insects. There are at least 900,000 that have been identified and named and goodness knows how many more that have never been classified or even seen.
Most insects have a very short life cycle and an insect only two weeks old can reproduce itself at that age. It has been calculated that in one year a single female Cabbage Aphid could produce over 1,560,000,000,000,000,000,000,000 offspring! This is only 16 generations. The termites (the ant family) are prodigious breeders; the queen termite lays one egg every two seconds, twenty-four hours a day throughout her life. There are authenticated reports of swarms of butterflies so large that over one and a quarter million butterflies flew across a 250 mile zone every minute for 18 days. Locusts have been seen in swarms over half a mile high, a hundred miles wide and three hundred miles long. The number of locusts in a swarm of that size would number over one hundred and twenty-four thousand million. Traffic was brought to a standstill in southern England a few years ago by columns of caterpillars marching across roads and plagues of ants are reported that can eat their way through lush undergrowth leaving nothing behind. One of the great plagues of Egypt mentioned in the Bible was a plague of locusts that stripped the Egyptian crops and locust plagues still cause immense damage to farms in Africa today despite the use of modern insecticides.

Insects are the toughest animals on earth

There is nowhere on earth that does not have its share of insects. From the highest mountains to the deepest lakes, from boiling springs to frozen arctic wastes, the insect world has learned to survive the harshest climates. There are insects which live hundreds of feet below the ground, blind and without colour. There are insects which dwell at high altitudes in the Andes mountains where the air is thin and cold. There are insects which live in the poisonous sacs of insect eating plants and yet come to no harm. There are even insects which live in cans of raw petrol. Insects are protected by their exoskeleton, their bones are outside the body, unlike other animals whose bones are internal. The hard covering of insects makes them impervious to many of the toxins and dangers that threaten soft skinned animals. Their eyes are multi faceted and have accurate and incredibly sharp vision. Many of them have antennae which allow them to sense not only food but danger as well. And of course, many of them fly, which is often the best escape route of all. Naturally the best survival mechanism is the ability to breed in huge numbers so that even though there is a very high death rate there are always enough to carry on the species. Most insects are very resistant to poison, even when eaten or carried back into the nests. The cockroach must be one of the hardiest in this respect, often taking many months to eradicate. The problem of cockroaches in New York is becoming so serious that studies are being made into 'birth control pills' that will make the cockroaches infertile and so cause them to die out. There has been little success in this field so far. Cockroaches will eat any kind of human food they can get but they will also eat a variety of substances not generally regarded as edible such as boot blacking, ink and whitewash.

The 'blindworm' is not blind and it is not a worm

The blindworm, sometimes also called the slow-worm, is, in fact, a legless lizard which has a perfectly good pair of eyes which have proper lids. It is often mistaken for a snake but the eyes of a snake do not have proper lids. The blindworm is quite harmless. It is usually about 40 centimetres (17 inches) long and feeds on earthworms and slugs.

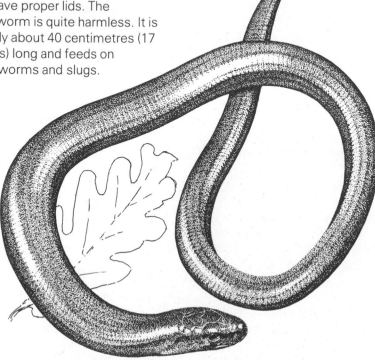

The blindworm, like all lizards, can cause fear in many people, but it is totally harmless to man.

There are between one and two million earthworms in every hectare of good pastureland

We may take the common earthworm for granted but we rely heavily on it to break down the dead vegetable matter in the soil so that the roots of plants can feed and grow. In any ordinary field there may be more than 200,000 earthworms to every hectare. In good meadowland there may be more than a million and in the richest pastureland there may be as many as two million earthworms to every hectare. They may pass anything between three and six tonnes of earth through their bodies per hectare every year and in some places they may pass more than 12 tonnes through their bodies. The largest earthworms are the giant earthworms of Gippsland, Australia. They are approximately one metre (three feet) long when contracted and up to three metres (ten feet) long when extended.

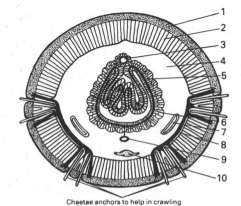

Chaetae anchors to help in crawling and burrowing

1 Circular muscle	6 Chloragogen Cells
2 Longitudinal muscle	7 Nephridium
3 Dorsal vessel	8 Retractor Muscle of Chaetae
4 Coelome	9 Ventral Vessel
5 Typhlosole	10 Ventral Nerve

Cross-section Earthworm around and about 20th segment

The Romans thought that the salamander could walk through fire without harm

The salamander looks rather like a lizard but it is more like an overgrown newt. Its skin is not rough and dry like that of a lizard but smooth and shiny. It was partly this, as well as their knowledge that the salamander was a cold-blooded, moisture-loving amphibian, that led the Romans to believe that the damp cold of its body would protect it against any fire through which it walked. They can never have put it to the test because the salamander cannot walk through fire. The European Fire salamander is about 20 centimetres (8.5 inches) long but the Japanese giant salamander can grow up to 1.5 metres (5 feet) long.

You can feed a grass snake from your hand

Grass snakes are quite harmless to man and can become acceptable pets that will eat out of your hand. They usually live near water and will feed on frogs and toads as well as newts and fish. They are generally about one metre (just over three feet) long and can be recognised by the yellowy-orange collar round their neck. The rest of the body is a fairly dull grey-green or brown. Grass snakes are found in several European countries and also in Asia.

The Gila monster stores its food in its tail

The Gila monster is one of the rare kinds of lizard that has a poisonous bite. It lives in the deserts of Arizona, Utah and New Mexico and grows to about 60 centimetres (24 inches). It is low-slung, short-legged, squat, brightly mottled and vicious when hungry or alarmed. The Gila monster can store food in its tail, so that it has a food supply when other food is scarce. When it is full, the tail makes the monster look bottom heavy.

Pythons and boas kill by suffocation

Pythons and boas both catch their prey by taking a grip with their mouths and winding their bodies round and round the victim. They squeeze and squeeze until the victim can no longer expand its lungs. Sometimes they burst the victim's blood vessels. Then they swallow their prey whole and spend several weeks digesting it. The anaconda is the largest of these snakes. It is a boa that lives mostly in water. The reticulate python is another large snake. It gets its name from the net-like markings on its body ('reticulate' means 'net-like'). Both the anaconda and the reticulate python can grow to nine or ten metres (29-33 feet) and can swallow a small antelope. Boas live in South America and Madagascar and have live young. Pythons live in Africa and parts of Asia and lay eggs. When the python is threatened, it rolls itself up into a tight ball as a means of defence.

The snake cannot hear the music of the snake-charmer

There are about 2000 different species of snake in the world and none of them have proper ears. They cannot hear sounds, as we hear them. Instead, they rely on vibrations through the ground, which pass through their body and are sensed by a delicate organ at the base of their jaw. When the snake charmer pretends to lull the snake with his music, the snake cannot actually hear him at all. The snake sways to keep his eyes on the man who is swaying himself and the snake feels the vibrations of the man's foot tapping on the ground or against the basket. Snakes have good eyesight and a good sense of smell but their keenest sense is on the end of their tongue. When they flick it in and out, they are testing the air for signs of danger or prey.

Some snakes can fly

Flying squirrels, flying frogs and flying lizards somehow sound quite natural when you learn that there is also a flying snake! This remarkable athlete can glide for up to 20 metres (60 feet) through the air, from branch to branch in the forests of Borneo. Apparently quite slender, it can bunch its body up into a series of S-bends, flatten itself by drawing up its ribs and slightly curve the underside of its belly until it presents a relatively flat, disc-shaped surface to the air. It can even, to some extent, control its direction of flight, or leap.

Below: *The spectacled Cobra is a member of the family* Elapidae *which includes the King Cobra of India which is the largest of all poisonous snakes, as well as being the most aggressive and most dangerous. When a cobra is about to strike it goes into a threat posture by raising itself up and spreading the ribs of its neck outwards.*

'Dragons' still live

Dragons of ancient times were supposed to have had scaley bodies, clawed feet, long tails and fiery breath. Look at any modern lizard and you will see a dragon in miniature, only without the fiery breath. There is even one kind of lizard that is called a 'dragon'. This is the Komodo dragon, a type of monitor lizard which grows up to three metres (ten feet) long that can be found in the East Indies. Other types of lizard include iguanas, skinks, geckoes and chameleons. One type, the flying dragon from south-east Asia, is about 25-30 centimetres (10-12 inches) long and can spread out the skin between its legs to glide from tree to tree – the nearest we can get to the mythical winged dragon.

Tropical forests contain more life than any other land area

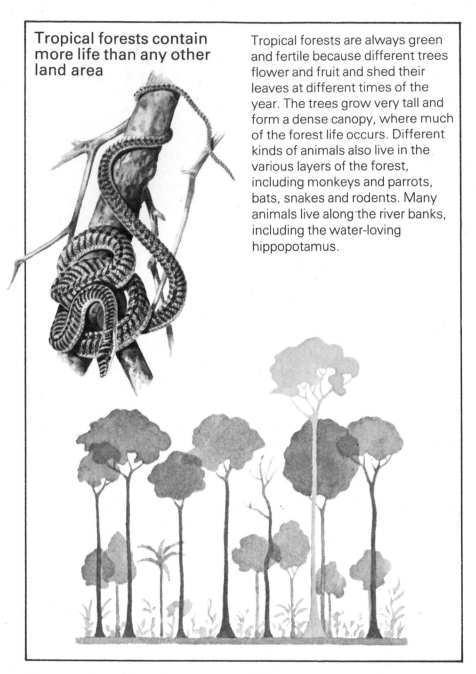

Tropical forests are always green and fertile because different trees flower and fruit and shed their leaves at different times of the year. The trees grow very tall and form a dense canopy, where much of the forest life occurs. Different kinds of animals also live in the various layers of the forest, including monkeys and parrots, bats, snakes and rodents. Many animals live along the river banks, including the water-loving hippopotamus.

The falling leaves of deciduous trees provide a rich environment for many small creatures

'Deciduous' means 'falling off' and deciduous trees lose their broad leaves in the winter. The fallen leaves provide a rich soil on the forest floor, and light filters through the bare branches to allow flowers and ferns to grow. Deciduous forests are excellent habitats for insects, and for birds that feed on those insects and on berries. Small animals such as shrews, woodmice and squirrels make their homes in these forests and woods, and so do larger creatures such as badgers, raccoons, wild pigs and deer.

Some trees and plants have very strange leaves

Victoria Regia, a giant species of water lily has leaves which grow up to one metre (3 feet) across. They are strong enough to support a young child. The Candle tree of Panama has flowers that look like huge candles. They can be as long as 1.2 metres (4 feet) long, and they contain a great amount of fat that is used for making lamp oil. The Traveller's tree of Madagascar grows in the shape of a giant fan. The sheaths of the leaves hold supplies of rain water – a blessing to thirsty travellers.

The needles of a pine tree are really leaves

Pine trees are conifers and like all conifers have small narrow leaves called needles. Most conifers are evergreens. These needles are very tough and are coated with thick cuticles. The breathing pores are well below the surface and this keeps water loss to a minimum, which is very important as most conifers exist in regions where water is in short supply, at least for part of the year. Conifers make up a large part of the vegetation in cooler parts of the world.

The banana tree is not a tree at all but a cluster of leaves

The stem of a banana plant consists of the tightly wound stalks of the leaves which spread out at the top in the shape of a palm tree. There is no proper tree trunk. Each plant produces a single stem of bananas after about two years' growth and then dies. The bunch of bananas may have about 100 bananas weighing between 30 and 40 kilograms (66-88 pounds). The bananas have to be cut when they are green, so that they do not ripen before they reach their destination.

Tea trees can grow to a great height

Tea is normally picked from low bushes about one metre (3 feet) tall. This is a convenient height for the pickers. But the plants are drastically pruned to keep them to this size and to produce a better crop of young leaves. If left to themselves, the bushes would grow into trees between five and ten metres (6-13 feet) tall.
The best tea comes from the tips of the small leaves at the ends of the branches; this gives the finest flavour and is the most expensive.

Conifer forests are not the empty places they may appear to be

Conifers are well adapted to the cold northern climate. Their needle-shaped leaves and flexible branches let the snow slip off easily and save them from being broken by its weight. Because they do not shed all their needles at once, conifers give year-long protection to an enormous range of animals. These include many birds and insects, and small animals such as pine martins, weasels, minks and stoats. Large creatures such as the Siberian tiger and the elk, or moose, are also found in the conifer forests of the far north.

What makes leaves fall?

Every year trees shed their leaves in the autumn, but it is not only then that trees lose leaves, there is a steady loss of leaves throughout the year, culminating in the complete loss of foliage for all deciduous trees during the autumn and early winter. What makes these leaves fall? It used to be thought that some trees grew a layer of cells at the base of the leaf stalks that cut the leaf off from the life giving sap of the trunk and branches, but this is not necessarily the reason for leaf fall since many plants do not have that layer and others, which grow it, do not lose their leaves from this point. The shedding of leaves is made more rapid by the shorter days (laboratory experiments which provided artificial light to make the days longer caused plants to keep their leaves longer), but this is not the full answer. New research has shown that fast growing leaves, particularly young ones, produce a substance called auxin which inhibits leaf fall, the more auxin present, the less likely the leaf is to fall. Further research showed that old leaves produce little or no auxin and a development of this research has shown that the plant not only produces auxin to keep healthy young leaves from falling but produces another substance, thought to be ethylene, which speeds up the fall of old or damaged leaves, thus allowing the supply of auxin to be concentrated in the leaves which most need it.

Some plants can travel at high speeds

It has always been thought that the difference between plants and animals is that animals move by themselves whereas plants do not. This is not true, most plants will turn to the light in order to gain the sun they need; this is called phototropism and most plants will respond in this way. Plants also open and close, depending on the time of day, these movements are called nastic movements and are caused by rises in temperature. Some plants have cells which will contract violently if irritated and cause the flower of the plant to snap shut - the insect-eating plants do this, but still relatively slowly. However there are groups of plants which move freely from place to place. Among these are the moulds which slide about much in the same way as an amoeba (one of the simplest animal organisms which moves by means of false feet). There are other groups of plants, among them the spores of algae and fungi which have long whip like structures called flagella (meaning whip-like) These plants are extremely small and yet they can move at speeds approaching nearly a metre an hour. Now this may seem very slow to us but in relation to the size of the plant it is an incredible speed. A man who can run 100 metres in 9 seconds is travelling at almost seven times his height per second, and a jet plane, travelling at 650 miles per hour covers its own length 25 times per second. The spore of a fungus is actually covering its own length as fast as the jet. The spore of the *Actinoplanes* has been measured moving at 99 times its own length per second and this is comparable to a man running at 400 miles per hour.

Powerful vegetable pumps

When you think that there are giant redwood trees and Douglas firs that can reach heights of almost 400 metres and still manage to supply the leaves at the top of these plants with water then these trees are raising water not only the height of the tree but also along the roots - a distance of some 430 metres. It has been calculated that to raise water to that height requires a pressure of 210 pounds per square inch, added to which is the friction between the walls of the tubes and the water which almost doubles this figure. The water is raised in the giant trees at the rate of about 30 metres per hour and may concern about 100 gallons of water a day. This is a stupendous feat, and little is known about the mechanism that these plants use to do this. One theory is that extremely high pressure in the roots forces the water upwards, but this is not tenable when the enormous heights of redwoods and Douglas Firs is taken into account. There must be a pulling mechanism somewhere. One theory surmises that the tension on growing shoots pulls the water towards them (this seems quite likely when you consider how many thousands of growing shoots a large tree bears).

The leaves of one plant can cure the sting of another

If you are ever stung by nettles, the best way to get rid of the sting is to rub dock leaves on to the sting. The juice of the leaves acts as an antidote to formic acid that causes the nettle to sting.

Men and Women

Facts about the evolution of man

Man along with monkeys, lemurs, lorises and apes is a primate and they all share certain characteristics. These are hands for grasping, forward facing eyes with which to judge distance, small noses (because smell is not as important as sight to them), teeth that are adapted to a variety of foods, a well-developed brain and well-developed social sense. Some of the primates also share to some extent man's more refined characteristics, such as the ability to walk on two feet and to use objects as tools or weapons.

Man's family goes back at least 65 million years. There are primate fossils even older than this, from shortly after the time when the dinosaurs disappeared. Man's closer relatives, the apes (gorilla, chimpanzee, orang-utan and gibbon) existed in Africa, Europe and Asia at least 15 million years ago. By that time, the jaws and teeth of the ape known to us as Ramapithecus had already begun to look more human than ape-like.

By about five million years ago, the first hominids, or man-like apes, had developed into a more advanced species known as Australopithecines ('southern apes') living in South Africa. But there was more than one type of southern ape. *Nutcracker man,* as he was nicknamed, had large teeth and was very robust. But he seems to have died out. *Handy man* was more slender and had a larger brain than nutcracker man. Remains of Handy man date from about 1-2 million years ago and have been found along with simple stone cutting tools.

Upright man or *homo erectus* probably developed from Handy man about 1 million years ago and we have the first signs of him in remains of Java and Peking man about 750,000 years ago. The body and brain of these immediate ancestors developed into those of Neanderthal man about 150,000 years ago. One group of Neanderthals developed further into Cro-Magnon man about 40,000 years ago and gradually spread all over the world. It was Cro-Magnon man who produced some of the marvellous cave paintings in southern Europe, during the Old Stone Age.

The earliest civilisations

While European men still struggled through harsh weather with no more protection than rough wooden shelters or damp caves, the Chinese civilisation was reaching its zenith. While the early Europeans used their fingers to eat with and cut up their food with crude flint knives, the Chinese ate from delicate porcelain bowls with dexterously wielded chopsticks. While Europeans buried their royal dead in shallow graves with only a few weapons as grave offerings, the Chinese buried their royal families in elaborate graves, clothing the bodies with jade armour and surrounding the dead with beautifully fashioned models of all the retainers who had served them during their lives. The sweep of civilisation has moved regularly round the globe, from the Far East to the Middle East where the early Egyptians built vast temples, burial monuments and tombs which even today almost defy the imagination in their complexity and vastness. The greatest of all these Egyptian monuments are the Pyramids, immense structures that each took many years to build and must have cost the lives of hundreds or even thousands of slaves. The accuracy of the building techniques would be difficult for us to duplicate today, even with modern high technology at our service. The great pyramids were built more than five thousand years before the birth of Christ, when England was still a barbaric land covered with forest and ravaged by wolves and wild animals. As the early tribes of Britain fought for survival the Egyptians lived in elegant palaces, diverted the course of the Nile to serve their own needs and built these marvellous edifices. As the sweep of civilisation moved ever westwards Western Europe developed and grew. The great ages of churchbuilding lasted for a thousand years from 500 AD up until almost the present day, society became more complicated and organised, exploration opened up new lands and with this, civilisation swept onwards, ever westwards to the Americas.

Perhaps the sweep of civilisation is coming full circle and we shall one day see China reaching upwards again to the greatness it once taught the world.

What happened to Atlantis?

For centuries, there has been a persistent belief in a great civilisation that was completely wiped out and lost to the world, this civilisation has been variously called Lemuria, Atlantis or just Mu. Certainly there is evidence in the Eastern Mediterranean, off the coastline of Greece, that a great cataclysm, either an eruption of a force never seen before or perhaps a gigantic earthquake which destroyed several islands and must have seriously affected the mainland, perhaps this was the original site of Atlantis. Other historians claim that Atlantis was situated in the North Atlantic sea and disappeared suddenly and completely. Yet another theory places Atlantis off the shore of southern North America, near to the notorious 'Bermuda Triangle' where strangely precise roads of stone lie under the waves. Probably the truth will never be known, but the myth of Atlantis is one of the most enduring mysteries of the world.

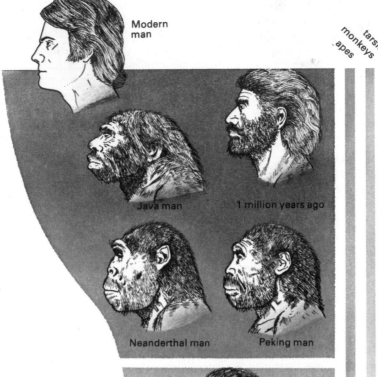

Modern man

Java man

1 million years ago

Neanderthal man

Peking man

monkeys
apes
tarsiers
lorises
lemurs
tree shrews

Australopithecus

10 million years ago

Ramapithecus

Cro-Magnon man
Homo habilis

Male sexual anatomy

The so-called external sexual parts of the male include the penis and the penile urethra, the tube with carries both urine and semen; the glans or tip of the penis; the foreskin or prepuce, which may or may not be circumcised or cut; the scrotum or sack, which holds the two testes where the sperm and male hormone are produced; and the epididymis, which is a tube attached to the testes and which transfers the sperm into the *vas deferens*, the tube which takes the sperm into the body.

The so-called internal sexual parts of the male include the *vas deferens*, where it enters the body from the scrotum, bearing the sperm; the prostate gland, the seminal vesicle and the bulbo-urethral gland, which all contribute secretions that help the sperm to move and to fertilise.

The penis is made rigid because it becomes engorged with blood. When flaccid, the penis may be anything between seven and eleven centimetres (three-four inches) long; when erect it may be between fourteen and eighteen centimetres (five-and-a-half to seven inches) long. Size when flaccid bears little relation to potential size when erect and neither bear any relation to sexual potency or fertility.

One reason that the scrotum hangs outside the body is to keep the testes a little below body temperature. In cold weather (or cold water) the skin of the scrotum contracts and draws the testes nearer the body for additional warmth. If the sperm become too warm, they may not be able to fertilise the egg.

Male sperm, or spermatozoa, are continually being formed in the testes from puberty to old age. One ejaculation produces about 100 to 400 million sperm and in his lifetime a man might produce as much as 400 or 500 thousand million sperm. In sexual intercourse, only about a dozen sperm actually reach the egg in the oviduct and of these only one hits the egg at the right angle to enter and fertilise it.

Circumcision occurs among many different peoples, as a religious ritual and for hygiene. The Jews perform it on newly born babies to symbolise Abraham's covenant with God. Aborigines perform it as an initiation into manhood and to keep the tip of the penis clean in the dust of the desert. In Ancient Egypt, it was usually the priestly class who were circumcised. Today, it is more a matter of habit or fashion. It is generally considered unnecessary and whether or not the foreskin is circumcised does not affect sexual sensitivity or performance.

Causes of infertility in the male

Infertility in the male can be assessed in many ways and can be divided into two types: Impotence, where no sexual performance takes place and infertility of the semen where sexual performance is physically possible but the sperm itself is infertile. In the case of infertility of the semen there are many causes. Clothing which is too tight and constricts the testicles causes a rise in temperature which can affect the fertility of the sperm.

Obesity, poor feeding and bad health also affect the production and vitality of the sperms, as do smoking and drinking to excess and emotional stress. Even prolonged abstinence causes infertility because this can increase the numbers of abnormal sperm present in the semen. Some childhood illnesses, such as mumps, particularly if it occurs in adulthood can cause infertility as can exposure to radioactivity, certain chemicals, fumes from vehicle exhausts and lack of vitamins.

Are boy babies more at risk than girls?

A baby's sex is determined at the point of conception. All human body cells contain 23 pairs of chromosomes - the building blocks of nature. In female cells all the chromosomes are identical, consisting of matched pairs of chromosomes of the X variety but in the male one of the pairs is mis-matched, consisting of an X chromosome and a Y chromosome. This single mis-matched pair of chromosomes is all that determines the sex of a baby. More male babies than female babies are conceived but of all the babies conceived, male babies are more likely to die in the womb - the earlier the miscarriage, the more likely it is that it is a male foetus that has miscarried. There are more male stillbirths than female but even so the ratio of full term live births of male babies to full term live births of female babies is one hundred and five to one hundred and six males to one hundred females.

The average man

The average height for a man is just over five feet nine inches.

The average weight is about one hundred and sixty two pounds.

The average chest measurement is thirty eight and a quarter inches with a waist measurement of thirty one and a quarter inches and a hip measurement of thirty seven and three quarter inches. These measurements are based on United States statistics. Since they are worked out by listing everyone's height, weight and measurements from the tallest to the shortest, heaviest to lightest, fattest to thinnest it is very unlikely that many people have these measurements. The tallest man

who ever lived was eight feet
eleven inches tall and the shortest
only twenty six and a half inches,
between these two extremes fall
the measurements of the rest of
humanity.

The male sex organs.

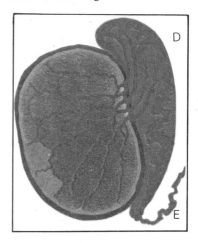

Key:

A Penis

B Erectile tissue

C Penile Urethra

D Epididymus

E Vas deferens

F Bladder

G Prosta

H Seminal vesicle

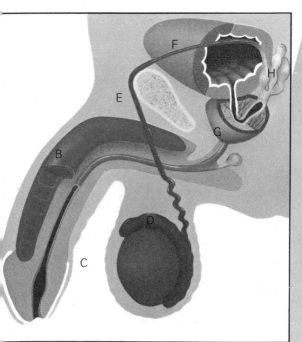

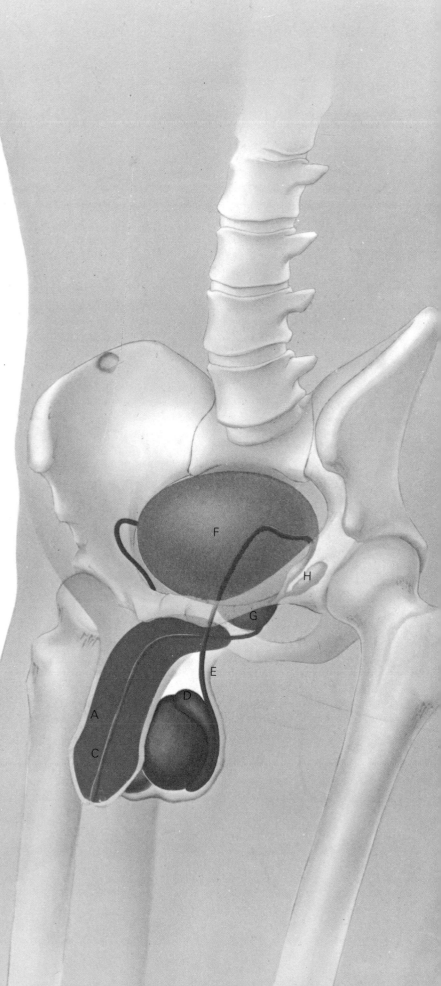

Female sexual anatomy

The female uterus or womb can expand in the most remarkable way. Normally it weighs about 60 grammes (2 ounces) and is about nine by six centimetres (two-and-a-half inches) in size. In pregnancy it weighs fifteen or sixteen times as much and extends to about 40 centimetres (15.8 inches) in length, so that it can hold a baby weighing between three and four kilograms (nine pounds). Even more remarkably, after pregnancy, it returns to its original size.

The female ovary of a young adult woman contains about 200,000 egg cells. Most of these die off during her lifetime and she will only actually produce about 400 mature ova during her reproductive life.

Menstruation may begin at any time between the ages of ten and sixteen. In the western world it is getting gradually earlier, largely due to good nutrition. A century ago the average in the west was fifteen; it is now about twelve to thirteen.

The menstrual cycle is said to begin on the first day of menstruation. The length of the cycle averages 29 days but may vary from 24 to 34 days. The ovum or egg leaves the ovary about 14 days after menstruation last began and must usually be fertilised within two days to make sure that it matures. At this time, the woman's temperature may jump by almost one degree Fahrenheit.

The so-called 'external' sexual parts of the female include the fatty mound known as the *mons pubis*; the larger and smaller pair of fatty lips known as the labia *majora* and *minora*; the clitoris, which enlarges during intercourse; the vestibule or opening between the labia minora; the hymen, an incomplete membrane which is often torn during the first sexual intercourse; and the vestibular or Batholin's glands, which help to lubricate the insides of the labia minora. The vulva is the overall name for this part of the body. The opening to the urethra, or urinary tract is directly behind the clitoris.

The *mons pubis* or pubic mound is also known as the *mons veneris* or mound of Venus. This is because Venus was the ancient goddess of love and the mound begins to develop at puberty.

The so-called internal sexual parts of the female include the vagina, a muscular tube about eight or nine centimetres (three to three-and-a-half inches) long; the cervix or neck of the womb; the womb or uterus; the uterine or Fallopian tubes (also known as the oviducts), which extend about ten centimetres (four inches) from the uterus to the ovaries and within which fertilisation takes place; and the ovaries themselves, where the eggs are produced as well as female hormones.

There are many primitive myths about menstruation, virtually all of which are untrue. Primitive people feared menstruation, largely because of the blood, and they believed that it was dangerous for a woman during menstruation to go near food or any growing plants or creatures. She must not cook anything or have anything to do with crops; she must not go near wine or milk in case it turned to vinegar or went sour. These myths were predominant among the Australian aborigines and among certain Indian cultures but they also appeared even in the west in earlier centuries.

Superstitions about women and children

There are several very interesting superstitions about women prevalent in Nigeria, many of these are very representative of all African beliefs and also compare closely with many European superstitions. All powerful events are surrounded by superstition and magical belief and none more so than the greatest event of all - birth. The last child in a family is credited with 'second sight' in Nigeria, this compares with the belief that the seventh child, or the seventh child of a seventh child in Europe will have the sight. Beliefs about the death of newly born children proliferate, if a child is born dead this is a sure sign that the parents have done something wicked and should the first child a woman conceives die, then it is believed that the first child born to her daughter will also die. Twins have always been regarded as magical, either for good or evil. In Africa they are considered an unlucky omen, and up until quite recently, one of them would have been left in the open to die. As if this is not enough the mother is segregated from the rest of the village in case she should bring bad luck to the settlement. In Europe, twins are thought to have an uncanny bond, knowing what the other is thinking and suffering. Some African superstitions seem surprisingly modern, for instance if a pregnant woman should walk under a ladder this will cause her labour to be difficult. Gipsies all over the world have their own superstitions about women, one of the strangest being that no gipsy will drink from a stream that has been walked over by a woman. The Amish people of America, a strongly religious group, have a complete set of beliefs about babies, some of which are very strange indeed. They believe that if the water a child is baptised in is saved and given to the child to drink when he or she is older, that child will grow up to be a fine singer. Children born in thunderstorms are doomed to die by lightning and putting an old nappy on a baby at birth condemns him to being a thief. Babies should be always carried on the left hand side or they will become left handed and if weaned early in the spring will have prematurely grey hair. Babies must never be stepped over for fear of stunting their growth and must never be tickled under the chin if they are to grow up without a stammer. Icelandic superstitions also contain several warnings to pregnant women - stepping over a cat during the mating season causes the birth of a hermaphrodite while eating a ptarmigan egg (a large quail-like bird) brings freckled babies and more seriously, drinking from a cracked cup will cause a hare lip in the baby. It is a wonder that some babies grow up at all when they are surrounded by so many potentially dangerous situations!

The female sex organs.

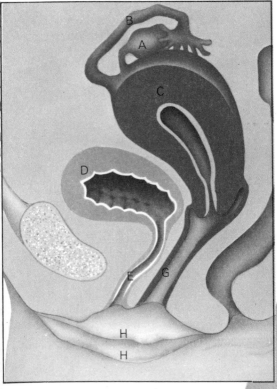

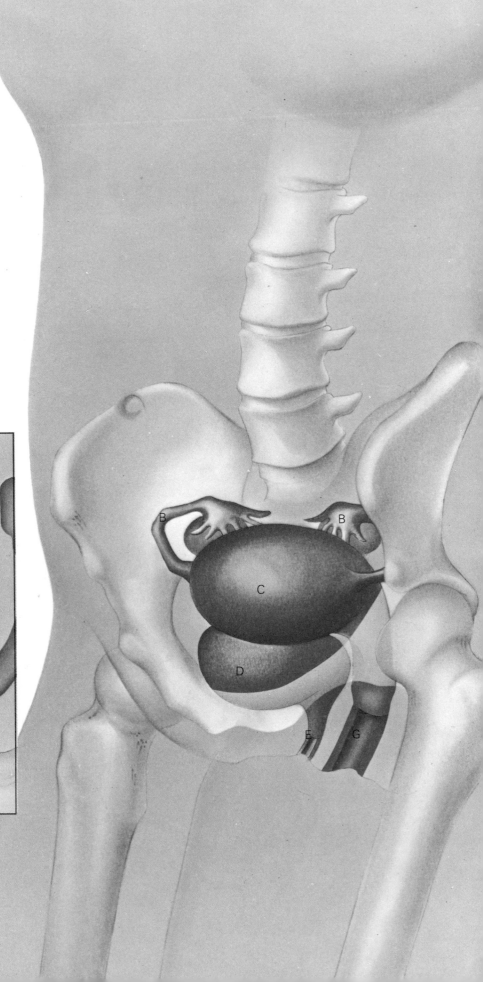

Key

A Ovary

B Fallopian tube

C Uterus

D Bladder

E Urethra

F Cervix

G Vagina

H Labia

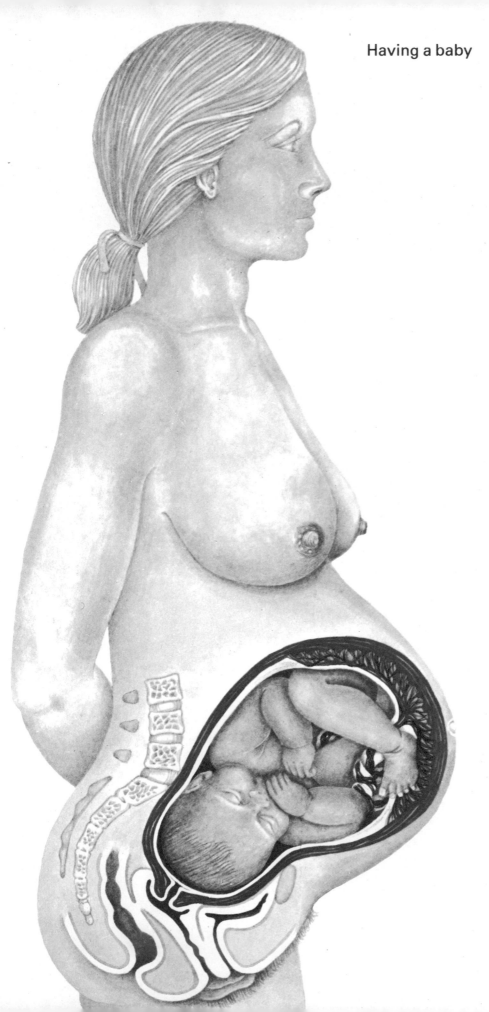

Having a baby

Babies are usually born head first. As the head emerges, it faces down, towards the back of the mother, and then turns to the side as the head and shoulders slip out. The head may be slightly elongated at first, to help it come out, but it will quickly return to a normal shape.

Many animals eat their afterbirth but humans do not need to. The animals do this for several reasons. The afterbirth contains certain substances that help to stimulate the flow of milk to the baby animal. It also provides basic nourishment so that the mother can survive without food for a few days and stay close to the baby. Animals also eat the afterbirth to hide the arrival of the baby from a predator.

A human pregnancy or gestation lasts about nine months, from conception to birth. This is approximately 266 days, although the average time may vary between 250 and 285 days. A baby that is born after about 196 days, or 28 weeks, can survive with the help of an incubator.

The longest gestation period of any animal is that of the Indian elephant, which takes about 22 months or between 650 and 660 days. The Virginian opossum needs only just over 12 days, a hamster about 16 days, a rabbit about one month, a whale about one year. Giraffes and camels take about 400 days, dogs and cats just over 60 days, a cow just over 280 days and a horse just under 340 days.

At the end of its first month in the womb a human embryo could fit on a smallish coin. After three months it could still fit inside a largish hen's egg. By then the fingernails are already developing and the embryo can move its feet around. It can hiccough at five months and after six months it will be sucking its thumb a great deal. The embryo gains more than half its birth weight in the last six to eight weeks in the womb.

A Caesarean birth is named after the Roman, Julius Caesar, who is believed to have been delivered in this way. In some cases it is not possible for a baby to be born in the normal way. A Caesarean section, as it is called, is performed and the baby is taken out through a carefully cut opening in the mother's abdomen.

Strange fancies do not only affect women during pregnancy

Cravings for odd food during pregnancy used to be thought to be due to the woman's body needing extra chemicals which might be found in such things as coal, grass and other peculiar sources. This is quite untrue. Even stranger than some of the cravings women develop during their pregnancies is the behaviour of the men of certain African tribes. When their wives are discovered to be pregnant, the men take to their beds, often appearing to swell as much as their wives. When the time comes for the birth the women leave the village and go into the bush to deliver their babies while the men stay in the huts, groaning and crying out with pain and appearing for all the world to be giving birth to the babies themselves. The swelling disappears and the men return to normal when their wives bring the newly born infants back to their husbands.

Multiple births

It is not uncommon for more than one baby to be born at a time; twins are born in one out of every 85 births, triplets are not so common, once in every seven thousand five hundred births, quadruplets are much rarer, once in every six hundred and fifty thousands births and rarest of all quintuplets once in every fifty seven million births. Sextuplets are very very rare and the babies are so

frail that very few survive.

With the advent of hormone treatments for infertility, multiple births are becoming more common and mothers who have undergone these treatments are monitored carefully to check that all is well.

Some twins are 'paternal', that is they are each formed from separate eggs, which are each fertilised by a separate sperm; paternal twins may be no more alike than other brothers and sisters in the same family. Maternal twins are born from a single egg which divides to form two babies; these twins are always very alike. Twins may not be born together, a month between the birth of each twin has been recorded. Multiple births carry more risk than single births and the babies are delivered by Caesarean section.

Inherited diseases

There are several disorders which are inherited and some of these come through the mother. The most common of these is colour blindness where most of the sufferers cannot distinguish between green and red. Most colour blind people do not realise that they have this defect and only discover this by testing. It is estimated that between two and eight per cent of all men are colour blind (ten times more men than women). Haemophilia is a disorder of the blood which affects the ability of the blood to clot after an injury - in severe cases of haemophilia even the slightest cut causes dangerous loss of blood, and bruises can cause serious internal bleeding. The gene which causes this disorder is carried on the X chromosome, the chromosome which is always passed on by the woman (women have no Y chromosomes). If the defective X chromosome is not matched by a healthy one the

disease can be passed on to her male children, the girls will not be affected but may become carriers of this gene.

If a woman is the carrier of this gene, half her sons are likely to suffer and half her daughters are likely to be carriers; if the father is a sufferer and the mother is a carrier, half the boys are likely to have the disease and half the girls will suffer from it, the other girls being carriers. If only the father is the sufferer then no boys will have the disease but all the girls will carry the defective gene.

Reproduction without Fertilization

In 1962 a doctor at Oxford University succeeded in producing identical frogs by transplanting the nuclei of cells from tissues in frogs intestines into frogs eggs from which the nuclei had been removed; several of these eggs developed into healthy adult frogs identical in all respects. In 1975 Dr Bramhall, again at Oxford, took this possibility one stage further by experimenting with rabbits eggs. These tests have never been concluded; the difficulties of producing a foetus from these eggs which need to develop inside a female rabbit are insurmountable.

How big will the world's population grow?

Every minute of the day and night two hundred and forty children are born somewhere in the world, although there are deaths too; by the end of the day there are two hundred thousand more children in the world. Between 1970 and 1975 it is estimated that the world's population increased by three hundred and thirty six millions. Surveys have shown that the total of all the world's urban population is doubling every twenty five years.

Each of our eyes give a slightly different picture of the world

Hold a pencil up and look beyond it to the wall. Shut one eye and the pencil will be in one place against the wall. Shut the other eye and the pencil will have moved in relation to the wall. This double image is important in judging distances. A stereoscopic camera has two lenses about the same distance apart as your eyes. When the photographs are put in a stereoscope, one view is seen by one eye and the other view is seen by the other eye, just as the scene would appear in reality. This gives a three-dimensional effect to the photographs taken by the camera.

Wrinkled peas led to the secrets of inherited eye colour

Gregor Johann Mendel was an Austrian monk who lived in the middle of the 19th Century. He wanted to discover how genes that determine individual characteristics are passed on from generation to generation and how some genes are stronger than others. He experimented at first with smooth and wrinkled peas in the monastery garden and discovered which of the peas had the dominant characteristics when he grew them. These experiments helped scientists to understand about genes in the human body. For example, if the genes that

determine eye colour are the same in both parents, then their child will have the same colour eyes. But if one parent has a stonger or dominant gene, such as brown eyes, and the other has a weaker or recessive gene, such as blue eyes, then the child will have brown eyes. But the child's genes will also carry the blue-eyed genes from its mother and if the child then marries someone else with blue-eyed genes, then their own children may well have blue eyes.

Research being carried out in the United States is beginning to show a strange relationship between the colour of the eyes and a person's personality, blue eyes seeming to often confer a more outgoing personality than brown eyes.

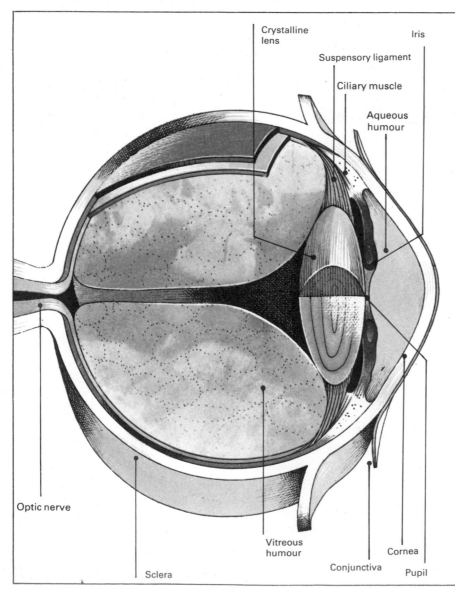

Crystalline lens
Iris
Suspensory ligament
Ciliary muscle
Aqueous humour
Optic nerve
Vitreous humour
Sclera
Cornea
Conjunctiva
Pupil

Most of the eye is made up of a salty jelly, called the vitreous or glassy humour

Vitreous humour helps to keep the eye the right shape. It forms the body of the eye, between the front part and the retina at the back. The retina is the inside film of the eye that records everything that enters through the lens and transmits the message through the optic nerve to the brain. The choroid membrane surrounds the retina and supplies the eye with blood. The sclera provides a tough outer skin to the eye and appears as the white of the eye at the front and as the clear cornea. Behind the cornea is the aqueous humour and then the iris (the circle of colour) and the pupil (the black centre), which are like the shutter and aperture of a camera. Within the pupil is the lens, which uses its muscles to adjust itself so that it focuses light on the retina.

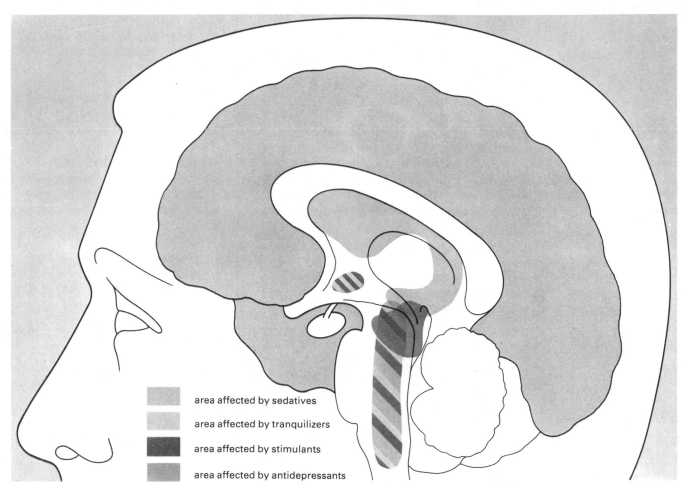

area affected by sedatives

area affected by tranquilizers

area affected by stimulants

area affected by antidepressants

Drugs can change the way you think

There are many different ideas about the causes and cures for mental illness. Drugs are commonly used to relieve some of the symptoms and to re-establish the right balance of chemistry in the brain. Drugs damp down some parts of the brain and stimulate other parts. Drugs known as tranquillisers are used for major illnesses such as schizophrenia and for minor illnesses such as anxiety. Anti-depressants can make a person less depressed. Hypnotics induce sleep but are now rarely used because they alter a person's sleep pattern and can become addictive. Sedatives calm a person without actually inducing sleep. Stimulants, like anti-depressants, speed up the working of the brain.

Electricity can be used to change the outlook of the brain

Severe depression can be treated with electroconvulsive therapy (ECT). This is only used in extreme cases and is now much more rare than it used to be. The patient is put under general anaesthesia and an electric current is passed through the brain. This produces excessive activity in the brain, which is meant to sort out the chemistry of the disordered brain and return it to normal. ECT also leads to loss of memory and a general confusion of the patient.

The ears are not just for hearing

Within the ear there is a twisted organ consisting of three U shaped canals; these are arranged so that they fall at right angles to each other. This organ is called the Cochlea and is possibly more important to a human being than the hearing part of the ear. It is the Cochlea which tells us which way up we are and gives us our sense of balance. The canals of the Cochlea are filled with fluid and the bases of these canals bear fine hairs: as we move, the fluid in the canals moves and the fine hairs sense this movement and send messages to the brain which are translated into our sense of balance. If there is any inflammation of the Cochlea, or damage to it, it becomes very difficult to stand or move about, since the body cannot tell whether it is balanced or not. Also in the middle ear, and within the Cochlea, are two other structures - the Saccule and the Utricle; these contain cells which are responsive to gravity and so inform us which way up we are. Any damage to these structures is very serious indeed as it can completely unbalance a person.

Heart attacks occur in several ways

Sometimes the heart muscle itself is diseased; sometimes the valves within the heart have become weakened by illness; sometimes there is a blockage in the arteries that supply the heart muscle with blood – these are called the coronary arteries. A heart attack is known as a coronary thrombosis. Bad diet, smoking, excessive tension and high blood pressure all contribute towards heart attacks, which are generally more common in old age and especially after sudden unaccustomed exercise.

Blood is not always red

Blood is mostly a straw-coloured substance called plasma, which contains little red and white cells called corpuscles. It is the red corpuscles that give the blood in the arteries its red colour and they in turn get their colour from a substance within them called haemoglobin. Haemoglobin is responsible for taking the oxygen from the lungs and distributing it to every part of the body. When the blood returns to the heart through the veins it is a blueish-purple colour because the haemoglobin in the red corpuscles has lost its oxygen.

There are 500 red corpuscles to every one white corpuscle in the blood

Red corpuscles carry oxygen through the blood. They are very small discs and there may be several million of them in a single drop of blood. They wear out quite quickly, within a few weeks, and are remade in the bone marrow. White corpuscles are much larger and rather shapeless. Their function is to fight disease in the body by crowding round bacteria and digesting them. The body makes more white corpuscles when necessary to deal with attacks by germs. The plasma itself, in which the corpuscles float, carries food and chemicals throughout the body and brings back carbon dioxide to be passed out through the lungs. If the bone marrow becomes disordered, leukaemia, a disease of the white corpuscles, can result, which is usually fatal.

The hardest working pump in nature

Every minute of every day a human heart beats from sixty to eighty times; a woman's heart beats faster than a man's because it is smaller. Each heart beat pumps about a quarter of a pint of blood through the heart - this works out at two thousand gallons a day - fifty million gallons in an average lifetime. The heart never rests but goes on pumping away whether we are awake or asleep. Obviously the heart beats more slowly when we are asleep and faster when we take strenuous exercise; during a running race a healthy heart may increase its beat to one hundred and eighty beats per minute, pumping more than thirty five pints through the chambers of this remarkable organ. The heart is not the only pump in the body, the arteries themselves pump the blood along too by contracting and expanding their muscular walls thus forcing the blood through to the tissues that need it.

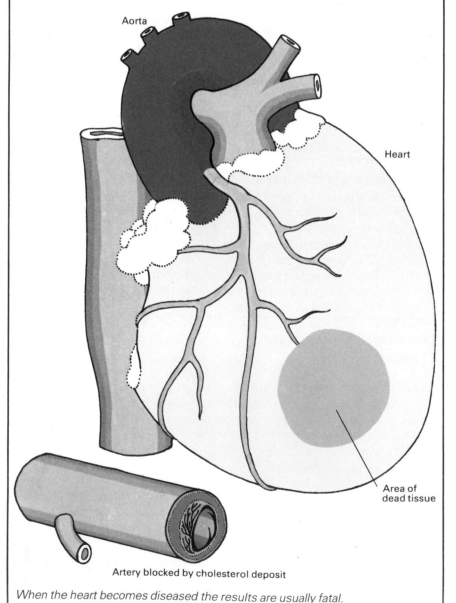

Aorta

Heart

Area of dead tissue

Artery blocked by cholesterol deposit

When the heart becomes diseased the results are usually fatal.

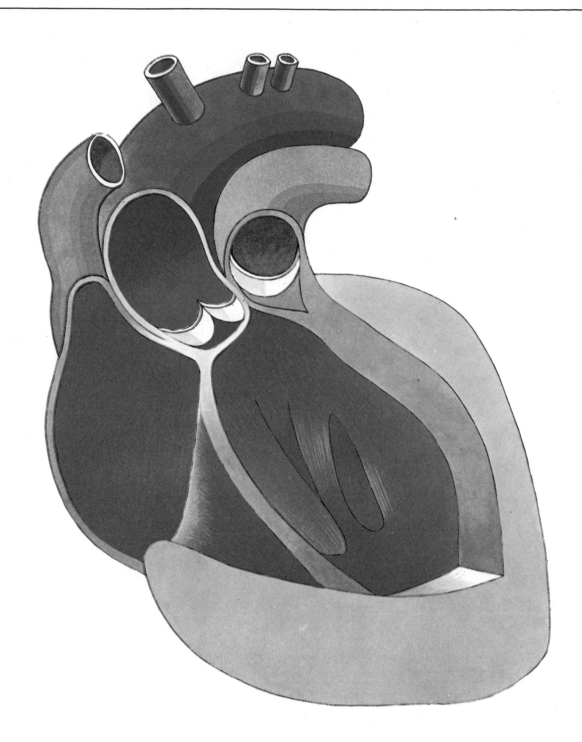

Broken hearts can be mended

Diseased hearts often beat too slowly. They can be speeded up by sewing into the skin, just by the heart, a tiny pace-maker, a motor that stimulates the heart with regular shocks. Some babies are born with holes in their hearts, which means that the blood does not get enough oxygen. These holes often grow over of their own accord but if they do not they can be sewn up in an operation. The most dramatic solution to a failing heart is to swop it for the heart from a healthy person who has died from some other accidental cause. This was first done by specialists led by Dr Christiaan Barnard in Cape Town, South Africa.

During a heart transplant operation the old heart must be removed. This involves cutting through all the veins and arteries that lead into it, the aorta, pulmonary arteries and the others in this drawing. The new heart must then be inserted and the veins and arteries stitched to the proper connections in the new heart.

Disease in one part of the body can be cured by treating another part of the body

Acupuncture is a very ancient form of medical treatment used by the Chinese at least 2,500 years ago. Small metal needles are pricked lightly into the skin at certain points of the body, along specific lines. The organs of the body have their own lines which run the length of the body. The needle may be stuck anywhere along the eye 'line', for example, to cure an eye complaint. The needle tends to relieve the nerves affecting a particular part of the body and acupuncture has been used with some success recently in the western world to control the pain of arthritis and migraine.

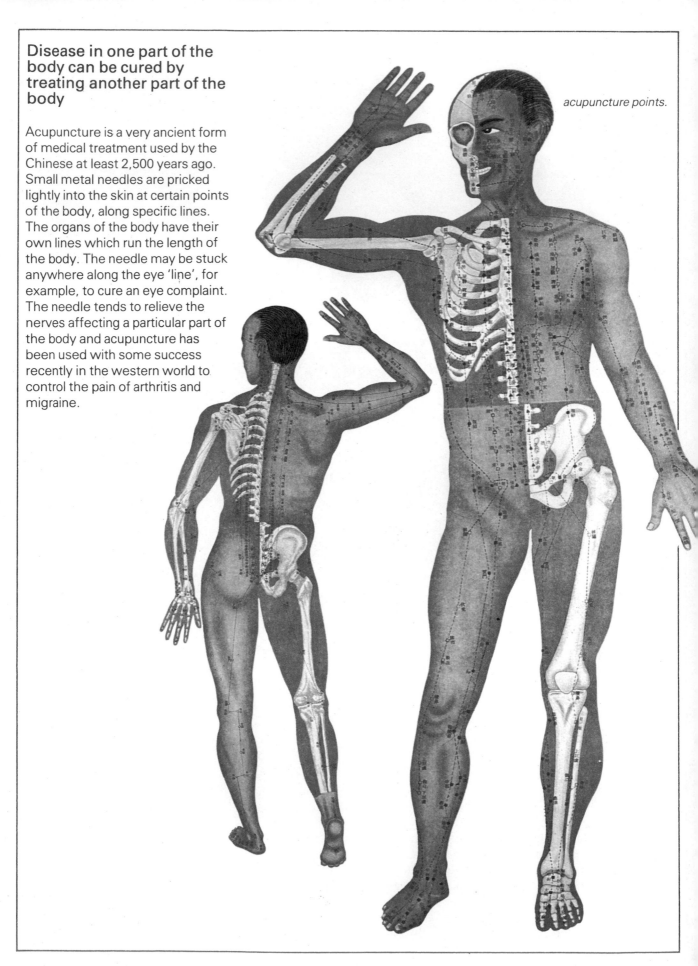

acupuncture points.

There are more than 200 bones in the human skeleton

Bones are a mixture of inorganic, mineral matter, such as phosphate of lime which give hardness, and organic, animal matter which promotes growth, strength and resilience. Some bones have marrow inside, where red and white corpuscles are produced. The bones in a baby are largely cartilage or gristle at first. They gradually ossify, or turn to bone, in the middle and then towards either end. As the child gets older, the ends of the bones close together. When the living tissue in the bones stops growing, so does the person. Water inside the bones tends to dry out as people get older, thus making the bones more brittle.

It is better to breathe through the nose than through the mouth

The nose performs two very important functions when you breathe in. It warms the air and cleans it. The air is warmed by passing over the many small blood vessels that lie close to the surface within the nose. It is cleaned by passing through tiny hairs and over slimy mucus that is produced by special glands. This mucus also helps to kill germs. The mouth should act as an air-intake only in emergencies, when the nose is blocked or when large amounts of oxygen are needed.

The inner linings of the lungs could cover the floor of a fair-sized room

The purpose of the lungs is to pass oxygen into the blood and to extract waste-water and carbon dioxide from the blood. Oxygen enters the lungs from the trachea, or breathing tube, and eventually reaches minute alveoli 'balloons' which cover the huge folded surface of the lung wall. The wall is also covered with the smallest form of blood vessels, the capillaries. The exchange of oxygen and carbon dioxide takes place between the alveoli and the capillaries. The lungs of birds are relatively small but they do have several air sacs in their bodies which take up much of the air that enters the lungs. Apart from helping breathing, these air sacs may also help to keep the bird cool.

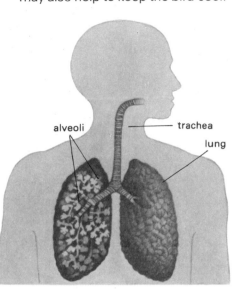

Birds have no diaphragms to help them breathe

Humans, like other mammals, have a diaphragm, which is a sheet of muscle that lies like a floor to the chest. When you breathe in, the diaphragm is drawn down, enlarging the space within the chest and allowing the lungs to expand and take in air. When you breathe out, the diaphragm rises, compressing the lungs and driving out the air. Since birds have no diaphragms, they have to use the muscles of the body wall to expand and compress their lungs.

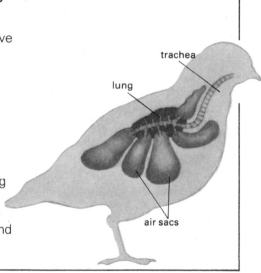

Insects have no veins or arteries

In birds and mammals, blood is pumped from the heart through arteries to all parts of the body, carrying food and oxygen to every single cell. The blood returns to the heart through the veins, having carried the body's waste matter to the kidneys. Insects, however, do not have this organised system of veins and arteries. The elongated heart pumps blood from the abdomen up to the head, from where it flows back down the body completely bathing the internal organs before entering the abdomen again. Additional pumps send blood to the wings and other extremities.

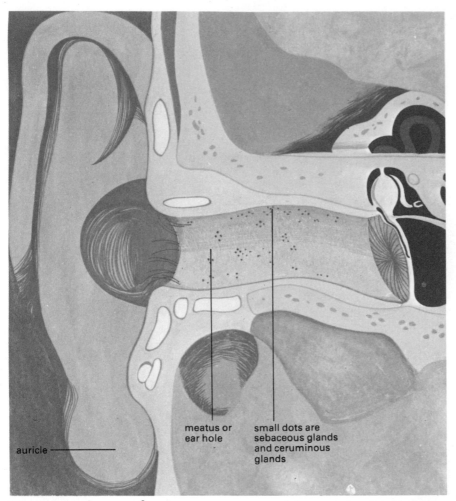

auricle

meatus or ear hole

small dots are sebaceous glands and ceruminous glands

The hammer, the anvil, the stirrup and the drum are all in your head

The ear is formed in this way: the outer flap, or auricle, leads into the earhole, or meatus, which reaches to the eardrum. The drum receives vibrations from the air. These vibrations are magnified in the middle ear, a cavity where there are three little bones known as the hammer, the anvil and the stirrup because of their shape. A tunnel from the middle ear to the back of the nose (the Eustacian tube) lets air in behind the eardrum to equalise the pressure of the outside air on the drum. The magnified vibrations meet the cochlea, which is a snail-shaped part filled with fluid and nerves that connect with the brain. Next door to the cochlea are three semi-circular canals which are also filled with fluid. These help to provide a sense of balance.

A quiet whisper in St Paul's Cathedral can be heard 30 metres away

St Paul's Cathedral is one of the most famous landmarks in London. Around the inside of the great dome there runs a gallery known as the whispering gallery. If you whisper quietly near the wall on one side, you can be heard quite clearly 30 metres (98 feet) away on the other side. The cathedral was designed by Sir Christopher Wren after the Great Fire of 1666, in which the old church had been destroyed. The reconstruction took 35 years. There are three domes, one within the other. Between the outer shell and the inner dome, there is a dome of brick that supports the great ball and cross that stand on top of the cathedral more than 111 metres (364 feet) above the ground. St Paul's Cathedral was the scene in July 1981 of the wedding of the Prince of Wales and Lady Diana Spencer, the first time for many years that a royal wedding has been held there.

Ears contain wax for protection

Wax helps to protect the ears. It catches dust and other matter that enters the ears from outside. There are special sweat glands in the skin of the earhole, or meatus. These are called ceruminous glands and they produce the wax. The hairs on the outer end of the meatus also help to catch dust.

Through the science of ultrasonics, doctors and scientists can built up pictures from sound waves

The human ear can hear sounds that vibrate from 20 to 20,000 times per second. A bat can hear sounds vibrating at more than twice that speed. Machines that use ultrasonics produce sounds that vibrate thousands of millions of times per second. These sounds are too fast to hear. They are used instead for 'seeing'. A beam of ultrasonic sound waves can detect cracks in metal that are invisible to the human eye. This is because the sound travels at a different speed through the metal than it does through the crack. A picture can be built up from these sound waves. In the same way, ultrasonics can be used to take 'photographs' of babies inside a mother's womb without using dangerous x-rays.

Deaf and dumb people can talk to each other

Although deaf people cannot hear and dumb people cannot speak they can communicate by using a sign language based on hand movements and finger positions. These are based on seventeenth century manual alphabets.

The sound of an approaching car is shriller than the sound of a car going away

This is because the sound waves from an approaching car are bunched closer together as they reach the listener. The car is coming nearer to the listener all the time and so the sound waves arrive at shorter and shorter intervals, reaching a steadily higher pitch. As the car goes away, the sound waves become spread out and come back to the listener at steadily longer intervals, creating a lower pitch. This was explained by Christian Doppler, an Austrian scientist who died in 1853. It is known as the 'Doppler effect'.

A blind, deaf and dumb girl graduated from university

Helen Keller was born in America in 1880. She became very ill and was blind and deaf by the time she was nineteen months old. She became mute as well shortly afterwards. When she was six, she began to receive instruction from a remarkable teacher called Anne Sullivan, who had herself suffered from a degree of blindness. Anne managed to teach Helen Keller to read, speak and write so well that in 1900 Helen went to Radcliffe College and graduated with the highest honours four years later. Helen wrote several books, travelled and lectured widely and helped many blind people at a time when very little was being done for people with such terrible handicaps.

Russian research shows evidence of paranormal powers

Dr Iosif M. Goldberg, a general practioner in the Ural Mountain town of Nizhniy had a most unusual patient. Rosa Kuleshova claimed that she could "see" with her fingers. When she was tested it was proved to be quite true. She could not only distinguish between colours but could actually read newspapers when heavily blindfolded and shielded from the paper by a large impenetrable cardboard shield. So startling were the results that Rosa was sent to the Soviet Academy of Science in Moscow where further tests showed that she could indeed do just what she claimed, she could even read small print with her elbows. Further research undertaken in Russia involved sixty children who had either been born blind or who had become blind in early childhood; Doctor Georgi Lozanov even blindfolded these children to ensure that there could be no fraud. After more than four hundred tests he discovered that three of the children had "skin sight" and what is even more remarkable he learned how to train other children to "see" this way.

Other sightless powers defy explanation

Dowsing or divining is not only used to find underground streams or water sources, although for centuries it has been known that certain people have this uncanny ability to find water that cannot be seen - dowsers can also find hidden metals and buried objects. Most dowsers use a pendulum to concentrate their minds, but it is the mind and not the pendulum which does the work. Some dowsers do not even need to be at the place they wish to search, they simply use a map and can locate what they are searching for with uncanny accuracy. In 1966 an Irish dowser, Thomas Trench was called in by the Belgian police to locate the body of a policeman who had ben killed during rioting and the body taken away and hidden by his murderers. Using first a small scale map and later a large scale map of the area he felt the body was hidden, he located the body from 500 miles away.

Lie detectors used on plants

The lie detector or polygraph machine detects minute changes in the temperature of a person's skin, the blood pressure and moisture of the skin - these changes can point to stress and possibly indicate when a person is lying. Cleve Backster, an American lie-detector expert, wired up one of his house plants to a polygraph and obtained the most startling results; not only did the plants respond to watering as he expected them to, but more strangely they responded to the death of an unrelated species - small shrimps. Backster dropped live brine shrimps into boiling water in the same room as a potted palm which he had wired up to a polygraph machine. The plant responded to the death of each shrimp, even though Backster had used a randomly automated machine to drop the shrimps. Even more strangely the plant did not respond when dead shrimps were dropped into the boiling water. Other researchers have carried on with this research and find that plants seem in some way to observe behaviour around them. In an experiment carried out by Lyall Watson, a plant was uprooted by a member of the research team in a room containing another plant of the same species which was wired up to a polygraph. When a group of five other researchers approached the surviving plant, there was no reaction, but when the researcher who had uprooted the first plant approached there was a significant response which seemed to prove that the wired-up plant had in some way remembered and identified the killer of its partner.

Perhaps this response gives us the reason for the belief that some people have "green fingers" and seem to be able to grow anything while others have little success in the garden - maybe the plants respond to people who approach them lovingly and flourish accordingly.

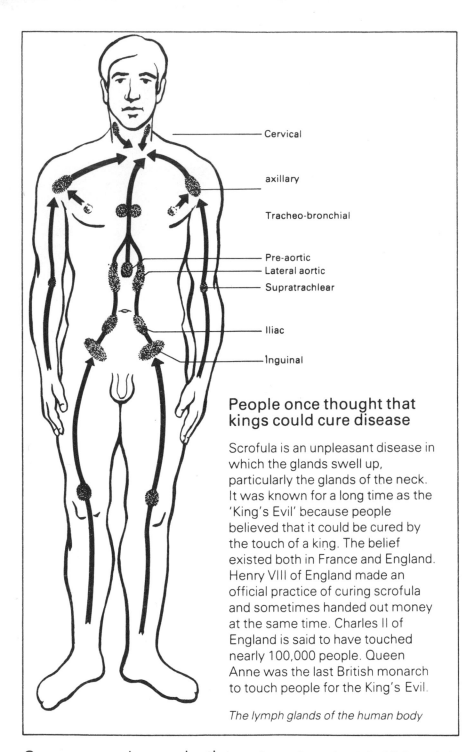

- Cervical
- axillary
- Tracheo-bronchial
- Pre-aortic
- Lateral aortic
- Supratrachlear
- Iliac
- Inguinal

People once thought that kings could cure disease

Scrofula is an unpleasant disease in which the glands swell up, particularly the glands of the neck. It was known for a long time as the 'King's Evil' because people believed that it could be cured by the touch of a king. The belief existed both in France and England. Henry VIII of England made an official practice of curing scrofula and sometimes handed out money at the same time. Charles II of England is said to have touched nearly 100,000 people. Queen Anne was the last British monarch to touch people for the King's Evil.

The lymph glands of the human body

Quarantine used to mean forty days of isolation

Anyone who has mumps or measles or any similar contagious disease has to be kept apart from other people during the period in which the disease can be caught by others. This period of separation is known as 'quarantine'. For most ordinary diseases, it lasts for only a few days or at the most a week or two. But the original Italian word 'quaranta' meant 'forty' and a period of 'quarantine' was a full forty days.

Children were once sewed up in their clothes to keep them healthy through the winter

It was once firmly believed by country people that this was the only way to make sure that their children stayed healthy throughout the cold months of winter. Washing of any kind was sure to bring about illness. Even in recent times, poor people have padded their children's clothes with layers of newspaper during the winter to keep them warm and made them keep their clothes on, night and day, for months on end.

The first hospitals were guest houses for pilgrims

The ancient Greeks and others often used their temples as temporary 'hospitals' for healing people. They relied as much on the help of the gods as on the help of doctors. The Romans later developed efficient military hospitals but had no real civilian ones. The word 'hospital' comes from the Latin 'hospitalia', which means a 'guest house' and during the Middle Ages there were many such guest houses attached to monasteries where pilgrims rested on their way to visit holy shrines. In time, these hospitals became more concerned with those who were sick.

Scurvy caused more deaths than sea battles did in the days of the old sailing ships

Scurvy was the sailor's curse between the 16th and 19th centuries. It was caused by the lack of Vitamin C (found in fresh fruit and vegetables) in the diet on the long ocean voyages of the time. When sailors had scurvy, their gums swelled, their teeth fell out and their skin became mottled. Sufferers often collapsed and died if they tried to get up. It was estimated that a large proportion of shipwrecks was caused by weakened crews unable to control their ships. On the longest voyages as many as half or even three-quarters of the crew sometimes died of scurvy. Towards the end of the 18th century, Captain Cook and others did a great deal towards controlling the disease by introducing lemon juice on board for sailors to drink.

There are curious cures for hiccoughs

Hiccoughs happen when the muscles in the chest and throat suddenly tighten. This can be caused by eating or drinking too much or too fast. Sometimes an attack of hiccoughs can last for several hours, in which case it becomes very serious, but usually an attack lasts for only a few minutes. Although hiccoughs would probably disappear if nothing is done about them, everyone has their favourite way of getting rid of them. Cures include a sudden shock, drinking water backwards out of the wrong side of the cup, holding the breath and trying to sneeze, or dropping a cold key against your chest or down the back of your neck. Hiccoughs were also believed to be caused by someone who had spoken your name. You had to say the name of everyone you knew until you got the right person and only then would the hiccoughs stop! Hiccoughs are however no laughing matter. If the attack goes on for any length of time they can lead to oxygen starvation and can be fatal.

Artificial limbs were in use a long time ago

Amputation, or cutting off a limb, is one of the oldest surgical operations. The earliest references to artificial limbs are in Hindu writings of about 1500 BC. One of the oldest artificial limbs in existence is a Roman leg made of bronze strips fitted to a central wooden stick. Peg legs were common in the Middle Ages but hinged legs were not developed until quite recently. Electronics is now used to transmit signals from surviving muscles to artificial hands, feet, arms and legs. This gives more movement to the artificial limb.

Every single fingerprint in the world is different

The ridges on the skin of your fingertips form a pattern that is unique to you. That is why fingerprints can be used as identification. Each of your fingers has a separate print of its own. There are nearly 4,000 million people in the world and so there are about 40,000 million different fingertips. This unique fact was understood by the Chinese more than 2000 years ago, when the emperors used their thumb print to sign important documents. But it was not until the 19th century that fingerprints were first used to identify criminals. At the beginning of the 20th century a proper method of classifying fingerprints was perfected, so that any one set of fingerprints can quickly be selected from the millions that are on file.

Barbers once did the work of surgeons and dentists

The traditional barber's pole, with its red and white spiral pattern, represented the patients' blood and the surgeon's bandage. Blood-letting, to let out 'bad' blood, used to be a common cure for many illnesses. This was always the job of the barber-surgeon. Many barbers were also the local dentist. A special Company of Barber Surgeons was founded in 1461 in England by King Edward IV. Barbers and surgeons were not properly separated into their special duties until the middle of the 18th century, when surgery became a little more scientific.

People once tried to cure meningitis by splitting a pigeon in half

Meningitis is an extremely unpleasant illness which is caused by the inflammation of the meninges, the membranes that surround the brain and the spinal column. There are different types of meningitis, some of which are easier to cure than others. One of the common symptoms is very painful headaches. In Mediaeval times, people believed that the sufferer should take a young pigeon, split it in half and spread out the halves, cut side down, on top of his head and leave them there for as long as possible. The smell was probably almost as unpleasant as the illness.

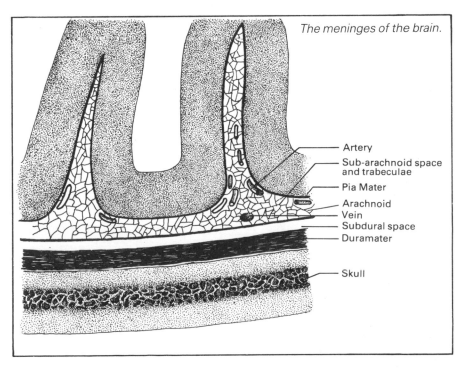

The meninges of the brain.

Artery
Sub-arachnoid space and trabeculae
Pia Mater
Arachnoid
Vein
Subdural space
Duramater
Skull

The rules of medicine were laid down 2400 years ago and are still obeyed today

The Hippocratic oath that governs the behaviour of doctors even today was the result of rules laid down by a Greek doctor. His name was Hippocrates and he was born in about 460 BC on the island of Cos. He was one of the first doctors to explain that illness and disease were caused by natural things rather than by the will of the gods, sorcery or magic.
Hippocrates taught his pupils how to treat their patients properly. He instructed them to always help the sick, never to poison anyone and to keep secret anything their patients had told them in private.
Hippocrates was often called "The Father of Medicine."

Hippocrates' pupil Aesculapius's staff was a symbol of early doctors.

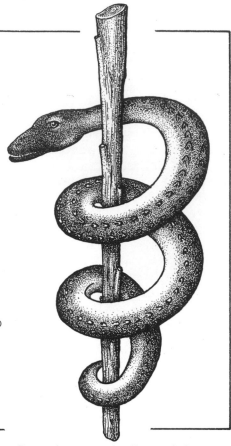

Sticking a boar tusk through the nose is a sign of importance

Many different kinds of people throughout history have worn decorations in their noses to show their importance. Sometimes the decoration is just a small precious stone worn on one side of the nose. Some tribespeople, however, thrust large pieces of tusk or bone right through the central part of the nose.

People once believed that flu was caused by the influence of the stars

Many people suffer from flu, or influenza, at some time in their lives. It is caused by a virus. The name influenza comes from the Italian word for 'influence' because people once believed that the influence of certain stars caused epidemics of influenza. Throughout history there have been serious epidemics of flu.

People once believed that malaria was caused by bad air

Malaria is a common and often fatal disease in hot, swampy climates near the tropics. The Italians believed it was caused by the foul atmosphere of the swamps and so they called it *mala aria* or 'bad air'. Now we know that malaria is caught from the infected bite of a mosquito. Control has been widely achieved by stopping the mosquitos from breeding and by spraying the larvae in their stagnant pools.

The royal doctor feared draughts

During the reign of Louis XVIII the court physician feared draughts so much that he forbade anyone to open windows when he was in the room. He travelled about in a wheel-chair, wrapped up in blankets with a clove of garlic in each ear and nostril. He lived to a ripe old age.

Tattooing the tongue was once a sign of grief

Tattooing is one of the oldest ways of decorating the body. It is usually done by puncturing the skin with a sharp needle to make a pattern or picture and then rubbing a coloured dye into the holes. Ancient Egyptians and Chinese, Red Indians, Maoris, sailors and many other kinds of people were traditionally tattooed. It is generally done now for decoration but it used to be done for religious reasons, or to show to which tribe a man belonged. In some groups women who had lost their husbands had their tongues tattooed as a way of showing their grief to others.

In the past, children's heads were sometimes bound tightly to alter the shape of their skulls

Some people in the past have on purpose tried to change the shape of their children's heads to make them more beautiful. American Indians used to flatten the heads of babies and small children by tying boards tightly to their skulls. They also used to bind the heads tightly with strips of cloth so that the head became long and pointed. This was often done for religious reasons.

Quinine comes from the bark of a tree

Quinine is used in medicines and also in tonic water. It used to be the main protection against malaria. The substance was originally obtained from the bark of the cinchona tree of South America and was later cultivated by the Dutch in Java. During the Second World War, the Japanese seized the island and stopped the major source of supply to the west. This forced the Americans and others to develop chemical substitutes which have since been widely used instead of quinine.

Man has conquered smallpox

The fight against smallpox, once the cause of many deaths, began in the 18th century when Edward Jenner noticed that dairy-maids who had had a milder disease known as cowpox seemed to be immune to smallpox. He deliberately gave a small boy a dose of cowpox and when he later gave the same boy a dose of smallpox the boy remained perfectly healthy. This 'vaccination' with cowpox to prevent smallpox slowly became widespread until there were only small areas in the world where smallpox occurred.

There was a baby with no brain

In 1788, Mary Clark aged 28 gave birth to a baby in Carlisle. The doctors noticed that although he was perfectly developed, he had a very soft head. After five days the baby died and an autopsy revealed that there was no brain in the child's skull.

Civilisation brought death to the savage tribes

When Captain Cook and other explorers discovered the South Sea Islands they brought not only Christianity but death to the inhabitants. The natives, never having had any of the infectious diseases so prevalent in Europe, had no resistance to the diseases and so succumbed fatally to ailments such as the common cold and influenza.

A Polish countess operated on herself for cancer

In the mid-nineteenth century, Countess Rosa Branicka was diagnosed as having cancer of the breast. The countess refused immediate surgery and instead went on a tour of Europe. At each town she bought a surgical instrument and when she arrived in Paris, she locked herself in her hotel room and removed the cancer from her breast. She lived until she was 82 years of age.

Cannibalism kills the cannibals

The act of cannibalism has always had ritual significance, eating the brains, heart, liver or flesh of an enemy was supposed to endow the victor with the intelligence, strength, stamina and good qualities of the vanquished. It was more likely to lead to severe illness however, since the flesh of a like species contains toxins that cannot be so easily broken down and are certain to be poisonous. Cannibalism was not regularly practised for this reason, and regular flesh eating was not widespread as some historians have claimed which has led to popular fallacies about cannibalism. In Mexico the religious importance of cannibalism was stressed at the feasts of harvest and seed time. The choicest morsels (the palms of the hands and the cheeks) being saved for the most powerful person attending the feast as a mark of respect of his position.

One bacterium can multiply to one million bacteria in less than one day

Bacteria are very small living things with only a single cell. They are so small that they can only be seen under a powerful microscope, but they exist everywhere: in the air, in the ground, in the sea and in all other living things. Some are rod-shaped, some look like corkscrews, some form in clusters, and some are linked like a chain. They multiply very fast, by splitting in two and then in two again and so on, so that a single bacterium can become a million bacteria in about 15 hours. Various factors then make the growth rate slow down a little. Some bacteria help us by breaking down dead matter into its original simple components and so keep the Earth clean of refuse. Others are harmful and cause diseases such as cholera.

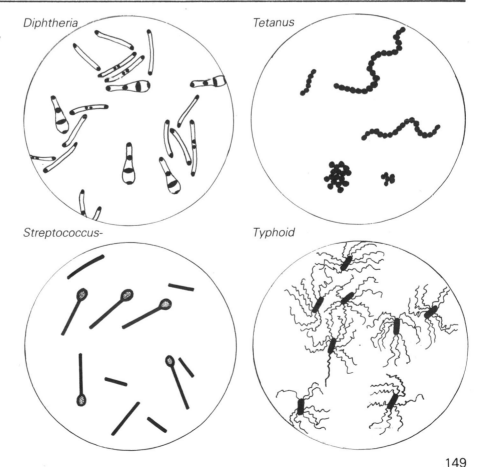

Diphtheria

Tetanus

Streptococcus-

Typhoid

Neck-stretching is another sign of beauty

Some tribeswomen stretch their necks on purpose by wearing metal rings about their necks. More and more rings are gradually added until the neck stretches to two or three times its normal length. At this stage, the rings can never be taken off because the neck is too weak to hold up the head.

Below left: *The neck of a normal torso.* Below right: *The giraffe women of Africa do not "stretch" their necks, rather they force the shoulders down which gives the effect of neck stretching.*

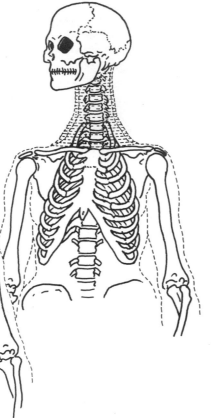

Lips are sometimes stretched to look more beautiful

In the search for beauty, some tribespeople stretch their lips by forcing larger and larger discs between the lips and the gums. Sometimes discs the size of dinner plates can be fitted into the lips, making them stick out far in front of the face. If the discs are taken out, the lips hang down uselessly. Teeth and gums are usually badly affected by the treatment and it may be impossible for someone with stretched lips to eat solid foods. Teeth filing is also the most important ceremony in Bali, because it marks the passage of child to adulthood. A woman's rank in society is shown by the filing of her teeth. This ritual has become a popular spectacle for tourists in Bali.

To prove manhood Mandam men were tortured beyond endurance

The Mandam tribe of North American Indians made their men go through the most painful initiation rights before they could call themselves men. The initiates had to starve themselves completely for four days; they were not even allowed to drink. They were then dressed in colourful clothes and had their bodies painted, before being led into the ceremonial hut. There, the chief medicine man carved slices of flesh from their chests, using serrated knives. They then pushed wooden skewers into the wounds. Leather thongs were attached to the skewers and the young man was hoisted from the floor by the thongs. Heavy weights were attached to his legs and he was spun round and round. If he recovered the youngster was then given a hatchet with which he had to chop off the little finger of his left hand. Unfortunately the tribe did not survive. In the 1840s it was wiped out by smallpox!

Teeth are often sharpened to points or decorated as a sign of beauty

Gold fillings are quite often used by modern dentists only because the gold is easy to shape and does not decay. In ancient Mexico, and other parts of the world, teeth were sometimes drilled with artificial holes and filled with gold plugs for decoration. In parts of Africa and Australasia, it used to be common to remove one or more teeth as a sign of beauty or maturity. Some African people still file their teeth to sharp points to show they belong to a particular tribe. In the Western world, straight white teeth are considered desirable and men and women pay large amounts of money for cosmetic dentistry which can have dramatic effects on their appearances.

People all over the world change the shape of their ear lobes or decorate them to look attractive

Ears are used for decoration almost everywhere in the world. They are often pierced for earrings when children are quite young, even in the most civilised societies. In some primitive tribes very large holes are made in the lobes. The holes are first made in childhood and larger and larger objects are gradually inserted until a fist or a cup can be pushed through the hole. Weights are also tied to the end of the lobe to stretch it so that it hangs down to the shoulders. In parts of Africa and Borneo, men and women make themselves more beautiful by doing this. Beauty, of course, is in the eye of the beholder.

A bone through the nose can be a sign of wealth

In New Guinea a man will adorn himself with a feathered headdress, striking white paint and a bone through his nose to take part in certain ceremonies. His sumptuous appearance is evidence of his wealth, but it also demonstrates his skill at decorating himself. Among the Aborigines of Australia, a boy's nasal septum may be pierced but only as part of a very intricate series of initiation rites.

People paint their bodies in some parts of the world instead of wearing clothes

People have always painted their bodies. The reasons are many: religious, ceremonial, to denote status or simply for decoration. In Brazil, the Kayapo Indians paint each other's bodies in geometric patterns using the blue-black juice of the genipap fruit. An unpainted body can mean that the person has no one who cares enough to do it. Other Indians regard an unpainted person as naked.

Sometimes body painting can be quite complicated because every colour and shape has a particular meaning. A popular design among the Thompson Indians in North America was to paint half the face red and the other half black; red brought the warrior good luck, while black gave his enemy misfortune. Sometimes stripes were painted on the chin of a warrior showing how many people he had killed. The Aborigines of Australia indulge in a great deal of body painting. In decoration for a religious occasion, traditional colours and patterns are used and are applied by a special person. For instance, when mourning, the mourners are covered in white paint. But for everyday occasions the Aborigines will use any colour and any pattern and families may spend hours improving one another's appearance. Patterns include concentric circles, transverse lines and lattices. Among the Nuba in the Sudan, body painting is art for art's sake: it has no religious meaning, it simply makes the body more beautiful. In fact, as a man gets older and less attractive, he replaces paint by clothing. Also a man suffering

illness or injury will wear clothes until he recovers. Even in the more sophisticated world, we paint ourselves. Women wear lipstick and put on eye make up. Throughout the world, people like to decorate themselves according to their own customs. Today, in the Western World the cosmetics industry is a multi-million dollar one, with vast amounts of money being spent on advertising campaigns to persuade men and women to spend money on cosmetics.

In New Guinea men will wear wigs to attract women

The men of New Guinea believe that spirits inhabit hair and a good growth means the spirits are favourable. Baldness is a sign that the spirits have abandoned a man. Men wear wigs as decoration and to attract women. They are made from hair cuttings and mounted on a long pointed bamboo frame. Making a wig is a ritual that only an expert can perform. Before the wig is started, a pig is sacrificed to the ancestors. Wigs are not meant to imitate human hair for they are decorated with scarab beetles and fur, and often brightly painted.

Leeches were once used to cure disease

In ancient times and during the Middle Ages, doctors often used leeches to suck their patients' blood. Many people believed that certain illnesses were caused by too much blood in the body. Leeches were specially bred for the purpose and doctors themselves were sometimes called 'leeches'. There are many different kinds of leech. Most of them live off the blood of other creatures. They attach themselves to their host, pierce the skin, and give out a substance that stops the blood from clotting. Then they suck the blood as it flows. Once attached to the skin, they are very difficult to remove.

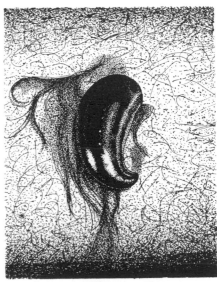

Above left: *Before the leech begins to suck blood, it is quite small, but once it begins to suck it gradually becomes full of blood and it becomes many times its* *normal size. Recent research has shown that the application of leeches may be of use today if applied to patients who have had organ transplants.*

151

Pythagoras stood behind a curtain when he gave his lectures

Pythagoras was a famous Greek philosopher and mathematician, some of whose rules are still used in mathematics today. He was born in Samos in the 6th century BC. When he gave public lectures, he used to stand behind a curtain and only a few of his disciples were allowed inside the curtain. These were his 'esoteric' disciples, meaning 'those within'. The others had to stay outside and listen through the curtain. These were the 'exoteric' disciples, or 'those outside'. Aristotle gave difficult or esoteric lectures in the morning for his more learned disciples and easier or exoteric lectures in the evening.

Pythagoras's theorem that the square on the hypotenuse of any right angled triangle is always equal to the sum of the squares on the two adjacent sides is shown by this diagram.

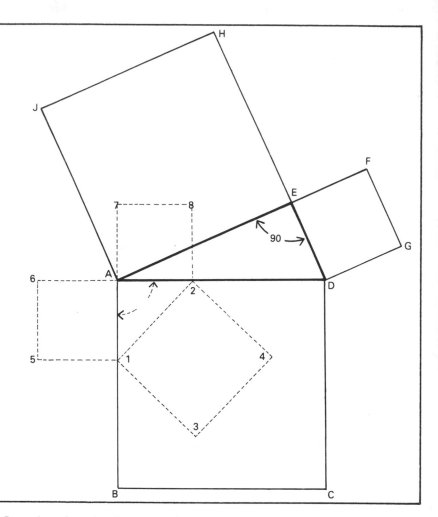

One of the world's greatest teachers was forced to commit suicide

Socrates was a great teacher and philosopher who lived in Athens during the 4th century BC. The philosopher Plato and the brilliant leader Alcibiades were among his pupils. Socrates' arguments about the truth of life made people think about what they were saying and doing. He would ask many questions until his students began to think more carefully. Many important people considered him dangerous and they accused him of corrupting the minds of the young men of Athens. He was put on trial and found guilty. He refused to admit that he had said or done anything wrong and was sentenced to death. Plato described Socrates' last moments when the great philosopher drank the poison, hemlock, which was given to him by his gaoler.

A Greek scientist invented machines powered by steam in the 1st century AD

Steam engines were first put to practical use in the 18th century, by men such as Newcomen, Watt and Fulton. But a Greek scientist in ancient Alexandria, called Hero, had already been playing with steam power in the 1st century AD. He had, however, never put it to any real use. For him, it was only a game. One of his devices was a water boiler with pipes leading the steam into a hollow sphere which had two jets on opposite sides. As the steam came through the jets, the sphere spun round. He also invented a process whereby a combination of hot air and water-filled buckets could open temple doors. We know about them from contemporary records which have been copied and recopied as generations passed and have been handed down.

Two of the greatest men the world has ever known were once tutor and pupil

The Greek philosopher Aristotle was possibly the greatest thinker there has ever been. He was famous even in his own time. At one period in his life he was hired by Philip of Macedon to be the tutor of Philip's son and heir, Alexander, who became the greatest soldier in the world. Alexander became king at 19 and by the time he was 32, he had conquered Greece, crossed the Hellespont, defeated the Persian Empire in a series of great battles, conquered Egypt and crossed the River Indus into India. He never lost a battle in his life. However, we now believe that Alexander lived a very dissolute life and that he died of drinking too much when he was still quite young aged 32 when he should have been at the height of his powers.

The Greeks celebrate their name day rather than their birthday

In many countries, people celebrate their birthdays, but the Greeks prefer to celebrate the day of the saint after whom they are named. Many Greeks are named after one saint or another and on their Saint's day all the people with the same name celebrate. All those named after the apostle Philip, for example, celebrate their name day on 1st May, St Philip's day. They go to each other's houses during the day, congratulating each other, and then have a big feast in the evening.

The Greeks once hoped that a change of name would calm the storm

The original Greek name for the Black Sea was the 'Axeinos' or 'Unfriendly' Sea. This was a very suitable name because there were constant storms and ships were often wrecked on the dangerously rocky shore. However, the Greeks later felt that if they called the sea by a more pleasant name, storms would calm down a little, so they called it the 'Euxine' or 'Friendly' Sea. This made no difference in the end, so we have returned to its gloomier name, the 'Black' Sea.

In the days of Ancient Greece, people believed that the Earth was the centre of the universe

The earliest known Greek scientists, like Anaximander, believed the Earth was flat and disc-shaped, with Greece at its centre. It floated on water and was surrounded by the sphere of the universe. The stars shone through holes in the dark sky. At that time, in the sixth century BC, the most important scientist was Pythagoras. He claimed that the Sun, Moon and planets all orbited the Earth in perfect concentric circles. The Greeks were so in love

with symmetry that they liked to see everything fitting in with this way of looking at things. So theories about the universe had to be in accordance with their idea of beauty and perfection. Because a regular unchanging motion was more elegant than one which varied, Pythagoras taught that the planets orbited the Earth in circles at a regular rate. Observations showed them that the movement of the planets did not necessarily agree with their theories, so they devised ingenious reasons for why this was so and backed them with mathematical equations. It was not until the seventeenth century that the German astronomer Johannes Kepler found out that Pythagoras had been entirely wrong. By that time too Copernicus had overturned the idea of an Earth-centred universe. So the Greek vision of the universe, despite its beautiful symmetry, was proved to be utterly mistaken.

A doctor in Ancient Greece set down rules of medicine which are still used 2300 years later

The Greeks thought a strong, healthy body was very important so they were careful about their diets and exercise. The earliest doctors used old remedies to cure the sick, which sometimes seemed to work and sometimes didn't. Many of the ill made pilgrimages to the temples of the god Asclepios, in the way people visit Lourdes today. In an attempt to learn more about illnesses, doctors began to collect information. They asked their patients questions about every aspect of their lives and noted it down. Then they were more able to diagnose the illness. After that, they would prescribe a medicine and over the weeks note down its effects. This is the same procedure followed by doctors today. The greatest of all medical men of ancient times was Hippocrates of Cos (born about 460 BC). He wrote the first medical text-books, setting

out the methodical approach that doctors should follow of thorough investigation and observation. He gave his name to the Hippocratic oath sworn by doctors all over the world, binding them to observe the code of medical ethics that in all probability Hippocrates himself drew up in the fifth century BC.

By taking a bath, Archimedes was able to solve a scientific problem

Archimedes, a Greek scientist, had been asked by King Hiero to find out if his new crown was of pure gold. Hiero suspected that the man who had made the crown had stolen some of the gold and replaced it by another metal. Archimedes pondered this for a long time. One day as he lowered himself into his bath tub, he noticed that the water level rose. Suddenly his problem was solved! He leapt out of his bath in excitement, shouting 'Eureka!' (Greek for 'I've found it!') What Archimedes had realised in a flash was that a body in water displaces a quantity of water equal to its weight. That means if he put the crown in water it should displace the same amount of water as the same weight in gold. If the crown displaced more water, then it contained other metal and was not pure. In fact, he discovered that the maker of the crown had cheated the king and was subsequently punished. This new law of physics was called Archimedes Principle.

Archimedes may have used solar energy to defeat Rome's navy

In 1973, Dr Ioannis Sakkas made some experiments that proved that an old story of Archimedes may have been true. According to several historians, Archimedes reflected the sun's rays at the Roman fleet at Syracuse and set it on fire. Sakkas focused 50 mirrors on a small rowing boat and within two minutes it was on fire.

A Roman aqueduct has remained in use for more than 1800 years

The Roman aqueducts are marvels of practical engineering. Built of stone blocks, many of them have remained standing for nearly 2000 years. The aqueduct at Segovia, in Spain, which was built in the reign of the Emperor Trajan, who died in AD 117, was still carrying water in the 20th century. It has two tiers, 800 metres (2650 feet) long. The

Pont du Gard, at Nimes, in France, has three tiers, nearly 50 metres (55 feet) high. Many of the earliest aqueducts were mostly underground, such as the Appia and the Anio Vetus. The Aqua Marcia, built about 144 BC, was more than 80 kilometres (50 miles) long in all, with about nine kilometres (6 miles) on arches. At the end of the 1st century AD, there were nine aqueducts bringing water to the city of Rome and its immediate environs.

Naval battles used to take place in the Colosseum in Rome

You can still see the remains of the great Roman Colosseum that stands proudly in the city of Rome. It was completed by the emperor Titus in AD 80, on the site of a previous amphitheatre of stone and wood which had been destroyed in Nero's fire. It is a four-storey oval building made largely of concrete with an arena approximately 92 metres (287 feet) by 55 metres (180 feet) and it is 55 metres (160 feet) tall to the top of the outer wall. The Colosseum could hold up to around 50,000 people. Beneath the floor of the arena there was a complex of animal cages and underground changing rooms and prisons. The opening ceremony lasted 100 days during which time 9000 wild beasts were killed. The arena was also flooded to a depth of about one-and-a-half metres (5 feet) and there was a display of fighting ships to amaze the crowd.

High-rise apartment blocks were the curse of ancient Rome

The ancient Romans had many of the same problems that we have today. One of these was the unpleasantness of living in high-rise blocks. Even in the 1st century AD, the emperor Augustus put a limit of about 24 metres (80 feet) on apartment blocks but a century or two later five and six-storey blocks were still quite common. The rooms were usually small, the rents were high and there was generally no plumbing or sanitation. Pots were emptied out of the window often onto the heads of unfortunate passers-by and water had to be collected from a communal well. Fires were common and caused many deaths. All this was very different to the luxurious villas of the wealthy which were beautifully laid out with cool, marble floors and spacious gardens where the owners spent much of their time.

Firemen once punished people who were careless

The earliest Roman fire-fighting force was an inefficient group of unpaid slaves, but after one-quarter of Rome was destroyed in the severe fire of AD 6, the Emperor Augustus organised the first professional fire brigade. This 'Corps of Vigiles', or Watchmen, was split into seven brigades of 1000 men, allocated to each of Rome's main areas. They were equipped with bronze syphons for squirting water, and with blankets, ladders, axes and ropes. They also patrolled the streets at night, acting as policemen, and they were entitled to punish anyone whose carelessness caused a fire, usually by a public beating on the spot.

The Romans made ice-cream without refrigerators

Since the Romans had no refrigerators, it was impossible for them to make ice. But wealthy Romans solved the problem by ordering their slaves to bring snow from the nearest mountains. This was kept cool throughout the journey in insulated clay pots. A delicious form of ice-cream was made by mixing the ice with fruits and honey. Ice was also used to cool wine. It was a luxury that only the richest could afford but it always served to impress the guests they wanted to flatter.

The original palace was on a hill in ancient Rome

The word 'palace' comes from the Palatinate Hill, one of the seven hills on which ancient Rome was built. It was a special building on this hill and it became the word used for the Emperor Augustus's 'palace' and then for the 'palaces' of other emperors and kings whether or not these were on the hill or even in Rome.

3000 men could all bathe in the same bath

There were about 1000 public baths in the city of Rome at the beginning of the 4th century AD. Many of those included gymnasia as well as hot and cold plunges and steam rooms. The largest baths of all were those built by the emperors Diocletian (about AD 305) and Caracalla (about AD 217). These had marble floors throughout, with marble columns and painted and elaborately decorated ceilings. There was space for about 1600 people in the halls and baths of Caracalla's building – and almost twice that number in Diocletian's Bath. Much

later, Michelangelo reconstructed and altered part of the baths of Diocletian to form the Church of Sta. Maria degli Angeli. Many provincial cities in the Roman Empire had public baths as well, including the well-known ones at Pompeii and at Bath, in England.

Lead water pipes were used from Roman until recent times

Plumbing involves both the provision of fresh water and the drainage of waste water. The Romans were excellent plumbers and built a magnificent system of aqueducts to carry fresh water long distances to their towns. They also built excellent drains. The word plumber itself comes from the Latin word *plumbum*, which means lead, because the Romans used lead pipes. Lead continued to be used for water pipes for many centuries and lead water pipes still exist, although pipes of copper and plastic are more common, as well as those of iron and steel.

Roman roads still survive today

The Romans believed that the shortest point between two towns was a straight line and when they built roads they made them as straight as possible, only deviating around an obstruction when there was no possible way over or through it. In Britain many of the roads they built formed the basis for many main roads, especially those leading from London.

The founder of Rome was raised by a wolf

Legend has it that the founder of Rome was its namesake, Romulus. He and his twin brother, Remus, were the sons of the god of war, Mars, and a human princess. They were abandoned in a forest as babies and nursed by a she-wolf. When they grew up they set out to found a city, but they quarrelled and Remus was killed. So Romulus founded the city of Rome in 753 BC, according to the well-known Roman historian, Livy. Although the story is regarded as myth, the date strangely enough has been confirmed by recent archaeological evidence. After World War II, remains of village huts were excavated on the Palatine, dating from the eighth century BC. They were the homes of farmers and shepherds. In the area surrounding Rome, evidence was also found of colonization by people from the Late Bronze Age, twelfth century BC, who came from the east by sea. This confirms another legend that Rome's environs were settled by refugees from Troy (now part of Turkey), led by Aeneas, hero of Virgil's *Aeneid* one of the great Roman classics which is still read today.

The 'tanks' of the Ancient World were elephants

Rome's great enemies, the Greek king Pyrrhus and the Carthaginian general Hannibal brought war elephants with them when they attacked the Romans. Hannibal's elephants are perhaps the most famous because of the historic journey across the Alps that they made. These huge beasts terrified their enemies in much the same way as an army of advancing tanks does today. These elephants are no longer in existence. They were African bush elephants which were much smaller than their bush cousins. They lived near the Atlas mountains in Morocco and in the oasis of Ghademes in Tunisia.

Many foreigners were citizens of Rome

Because Rome was the centre of a huge empire, the Romans appointed governors to rule over their territories. These governors often appointed local people to important positions, hoping that the local people would respect them and obey what they said. These people were often made citizens of Rome. St Paul, for instance, although he was a Jew, was a Roman citizen.

Roman purple came from a shellfish

The richest and rarest colour with which wool was dyed in Greek and Roman times was purple. It was the colour for Greek generals and Roman emperors. The dye itself came from a shellfish known as Murex and the word 'purple' came from 'purpura', a particular type of this kind of shellfish. Tyrian purple was the most popular and the most expensive of all. This was a mixture of shellfish dyes from the prosperous Mediterranean port of Tyre.

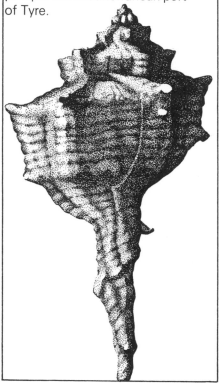

Decimation was once a form of punishment

If soldiers are said to be 'decimated' in battle, we mean that a large number of them have been killed. In fact, it should mean that exactly one in ten of them have died for 'decimate' comes from the Latin word 'decem' meaning 'ten'. If there was a mutiny or general signs of cowardice in a Roman army, the soldiers were sometimes punished by being 'decimated'. This meant that one in every ten men was killed as a warning to the others. Sometimes, one in a hundred was killed.

You cannot turn back once you have crossed the Rubicon

'To cross the Rubicon' means to take a step that will lead to great changes. The Rubicon is a small river that once separated Italy from part of ancient Gaul. When Julius Caesar was governor of Gaul no provincial governor was allowed to bring his legions into Italy. Caesar believed that his enemy Pompey was plotting against him and so he disobeyed the Roman Senate and crossed the Rubicon into Italy with his soldiers in 49 BC. This was the start of the Civil War that led to the defeat and death of Pompey and Caesar's victory.

First gladiators fought at funerals

Gladiatorial fighting was originally a religious custom rather than a performance. Later, Roman gladiators were organised to fight in arenas and amphitheatres before large crowds. Usually they had to fight to the death and if they were badly wounded and about to be killed by their opponent, the crowd would shout whether the fallen man should be slain or not. Often, the gladiators fought with different weapons — short swords against long swords; knives against spears; nets against broadswords. Sometimes they fought against lions and other wild beasts. Gladiator fighting went on until the 4th and 5th centuries AD, even though it was officially forbidden in about AD 325.

The Romans believed that everyone had genius

The only people who we call 'genius' are very clever people, but the Romans thought that everyone had a kind of genius. Their 'genius' was a friendly spirit that kept an eye on a man throughout his life, helping his good fortune. Some believed that there were two geniuses, or genii. One was good and brought good luck. The other was evil and brought bad luck. Sometimes one got the upper hand and sometimes the other did. Only men had genius, women were watched over by their own special Juno. She was a representative of the chief of the Roman goddesses, Juno herself.

Romans took their holidays at seaside resorts

The well-to-do Romans had summer holidays just like we do. Some went to their country villas in the hills surrounding Rome. Others went further north to Tuscany, as some English people might go to Scotland, to hunt deer.

By far the most popular place was Campania - the area around the Bay of Naples. Here rich Romans built beautiful seaside villas in lovely gardens, with private jetties for boating and fishing. One villa described by the poet Martial was so near the sea that one could fish while lying in bed! In the evening, they would dine on the wide variety of seafood available.

The cities of Campania, like Pompeii and Herculaneum, lived under the shadow of the great volcano, Vesuvius. On August 24, AD79, it erupted and buried the cities under a layer of lava and ash, killing 10 per cent of the population. When modern archaeologists came to excavate these cities, they discovered a unique record of daily life from what had been left just as it had been on the day Vesuvius erupted. Pompeii is one of the major tourist attractions of Italy today.

Although most Romans could not read, Rome had several public libraries

There were many bookshops in Ancient Rome, and by the fourth century AD Rome had 29 public libraries. But the printing press had

A symbol of justice became a byword for terror

In ancient Rome, the senior magistrates had their symbol of office. It was a bundle of rods with an axe, tied together by a red thong and carried before them when they walked through the streets. This bundle was called the 'fasces' and it symbolised the authority of the magistrate over life and death. We get our modern word 'Fascism' from that origin but in 20th century Italy and Germany 'Fascism' did not mean 'justice'; it meant the totalitarian nationalist state, which swept away all opposition and was prepared to wipe out all its enemies. The movement was initiated in 1919 by Benito Mussolini in Italy. In 1925, he became Dictator of Italy and called himself 'Il Duce', the Leader. He controlled Italy until 1943 and died in 1945.

Roman fasces like the ones above, were the symbol of authority of Roman magistrates and were carried by them wherever they went.

not then been invented, so how were books produced in any number? They were made by skilled copyists, usually slaves. Although the process was slow and books could not be produced in great numbers as they are today, the need for books was catered for. After all, only the rich men in Rome were educated and that was only a small minority of the population. A book did not look like a modern one; it was a length of papyrus or parchment about 10m long and rolled round a wooden spindle. The copyists wrote on it with pen and ink. These books were collected by rich men like Libanius of Antioch for their own libraries. However, there were also schoolbooks mainly for young boys - and people could borrow books from the public libraries.

Betting at the races was a favourite pastime of the Romans

The Romans were great enthusiasts of spectator sports.

The official games were known as the *ludi* and consisted mainly of chariot racing. The Circus Maximus, Rome's main stadium, could hold 250,000 people; its oval arena was 600m long and 87m wide. Each day's chariot racing was begun by races between *bigae*, two-horse chariots driven by the less experienced charioteers, each one known by its colours - the reds, the greens and the blues. Like football supporters today, the Romans supported one or other of the teams. As at all races, they backed the teams they thought would win. Great fortunes could be lost or won at the games.

Today Rome can be seen as the centre of Christianity, but once the Romans worshipped a variety of gods

The Romans had gods and goddesses which governed every aspect of their lives. Generally they could be divided into two

categories: gods who looked after the state and those who watched over the family. Some of the state gods had months or days of the week dedicated to them because they were so important: Mars, god of war, gave his name to March, Saturn, god of agriculture to Saturday. These great gods were worshipped in public ceremonies. Each one had its own temple where sacrifices were made. This was usually food - but if someone wanted a big request granted, he would sacrifice an animal. A priest would examine the liver of the dead animal to see if the god had accepted the sacrifice and then the meat would be cooked and eaten. The household gods were spirits called *lares* and *penates* and many Roman homes had a lararium or shrine where they left offerings. These spirits had to be humoured because they protected the house against burglars and bad luck. It was only in 312 AD when Constantine the Great had a vision of the Cross, that the Roman Empire became Christian. Since then Rome has been the centre of the Roman Catholic faith, one of the most important in the world.

The Romans had very strange ways of washing togas

Many wealthy Roman families took their clothes to the fuller or washerman to be cleaned and repaired. First the cloth was washed in fuller's earth, a type of clay that absorbed the grease. Then it was bleached by being hung over a wickerwork frame above burning sulphur. Then the cloth was trodden in a vat of urine from the public lavatories. The chemical in the urine helped to thicken the cloth. Afterwards, it was fluffed up by combing it with teasels or hedgehog skins and then sheared to make it smooth and sprayed with water from the fuller's mouth. Only then was it ready to wear again.

Tuareg tribesmen wear veils

The Tuareg are tribesmen of the western and central Sahara. They travel out from places such as Timbuktu along the old desert trade routes. The Tuareg are a strong and graceful people with long black hair and black tunics. The men wear the end of a cloth as a veil over their face day and night, and are therefore often called by the Arabs the 'veiled people', or *muleth themin*. In contrast, the women never wear a veil.

Women once wore their hair piled one metre high

Some of the most elaborate fashions in hairstyles were in the 18th century, when they became ridiculously elaborate and top-heavy. Women's hair was often shaped over a wire frame, almost a metre high, and thickened with grease to keep it in shape. The hair was then often topped with some decoration, such as toy soldiers, ships, flowers or animals. Ladies who had their hair dressed like this had to keep the style for weeks and slept with their heads on wooden props so as not to disturb anything. Such fashions disappeared very quickly at the end of the 18th century, with the French Revolution.

Heated rollers were used to style hair more than 4000 years ago

Fashions in hair styles were as important in very ancient times both to men and women as they are today. Some of the styles of ancient Greece and Rome were remarkably elaborate and beautiful. Egyptians and Assyrians from even earlier times took just as much trouble. Four thousand or more years ago it was already possible to have a 'permanent' wave by shaping the hair and leaving it to dry in cakes of mud, or by winding it on heated irons. Men's beards were given a careful 'permanent' curl, especially the beards of the aristocracy.

Hats were worn back-to-front and side-to-side to distinguish between two different armies

The traditional military hat of the 18th century was the tricorne. This had three corners and was generally worn with one corner forward and the other two corners to the sides. It was replaced by the bicorne hat, which became popular during the Napoleonic Wars, generally worn by officers. The French wore it with the two corners sticking out on either side of their head. The British wore it with the two corners sticking out front and back, it was occasionally worn with formal evening wear in the nineteenth century.

An Englishman founded one of the most famous French fashion houses.

In 1845 a young Englishman named Charles Worth arrived in Paris, with only 117 francs in his pocket. In 1858 he opened a salon in the Rue de la Paix and became the founder of modern *haute couture*. Two years later, his wife introduced him to the influential Countess Metternich, whose husband was one of the most important men in Europe. The countess enthused about Worth's dresses to Eugénie, wife of the French Emperor, Napoleon III, and she became one of his clients. When she attended the opening of the Suez Canal it is said that she had 150 of Worth's dresses with her. Worth eventually numbered nine queens among his clients, and his designs were the most admired of the day. His success encouraged other designers to open salons in Paris, making it the fashion centre of the world. Today his name is still with us as his house created famous perfumes which are still sold around the world.

Shoes once had points so long that they had to be tied up to the knees

Fashions in shoes have altered over the centuries as much as fashions in other kinds of clothes. One of the most extreme fashions that existed in the 14th century was a short leather boot or shoe with a toe so long and pointed that it was curled back and attached by a decorative chain to a garter just below the knee. Not surprisingly, this awkward style did not last for long and was probably only popular among the rich and leisured few.

Beauty spots come in every shape and form

We know from writers like Ovid and Martial that Roman women wore beauty spots on their faces. The purpose was probably to show up the delicate complexion of the rest of their face. Perhaps the spots were also meant to hide blemishes on the skin. The custom was revived in the 16th century and grew increasingly in the 17th and 18th centuries. Political party supporters often wore them to show which side they supported. Stars, moons, lovebirds, even horses and coaches made out of silk, velvet or taffeta were stuck on and moved about the face depending on where the wearer, man or woman, wanted.

Little boys were once dressed as little girls

Up until the beginning of this century, it was usual for the sons of aristocratic families to be dressed in frocks and wear their hair long and curled, similar to a little girl. It was only when they were sent off to school at the age of six or seven, or left their nurseries for the schoolroom that they were allowed to wear trousers.

Chinese women used to bandage their feet tightly

In China, up until the beginning of this century, small feet were considered to be very beautiful and in order to stop their feet growing too large, the women used to bandage their feet incredibly tightly. Little girls' feet were also tied up in this way. This naturally distorted the feet badly and the practice was outlawed by the Chinese government.

Dark clothes should be worn in winter

Dark clothes, especially black ones, absorb the heat of the winter's sun much more efficiently than light coloured ones, and are therefore warmer to wear in winter time. A Swiss scientist and explorer, de Queverain, painted a thermometer black when it was registering 10 degrees, within a few minutes in the sunshine, it had shot up to 60 degrees.

Venetian women wore platform shoes

In the seventeenth century, high-heeled shoes were the height of fashion in Venice. The fashion was taken to ridiculous lengths and the heels became so high that the women had to hire servants to walk at their sides to stop them toppling over.

A Florida man took a size 42 shoe

Harley Davidson, who lived in Florida, had feet 22½ inches long. He had to have his shoes specially made for him — size 42. This is enormous when one considers that the average size is around size nine.

Shoe sizes were measured in barleycorns

In 1324, Edward II of England decreed that an inch was equal to three barleycorns laid end to end. The normal shoe size was laid down as 39 barleycorns and was said to be a size 13. Other sizes were graded from this and each size was one barleycorn more or less than the normal.

Scots were banned from wearing the kilt

After the 1745 rebellion, led by Bonnie Prince Charlie, the British Government made it illegal for Scotsmen to wear tartan kilts — their national dress. The ban remained in force until 1832.

Only the Plains Indians wore the trailing feather head-dress normally associated with American Indians

The American Indians had many tribes and lived in many different ways in various parts of North America. The great long trailing feather head-dress was worn by the Indians of the Central Plains, particularly the Dakota Sioux. Other Plains Indians were the Cheyenne, the Pawnee, the Crow and the Comanche. The Shoshone lived to the west of the Plains and there were many lesser-known tribes along the Californian coast. Farther north, lived the Cree. To the south-west, in the desert, lived the Pueblo Indians, the Navaho, Hopi and Apache. In the north-east lived the Iroquois, the Mohawk, Algonquin and Huron. Farther south were the Shawnee, Cherokee and Creek. Besides these major tribes there were many smaller tribes.

Hurling is a mixture of hockey, lacrosse and rugby

Hurling is the national sport of Ireland and has been played since ancient Gaelic times. In Gaelic, it is called 'iomain' and many of the old chieftains were famous for their skill and courage in the game. It is fast, dangerous and exciting. The stick is like a hockey stick with a much wider, oval-shaped head, and the ball can be hit from man to man overhead as well as along the ground. There are 15 men on each side, as in rugby, and the goal posts are similar to rugby posts in that they rise up on either side of a central bar. One point is scored for sending the ball over the bar and three points for sending it below the bar. The ball can be caught in the hand but it cannot be thrown or picked up.

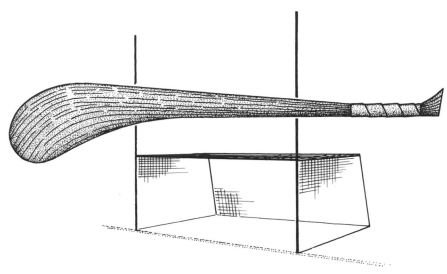

The first ascent of the Matterhorn cost the lives of four out of the seven climbers

The Matterhorn in the Alps is about 4480 metres (14,700 feet) high, an almost perfect pyramid shape that rises proudly between Switzerland and Italy not far from the Swiss town of Zermatt. It has been considered a great challenge by many generations of enthusiastic climbers. It was first conquered in 1865 by an Englishman, Edward Whymper, with three English companions and three guides. They started from Zermatt, reached the summit, and met with tragedy on the way down. One of the Englishmen fell, dragging three other climbers with him to their deaths. Whymper and two of the guides were saved only because the rope broke, so preventing them from being pulled down as well. Three days later, a party of Italians climbed the mountain successfully from the Italian side.

The first game of tennis was played in a cloister

Real tennis, the forerunner of tennis, originated in France. It was first mentioned in French ecclesiastical documents of the twelfth century, so the first tennis game was most likely played in a cloister! It is still played today and there are about thirty courts in the world. One of them is at Hampton Court, built by Henry VIII. The court is marked out with a number of lines that have extraordinary names like 'Hazard Chase', 'The Door' and 'Half a Yard Worse Than the Last Gallery'. The racket looks like a lopsided tennis racket and the ball is a hard one. The scoring is similar to lawn tennis, but that is where the similarity ends. The game is still played today, but is not as popular as lawn tennis, because there are less courts. However, it is growing in popularity again as more and more people take up the sport.

Boxing gloves were introduced to prevent aristocrats from being disfigured

Boxing was a game enjoyed at the Greek Olympic Games, but the Greeks boxed with bare hands. The Romans, always found of fighting, took it up, but introduced the *cestus*, the original 'knuckle duster'. The craze for boxing spread throughout Europe finding a ready home in England. In 1723 a 'ring' was made in Hyde Park for boxing contests. In 1745, the first rules for boxing in the Prize Ring were made and boxing gloves were introduced. They were called mufflers and were there so that the aristocratic patrons could not be disfigured. It was an aristocrat, the Marquis of Queensberry, who was responsible for drawing up the rules which are the basis of the sport today. Today, of course, boxing is a professional sport, fought for large money prizes.

Racing cyclists can reach speeds faster than some cars can achieve

Racing cycles, made of light-weight alloy, can go faster than some cars. In sprint races, cyclists may reach final speeds of more than 60 kilometres (37 miles) per hour. If a motor cycle or a car rides in front of a cyclist, breaking the wind resistance with a shield of some sort fitted to the back of the vehicles, then the cyclist can go even faster. The greatest distance covered by a cyclist in one hour is almost twice as much when he is following behind such a 'pacer', than when he is on his own. The world speed record for a cyclist travelling behind another vehicle is more than 140 kilometres (87 miles) per hour. The most famous cycle race is the *Tour de France* which lasts for one week, taking the competitors from all over the world all round France!

Boxing matches once lasted several hours and consisted of more than 100 rounds

Although boxing was known in ancient Greece and Rome, it did not become a popular sport until about AD 1719, when a man called James Figg set himself up as the London champion and took on all challengers. Prize fighting, as it was called in those days, was a little different to modern boxing. The fighters used bare fists, and kicking, biting, wrestling and scratching were allowed. Contests lasting 100 or 200 rounds were known. They continued for several hours until the contestants were exhausted. Up to 30 seconds or more were allowed for a prize fighter to get up after being knocked down. Boxing gloves, or mufflers, were first introduced by Jack Broughton, one of Figg's pupils, but the modern rules of boxing were not drawn up until about 1867 and these were not confirmed until 1872. The Marquis of Queensberry was responsible for their introduction.

Three different types of sword are used in the sport of fencing

Fencing is a popular sport that demands agility and quick reflexes. In a way, it is the modern version of the traditional duel and the weapons that are used are the modern equivalents of the everyday swords of the past. The foil is the lightest weapon and hits are made only on the trunk of the body, not the limbs or head. The epée is most like the old duelling sword and is stiffer and more solid. Hits may be made anywhere on the body, head or limbs. The sabre is the equivalent of the old cavalry sword and is used for cutting as well as thrusting. Fencers wear masks and thick waistcoats for protection from injuries which can occur during matches.

All modern Thoroughbreds can trace their ancestry back to three Arab stallions

The Thoroughbred is one of the fastest of all horses and is used largely for racing. Although there are thousands of Thoroughbreds, all proper Thoroughbreds throughout the world today can be traced back to one of three Arab stallions brought into Britain between 1689 and 1728. These three were the Byerley Turk, the Darley Arabian and the Godolphin Arabian, all of whom had exciting histories.

'Steeple chase' describes exactly what early steeplechases were

Steeplechasing became popular in the 18th century, when eager horsemen raced across country from one landmark to another. As the clearest landmarks were the local church steeples the sport became known as steeplechasing. When the sport became more organised fences, or hurdles, took the place of hedges.

Steeplechasing is also an athletic event for runners. The course is usually about 3,000 or 5,000 metres and has only a few, heavy hurdles set about the track.

The Grand National steeplechase course at Aintree.

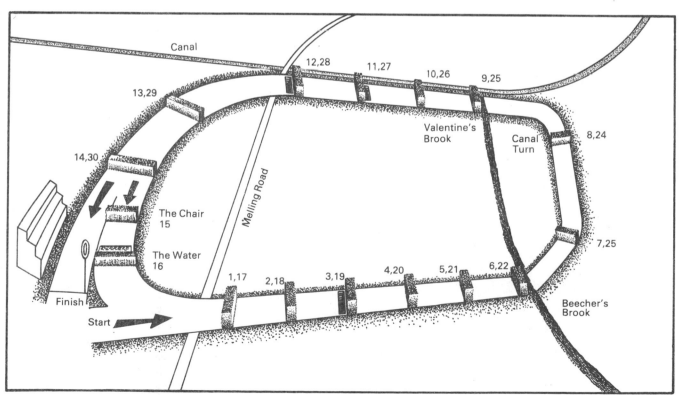

Quoits was once played with iron horseshoes

Quoits is a very old game indeed. It was played in ancient times using a metal ring to throw over an upright post from a distance. Horseshoes were often used instead of rings because they were more readily available but the game was the same, to drop the shoe over the post. Although quoits are now more usually played with rings of rope or rubber, there are still players who use old horseshoes.

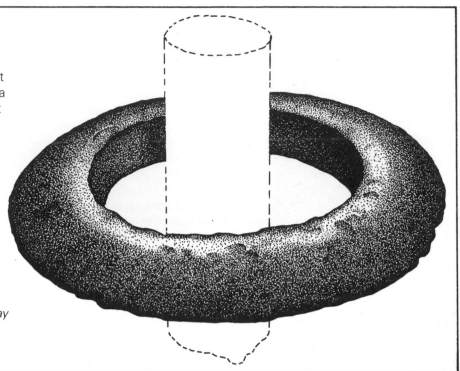

A cast iron quoit from the island of Islay in Scotland. It weighs around three pounds and is shown two thirds of its actual size.

Conjuring is one of the oldest forms of entertainment

In a way, priests of ancient days were conjurors, performing magic in their temples to impress the worshippers. But there were real conjurors, too, in ancient Egypt, Greece and Rome. One of the tricks most often mentioned in old records is called the Cups and Balls. It is still performed today. Three cups are turned upside down on the table and a ball is placed beneath one of them. When the cups are taken away, the ball has mysteriously moved from one cup to another, or else a second ball has appeared. The trick, of course, is to distract the audience's attention while the balls are moved or an extra one is added. It is a trick that has been puzzling audiences for several thousand years.

Playing cards originally came from the East

Playing cards were introduced into Europe by the Moors. Originally the cards came from China, India and Egypt. The first packs included Tarot or picture cards, which were used to tell fortunes according to the way in which they were laid out. Symbols included such gloomy characters as the Hanged Man. The 52-card pack was probably developed in France, using pikes, hearts, squares and trefoils for symbols. In England, these became spades, hearts, diamonds and clubs. The pictures were made double-headed in the 19th century, so that they could easily be seen upside down. The extra symbols on the corners of the cards were added to make it easier to see the cards when held closely in the hand. The number of games that can be played with a pack of playing cards is incredible, ranging from various simple games of patience for one person to contract bridge, a complicated card game for four.

Cards were once taxed

The tax on a deck of playing cards in England in the sixteenth century was two and sixpence – as much as many people earned each week.

'Knucklebones' were never made from human knuckles

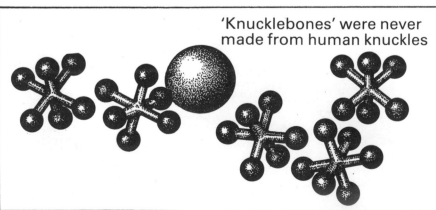

Knucklebones were the first form of dice and were used from very ancient times for gambling. They were usually taken from the anklebones of sheep and marked on four sides. Proper dice, carved out of bone to give an even, six-sided shape, were used by the ancient Egyptians in about 2000 BC, and also by the ancient Chinese. Greeks and Romans also enjoyed playing with dice.

Pall Mall is a game with bat and ball

Pall Mall is a famous London Street that lies close to St James's Park, where another road called The Mall runs down from Buckingham Palace to Trafalgar Square. The street was named after a game played in the time of Charles II, at the end of the 17th century. The name itself came from the Italian *palla*, which meant a ball, and *maglio*, which meant a mallet or bat. The aim of the game was to strike the ball with the mallet through an iron hoop in as few strokes as possible.

The ace of spades had the largest symbol of all the cards

Several centuries ago, packs of playing cards carried heavy taxes. The Ace of Spades was the card that was stamped to show that the tax on the pack had been paid. Today, the ace of spades usually carries the maker's trademark. The ace of spades is also regarded as the death card when a fortune teller uses cards.

The Romans played hopscotch

Hopscotch is one of the simplest of children's outdoor games and also one of the oldest. Even so, it needs quite a lot of skill. Several squares are marked out with chalk on the ground in a variety of patterns. The players throw a stone into each of the squares in turn. They have to hop and jump to reach the stone and then hop back to base, going through each square in the proper order. Marks of hopscotch games have been found scratched on stone in the remains of Roman towns.

The Japanese cut down billiard tables when they learned to play

When the Japanese learned to play billiards after they captured Singapore during the Second World War, they found that being smaller than the British, the tables were too high for them to play comfortably. So they cut six inches off each leg to make it easier for them. It is now one of the most popular indoor games in Japan with many thousands of billiard parlours being built each year.

People toss a tree-trunk for fun

The Highland Games are a sort of athletic meeting held in Scotland. They began as friendly competitions that were held at clan gatherings and now they are held regularly throughout Scotland and in many parts of the world where there are Scotsmen gathered together. Apart from the running races, hurdling and jumping, there is also throwing the hammer and tossing the caber. The hammer is an iron ball on the end of a wooden rod. The caber is the trunk of a small fir tree, about five metres (17 feet) long, which is held upright in the arms and then tossed so that it lands some distance away on the other end.

Plato played dice

Plato, the famous Greek philosopher was a keen diceplayer. The dice that he used were made of bone or ivory. He said that to be good at dice, it must be played from childhood, but should only be played for pleasure, not for money.

The game of dominoes is played throughout the world

Early domino pieces were of black ebony with white ivory dots, which resembled white eyes shining out of the black hood and mask that was known as a domino. Most dominoes have any number between nought and six at each end but some versions have anything up to nine or twelve dots and Eskimos gamble with even more dots on their pieces. The most ancient form of the game is probably from China, where the pieces have figures, like playing cards, as well as dots. The game was introduced into Europe in the 18th century.

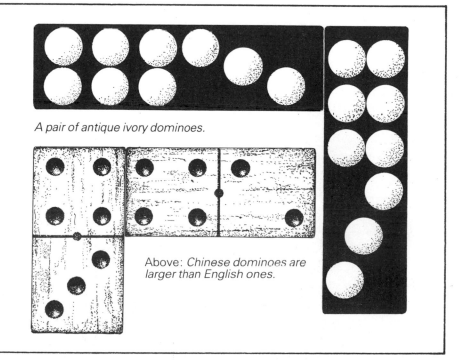

A pair of antique ivory dominoes.

Above: *Chinese dominoes are larger than English ones.*

The ancient game of polo was once used for training cavalry

Polo was played in Persia as long ago as the 6th century BC, when it was probably used to train horsemen in quick, skilful movement and control of their mount. It was not brought to Europe until the 19th century when many cavalry regiments adopted it as a sport. A small, light ball is used, which is hit by a narrow-headed, long-handled stick. Each player needs to own more than one horse, because each horse is used for only a short time during the game. The game is so fast that the horses soon tire.

Golf was made illegal because it interfered with national archery practice

It is said that golf began in northern Germany or Scandinavia but the earliest references to golf come from Scotland, where it has been popular since the middle of the 15th century. Indeed, it became so popular that King James II of Scotland passed a law forbidding his subjects to play golf because it interfered with their regular archery practice. Mary Queen of Scots later founded the royal golf course at St Andrews. It is believed that she first referred to the pupils of the game as 'cadets', which gave rise to the word 'caddies'.

There was only one event in the first Olympic Games

It is believed that the first Olympic Games were held 776 years before the birth of Christ, at a stadium at Olympia in southern Greece. They were then held every four years, in honour of the Greek god Zeus. At first there was only one race, down the length of the stadium, and the Games lasted only one day. Later, there were seven days of running, jumping, discus and javelin throwing, wrestling and chariot racing, with prizes of olive wreaths for the winners. These ancient Games were abolished in AD 393 by the Roman emperor, Theodosius. They were revived 1500 years later, in 1896, by a Frenchman, Baron Pierre de Coubertin. Since then, with a few interruptions, they have been held every four years in a different country each time.

There were no stumps in the earliest games of cricket

Some people say that cricket began in England, some say it was developed from the French game of croquet. Whatever the truth, a form of cricket was played in the time of Queen Elizabeth I, although there were probably no wickets. Instead, there were holes dug in the turf and the fielders had to get the ball into the hole before the batsman had finished running back to his crease. An English county cricket game was first recorded between Kent and Sussex in 1728 but even then there were only two stumps. A third was added in 1777. The game was revised and rules were set up by the MCC in London in 1788. Tests between England and Australia began in 1876. The Ashes were introduced in 1882, after England had suffered a disastrous defeat by Australia and one of the stumps was ceremoniously burnt.

The very first marathon runner died at the end of his race

When the Athenians defeated the invading Persians at the battle of Marathon, in 490 BC, they sent a messenger to run almost 37 kilometres (23 miles) to the city of Athens. He was sent to announce the victory and to warn the Athenians that the Persian fleet was sailing along the coast to launch another attack. The runner reached the city in time but collapsed and died as soon as he had given the news. The victorious Greek army also managed to get back to the city's harbour before the Persians landed, and the enemy fleet quickly sailed away again. The modern marathon race was begun in 1896, with the revival of the Olympics. Eventually it was set at a standard of a little more than 40 kilometres (25 miles).

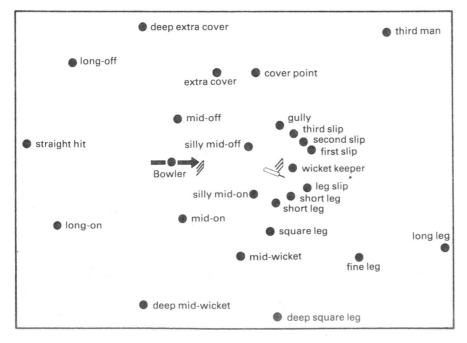

The fielding positions on a cricket field.

Marathon runner accepts a lift

At St Louis in 1904, the marathon was contested mainly by Americans and Greeks, who had to contend with a hilly 40 km course, extremely hot weather and dust and exhaust fumes thrown up by the cars accompanying them. An American, Fred Lorz, got cramp and accepted a lift in one of the cars. However the car broke down and he decided to run the remaining kilometres of the race. As he entered the stadium he was greeted by cheers and even accepted the winner's wreath before being disqualified. The real winner, Thomas Hicks (also American), almost fainted when he saw Lorz pass him, only reviving when he was told Lorz was no longer in the race. Lorz was not allowed to run for a year for his unsportsmanlike behaviour. However there was a bright aspect to the ending. Felix Carvajal, a Cuban postman who had had to beg his way to the Games, finished fourth. This was after a very unauspicious start and several stops on the way to chat to spectators.

The hero of the 1908 Olympics never won a medal

The Italian sweet-maker, Dorando Pietri, stole the hearts of the spectators although he never won a medal. His running career had started by accident when he ran a distance of 48 km in 4 hours to deliver a letter for his employer. At the end of the marathon he was one of the first runners to enter the stadium, but he most unfortunately started to run round the track the wrong way. He was turned round and started to go for the tape, but kept falling and being helped to his feet again; this meant that he had to be disqualified although he had touched the tape first. However he was given a special gold cup from Queen Alexandra of Britain.

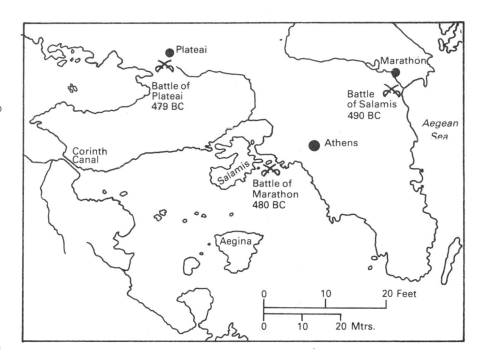

Above: *The original marathon was run from Marathon to Athens.*

A man who had been crippled won three Olympic titles

At the Games in Paris 1900, American Ray Ewry won three gold medals for all three standing-jump events. Although this is achievement enough for most people, it is particularly amazing when we realize that Ray Ewry had been paralysed as a child. He was confined to a wheelchair and told he would never walk again. But the young boy would not admit defeat. Instead he made up exercises for himself and practised them regularly. As a result he developed very powerful leg muscles and this combined with perfect timing made him the greatest standing jumper the world has ever seen. These events are no longer on the Olympic Games schedule, the triple jump having been abandoned in 1904 and the long and high standing jumps in 1912.

A Scottish athlete refused to run on a Sunday during the 1924 Olympics

In the Paris Olympics in 1924, Eric Liddell, a deeply religious Scotsman was due to run in the 100 metres and was one of the favourites for the event. However when he arrived in Paris he found that the heats were to be run on a Sunday and his religious principles would not let him compete. There was a great deal of pressure put on him by the committee of the British team, but he was quite adamant. A solution was eventually reached. It was decided that he should run in the 400 metres instead. It was a good decision, for Liddell won the Gold Medal and Britain won the 100 metres, too, when Harold Abrahams was first past the tape. Liddell eventually became a missionary in China where he died. He is still remembered in Scotland today as one of the greatest athletes that country has ever produced. The story of Liddell and Abrahams was made into a film called *Chariots of Fire*, which won the Oscar for the best film of 1981.

The length of the marathon was changed to suit a queen

Queen Alexandra of Britain was so keen to see the finish of the Olympic marathon of 1904 in London that the finishing line was moved 385 yards so that it was opposite the royal box.

William Shakespeare was born at Stratford-upon-Avon in 1564. Most people believe he was the greatest English dramatist and poet that ever lived. But some people think he could never have written all his plays by himself. They suggest that the plays were written by a team of people led by Shakespeare. Others suggest that Shakespeare did not write them at all, but that they were written by Francis Bacon, who lived at the same time.

William Shakespeare as the artist Droeshout sketches him for the first folio of his work. Shakespeare wrote 37 plays including Hamlet, Julius Caesar, Romeo and Juliet *and* A Midsummer-night's Dream *among those most often performed and* Timon of Athens, Cymbeline *and* Pericles *among those that are not so popular. He also wrote some long poems such as* Venus and Adonis, *as well as 154 fourteen-line sonnets.*

Don Juan is a fictitious character who has appeared in many stories and plays

Don Juan is a popular figure in fiction and romance, a light-hearted fellow who attracts women but never stays with any one of them for very long. He is an imaginary character who has probably existed in folklore for a long time. When he made his first appearance in a proper story in the Spanish play, *The Rake of Seville*, in 1630, he was a great deal more evil than he later became. In the play, he kills the father of one of his girlfriends when the father tries to interfere. When he later sees a statue of the man standing on his grave, he jokingly invites the dead man to dinner. Imagine his terror when the man appears and warns Don Juan that he, too, will soon die.

The original Pygmalion was a king of Cyprus

The story of Pygmalion is best known through Bernard Shaw's play of the same name, and the musical and film of *My Fair Lady*, which set the story to song. The original tale comes from classical myth. Pygmalion was King of Cyprus and a brilliant sculptor. He made a statue of his ideal woman and fell in love with it. He called it Galataea and begged the gods to give it life so that he might marry it. They granted his wish. In Shaw's play, and in *My Fair Lady*, the theme is matched by the poor, uneducated girl who is suddenly given money and an education and a place in society by a rich man who takes a bet that he can improve her and then falls in love with her having won his bet triumphantly and infuriating the girl in the process.

The first great playwright wrote nearly 90 plays but only seven have survived

Aeschylus was born in Athens in about 525 BC and is generally thought of as the first true playwright, using characters and dialogue instead of merely songs and choruses. He is sometimes called the 'Father of Greek Tragedy' because most of his plays have tragic plots, like 'The Persians' and the trilogy known as the 'Oresteia', about Agamemnon and his family. We know that Aeschylus wrote at least 80 plays and probably nearer 90 but only seven of them have survived and are still played today. There is an old and probably untrue story that Aeschylus was killed by an eagle who thought that his bald head was a stone and so dropped a tortoise on it to crack the shell so it could eat it.

Chaucer died before he finished *The Canterbury Tales*

Geoffrey Chaucer was born in about 1341 and is thought to be one of the greatest English poets and story-tellers. As well as being a writer, he had a busy career as a civil servant and also went on several important foreign missions on behalf of the king. His most famous work is *The Canterbury Tales*. This is a collection of stories which a group of imaginary pilgrims tell to each other on their way from the Tabard Inn in Southwark, London, to the shrine of St Thomas à Beckett in Canterbury. There is a Prologue, which introduces all the characters. This is followed by such famous stories as the Knight's Tale, the Wife of Bath's Tale, the Nun's Priest's Tale about the cock, the hen and the fox, and the bawdy Miller's Tale, a total of 22 complete tales. But there were originally meant to be 30 pilgrims, each of whom was to have told two stories, one going to and one returning from Canterbury – a huge collection of 60 tales that Chaucer never had time to finish before he died.

A playwright died after acting in one of his own plays

Molière was the name adopted by Jean Baptiste Poquelin, a French actor and playwright, during the reign of Louis XIV. His brilliant plays are both funny and serious. They laugh at people's habits and they also criticise them. Two of his best known plays are 'L' Avare' (The Miser) and 'Le Malade Imaginaire' (The Imaginary Invalid). Molière fell ill while acting in 'Le Malade Imaginaire' and died that same night, in 1673. His plays were so well constructed that they lose none of their sting in translation.

Ring a ring o'roses acts out the terror of the Plague

Ring a ring o'roses,
A pocket full of posies,
Atishoo! Atishoo!
We all fall down

This may sound innocent enough but it is a reminder of the terrible days of the London Plague of 1665. The 'ring o' roses' refers to the red rash and spots that appeared on people with the disease. Nosegays and posies of sweet-smelling flowers were carried to drive off the Devil and the Plague. But this did not often help. Soon the victims began to sneeze as well – 'Atishoo! Atishoo!' – and in a very short while they all fell down – dead! Thousands of people died in the crowded London streets and houses. The following year there was a dreadful fire that burnt out the heart of London and cleared the streets and happily, despite the fire's damage, the plague was over.

The novels of Charles Dickens were first written as serials

Charles Dickens's first successful novel was *Pickwick Papers*, which appeared in regular magazine instalments between 1836 and 1837. It was all about the adventures of an odd collection of characters that called themselves the Pickwick Club. All Dickens's novels were written at first in this serial fashion. This partly explains why each chapter ends on a high note to keep the reader in anticipation for the next issue of the magazine. As well as writing such famous novels as *Oliver Twist, Nicholas Nickleby, David Copperfield* and *Great Expectations*, Dickens later gave public readings and lectures in a highly dramatic style. He never finished his last book, the *Mystery of Edwin Drood*.

An illustration by Cruikshank of The Last Cabdriver, *one of Dickens' early stories.*

Robinson Crusoe really existed

One of the earliest novels in the English language and one of the best-loved stories is *Robinson Crusoe* by Daniel Defoe. It was published in 1719 and tells how Robinson Crusoe was shipwrecked on a lonely island where he lived for several years with his companion, Man Friday. Fifteen years before, a Scottish sailor, Alexander Selkirk, was abandoned on the island of Juan Fernandez, off the coast of Chile. The island was uninhabited. He lived there for more than four years, quite alone, until he was rescued by a British captain. The captain wrote an account of Selkirk's adventures. Defoe based his story on this account.

Jack and Jill went up the hill to bring the tide in to the shore

This well-known nursery rhyme:
Jack and Jill went up the hill
To fetch a pail of water;
Jack fell down and broke his crown
And Jill came tumbling after
it is thought to have represented the incoming and outgoing of the tide. Jack and Jill were drawn up the hill by the pull of the Moon, just as the tide came up the shore. But when the Moon's pull weakened and the tide went out, Jack and Jill went tumbling down the hill again. A similar image occurs in several languages.

Aesop was a slave who became an adviser to kings

Aesop was a slave who lived on the island of Samos in the early part of the 6th century BC and died in about 564 BC. He won his freedom and became an advisor to several kings, all because of the witty animal fables that he told, reflecting the ways of the world and men's weaknesses. His name was used for a collection of such fables put together about 200 years after his death, and again for a collection in verse published in the 1st century BC. It is quite possible that he did not originally tell all the fables in the collection. They had become a popular type of story and his name was convenient for putting to a general collection from various sources. Among the best known fables are 'King Log and King Stork' and 'The Fox and the Grapes'.

The author of Moby Dick was captured by cannibals

Herman Melville is best-known as the author of *Moby Dick*, a tremendous story of the terrible Captain Ahab and his great search for the white whale, Moby Dick. The book was published in 1851. Melville had first-hand experience of sailing ships. One of his greatest adventures happened when he jumped ship from the whaler *Acushnet* in the South Seas. He was captured by Taipi Indians on the island of Nukuhiva. These Indians had a reputation as cannibals but it seems that they treated Melville reasonably well. After a short time he escaped on a passing ship and had several more adventures. He was sometimes jokingly known as 'the man who had lived among cannibals'.

'Sour grapes' comes from an Aesop fable

This is a phrase from the fables of Aesop. It means that you pretend not to want something that you want very much but cannot get hold of. In the fable, a fox passes beneath a bunch of grapes and tries to reach them. He tries jumping again and again, imagining all the time how juicy and good they will taste but he still cannot reach them. In the end he walks away, muttering to himself that they were probably sour in any case and he never really wanted them.

It is dangerous to cry 'Wolf!'

'To cry "Wolf!"' is one of the many phrases that we get from the fables of Aesop. The story is about a young shepherd boy who was out guarding his sheep. He became bored and thought he would have some fun. So he ran to the village, crying 'Wolf! Wolf!'. The villagers ran out to help but, of course, there was no wolf. The boy did it a second time and again the villagers ran out but there was no wolf. The third time the boy cried 'Wolf! Wolf!' the villagers ignored his cries but this time the boy was serious and there was a real wolf and he got killed and eaten. The phrase therefore means, to give a false warning.

No one knows whether the great poet Homer ever existed

Homer is believed to be the author of the two great ancient Greek poems, the *Iliad* (about the fall of Troy) and the *Odyssey* (about the adventures of Odysseus after the fall of Troy). It is said that Homer was one of a group of wandering poets who lived in about the 8th century BC. But some people think that the stories of the *Iliad* and the *Odyssey* were collected from a number of poets and story-tellers and brought together under one name for convenience.

Virgil ordered the *Aeneid* to be destroyed when he died

Publius Vergilius Maro, better known as Virgil, was born in 70 BC and became one of the most famous of all Roman poets. He took seven years to write the *Georgics*, a long poem about the countryside. For the last 20 years of his life he worked on an even longer poem about the legendary history of Rome and the ancient hero *Aeneas*. This poem is called the Aeneid. It was partly written to flatter the Emperor Augustus, who gave presents to Virgil. In 19 BC, Virgil intended to spend three more years improving and altering the poem but he fell ill and died suddenly. Before he died, he ordered the unfinished work to be destroyed but Augustus and his friends saved the poem. The *Aeneid* is still considered to be one of the greatest works of literature.

There is a book with no 'e's in it

In 1939, Ernest Vincent Wright published a novel called Gadsby. Although there are more than 50,000 words in it, the only 'e's that appear are those in the author's name.

The manuscript for Ulysses was thought to be a spy's message

The handwriting of James Joyce, the Irish author, was so illegible, that when he sent the manuscript for his classic novel Ulysses to his publisher, the censor who, because England was at war with Germany at the time and went through the mail for security purposes, thought it was a coded message from a spy and confiscated the book. The manuscript was eventually released and has become one of the most influential books of the twentieth century, and Joyce is regarded as the leading prose innovator.

Mother Goose's Nursery Rhymes more than 300 years old

Mother Goose's Nursery Rhymes were first produced by the French story-teller Charles Perrault in 1697, but they were in fact a collection of all sorts of fairy stories that already existed in one form or another long before that. They got their name from the frontispiece in his book, which showed a picture of an old woman with several children and the title 'Mother Goose's Tales'. These were later translated into English and the collection was added to and changed many times. The collection includes such favourites as 'Sleeping Beauty', 'Red Riding Hood', 'Puss in Boots', 'Bluebeard', 'Cinderella' and 'Hop o'my Thumb' and have been favourites with children since they were published.

Egyptian 'writing' was not understood for thousands of years

The Egyptians used a form of picture writing known as hieroglyphics, or 'sacred carvings' which they painted and carved these pictures on the walls of temples and tombs. Later people could not understand these hieroglyphics until, in 1799, a remarkable stone was discovered near Rosetta, on the mouth of the River Nile. There were three different forms of writing on the stone, saying the same thing in three different languages – hieroglyphic, another form of Egyptian writing and Greek. But it was still not until another 23 years had passed that a young Frenchman called Jean François Champillon managed to translate the hieroglyphics by using the Greek and Egyptian versions that he already knew. Once the Rosetta stone had been translated, many other hieroglyphics could also be translated.

A famous story was written in a week to pay for a mother's funeral

Dr Samuel Johnson was a great 18th-century writer and talker. He is probably best known for the biography of him written by his friend and companion James Boswell. Boswell's *Life of Johnson* is full of the great man's ideas, opinions, prejudices and humour, and everyone knows him as a man who enjoyed food, drink and good conversation. One tale tells how he wrote the story of 'Rasselas' in a single week to pay for his mother's funeral. 'Rasselas' is a romance about a prince of Abyssinia who gets bored of pleasure and sets out to travel the world to find how others live. The story was published in 1759. It earned £100 for Dr Johnson which was more than enough to pay for the funeral.

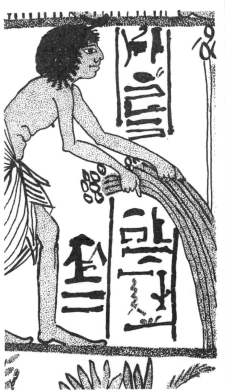

Part of an Egyptian tomb painting showing a farmer harvesting flax, and some typical Egyptian hieroglyphics.

The original Rip van Winkle was a teacher in Crete in the 6th century BC

The story of Rip van Winkle was told by Washington Irving in his 'Sketch Book' of 1819/20. It is about a hen-pecked fellow who goes for a walk in the Catskill Mountains and takes a drink from some strange people he meets. He wakes up 20 years later to find his home deserted and his fellow villagers astonished to see him. But they welcome him back and he lives to a ripe old age. The story was not entirely new. The Roman author, Pliny, mentioned a religious teacher from Crete, called Epimenides, who fell asleep in a cave when he was a boy and woke up 57 years later. He went on to live another 200 years or so, according to the story.

Mark Twain took his name from a paddle-steamer phrase

Mark Twain's original name was Samuel Langhorne Clemens. He was born in 1835 and grew up in the Mississippi. He worked for a while on the Mississippi paddle-steamers before he wrote his famous books *Tom Sawyer* and *Huckleberry Fin*. When the Mississippi pilots called out the depth of the water, they used the word 'twain' for 'two'. The call 'mark twain' meant that the water was up to the two-fathom mark on their lead-line, or depth-finding line.

A Scottish writer ended his life in Samoa

Robert Louis Stevenson was born in Edinburgh in 1850 and studied law at university. Because he was unhealthy and had trouble breathing, he spent much of his time travelling to Europe and America. Then he settled down in Scotland with his wife to write such famous books as *Treasure Island*, *Kidnapped* and *Dr Jekyll and*

Tweedledum and Tweedledee were two rival musicians

Tweedledum and Tweedledee are best known as the two fat men in Lewis Carroll's *Alice Through the Looking Glass*, which was published in 1872. But Carroll got the names from John Byrom, who lived about 100 years earlier. Byrom invented them in a mocking reference to two rival types of music which he said were virtually the same. The verb 'to tweedle' was already in existence and meant 'to produce a high, shrill musical sound'.

Tweedledum and Tweedledee by Tenniel.

Mr Hyde. His illness proved to be tuberculosis and in 1888 Stevenson sailed to the South Seas, still searching for fresh air to regain his health. He and his wife settled in Samoa, where he continued writing and became very interested in the life of the Samoans. He died in 1894, when he was only 44, and was buried on the island.

Dr Faust sold his soul to the Devil

The story of Dr Faust is about a man who sold his soul to the Devil in exchange for all the pleasures and treasures of the world. But in the end the Devil comes to claim Faust's soul and takes him off to Hell. The tale was first put into literature in Christopher Marlowe's play, *The Tragical History of Dr Faustus*, in about 1592. It was recreated by Goethe 200 years later in *Faust*. The original Dr Faust may well have been Johann Faustus, an astronomer who was born in Wurttemberg and died in about 1538. Many people believed that he had supernatural powers and could perform magic and make spells. Others said that he was merely a swindler who only pretended. Whatever the truth is, his name has come to symbolise the conflict between good and evil.

Who was the man in the iron mask?

Alexandre Dumas wrote a magnificent story called *The Man in the Iron Mask*. The hero lived during the reign of Louis XIV, and spent most of his life wearing an iron mask to hide his identity. There really was such a man but he wore a velvet mask, not an iron one. He died in the Bastille and was buried under a false name. No one knows who he was or why he was kept hidden. Some people think he was a treacherous but important foreign agent. Others think he was either the elder brother of Louis XIV, or his real father.

Mrs Beeton, the author of one of the world's most famous cookery books, died when she was only 29

Mrs Beeton took four years to write her famous *Household Management*. She was married with four children but died at the early age of 29, in 1865. Her book has remained one of the most popular and lasting of all cookery books, even though it is now more than 100 years old. It contains recipes for cooking, hints on running a large house, and advice on managing the servants, the nursery and the sick room.

Keats spent only five years writing poetry yet became one of the best-loved poets in the world

John Keats wrote some of the most beautiful poetry in the English language. It includes such poems as the odes 'to Autumn' and 'to a Nightingale'. Keats trained as a doctor but gave up medicine for poetry at the age of 21. He died of tuberculosis five years later. Tragically, he had already nursed his brother Tom while he lay dying of the same illness. Keats believed that the most important thing in the world was the beauty that he saw in almost everything around him. Many of his letters and earlier poems show that he had a good sense of humour as well.

Iceland once had the greatest literature in Europe

Iceland now has about the smallest population of any country in Europe, with just over 200,000 people. Long ago, the Vikings who lived there told marvellous stories of their homeland in Norway and of their adventures in Iceland and elsewhere. These stories, or 'sagas', were passed on by word of mouth until they were written down in the 12th and 13th centuries. The sagas are in prose and the most famous writer of them was Snorri Sturluson. One of his most exciting stories is about the hero Egil Skallagrimsson. Another well-known saga is about the burning of Njal and his family. Gudrun is one of the great heroines of the Icelandic sagas.

The first Encyclopedia Britannica had only three volumes

The oldest surviving encyclopedia is Pliny's *Natural History*, which was written in the 1st century AD. It has 37 volumes with (according to Pliny) 20,000 facts taken from 2000 books by more than 100 authors. There have been many encyclopedias since then.

One Chinese encyclopedia had more than 5000 volumes. One of the best-known modern encyclopedias, the Encyclopedia Britannica, was first published in 1768 in three volumes. New editions were brought out every now and then, extending to about 24 volumes plus one volume that is nothing but index.

A French dictionary took more than 50 years to write

The Académie Française was established in the middle of the 17th century by a small group of people who enjoyed discussing books and writers. The Académie was given the task of writing a dictionary of the French language and of keeping the dictionary up to date in order to preserve the language. The dictionary was begun in 1639 and completed in 1694, more than 50 years later. There are never more than 40 members of the Académie and they are all the most important French literary figures of the age.

A 'bestiary' was a book about strange and mythical creatures

A popular type of book in the Middle Ages was the 'bestiary'. This was a nature book with a difference because it was generally about strange and mythical creatures. Every story had a picture of the particular animal or bird and there was usually a moral at the end. Bestiaries are full of salamanders passing unharmed through fire, of phoenixes rising from the flames, strange sea beasts and camelopards (giraffes). The accounts of these animals were often based on rumour and the tales of travellers returning from far-off lands. Such stories were often exaggerated the more they were told. People today still believe in mythical creatures such as the yeti (abominable snowman) of the Himalayas, and the Loch Ness monster of Scotland.

An illustration from a twelfth century bestiary in the British Museum at London.

171

Man-Made Wonders

Stonehenge was probably an astronomical observatory

Many people believe that it was once possible to make extremely accurate astronomical observations by means of the great standing stones at Stonehenge, in England.

The circles of stones and the huge lintels were set up in several stages between 1800 BC and 1400 BC. Many of them were dragged long distances to the site. Originally Stonehenge may have been used as a kind of computer to record sunrise and sunset, moonrise and moonset, both at

mid-winter and in mid-summer. This was done by looking along certain alignmens of the stones. The most important alignment was from the centre through the 'heel' stone to the mid-summer sunrise. Four 'station' stones marked the points from which a number of other observations could be made.

France has its own 'Stonehenge'

The mysterious stones at Carnac, in Brittany, date from about the same time as the stones at Avebury and Stonehenge. No-one knows who set them up or precisely for what purpose. There are three separate systems of stones, each system broken at some point, and it is thought that perhaps at one time they all belonged to a single system. Many thousands of the stones have been removed for building in comparatively recent times. But the remainder are still an

impressive sight, standing together in long lines. One system has 10 lines about 1200 metres (1312 yards) long, one has 11 lines about 1000 metres (1093 yards) long and one has 13 lines about 800 metres (875 yards) long.

At Avebury, England, there were stone circles larger than Stonehenge

England is famous for the great prehistoric stones of Stonehenge, on Salisbury Plain. But not far away there is another circle, with more stones and covering a larger area. This is at Avebury, in Wiltshire,

which once had an outer circle of 100 stones up to 50 tons each in weight, with a steep ditch and bank more than 400 metres (1312 feet) in diameter. Two smaller circles, each with 30 stones and a diameter of more than 100 metres (328 feet), and possibly a third circle, stood inside the great circle. An avenue of vast stones linked Avebury with another monument nearly 1.5 kilometres (1 mile) away. The stones were set up in about 2000 BC and were probably used for religious rites by the ancient people. Later, a village was built within the circle and many of the stones were used for building.

172

A butterfly hunter discovered a beautiful lost city

In 1861 a French naturalist, Henri Mouhot, was searching for butterflies in the jungles of present-day Cambodia, when he came across the lost city of Angkor Wat. It contained the largest building in Asia. From the ninth to the fourteenth centuries Angkor was the capital of the Kymer empire. The city stretched more than 40 square miles into the jungle and was home for more than two million people. In the fourteenth century, the Kymers were beaten in battle and their capital was sacked. They fled into the jungle and the town became overgrown with plants and trees, and totally deserted except for jungle animals, until Mouhot came across it. The main temple at Angkor is the largest religious structure in the world. It has an amazing network of galleries, colonnades, courtyards and stairways and is crowned by five acorn-shaped domes, the tallest of which is 76 metres (250 feet) high. To get to Angkor Wat, tourists must travel across a long stone causeway, over a moat. Each side of the causeway is guarded by 54 stone statues. At the end of the causeway, a large entrance tower leads into the temple. It is extraordinary that such a breathtaking building should have remained undisturbed for so long.

The foundations of one door are worth more than twenty million pounds

The fortress of Purandhar near Poona in India looks like an ordinary Indian fortress, but the gateway to it is built on a foundation of solid gold. The building was begun in 1290 under the orders of the Rajah of Bedar. Soon afterwards the engineers told him that the place where the gateway was to be built was too marshy to support its weight and that it would sink into the ground; so the Rajah had two large cavities dug into the earth and into them 50,000 gold bricks. The plan worked for the gate still stands today. At today's price of gold, the foundations are worth more than £20,000,000.

The Great Pyramid of Cheops is the largest tomb in the world

The Great Pyramid was built more than 5,000 years ago, and is rated as one of the seven wonders of the world. Each of the stones weighs around two-and-a-half tons and was quarried many miles away from the other side of the River Nile. They were dragged on sledges and then pulled up a ramp to be put into position. This had to be done more than two-and-half million times before the pyramid was completed. The temple probably took up to thirty years to build and it required more than 100,000 men to build it.

There was a pyramid built of human skulls

Tamerlane was the son of an obscure chieftain who lived near Samarkand in Central Asia. Despite his background Tamerlane set out to create the mightiest empire the world has ever seen. It stretched from the Ganges in India to what is today Russia. Tamerlane was a ruthless tyrant. He felt nothing about destroying huge cities and putting the citizens to death. At Isfahan he built a pyramid out of the skulls of 70,000 of his victims. He went even further at Baghdad when he used 90,000 skulls and at Delhi he used 100,000 skulls to build his ghastly pyramid. He was originally called Tamar, but was crippled by an arrow when he was quite young. He came to be called Timur (the name he was given)-i-Leng which means Timur the lame. This has gradually been changed to Tamerlane. Christopher Marlow wrote a famous play based on this character.

Giant heads guard an isolated island in the middle of the ocean

The first European to land on Easter Island, in the South Pacific, was a Dutch admiral called Jacob Roggeven, in 1722. There he found a primitive, dark-skinned Polynesian people surrounded by about 600 giant statues. The heads had long ears and faces quite unlike the native Polynesians. The heads measured 3.6-6.1 metres (12-20 feet) tall, with blocks of red volcanic stone, like hats, standing 1.8 metres (6 feet) high on top. Each statue weighed about 50 tons and had been cut laboriously with hand-held stones from the solid rock and then heaved into place by manpower. Most of the statues date from the 13th and 14th centuries and they are believed to have been associated with religious and burial customs but no-one knows for sure, not even the natives. Many of the statues have fallen over but some still stand.

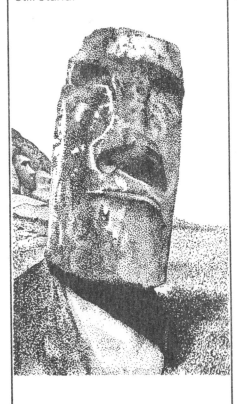

One of the statues on Easter Island.

One of the greatest Crusader castles still stands almost unchanged

Not surprisingly, most of the castles of the Middle Ages are now in ruins, but one of the greatest of all still stands. It is on a hilltop in the Syrian desert, commanding the route from Damascus to Jerusalem. It is the Crusader castle of *Krak des Chevaliers,* built and rebuilt during the 12th and 13th centuries to withstand the most formidable of Saracen sieges. It could, if necessary, support a whole garrison for a year without fresh supplies. The strong natural position on top of a hill is further strengthened by a zigzag, defensible approach path, a double set of walls and towers, ramparts of rubble and stone in parts up to 24 metres (80 feet) thick. The castle was so strong and so well defended that it took a trick to drive the Crusaders out in the end; in 1271, the sultan Baybars sent a forged message by pigeon from the Christian leaders, telling the soldiers to surrender.

The underwater cable that joins together Canada and Australia is more than 12,000 kilometres (6250 miles) long

This telegraph cable is not, in fact, one continuous length of cable, as it is broken by a number of relay stations to boost the signal at various islands on the route. The longest unbroken stretch of cable runs 5800-kilometres (3625-miles) from Vancouver Island to Fanning Island in the Pacific. The first transatlantic cable was laid in 1857-1858 by an American and a British warship, each of which carried half the cable. They spliced it together in the middle of the Atlantic and then sailed back in opposite directions, unloading the cable as they went. This cable did not last for long, however, and the *Great Eastern* laid another in 1866, having failed to do so at first.

The famous tower of Pisa began to lean even before it was completed

The leaning tower of Pisa, in Italy, was begun in 1174, as a bell tower, or campanile, for the nearby cathedral. The foundations were laid in sand and only three of the eight storeys were finished before it began to lean. The plans were altered to compensate for the problem and the building was eventually completed in 1350. The 54.5-metre (179-foot) tower has continued to lean a little more each century and it is now between 4.9 and 5.2 metres (16-17 feet) out of the perpendicular. Experts believe that whatever they do, the tower will steadily go on leaning over until one day it falls.

Galileo dropped stones from the tower, and by timing their falls he formulated his laws of motion.

A ship sailing through the Panama Canal, from the Atlantic to the Pacific, is actually sailing *east*

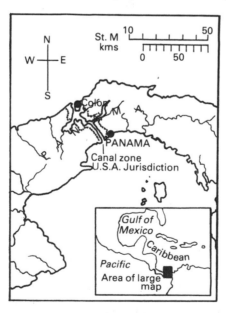

A careful look at a large map of Panama, between North and South America, will show you that the isthmus runs roughly horizontally from east to west. The Atlantic entrance to the Canal is about 20 miles farther west than the Pacific entrance, so that a ship going through the Canal from east to west will in fact be sailing east – the direction from which it has come. Attempts to build a canal in the 19th century were defeated by yellow fever. The modern canal was not officially opened for regular use until 1920. It is a little more than 50 miles long and has three locks stepping up from the Atlantic and three locks stepping down to the Pacific. Each is about 1000 feet long and 110 feet wide. About 15,000 feet sail through the canal each year and the number is constantly increasing.

Left: *The Panama Canal. To navigate the canal a ship must rise or fall more than 26 metres (85 feet). To allow this to happen, large locks were built. Ships travelling west are first of all raised to the level of an artificial lake, Lake Gatun.*
They then sail along to the canal at Lake Miraflores which is over 330 metres (1000 feet) long. At the Pacific end, the ship is then lowered to sea level at another lock. If a ship is travelling east, the process is reversed.

The Suez Canal was first used more than 3000 years ago

The ancient Egyptians dug a canal to join the Mediterranean with the Red Sea, thousands of years ago. It did not follow quite the same route as today's canal which runs directly from the Mediterranean across the narrow neck of land to Suez. Instead, it ran from the River Nile across to where the Bitter Lakes now are and thence down to the Red Sea. Romans and Arabs also made use of this route but eventually it was abandoned. In 1859 a French engineer, Ferdinand de Lesseps, began work on the modern canal. It took 10 years to build and is a little more than 160 kilometres (100 miles) long and about 46 metres (150 feet) wide. It was once believed that there was a difference in the levels of water in the Mediterranean and the Red Sea but this is not so – there are no locks in the Suez Canal. The canal was closed for a long time following the Suez crisis of 1956, which, indirectly, led to the growth of super-oil-tankers.

Hamlet's castle of Elsinore still stands guard over the entrance to the Baltic Sea

Elsinore is best known as the grim castle where Shakespeare set his play *Hamlet*. This is the story of the Prince of Denmark who hears his father's ghost telling him to revenge his murder. The castle has an important place in real history, too. It stands on the north-east corner of the Danish island of Zealand, looking out at the coast of Sweden only five kilometres (three miles) away across the narrow entrance to the Baltic. The castle guarded that entrance for many years and was able to demand payment from ships that passed through. The Kronborg castle still stands there, not far north of Denmark's capital of Copenhagen. One of the best films of *Hamlet* was made by a Rumanian director and was shot on location at Elsinore.

The World's Fair was once held in a giant greenhouse with 300,000 panes of glass

Every few years a capital city holds a World Fair, to which exhibitors come from all over the world to display their goods. In recent times, Tokyo, Montreal and New York have all played host to such a fair. One of the first of these great fairs was held in London in 1851, early in the reign of Queen Victoria. There were 13,000 exhibitors, half of whom were foreign. Joseph Paxton, a self-taught architect, designed the exhibition hall for London's Hyde Park. It was the largest glass building ever made, with nearly 300,000 panes of glass and 3300 columns supporting three storeys. After the exhibition, it was taken down and re-erected in south London, where it became known as the Crystal Palace. It was destroyed by fire in 1936.

Two thousand five hundred kilometres of highway were built in only six months

During the Second World War, the Americans feared that the Japanese might approach North America along the Aleutian Islands. This would threaten sea communications between the States and US bases in Alaska so an overland road link was planned to go through Canada to Fairbanks, Alaska. It was begun in the spring of 1942. Ten thousand engineers from the US Army, as well as 4,000 civilians, built more than 12 kilometres (seven-and-a-half miles) of road a day through forests and marshes and over rivers, to finish the road in November of the same year. By the following spring, many of the temporary bridges had been washed away but they were replaced by more permanent constructions. The Alaska Highway finally linked up with the Pan American Highway which runs North to South America.

The Alaska Highway.

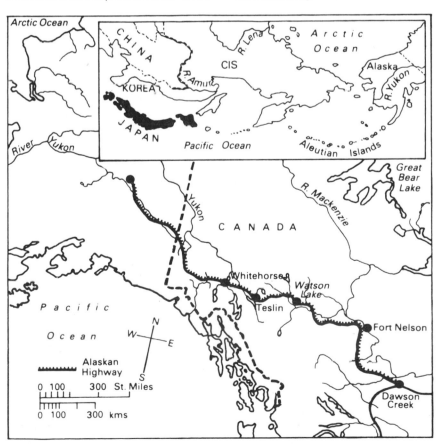

This famous lighthouse was one of the wonders of the ancient world. It was built in the time of the pharaoh Ptolemy II in the 3rd century BC, on the island of Pharos near Alexandria. Estimates of its height vary but it was at least 130 metres (426 feet). Its light was said to have been visible from a ship at least 65 kilometres (40 miles) out into the Mediterranean. The lighthouse was partly destroyed at the end of the 8th century AD but some of its remains were still visible even in the 14th century AD.

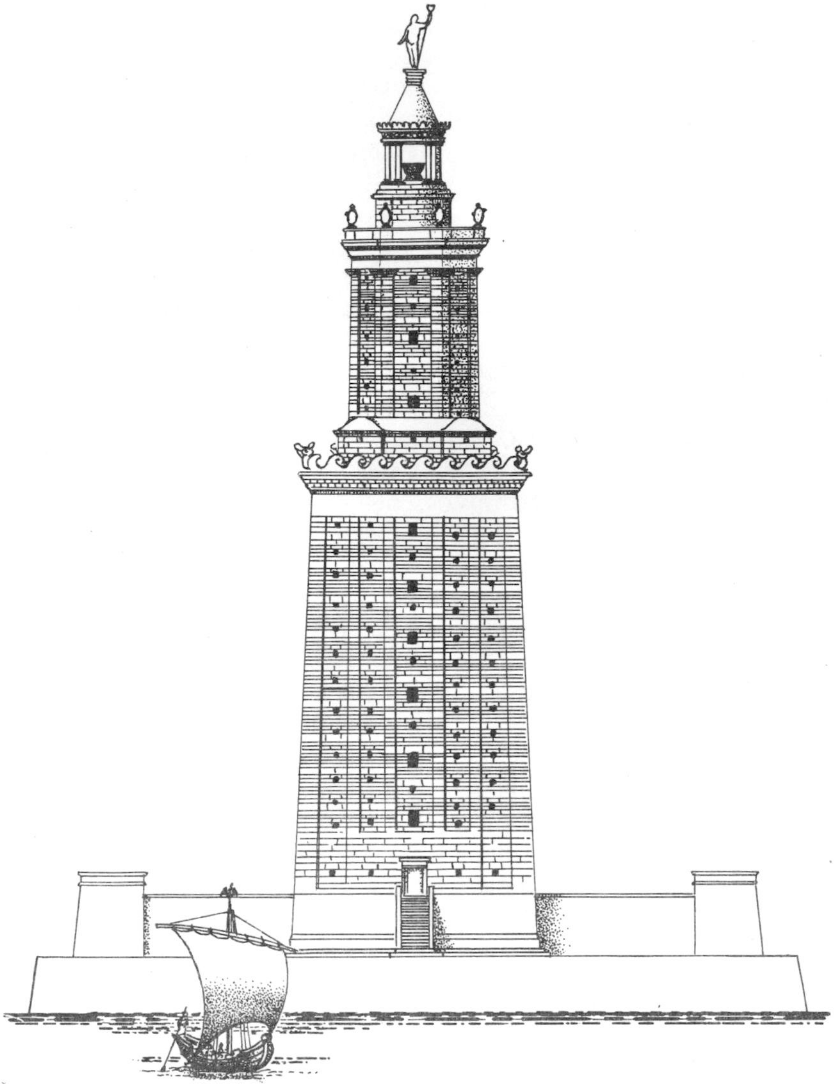

Left: *An artist's impression of the lighthouse of Pharos which was one of the seven wonders of the ancient world. The others were the Hanging Gardens of Babylon, the Great Pyramid of Khufo, the Statue of Zeus at Olympia, the Temple of Artemis at Ephesus, the Mausoleum at Halicarnassus and the Colossus Rhodes. Only the Great Pyramid survives today.*

The Great Pyramid is as tall as a modern skyscraper

Four and a half thousand years ago it was the custom of the pharaohs of ancient Egypt to have themselves buried in enormous pyramids. The greatest of these is the Great Pyramid of Cheops, or Khufu, at Giza, about five miles from Cairo, built about 2700 BC. Its base covers (13 acres), it is more than 480 feet high, contains 2,300,000 blocks of stone (ranging from 2½ to 15 tons) and took 100,000 men 20 years to build, without the help of any wheeled transport. The entire pyramid was once faced with polished limestone but that has long since been stripped off. Great care was taken to seal off the pharaoh and his treasure safely in his chamber deep in the centre of the pyramid but these efforts did not prevent the chamber being robbed and now only the tomb remains, a gigantic monument to a proud and powerful man.

A 3200-year-old temple was sawn down and rebuilt so that it would not be flooded

When the Aswan dam was built across the Nile and completed in the 1960s, the waters of the river began to rise and threatened to drown some of the marvels of ancient Egypt. Chief among these was the rock temple of the pharaoh Ramesses II. It was built in the solid rock 3200 years ago, and was guarded by statues of the pharaoh, 20.4 kilometres (67 feet) high, also cut out of the solid rock. The only way to save the temple was to saw it into great blocks, some of them weighing up to 30 tons, and to raise it piece by piece several hundred metres up the cliff face. There it was reassembled out of reach of the water. This extraordinary engineering feat took four whole years to complete, and even then only just in time. Now the statues sit as serene as ever, with a lake at their feet.

Tower Bridge opens up

Tower Bridge, on the River Thames in London, divides across the middle and swings upward to allow ships to pass between its towers.

The Wailing Wall is all that remains of a great temple

The Romans destroyed King Herod's Great Temple in Jerusalem in AD 70. All that was left was a part of the old wall, known to Jews as the 'Western Wall'. Since they had previously gone on pilgrimage to the Temple, they continued to pray at the 'Western Wall', and as many of their prayers were in the form of grief at the loss of the Temple the wall came to be known as the 'Wailing Wall'.

The Sydney Opera House cost ten times more than was planned

Sydney Opera House stands on a peninsula jutting out into Sydney Harbour. It can be seen from every side, and from above as the shore slopes up steeply behind it. The roof is made of ten shells, the highest 75 metres (221 feet) above the water. When work started in 1959 it was estimated that the cost should be £5,000,000. When Queen Elizabeth II opened it in 1973, the cost had soared to more than £50,000,000. Even then everything was not finished. The access roads had still to be built and the car parks had still to be paved. Another £5,000,000 was to be needed to meet the final cost.

The capital of Brazil did not exist twenty years ago

Until just after the Second World War Rio de Janeiro was the capital of Brazil, but the Brazilians decided to build an entirely new capital. They spent millions of dollars clearing a site in the jungle and building roads into it, and then created office blocks, factories and houses for the hundreds of thousands of people who were to work there.

A greenhouse builder built a glass palace

In 1850, the British decided to hold a great exhibition to show the world what its industries were capable of producing. Prince Albert, Queen Victoria's husband, became patron and the committee began to look for a suitable building to house this 'Great Exhibition'. 250 plans were submitted but they were all too costly or impractical. Then a self-taught architect who made a living designing and building greenhouses, bridges, reservoirs and even a gasworks, promised to design and plan the construction of the building in nine days. He was called Joseph Paxton. The building was to be 33 million cubic feet. For the first two days he visited the Menai Straits where Robert Stephenson was supervising the building of the Britannia Bridge. On the third day he sketched on an ink blotter, a rough plan of the building that was eventually built. The final designs were delivered within the promised time. It was 1848 feet long and 450 feet wide. 205 miles of iron bars were needed along with 293,655 panes of glass to cover an area of 900,000 square feet, and 600,000 cubic feet of timber. A vast iron framework was assembled without any scaffolding as all the girders supported each other. When the project started there were 39 men working at the site in Hyde Park in Central London. Within a few months, the work was proceeding at such a fast rate that the workforce had expanded to more than 2,000. The glazing was made easier by the clever use of trolleys, in one week 80 men managed to fit 18,000 panes of glass. The building was complete within eight months. When the exhibition opened in 1851, the Crystal Palace became one of the most famous of all the things that could be seen there. After the exhibition had closed, the whole structure was taken down and moved to South London. It was constantly used until 1936 when it was destroyed by fire.

The Eiffel Tower was once the tallest building in the world

The Eiffel Tower, with its framework of struts reaching up into the sky towards a sharp point, is one of the best-known symbols of Paris, where it stands. Alexandre-Gustave Eiffel built it in 1889 for the Paris Exhibition of that year. It was the tallest building of its time and now, with its TV aerial on top, it measures 322 metres (1060 feet). There are several taller buildings in the world today but the Tower still provides a magnificent view over Paris and is well worth visiting.

Weird and wonderful faces spout water from the roofs of churches

Gargoyles are stone-carved gutters that project from the walls of churches and cathedrals so that the water from the roof is made to fall well clear of the building. Stone masons in the Middle Ages often carved these gutters in the shapes of strange animals with grim or funny faces and so designed them that the water from the roof poured out of their mouths. The word *gargoyle* is an old French word for 'throat'. Some modern churches and buildings made of stone still have these gargoyles and sometimes the gargoyles are shaped like the faces of the people who have worked on the building or the people who have ordered the building to be made.

Flight

The first cross-Channel balloon flight was made by men stripped to their underpants

The first manned flight in a balloon took place over Paris in 1783. Two years later, the Frenchman, Jean-Pierre Blanchard, attempted to fly across the English Channel for the first time, going from England to France. He persuaded a wealthy American, John Jeffries, to pay all his expenses and to join him on the flight. The 'car' or basket beneath their balloon had flapping wings and a rudder but these were jettisoned nine-and-a-half kilometres (six miles) out from Dover when they began to float dangerously close to the sea. They continued to fly perilously low. To lighten their load Blanchard threw away his coat, Jeffries did the same. This was not enough and the two men had to take off their trousers. Their efforts were successful. They landed 19 kilometres (12 miles) inland, in the Forest de Felmores, wearing only their underpants, they had with them only a bottle of brandy and the first-ever letters to be carried by air – 'air mail' was born.

The first successful flight of a heavier-than-air machine took place in 1903

The Wright Flyer achieved the first successful flight of a heavier-than-air machine in 1903. Its engine was built by the Wright Brothers and their talented mechanic, Charlie Taylor. The engine had four water-cooled cylinders set in line, lying horizontally, a large flywheel and two gearwheels to drive the pusher propellers in opposite directions. The Wrights reported that the engine was 12 horsepower but it is believed to have been nearer 13 horsepower.

Other people besides Orville and Wilbur Wright had been practising with gliders for many years but these two brothers were the first to produce a plane that made a successful powered flight. On 17th December, 1903, their biplane *The Flyer*, flew for 12 seconds at a height of about three metres (10 feet).

The first drawings of helicopters are nearly 500 years old

The painter and inventor, Leonardo da Vinci, made the first technical drawings for a helicopter in about AD 1500, but he did not have the necessary power to drive the machine. In fact, toy helicopters, later called Chinese tops, had existed before Leonardo's time. The toy had four blades on a spindle, which sat in a hollow holder. A string was wound round the spindle and passed through a hole in the holder. When the string was pulled, the toy went flying into the air. The first powered helicopter to rise off the ground in free flight was designed by Paul Cornu in 1907. It rose about 30 centimetres (one foot) and hovered for about 20 seconds. The first really successful helicopter was produced by Igor Sikorsky at the beginning of the Second World War.

The first attempts at powered flight were made in the 19th century

W. S. Henson made a model steam engine for an airplane as early as 1843, and in 1852 Henri Giffard's steam-powered airship cruised at about 11 km/h (7 mph). Coal-gas taken from the envelope of the airship itself was tried in one engine. Electric motors, clockwork and compressed air were tried in other engines. In 1888 a Daimler petrol engine was used to drive an airship.

The Italians first used aircraft for warfare

Balloons had been used for observation purposes in the American Civil War, for carrying despatches out of Paris during the Franco-Prussian War of 1870-1871, and by the British in South Africa.

But the first time that heavier-than-air machines were used for war was by the Italians against the Turks in Tripolitania in the war of 1911-1912. French Bleriots and Nieuports were used for reconnaissance, along with non-rigid airships which dropped some grenades.

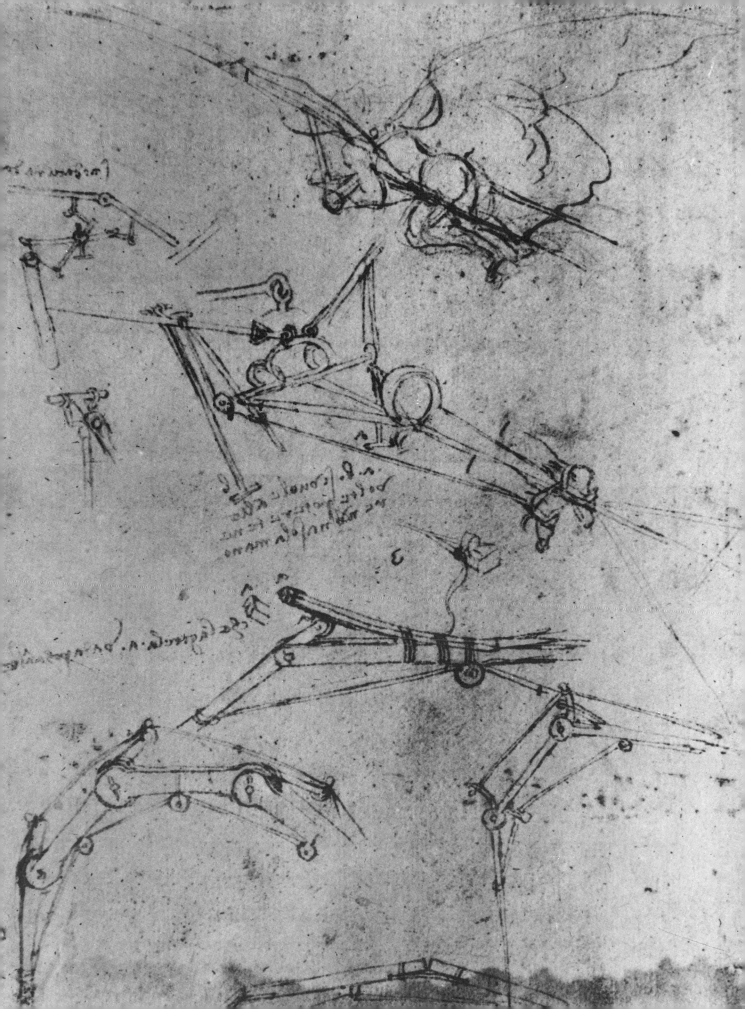

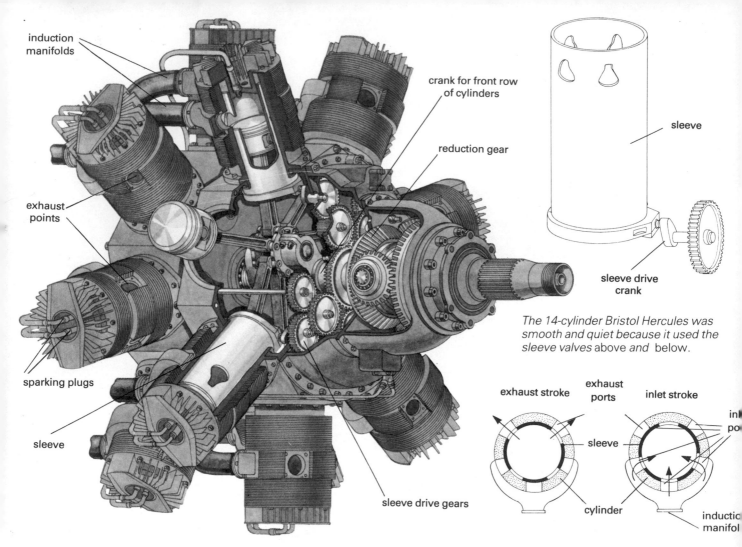

induction
manifolds

crank for front row
of cylinders

reduction gear

sleeve

exhaust
points

sleeve drive
crank

*The 14-cylinder Bristol Hercules was
smooth and quiet because it used the
sleeve valves above and below.*

sparking plugs

exhaust stroke

exhaust
ports

inlet stroke

inl
po

sleeve

sleeve

cylinder

sleeve drive gears

cylinder

inductic
manifol

Before 1917, most First World War aircraft had rotary engines

In a rotary engine the cylinders are fixed radially around crankshaft and rotate together with the propeller. The Gnome rotary engine, designed by the Seguin brothers of France, appeared in 1908. It was reliable and had a good power-to-weight ratio. The first design had five cylinders but later versions had seven cylinders. These were self-cooled through fins attached to the cylinders. Castor oil was added to the fuel to act as a lubricant. Unfortunately the oil often sprayed over the pilot sitting behind the engine. The Gnome and other engines of its type were used in almost 80 per cent of First World War aircraft before 1917 but were replaced by more sophisticated engines when the war finished in 1919.

Radial engines powered many aircraft in the Second World War

Air-cooled radial engines have their cylinders arranged radially around the crankshaft, in much the same manner as the rotary engine. In a radial engine, however, the cylinders do not turn with the propeller. They remain fixed. One of the best-known radial engines was the Bristol Hercules, which was first produced in the late 1930s. It was widely used in British aircraft during the Second World War. A later version developed more than 2000 horsepower. The 14-cylinder Hercules was one of the first engines to use sleeve valves. This made for a smoother and quieter engine. The more powerful 18-cylinder Bristol Centaurus was used in many fighters and large aircraft after the war but was gradually phased out.

The turbojet is the basic form of jet engine

Air is drawn in at the front of the engine and compressed by a compressor. The compressed air is mixed with fuel for combustion. The hot gases expand and produce thrust at the rear of the engine, having turned the blades of a turbine which is attached to a shaft that drives the compressor at the front. Turbojets are good for high speeds and high altitude planes.

Turbofans have propeller-like fans added to the front or rear of the turbines

Additional thrust can be obtained from air that by-passes the main engine and is accelerated by the fan. This air can be deflected back on landing to reverse the engine thrust to reduce the landing run.

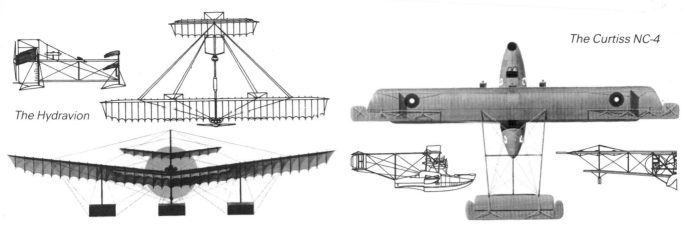

The Curtiss NC-4

The Hydravion

The first seaplane flew in 1910

The first airplane to take off from water was developed by Henri Fabre of France. His first Hydravion, as he called it, was built in 1909 but never took off. The second Hydravion was a back-to-front design with the 'tail' at the front and the main wings and the pusher propeller at the rear. It was extremely flimsy, with a couple of wooden girders for a fuselage,

three small floats and sail-like flying surfaces. The Hydravion flew 500 metres (1640 feet) near Marseilles on 28th March, 1910.

The first flying boat crossed the Atlantic in 1919

Glenn Curtiss developed the flying boat in America. He achieved his first success on 26th January, 1911, with a pusher biplane on a central float with two outriggers. Curtiss immediately saw the

usefulness of the flying boat to the US Navy. His hopes of flying the Atlantic in 1914 were frustrated by the First World War. In 1919 three NC (Navy Curtiss) flying boats attempted a crossing with navy support. Navy destroyers were placed at 80 kilometre-intervals to assist with radio, smoke and flares for guidance. *NC-4*, piloted by Lt-Commander Read, left Newfoundland on 16th May and reached Lisbon on 27th May, after refuelling in the Azores.

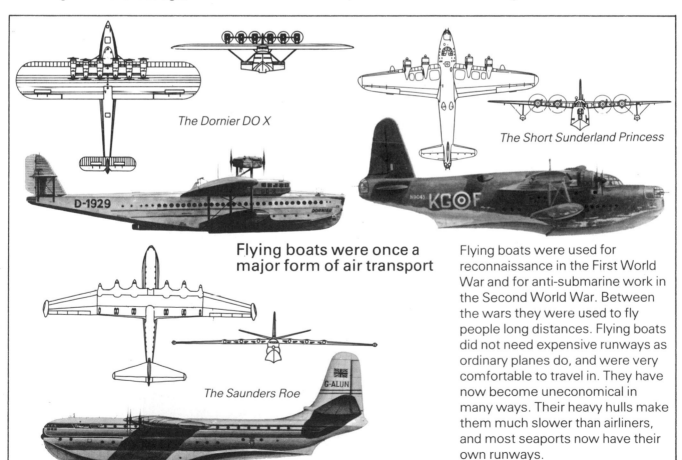

The Dornier DO X

The Short Sunderland Princess

Flying boats were once a major form of air transport

The Saunders Roe

Flying boats were used for reconnaissance in the First World War and for anti-submarine work in the Second World War. Between the wars they were used to fly people long distances. Flying boats did not need expensive runways as ordinary planes do, and were very comfortable to travel in. They have now become uneconomical in many ways. Their heavy hulls make them much slower than airliners, and most seaports now have their own runways.

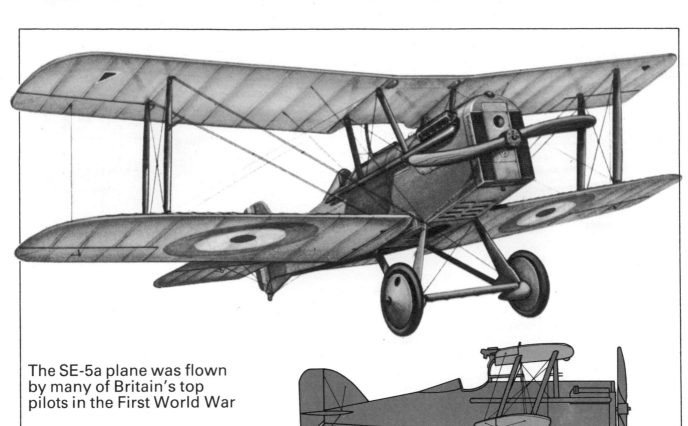

The SE-5a plane was flown by many of Britain's top pilots in the First World War

The Royal Aircraft Factory SE-5a was not as agile as the Sopwith Camel but it provided a fast and stable gun platform. It was first delivered in June, 1917, and 5205 planes of the SE-5/5a type were built. SE stands for Scout Experimental.

Type: single-seat fighter
Engine: a variety, including the
   200 hp Wolseley W.4A Viper
Armament: one fixed synchronised
   .303 inch Vickers machine gun
   and one .303 Lewis machine
   gun, with 4 x 25 lb Cooper
   bombs
Speed: 203 Km/h at 3048 metres
   (126 mph at 10,000 feet)
Climb: 13 minutes, 15 seconds to
   3048 metres (10,000 feet)
Ceiling: 5334 metres (17,500 feet)
Endurance: 2¼ hours
Weight: 694 Kg empty, 929 Kg
   loaded (1,531 lbs empty,
   2,048 lbs loaded)
Span: 8 metres (26 ft 7.4 ins)
Length: 6.4 metres (20 ft 11 ins)
Height: 2.9 metres (9 ft 6 ins).

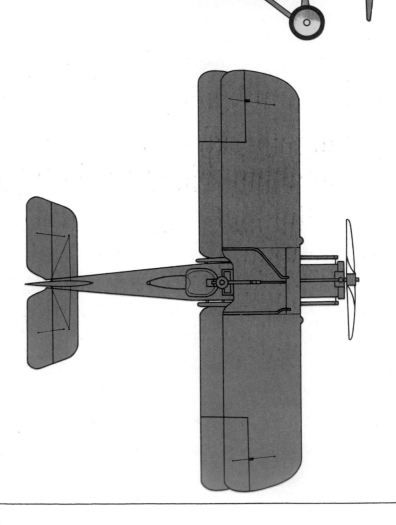

Many fighter pilots in the First World War became known as 'aces'

An 'ace' was a First World War pilot who had scored more than a certain number of victories over other aircraft. The French demanded five victories before calling a pilot an ace. The Germans demanded ten victories. The greatest ace of the war was Manfred von Richthofen, the Red Baron, who claimed 80 victories before he was eventually shot down and killed. Fonk of France, Mannock of Britain and Bishop of Canada all claimed more than 70 victories.

When propeller-driven planes were fitted with guns the pilots were in danger of shooting off their own propellers

In the earliest First World War planes, pilots had the problem of how to fire their guns without shooting off their propellers. Solutions varied from fitting the gun in front of the propeller to fitting the propeller behind the pilot. In the spring of 1915 a French pilot, Roland Garros, fitted steel deflectors to the blades of his propeller to solve this problem. On 19th April he was captured by the Germans the lead in air warfare. The onslaught became known as the 'Fokker scourge'. Other Fokkers included the Fokker Dr 1 triplane, which was the favourite machine of Manfred von Richthofen, and the Fokker D. VII, which was probably the best of the German First World War fighters.

Germans. His plane was given to the Dutch designer Anthony Fokker to copy. Instead, Fokker came up with a different idea. He designed an interruptor gear. This synchronised the firing of the gun so that it stopped as the propeller blade passed in front of it. He fitted this interruptor to his Fokker E.1 monoplane. Fokker was one of the greatest aeroplane designers of his or any other day. As well as being remembered as a designer of the fighter aircraft, he also developed a superb family of transport aircraft when the war ended.

The 'Fokker scourge' took place in 1915-1916

The Fokker E.1 (Eindekker, or monoplane) destroyed its first victim using its new interruptor gear in August 1915. During the winter months of 1915-1916, the Fokkers E.I, E.II and E.III gave the

Fokker Dr 1
Engines: one 110 hp Le Rhone rotary
Armament: two 7.92mm Spandau machine guns
Speed: 165 km/h (102 mph)
Initial climb: 220 m/min
Ceiling: 6,100m (20,013ft)
Range: 210km (130 miles)
Loaded weight: 586kg (1292lb)
Span of upper wing: 7.19m (23ft)
Length: 5.77m (18ft 8in)
Height: 2.95m (9ft 6in)

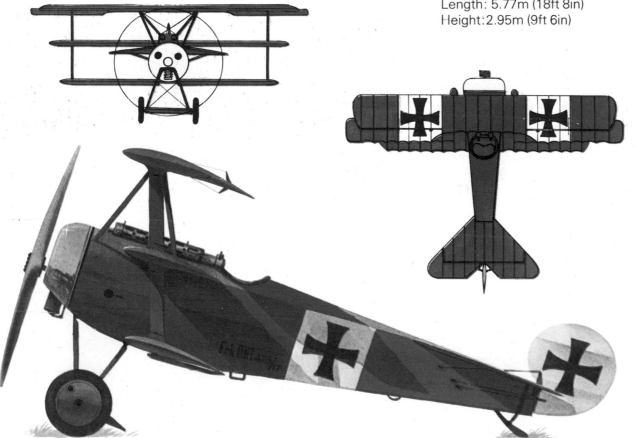

The first Moth biplane, the DH60, was produced by Geoffrey de Havilland in 1925. It had a 60 horsepower engine and was used as a trainer between the wars and during the Second World War.

The Moth biplane was made in several different versions

a) DH60G Gipsy Moth G-AAAH. This was the plane flown by Amy Johnson in the first solo flight by a woman from England to Australia in 1930.

b) DH60 Genet Moth. This had a 75 horsepower Armstrong-Siddeley Genet I five-cyclinder engine and was used by the RAF as a trainer in the 1920s.

c) DH60GIII Moth Major. This type had a 130 horsepower engine.

d) DH82a Tiger Moth. This entered service with the RAF in 1932 and about half the Commonwealth pilots of the Second World War learned to fly in Tiger Moths.

Pulse jets were used in the Second World War for German V.1 flying bombs

Pulse jets are quite unlike turbine jets. Air enters at the front of the engine and is taken into a combustion chamber where it burns with fuel in a series of rapid explosions, or pulses. As it burns, the pressure automatically closes the spring-loaded shutters at the front of the air intake so that the gases can only escape backwards. Then the shutters re-open and allow more air in for another combustion. In general the pulse jet is unsatisfactory because of noise and the difficulties of control.

The First World War was responsible for a great boom in aircraft

In November 1918 the First World War officially ended. Only fifteen years had passed since the Wright Brothers had begun powered flight and for the first eleven of these years, there had been little development. But as the war progressed, the need for faster and more efficient aircraft was seen by all governments involved, and the years between 1914 and 1918 saw a revolution in airplane performance and design. By the end of the war the Royal Air Force had grown from 160 aircraft to a massive 22,647 and its strength in officers and men from 2,000 to 300,000. These men and their equivalents in Europe, and all the 'planes that were lying idle were the men and machines that opened up the world during the 1920s and 1930s and made it the much smaller place that it is today.

A great fighter ace had no legs

Group-Captain Douglas Bader lost both his legs in a dreadful plane crash, but despite this he became one of the greatest fighter pilots of the Second World War.

The Sopwith Camel probably destroyed more aircraft than any other airplane in the First World War

The Sopwith Camel entered service in 1917 and was the main rival of the German Fokker D-VII. Its main asset was its manoeuvrability and it could make very tight turns. In all, 5490 Camels were built.

Type: single-seat fighter
Engine: several types were used, from the 100 hp Gnome Monosoupape to the 170 hp Le Rhone 9R
Armament: two fixed synchronised 303 inch Vickers machine guns
Speed: 169 Km/h at 3048 metres (104.5 mph at 10,000 feet)
Climb: 11 mins 45 secs to 3048 metres (10,000 feet)
Ceiling: 5791m (19,000 feet)
Endurance: ½ hour
Weight: 436 Kg empty, 672 Kg loaded (962 lbs empty, 1,482 lbs loaded)
Span: 8.5 metres (28 feet)
Length: 5.7 metres (18 ft 9 ins)
Height: 2.5 metres (8 ft 6 ins)

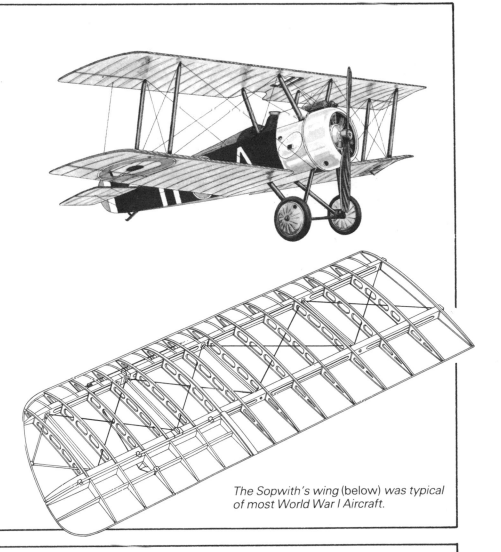

The Sopwith's wing (below) *was typical of most World War I Aircraft.*

Turboprops are better for heavier planes, lower speeds and lower altitudes

There is a smaller amount of thrust at the rear, as in the turbojet, but the turbine also drives a propeller in front of the compressor. Extra fuel is sometimes added behind the turbine to burn in the jet pipe to give additional thrust for take-off. This is called an afterburner. Two of the most successful turboprop engines have been the Rolls-Royce Dart (1,700 horsepower/1,260 kilowatts), which was the first turboprop to go into use, and the Bristol Proteus (4,000 horsepower/ 3,000 kilowatts). The Bristol Proteus in the photograph is a Mk 765, used in the Bristol Britannia, and also in fast naval craft and in air-cushion vehicles.

Trains

There were different types of valve gear in the pistons of early locomotives

The illustrations show three different systems of valve gear in early locomotive pistons. The two most important types are Walschaert's (shown above) and Stephenson's link motion (below left), which was more common before 1900. The Joy valve gear is

also shown (below right). The valve gear controls the valves which admit steam to, and exhaust it from, each side of the pistons in turn. The valve gear makes it possible to change the valve timing for reversing and also for early cut-off of the steam supply. The illustrations show the positions of the rods in forward and reverse gears in a typical early locomotive of the nineteenth century.

One of the earliest trains went round in circles

Richard Trevithick produced a steam locomotive in 1804. His second one, the Penydarran, produced the same year, was the first steam locomotive to pull a train successfully. In 1808 his 'Catch-me-who-can' was used to pull a coach on a circular track in North London.

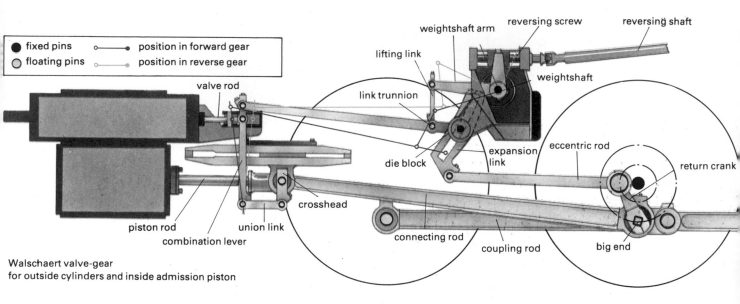

- ● fixed pins
- ○ floating pins
- position in forward gear
- position in reverse gear

Walschaert valve-gear
for outside cylinders and inside admission piston

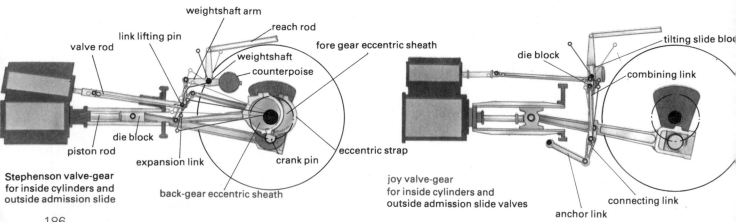

Stephenson valve-gear
for inside cylinders and
outside admission slide

joy valve-gear
for inside cylinders and
outside admission slide valves

The first public railway was originally going to use horse-drawn carriages on rails

George Stephenson's first locomotive was the 'Blucher' of 1814. He had built several other designs by the time he achieved his major success in 1825 with the opening of the Stockton and Darlington Railway. It had originally been proposed to use horse-drawn carriages on the rails but Stephenson built his famous 'Locomotion No 1' for the opening ceremony. The event is now regarded as the beginning of public railways. In 1829, Stephenson's even more famous 'Rocket' won a £500 prize in competing against other locomotives in the Rainhill trials in Lancashire. George's son, Robert, helped in the construction of the 'Rocket'. Robert later became more famous for building bridges.

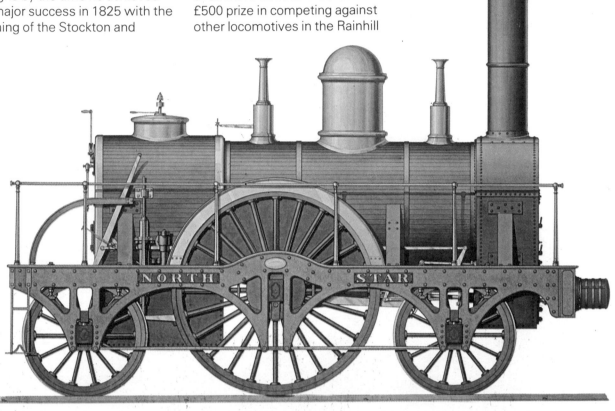

Railway engines have different wheel arrangements

The 'Rocket' had a wheel arrangement with one larger pair at the front and one smaller pair at the back. The drive went to the larger wheels. Two main axles coupled by a rod gave greater grip and looked like this: OO. Small leading axles gave a smoother ride and small axles both at the back and the front distributed the weight better, giving variations such as oOO and ooOOo. Greater weight and steeper climbs required more driving wheels and variations such as oOOO and the Pacific arrangement of ooOOOo. Thus trains are often identified by the arrangement of their wheels.

Some of the earliest steam locomotives were used for hauling coal carts

In 1812, Blenkinsop's track railway used a steam locomotive that drove on a cogged wheel that fitted to the track. The locomotive was used for hauling carts in a colliery. William Hedley's 'Puffing Billy' of 1813 was used on a colliery near the River Tyne. 'Puffing Billy' used a smooth wheel on a smooth rail. This is the oldest steam locomotive in existence and it remained in use until 1861. It went at a walking pace and hauled trains of up to 50 tons. As soon as people realised the potential of locomotives for pulling passenger cars, the railway boom was under way.

In a steam locomotive, water heated by burning coal is turned to steam

Coal is shovelled by hand through the fire door and burns on the grate or firebars. The fire passes around the brick arch across the centre of the chamber and goes through the fire tubes. The fire is drawn by the suction effect of exhaust steam passing from the blast pipe to the chimney, or by steam jets from the blower ring when the engine is not working. Water around the fire tubes is turned to steam by the heat and passes into the steam pipe. The steam is superheated by being passed back along superheater flues. The steam is then forced into the cylinders and drives the pistons.

The basic source of power for a steam locomotive was fire

The source of power is the fire burning on the grate (43). Air for combustion enters the ashpan (44) through damper doors (42). Coal is fired (by hand shovel in this small locomotive) through the firedoor (23) which also admits a little warmed air. A deflector plate (21) prevents cold air entering the tubes when the door is open. The fire passes round the brick arch (16) and through the fire tubes (10) and superheater flues (9), drawn by the suction effect of exhaust steam passing from the blastpipe (3) to the chimney. If the engine is not working, steam jets from the blower ring (4) produce the suction. The firebox crown sheet (15) and other flat surfaces are tied to the boiler shell by stays (18) and the whole boiler is lagged (11). The regulator handle (22) operates the main steam valve (12) in the dome. There is a 'steam stand' or 'fountain' (20) supplied by a collector pipe (14), from which steam is taken for auxiliaries, such as the injector (48) for feeding water to the boiler, and the vacuum brake ejectors working the locomotive brake cylinder (47) and the train brakes via the train pipe connections (1) at both ends of the locomotive. Steam is also taken for train heating via a reducing valve, to heating hose connectors (24) at both ends, and for the whistle (19). There are two safety valves (17). When the locomotive is working, steam from the regulator valve (12) passes to the saturated or 'wet' steam header (7) of the superheater, then through numerous small pipes or 'elements' to the superheated steam header (5). In each element, the steam makes four passes along the flue, the element having three 'return bends' (8, 13). A 'snifting

valve' (6) on the wet steam header allows the elements to be cooled by air drawn in when the engine is coasting with the regulator valve shut.

Steam enters all three cylinders (only the middle one is shown) via two-headed piston valves (26) moved backwards and forwards by the Walschaert valve gear, which derives its motion from a single eccentric (38) and the crosshead (33), which is the junction of the piston rod (30) and the connecting rod (39) and is guided by slide bars (32). The connecting rod drives a crank (41) incorporated in the driving axle (40). The motion from the eccentric is taken forward by the eccentric rod (37) to the expansion link (36) which is pivoted in the middle. From this the radius rod (34) takes a movement variable in amount and also reversible, because its connection to the slotted link can be shifted up and down by the driver, via a lifting link and a 'weighshaft' (35). The radius rod movement is combined with that of the crosshead by a combination lever (28) connected through the union link (31). The resulting movements of the valves allow the running in either direction and for expansive working. Valve and piston rods enter steam chests and cylinders through steamtight glands (27).

The brake shoes (45) are connected to the brake cylinder (47) by beams and rods, known as brake rigging. The driving and coupled wheels are sprung with laminated plate springs (46), while the bogie has coil springs (25). In addition to pivoting at its centre, the bogie can move sideways controlled by transverse springs (29).

Deflector plates (2) at the front of the locomotive help to lift exhaust steam clear of the cab windows.

Electric trains are cleaner than steam locomotives

Although it has never been proved that electricity is a cheaper power source than steam, there are several advantages that electric trains have over steam ones. The main advantage is electricity is much cleaner. This is important for trains in urban areas and undergrounds. The other advantages are that with an electric train, the power source is stationary, which makes it more efficient on gradients as more power can be drawn from the power source on demand; high power is available at low speeds to assist acceleration. The locomotive shown here is an electric locomotive of Swedish State Railways, built in 1942.

Modern trains run at extremely high speeds

Modern trains travel at speeds which would have astonished the railway pioneers of the nineteenth century. In France, the TGV (Très Grande Vitesse, which means very high speed) runs at speeds averaging 212 kph (132 mph) between Paris and Lyons. In Japan the Bullet Trains cover the 160 kilometres (100 miles) in less than one hour. British Rail's 125 express trains top 200 kmp (125 mph), and the 225 engines introduced in the early 1990s reach even higher speeds.

Future developments that will revolutionise rail travel in the coming years are a more widespread use of monorail, with the trains either riding above the rail or slung underneath it. Underslung carriages are suspended from wheeled bogies that run along the top of the concrete beam which constitutes the track. The bogies are kept on the track by guide wheels. More futuristic are the magnetic levitation trains being developed in some countries. A Russian prototype has carried passengers at over 400 kmph (250 mph) for a short distance.

The numbered parts of the electric locomotive shown below are:

1. the driving cab
2. transformer oil cooler
3. traction motor blowers
4. traction motors
5. transformer compartment and switchgear
6. transformer cooling oil pump
7. air compressor
8. pantograph
9. high tension busbars connecting pantographs
10. high tension busbar carrying current to transformer
11. main circuit breaker
12. pantograph operating cylinder and springs
13. relay cabinet
14. carrying wheels
15. driving wheels with elastic drive
16. main gear face
17. hollow axle
18. driving axle
19. sandboxes
20. sand delivery pipes
21. axle boxes
22. springs
23. compressed air reservoirs
24. brake shoes and hangers
25. buffers
26. drawgear
27. jumper cables
28. mainframes

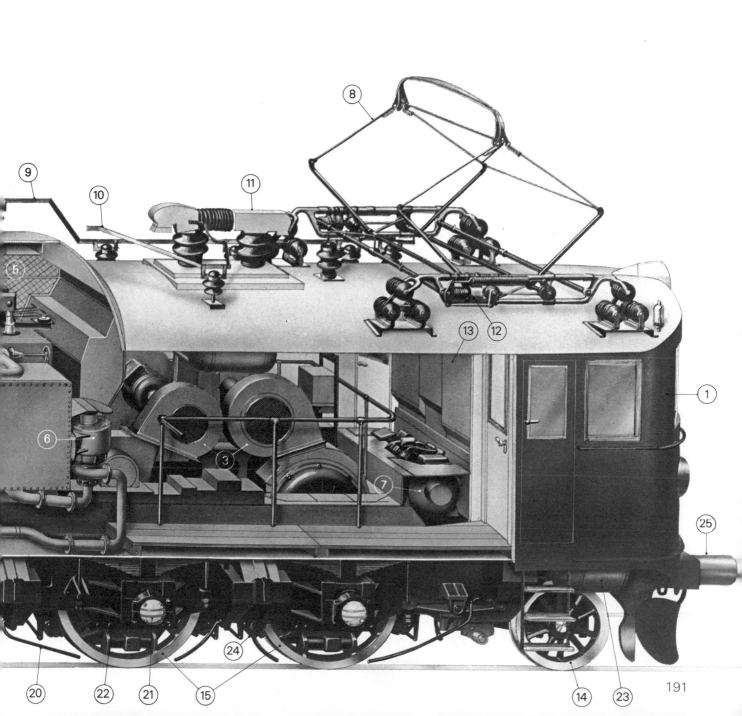

Ships and Boats

The Roaring Forties – the fast and slow way round the world

The Roaring Forties are strong, constant, ocean winds blowing from west to east in latitudes 40^0-50^0 south of the equator. In the days when sailing ships depended entirely on the wind, the Roaring Forties were very important. Ships sailing eastward, with the wind behind them, went fast. Ships going westward, against the wind, sailed slowly. Therefore instead of taking the shorter, westward route and battling round the Cape of Good Hope into the Atlantic, ships from Australia usually sailed eastward across the Pacific and round Cape Horn, keeping to the Roaring Forties as long as they could before turning north towards Europe.

Wind-powered ships may be a thing of the future

Once again, as in the old days of the great sailing ships, wind may be used as a cheap source of power for transporting goods by sea. Square-rigged 'dynaships' are now being designed in Germany and elsewhere. But whereas in the old days it took hundreds of men to raise the canvas sails, in the new ships one man will be able to raise or reef sail at the flick of a switch. These ships are planned to be 16,730 tonnes (17,000 tons) or more and will also be equipped with a small auxiliary engine to enable them to reach areas of advantageous wind as predicted and signalled by weather satellite launched into the atmosphere.

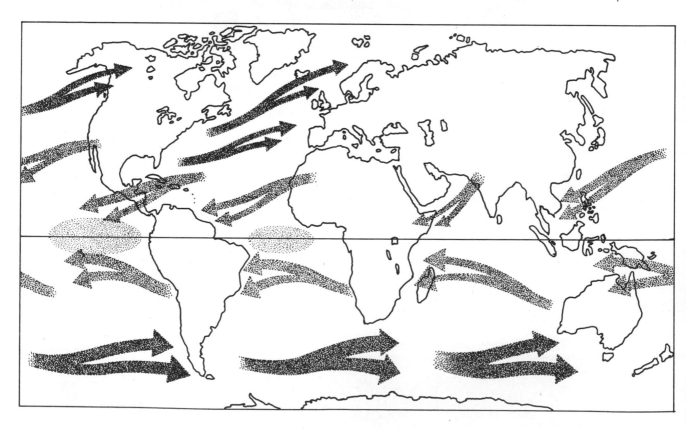

The prevailing winds of the world. The Roaring Forties blow along the bottom right of the map.

The first submarine was rowed beneath the surface by sets of oars

The idea of an underwater diving bell goes back to ancient Greek times but the first mention of a boat that could be *propelled* underwater was in the 16th century, when William Bourne put forward a plan for a wooden submarine covered with leather and rowed by oars. A more successful attempt at the same sort of thing was made by the Dutchman, Cornelius van Drebbel. In about 1620 he built a similar wooden frame covered with greased leather and managed to row four-and-a-half metres (15 feet) below the surface of the River Thames. A more advanced design was built by David Bushnell, during the American War of Independence, in 1776. His *Turtle* was driven by two hand-cranked propellers, one to move it forward and one to submerge it. The first really successful 'modern' submarines were the Holland type built at the very end of the 19th century.

An artist's impression of Halley's diving bell and helmet based on an early print.

Cushions of air can provide a fast and comfortable ride

In the last ten or twenty years, the hovercraft has become a familiar method of transport in certain parts of the world. Generally boat-shaped with rounded ends and a flat bottom, it rides on a cushion of air forced downwards by its motors. The idea was patented and developed by a British engineer called Christopher Cockerell and the first model, the SR-N1, was tested in 1959. Cross-channel hovercraft can now carry up to 600 passengers and can cruise at well over 100 kilometres (62.5 miles) an hour, and can reach speeds of about 130 kilometres (82 miles) an hour. Since they can travel over both land and water, hovercraft have been used to explore swampy rivers like the Amazon.

There was once a ship that was seasick-proof

Sir Henry Bessemer is famous for inventing a process for manufacturing steel. He also invented a special passenger ship with a saloon so built that it always remained level no matter how much the ship was rolling. The *Bessemer*, as the ship was called, was built in 1875 for cross-Channel ferry work from Dover to Calais but it never worked successfully. The engineer who operated the hydraulics system that kept the saloon level had to keep his eye fixed on a spirit level that told him how much to compensate for the roll of the ship. But he could not keep pace with the roll and the passengers were soon even more uncomfortable than they would have been on an ordinary ship.

A 19th-century stage coach was fitted with sails

Modern sand yachts run on wheels and are driven by the wind in their sails. They move very fast and need a lot of space in which to turn. The idea of harnessing wind power for wheeled transport was tried in the 19th century on a traditional stagecoach. The French experimented with 'L'Eolienne' in the 1830s. It had two masts fixed to the top of the coach, each with two or three square sails. Horses were not used at all. The coach was fast but extremely dangerous. It was impossible to steer the vehicle along the twisting roads. When men were sent up the rigging to raise or lower the sails to control the speed, the whole coach was put out of balance. The brakes were not strong enough to stop the coach.

The Jolly Roger may have been red, not black

The Jolly Roger was the traditional flag of the pirates of the Spanish Main (the Bahamas and the Caribbean) during the 17th century. It was once believed to be a black flag with a skull and cross bones. There is little or no evidence that the skull and cross bones ever existed, and there is some doubt as to whether the flag was always black. It is possible that the flag was more often red and that the phrase came from the French, *jolie rouge*. This literally means 'pretty red' and came to be called Jolly Roger.

Cannons changed war at sea

Cannons were introduced early into warships but were not of great importance until the beginning of the sixteenth century. Until then they had been too unreliable to be depended upon as the sole weapon. They were liable to shatter under stress and the gunpowder was liable to explode or become inefficient. Firearms were considered as auxiliary weapons and were normally sited in the fore and aft castles. But during the fourteenth and fifteenth centuries guns became more efficient and the powder less volatile. Henry the Eighth of England saw the potential of artillery and ordered ships with gunports cut into the sides of the hull like the one below. By importing guns from the best smiths in Europe and encouraging English gunsmiths to copy them, and by building fine ships, he laid down the basis of England's naval supremacy which lasted well into the twentieth century.

Sailors used to face severe punishments if they behaved badly

Keel-hauling was a fairly common form of punishment for severe crimes on board ship during the 16th and 17th centuries. A rope was passed from one end of the main yard (the spar that ran across the mast, holding up the square mainsail), then below the ship and up to the other end of the main yard. The victim was tied to the rope, with weights fixed to his body, and dragged to and fro beneath the ship from one side to the other. A gun was often fired while he was under the water, to frighten him still more, and his body would get torn and bruised by the marine growth on the hull of the vessel. At the beginning of the 18th century, keel-hauling was replaced by the cat o'nine tails, a knotted rope with nine ends, with which the victim was whipped

The idea for the seaman's hammock came from the Indians of the Caribbean

A hammock is a form of hanging bed, usually made of netting or cloth. It is the traditional bed for the seamen, hanging from the beams of the ship and swaying to the motion of the sea. The hammock was unknown in Europe until Christopher Columbus brought it back from the West Indies. He had seen the Carib Indians using hammocks slung between the trees.

An admiral gave his name to a method of carving

Scrimshaw is the art of carving on a piece of whale jawbone or walrus tooth. It was done by sailors with time on their hands as they crossed the oceans in search of whales. The work was often very delicately done, with scenes of ships, mermaids and monsters. The word 'scrimshaw' is probably derived from the name of Admiral Scrimshaw, who was apparently an expert in the craft.

An admiral gave his name to 'grog'

Sailors and officers on British and many other warships used to have a daily ration of rum, to keep them warm and cheerful. In 1740, Admiral Vernon of the British West Indies fleet ordered that this rum ration should be diluted with water. Admiral Vernon used to wear a coat made of grogram, a thick material made of silk and wool stiffened with gum. His nickname was 'Old Grog', because of his coat, and the diluted rum became known as 'grog'. British sailors went on drinking grog for another 200 years.

No one has solved the mystery of the *Mary Celeste*

One of the greatest of all ocean mysteries is the question of what happened aboard the *Mary Celeste*, long ago in 1872. The two-masted, square-rigged bark was sailing from New York to Genoa with 1700 barrels of alcohol in her hold. She was discovered by another ship, 480 kilometres (300 miles) west of Gibraltar, with her sails set, a meal laid on the table, and not a soul on board. There has never been a satisfactory explanation of the disappearance of the crew, but there have been plenty of theories. Some say that everyone got drunk, mutinied and jumped overboard – but scarcely any of the alcohol had been touched. Some said the ship had been attacked by pirates – but nothing of value had been stolen (only the chronometer had disappeared). Some said they had all landed on a volcanic island which had suddenly sunk beneath the waves. Some said they had all gone for a swim and been devoured by sharks. But no one really knows the truth.

The British fleet mutinied in 1797

Life in the Navy was so bad that in 1797 the men at Spithead and the Nore mutinied. As a result of the mutiny, conditions became better and sailors became respectable

The Plimsoll Line appears on all ships

Samuel Plimsoll was a Member of the British Parliament in the second half of the 19th century. He did a great deal to make ships safer for the men who sailed in them. The safety mark, the Plimsoll Line, that he introduced is still shown on all ships. The mark appears near the water-line, with the initials of Lloyd's Register of insurance above it. The line shows the average depth below which loaded ships should not sink. Other marks beside the Plimsoll Line show the maximum depth of water-line for different types of water, such as 'Tropical Fresh', 'Fresh', 'Tropical', 'Summer', 'Winter' and 'Winter North Atlantic'. Before Plimsoll introduced his line, some owners had overloaded their old ships and sent them out to sink, together with their crews, so that the insurance could be claimed. After the Plimsoll line was made legal, this practice stopped.

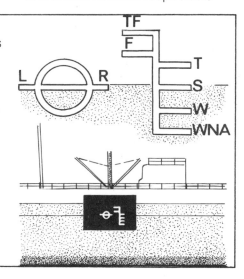

The Devastation was the first of the modern battleships

In 1872, the British ship *Devastation* was built. It was powered by steam and had an iron hull. There were four 12-inch muzzle-loading guns in two turrets fore and aft. Twin propellers gave the ship a speed of 12 knots. In length it was 86.8 metres (285 feet) and measured 18.8 metres (62 feet) in the beam. Its low freeboard gave the ship a clear field of fire. The freeboard was raised later to avoid the sea washing over it and damaging the guns.

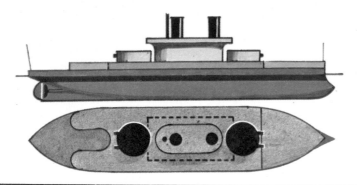

Some boats can speed across the water on stilts and wings

A vessel fitted with hydrofoils looks much the same as any other boat when at rest in the water. But when it starts to go at speed, the hull lifts clear of the water, rising on stilts supported by small underwater 'wings'. The forward speed of these wings lifts the hull and in this way the vessel's resistance to the water is greatly reduced. Hydrofoil boats can go at speeds of 70-80 kilometres (45-50 miles) an hour. They are especially used by river police.

A 19th-century ship had hinged joints

Designers are constantly trying to find new ways of handling large ships. A 19th-century ship, called the *Connector*, had three or four hinged sections that enabled her to ride the waves more easily, without any danger of breaking her back. These sections could also be disconnected and loaded and unloaded separately. It is not known what happened to the *Connector*, so we can assume that her design was not as successful as had been hoped.

Press gangs once legally forced people to join the British navy

The 'press gang' was usually a group of tough sailors with an officer in charge who was responsible for seizing men on shore to make up the crew of his war ship. Some men were taken from prisons but many were snatched in the streets at night and taken away without a chance to tell their wives and families what had happened to them. Often they knew nothing about the sea but they learnt quickly enough. Merchant ships were often stopped by warships and men seized from their crews as well. The practice of press-ganging started in mediaeval times and became common in the 16th century. It reached its peak when crews were desperately needed during the Napoleonic Wars at the beginning of the 19th century.

Devastation served in the Crimea with armour plating added to her hull to give her extra protection from shells.

Cars

Cars still work in much the same way as they did more than 80 years ago

Although the 19th century Panhard et Levassor shown here may look primitive, it works in basically the same way as a modern car. There are four wheels. The drive goes through the rear wheels, which are held parallel by a rigid axle. It has a four-stroke 'Otto' cycle engine at the front with a crankshaft aligned fore and aft. It has a friction clutch, change speed gearing and bevel gearing to turn the flow of power 90 degrees to the rear wheels. There are steel springs on all four corners and friction braking. Modern improvements add mostly to safety and streamlining.

Cugnot's giant steam-tricycle knocked down a wall on its first outing

Perhaps the first successful steam-powered vehicle to run on the road was the great steam-tricycle built by Nicholas Cugnot in 1769. This extraordinary machine had a vast boiler over the front wheel and travelled at walking pace. It was designed as a vehicle for pulling army guns. However, it was only able to travel for about 15 minutes before it had to get up steam again. A second version, built in 1770, could haul about four tonnes.

The Panhard et Levassor.

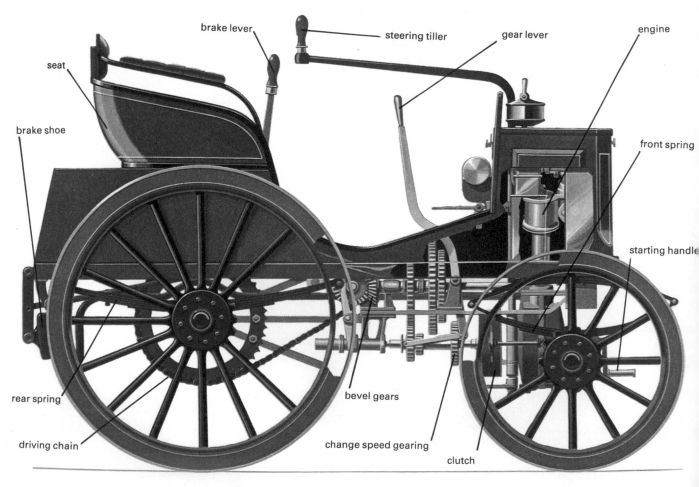

seat · brake lever · steering tiller · gear lever · engine · brake shoe · front spring · starting handle · rear spring · driving chain · bevel gears · change speed gearing · clutch

Most cars have four cylinders

Most small cars have a four-stroke 'Otto' cycle engine. Each cylinder in this type of engine develops power on only one stroke in every four. Therefore it is necessary to have at least four cylinders to ensure that one cylinder is developing power immediately after another in order to achieve smooth running. Each cylinder goes through the four strokes in turn. The petrol and air mixture is drawn through the inlet valve. It is then compressed into the combustion chamber, ignited by a spark and allowed to expand. Finally it is pumped out through the exhaust valve and the fumes are passed into the atmosphere.

A four stroke 'Otto' cycle engine.

1. Air filter. 2. Carburettor. 3. Inlet and exhaust valves. 4. Piston. 5. Thermostat. 6. Cooling pump. 7. Fan belt. 8. Camshaft driving chain. 9. Camshaft. 10. Dipstick. 11. Lubricator. 12. Oil filter. 13. Ignition distributor. 14. Push rod to open valve. 15. Fuel pump. 16. Flywheel.

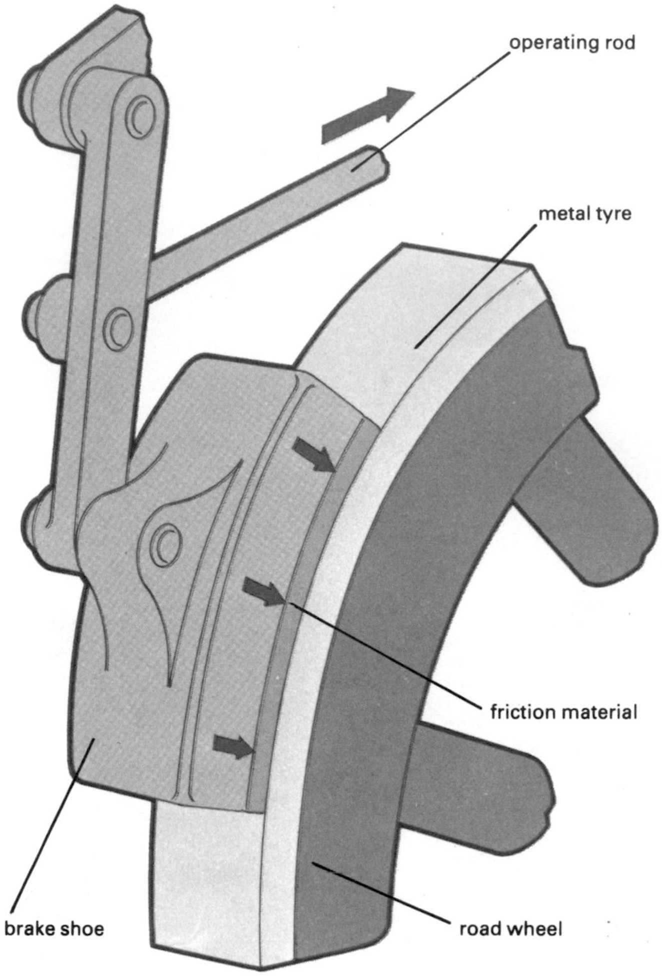

![operating rod, metal tyre, friction material, brake shoe, road wheel diagram]

operating rod

metal tyre

friction material

brake shoe

road wheel

The earliest brakes on motor cars were not much different from the brakes on horse-drawn carriages

The earliest brakes were known as block brakes. The tyre was made of metal and the face of the brake was leather, backed by a metal shoe. The shoe covered only a small part of the circumference of the wheel. As cars went faster, the contracting band brake was designed. Special brake drums were fitted to the wheel, around which brake bands could be tightened. The internal expanding drum brake was safer on wet roads. It pressed outwards on the inside of the drum using a hydraulic piston. Modern disc brakes squeeze metal discs between two friction pads. One new development which is becoming more common is anti-lock braking which ensures that wheels do not lock and skid no matter how much pressure is applied to the pedal. These work by sensing when the wheel is tending to lock up and immediately relaxing the hydraulic pressure.

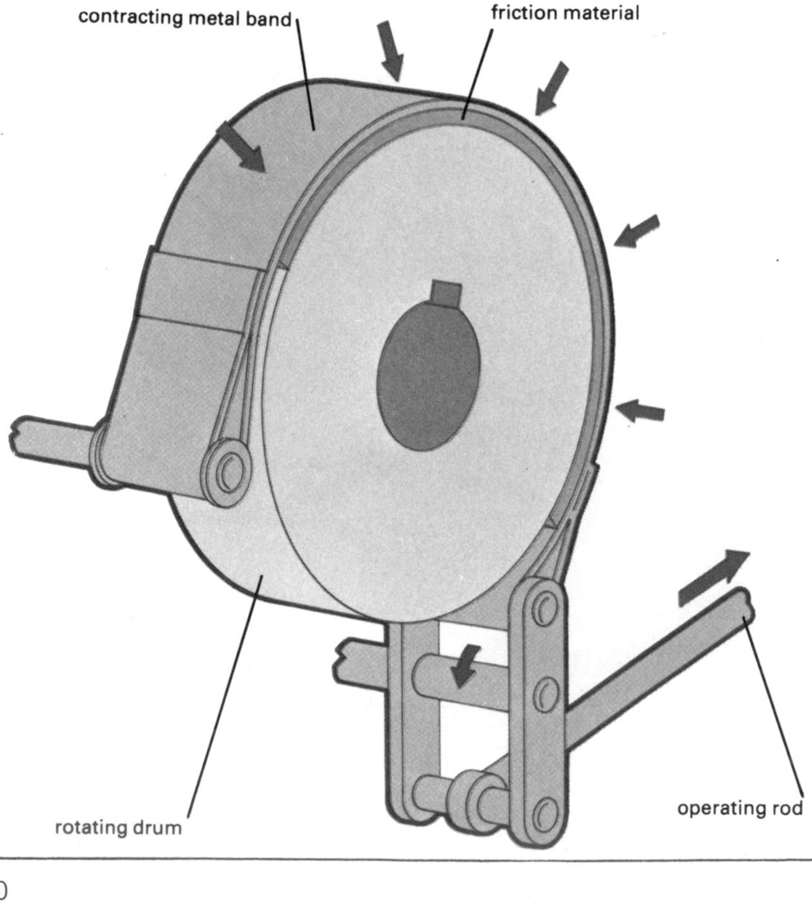

contracting metal band

friction material

rotating drum

operating rod

Top left: *A leather faced shoe brake is pressed against the solid tyre to slow the vehicle down. Although this was effective, the disadvantage was that after constant use, the leather and tyre became worn and had to be replaced.* Left: *As cars became more powerful, better brakes were required and special brake drums were provided around which a brake band could be tightened. Both of these braking systems worked well in dry weather, but were less efficient when conditions were wet. To solve this problem, internal expanding drum brakes were introduced. The one illustrated here* (upper right) *had a hydraulic piston and cylinder which pressed the brake shoes outwards. This was made even more efficient when modern disc brakes were introduced* (right).

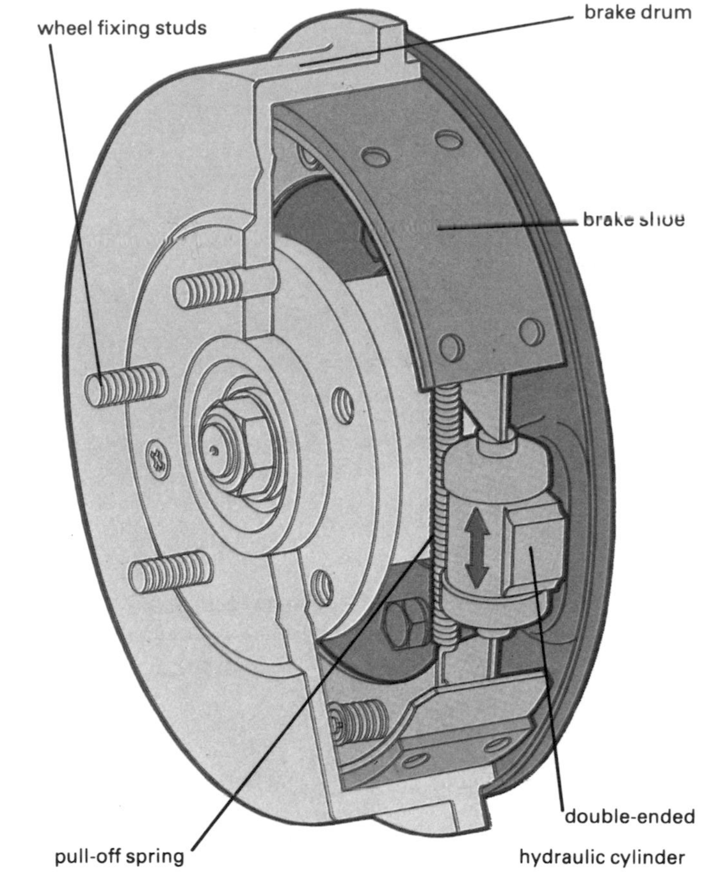

wheel fixing studs

brake drum

brake shoe

double-ended
hydraulic cylinder

pull-off spring

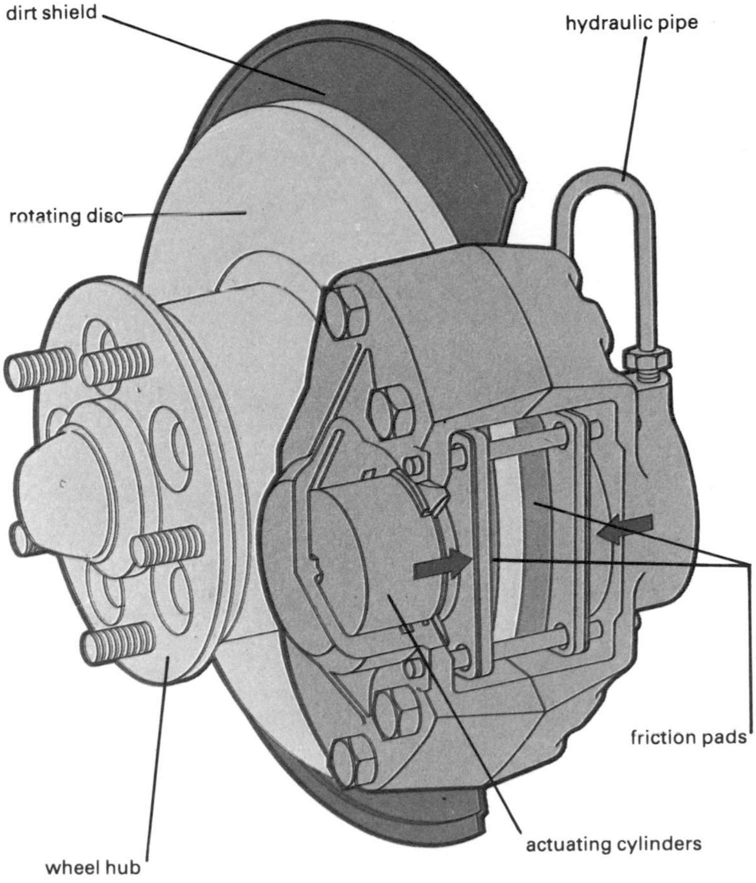

dirt shield

hydraulic pipe

rotating disc

friction pads

actuating cylinders

wheel hub

There were several designs for self-propelled vehicles

There were some imaginative designs for self-propelled vehicles long before any were successfully constructed. Leonardo da Vinci designed a model for a horseless carriage driven by clockwork. Father Ferdinand Verbiest is reported to have constructed a steam-driven vehicle for the Emperor of China towards the end of the 17th century. A model of a steam carriage was designed by the Frenchman, Denis Papin, in 1698. The first successful steam-powered vehicles did not appear until the 18th century.

Engines at the rear and front-wheel drive were two major developments in car design

Most cars have their engines at the front, but the first car built by Karl Benz in 1885 had its engine between the rear wheels. This idea was copied in Dr Ferdinand Porsche's Volkswagen of the 1930s. Rear-engined cars became popular in the 1950s but they were sometimes difficult to control because of the extra weight at the rear. Front-engined cars usually transmit their power to the rear wheels, but front-wheel drive was more compact and gave greater stability – it pulled the car round corners instead of pushing it. Front-wheel drive cars were made by Citroen and became popular when the Morris Mini-Minor was introduced in 1959.

1896 was the year of the car

1896 was the year that the first motorist was fined for speeding, the year a member of the royal family first rode in a car, the year the first car-hire firm began operating, the first motor show, the first car theft, the first race track event, the first motoring magazine and the first parking offence!

Modern Warfare

The first massed tank attack took place in 1917

Tanks were first used in mass formation at the Battle of Cambrai in November 1917. British Mark IV tanks, in groups of three, breached the German Hindenburg Line, a strong system of trenches and other defences. At the end of the first day they had made a breach 9.6 kilometres (6 miles) wide and 3658 metres (4000 yards) deep. Ten days later the Germans counter-attacked and regained what they had lost. This was largely because of the failure of the Allies to exploit their first advance. The illustrations show the Mark IV tank of 1917, which carried two 6-pounders and four Lewis machine guns. It weight 28 tons, could cross a 3 metre (10 feet) wide trench, had a speed of 6 km/h (3.7 mph).

A battle plan of Cambrai where Mark IV tanks were used en masse *to force an extensive breach in the Hindenburg Line. The Hindenberg line had three lines of mutually supporting trenches, ample artillery fire support and avenues of barbed wire. The top inset shows the front before the battle (the solid red line) and the broken red line shows the front on 29 November.*

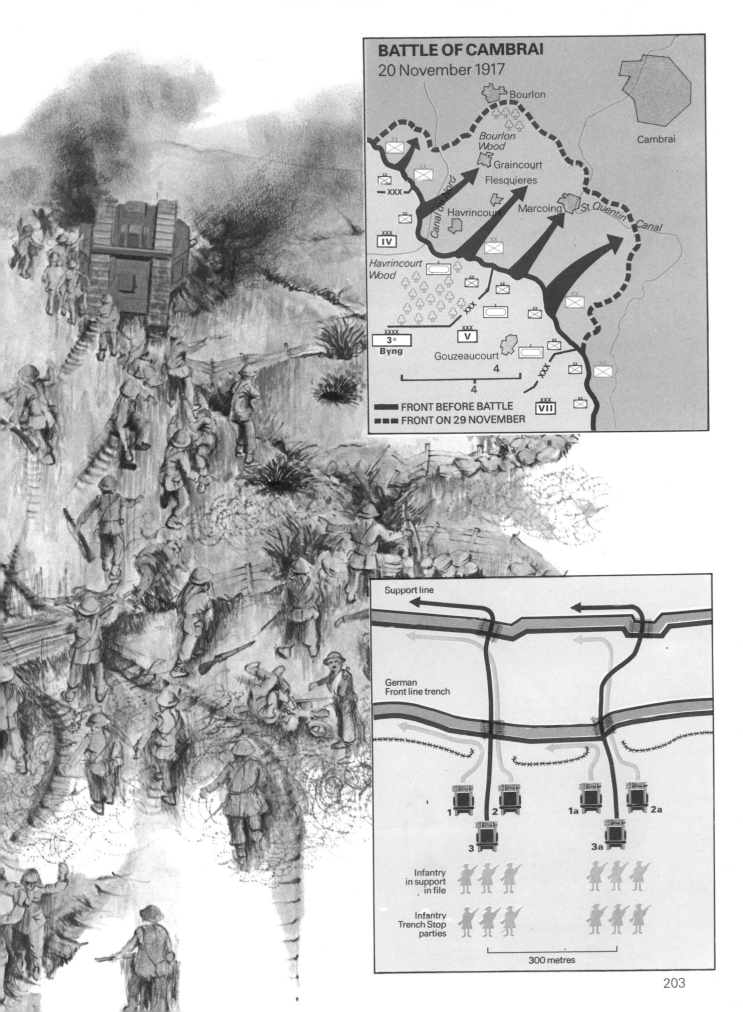

BATTLE OF CAMBRAI
20 November 1917

Bourlon

Bourlon
Wood

Graincourt

Flesquieres

Canal du Nord

Havrincourt

Marcoing

St Quentin Canal

Cambrai

Havrincourt
Wood

XXX
IV

XXX
V

XXXX
3ᵉ
Byng

Gouzeaucourt

4

4

XXX
VII

▬▬▬ FRONT BEFORE BATTLE
▬ ▬ ▬ FRONT ON 29 NOVEMBER

Support line

German
Front line trench

1   2   1a   2a

3   3a

Infantry
in support
in file

Infantry
Trench Stop
parties

300 metres

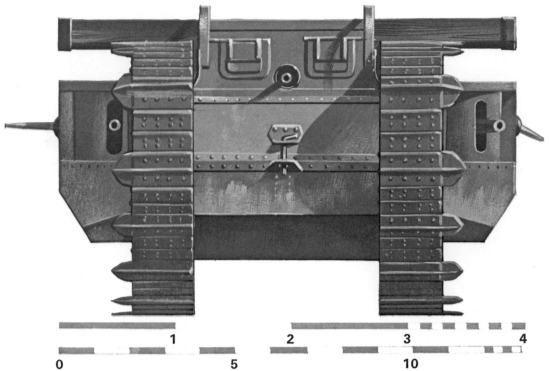

Tanks were male or female

The Mark IV was the first tank to be used en masse. It was basically the same shape as its predecessors but it had thicker armour, a more efficient gun and an excellent machine-gun. The front view (left) shows the observation ports for the driver and the commander. Tanks were designated 'male' or 'female'. Each model of tank made was made in two versions, one lighter than the other. The heavier one was called 'male' and the lighter was called 'female'.

The side view of the Mark IV shows the cylindrical exhaust silencer on top of the tank. Behind it are the manhole turret, and beneath the undirching beam, the box for the towing rope. The crewman had to wear leather helmets and visors to guard against the metal splinters which flew about the vehicle's interior after a hit.

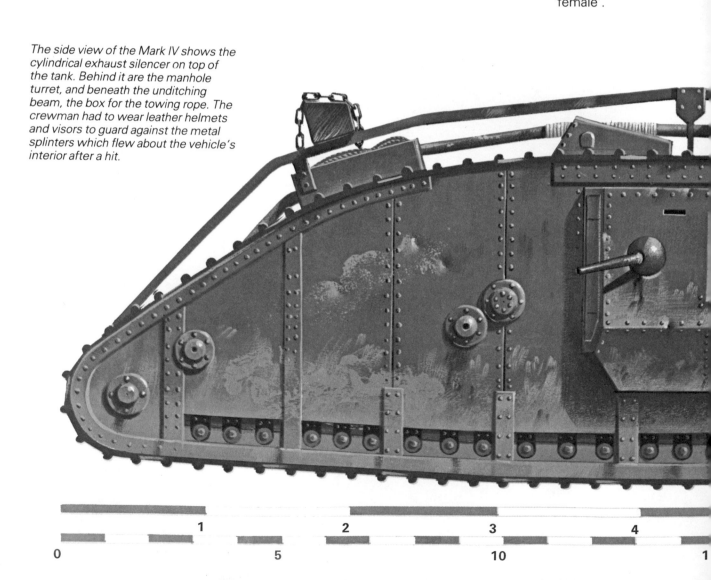

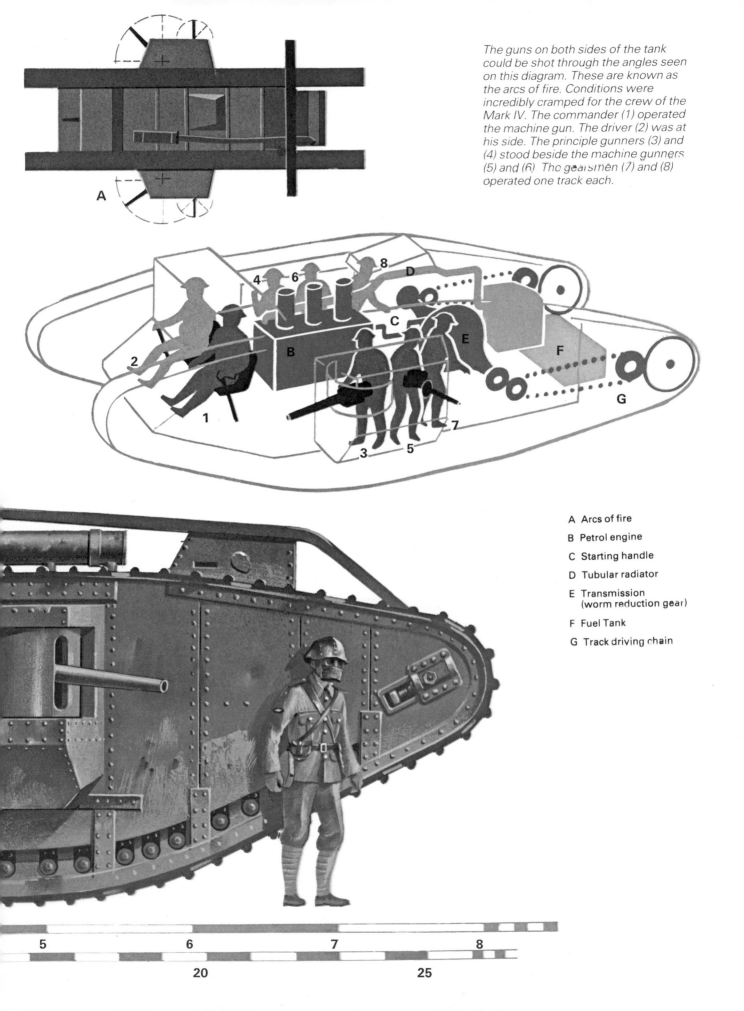

The guns on both sides of the tank could be shot through the angles seen on this diagram. These are known as the arcs of fire. Conditions were incredibly cramped for the crew of the Mark IV. The commander (1) operated the machine gun. The driver (2) was at his side. The principle gunners (3) and (4) stood beside the machine gunners (5) and (6). The gearsmen (7) and (8) operated one track each.

A Arcs of fire

B Petrol engine

C Starting handle

D Tubular radiator

E Transmission
   (worm reduction gear)

F Fuel Tank

G Track driving chain

The Russian T-34 was probably the greatest tank of the Second World War

The T-34 outgunned and outmanoeuvred the Germans on the eastern front. It went into production in 1940 and remained in service as the standard Russian medium tank throughout the war. The first type was armed with a 76 mm gun but this was replaced by an 85 mm gun in late 1943. The sloped armour gave extra protection. The T-34/76B shown here weighed 27 tons, was 6.5 metres (21 feet 7 inches) long, 3 metres (9 feet 10 inches) wide and 2.4 metres (8 feet) high. It had a maximum speed of 51.5 km/h (32 mph).

The T-34 was a robust and well designed tank which had good firepower, mobility and gave its crew decent protection.

Once the crew were inside the T-34 vision was limited to narrow vents cut into the armour and to the commander's periscope mounted on the turret. The broad tracks of the T-34 enabled it to keep going on soft conditions which defeated its German rivals.

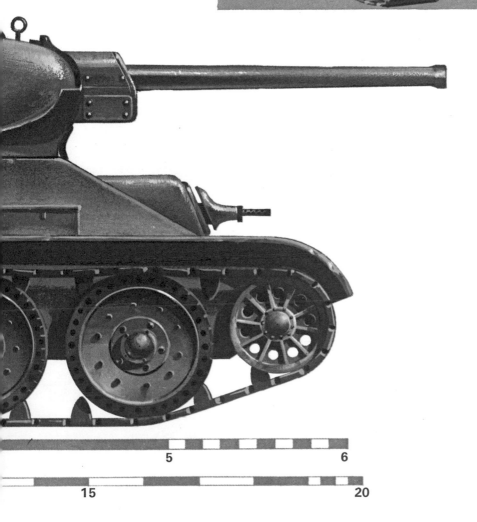

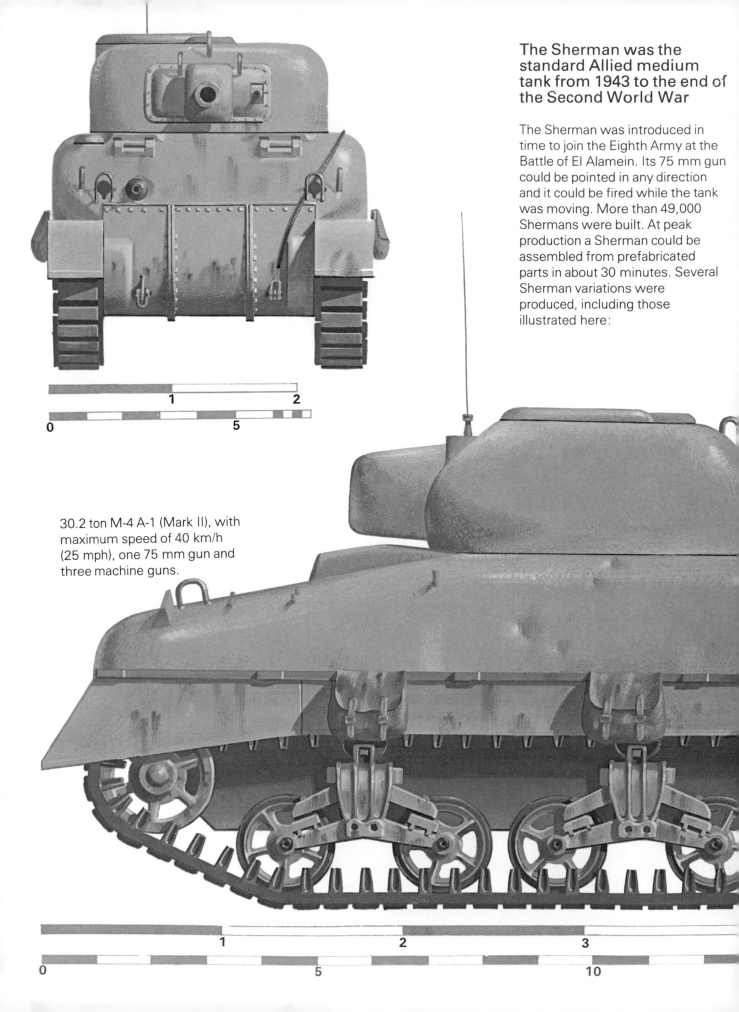

The Sherman was the standard Allied medium tank from 1943 to the end of the Second World War

The Sherman was introduced in time to join the Eighth Army at the Battle of El Alamein. Its 75 mm gun could be pointed in any direction and it could be fired while the tank was moving. More than 49,000 Shermans were built. At peak production a Sherman could be assembled from prefabricated parts in about 30 minutes. Several Sherman variations were produced, including those illustrated here:

30.2 ton M-4 A-1 (Mark II), with maximum speed of 40 km/h (25 mph), one 75 mm gun and three machine guns.

Sherman Jumbo with heavier armour.

M-4 A-3, also known as Mark IV, upgunned to 76 mm and with improved suspension system.

M-4 A-4 Firefly, Mark V, used by the British with a 17-pounder gun (76.2 mm).

5   6

15   20

The effect of the German *blitzkrieg* in 1940 was overwhelming

In May and June 1940, German *blitzkrieg* tactics achieved one of the swiftest and most remarkable victories in history. Their attack began on 10th May. Within five days the Germans had over-run Holland. Within 18 days, Belgium had surrendered. By the end of May, more than 330,000 British and Allied soldiers had been evacuated from Dunkirk. The Germans entered Paris on 14th June and on 22nd June the French signed a truce with them. It had taken the Germans six weeks to conquer Europe.

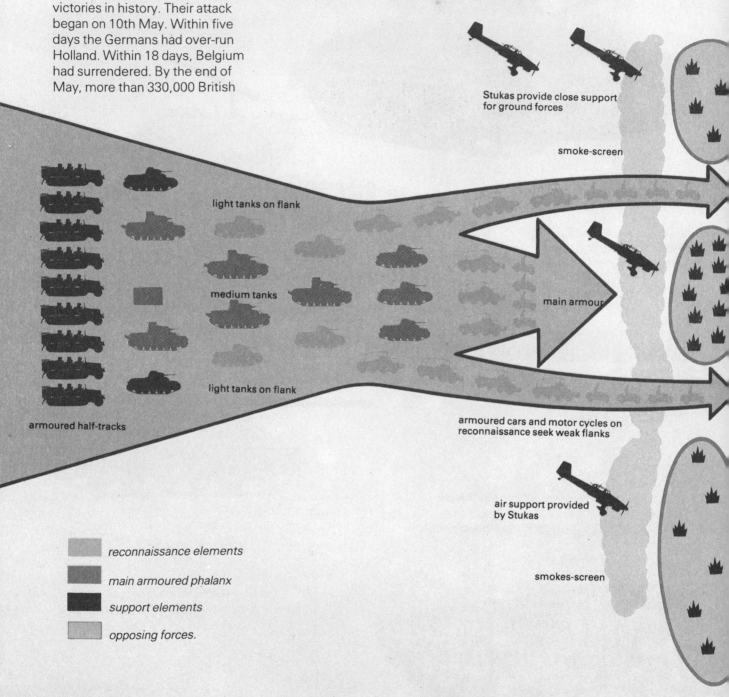

Stukas provide close support for ground forces

smoke-screen

light tanks on flank

medium tanks

main armour

light tanks on flank

armoured half-tracks

armoured cars and motor cycles on reconnaissance seek weak flanks

air support provided by Stukas

smokes-screen

reconnaissance elements

main armoured phalanx

support elements

opposing forces.

In the opening stages of Blitzkrieg, motor cycles and armoured cars profited from a heavy smoke screen and the close support of their dive bombers. They surged towards enemy positions, sought out weaknesses and infiltrated their lines. They were followed by Mark II Panzers, followed by more powerful Mark III and IVs. While the outlying enemy forces were being engaged, the recce units sped on towards the enemy's industrial and administrative centres, which they isolated, making them easy for the infantry and artillery to take. Stukas attempted to destroy enemy aircraft caught on the ground, and factories and to disrupt communications.

Blitzkrieg means 'lightning war' in German

Blitzkrieg was a form of military tactics used by the Germans with great success during the Second World War. It consisted of a co-ordinated attack by aircraft, tanks and motorised infantry that relied on speed and surprise to break through enemy lines.

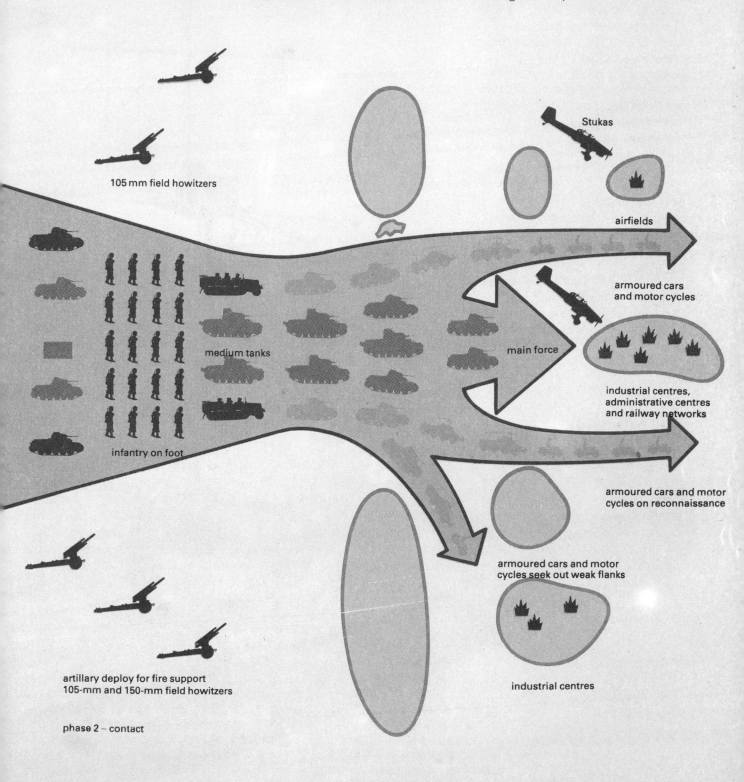

105 mm field howitzers

Stukas

airfields

medium tanks

main force

armoured cars and motor cycles

industrial centres, administrative centres and railway networks

infantry on foot

armoured cars and motor cycles on reconnaissance

armoured cars and motor cycles seek out weak flanks

artillary deploy for fire support 105-mm and 150-mm field howitzers

industrial centres

phase 2 – contact

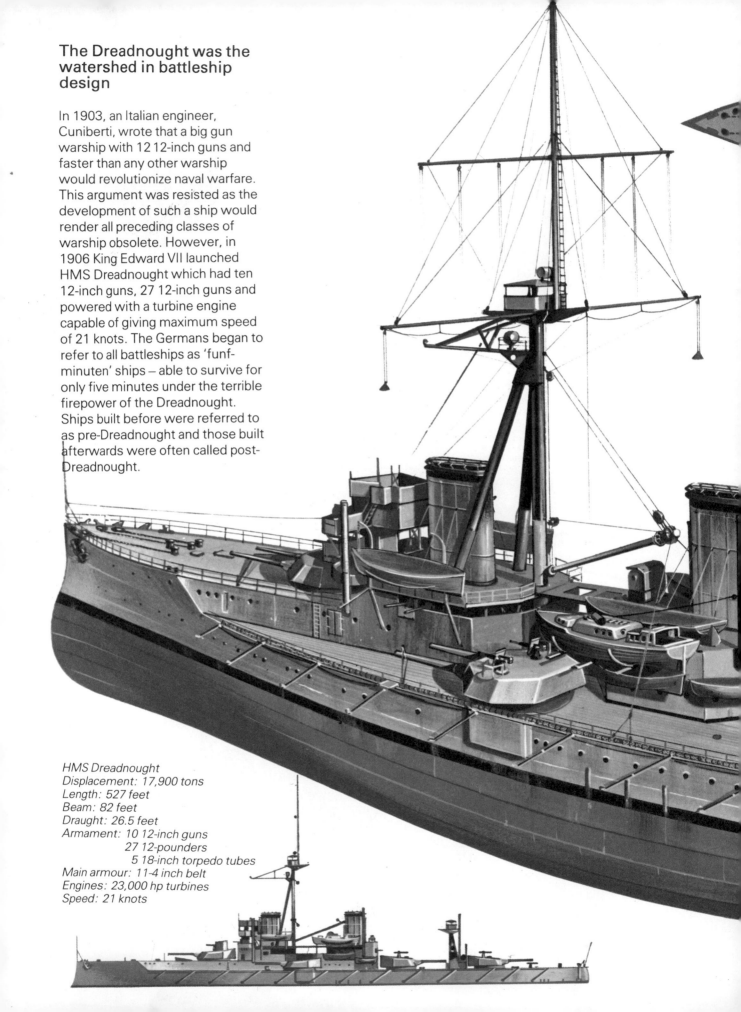

The Dreadnought was the watershed in battleship design

In 1903, an Italian engineer, Cuniberti, wrote that a big gun warship with 12 12-inch guns and faster than any other warship would revolutionize naval warfare. This argument was resisted as the development of such a ship would render all preceding classes of warship obsolete. However, in 1906 King Edward VII launched HMS Dreadnought which had ten 12-inch guns, 27 12-inch guns and powered with a turbine engine capable of giving maximum speed of 21 knots. The Germans began to refer to all battleships as 'funf-minuten' ships – able to survive for only five minutes under the terrible firepower of the Dreadnought. Ships built before were referred to as pre-Dreadnought and those built afterwards were often called post-Dreadnought.

HMS Dreadnought
Displacement: 17,900 tons
Length: 527 feet
Beam: 82 feet
Draught: 26.5 feet
Armament: 10 12-inch guns
27 12-pounders
5 18-inch torpedo tubes
Main armour: 11-4 inch belt
Engines: 23,000 hp turbines
Speed: 21 knots

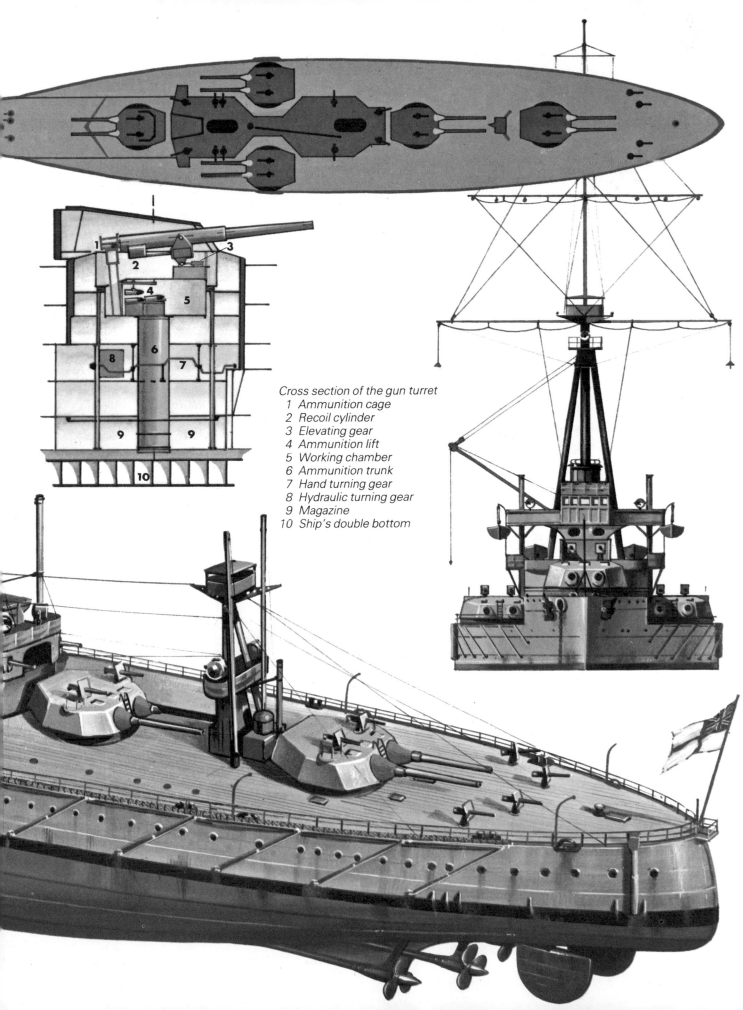

Cross section of the gun turret
1 Ammunition cage
2 Recoil cylinder
3 Elevating gear
4 Ammunition lift
5 Working chamber
6 Ammunition trunk
7 Hand turning gear
8 Hydraulic turning gear
9 Magazine
10 Ship's double bottom

A variety of the aircraft flew from a Second World War Essex aircraft carrier

Top: Curtiss SB2C Helldiver. The SB2C-3 model had a maximum speed of 470 km/h (294 mph), a maximum range of 3100 kilometres (1925 miles), and an armament of 2 x 20mm cannon, one 0.5 inch machine gun and up to 453kg (1,000lbs) of bombs.
Middle: Grumman TBM Avenger, torpedo bomber; speed 434 km/h (270 mph); range 1641 kilometres (1,020 miles); armament five machine guns and up to 680kg (2,000lbs) of bombs; one 971kg (1,920lbs) torpedo or eight rockets.
Bottom right: Chance Vought F4U-1D Corsair fighter bomber.
Bottom left: Grumman F6F-3 Hellcat fighter; speed 602 km/h (375 mph); range 1753 kilometres (1,090 miles); armament six 0.5 inch machine guns.

During the Second World War the Americans relied heavily on aircraft carriers in the Pacific

Between 1941 and 1945 the American forces in the Pacific relied heavily on aircraft carriers as bases from which to attack Japanese-held islands. The United States entered the Second World War after a dramatic assault by the Japanese on the US base at Pearl Harbor in Hawaii, on 7th December 1941. In May and June the following year, Japanese and American fleets fought in the Coral Sea, south of New Guinea, and off the island of Midway, west of Hawaii. With the support of their aircraft carriers, the Americans then started a counter-offensive to win back the islands that the Japanese had already taken. It was a long and hard-fought struggle.

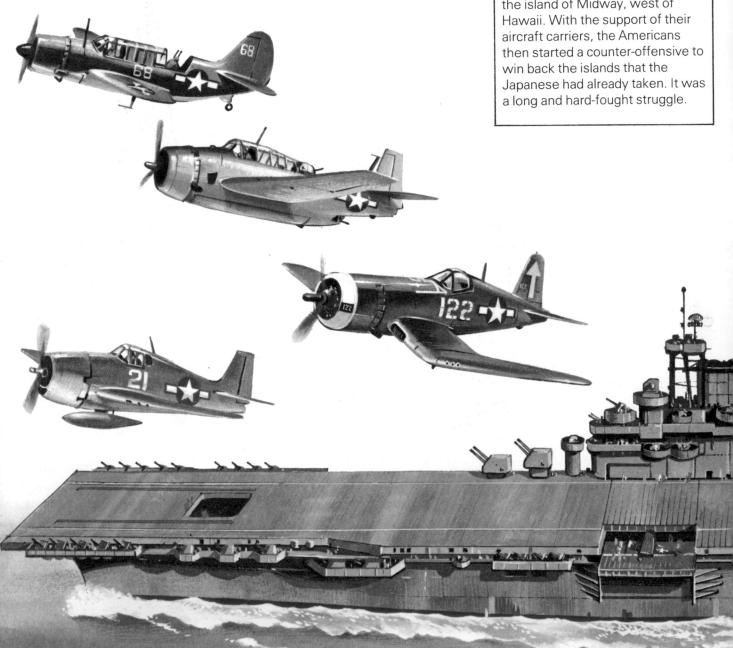

The Essex class aircraft carriers spearheaded the American offensive in the Pacific

In 1943, Essex class carriers spearheaded the American offensive through the Carolinas and Marianas Islands. They were better ships and had better aircraft than those used by the Japanese. The first of the class was the *Essex* itself, which was completed in December 1942. Twenty ships in all were built.

Displacement: 27,433 tonnes (27,000 tons)
Length: 250 metres (820ft)
Beam (extreme): 45 metres (147ft 6ins)
Draught: 6 metres (20ft)
Armament: 12 x 5-inch guns; 40 x 40mm AA guns; 50 x 20mm quadruple mounts
Armour: 5-7 inches (2-3 inches)
Engines: 150,000 hp, geared turbines
Speed: 32 knots
Capacity: 100 aircraft

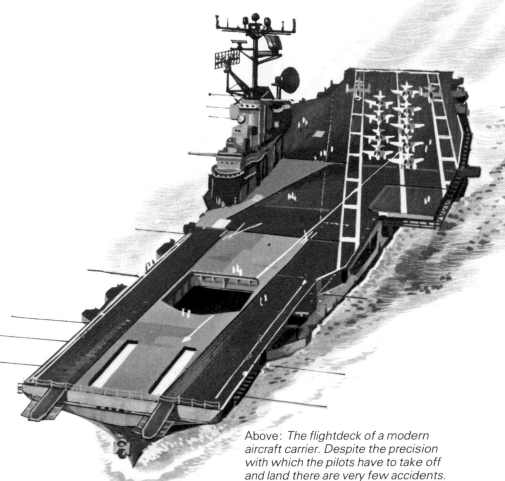

Above: *The flightdeck of a modern aircraft carrier. Despite the precision with which the pilots have to take off and land there are very few accidents.*

Heat, Light and Power

Insulators protect us against the cold

Metals such as silver and copper are good conductors of heat. Other materials are bad conductors. Some of these are used as insulators to prevent heat escaping. Wood, plastic and rubber are all good insulators. Air is also a good insulator. Woollen clothing traps air to keep the body warm. A string vest creates pockets of warm air. Two thinner layers of clothing, with air trapped in between, are often better than one thick layer. A duvet, or quilt, keeps you warm at night because the feathers trap warm air. Double-glazing on windows keeps a room warm, because a layer of air is trapped between two panes of glass.

Heat is transferred from one object to another in three different ways

Conduction is the way in which heat passes through a solid substance. An iron conducts heat to the clothes on an ironing board. Metals such as silver and copper are good conductors of heat. *Convection* occurs in liquids and gases, when the hot substance rises and is replaced by cold matter which itself then becomes hot and rises. This happens in a convector air heater. *Radiation* occurs when heat is transferred from one body to another without necessarily affecting the space in between. The Sun radiates heat in electromagnetic waves and so does an electric fire. Darker surfaces radiate more heat than lighter ones. Dark surfaces also absorb more heat, making dark clothes ideal for winter.

There are several primitive ways of making a fire

One way to start a fire without a match is to use a shiny piece of metal or a mirror to reflect the rays of the Sun on to dry tinder until the heat from the Sun makes the tinder smoulder and burn. Another way is create heat from friction, either by striking a spark from a flint or by rubbing two pieces of wood together. Primitive people had several ways of doing this. In a fire-drill and a bow-drill one upright piece of wood was rubbed in a wooden socket. In a fire-plough and a fire-saw one piece of wood was rubbed from side to side, either in a groove or across another piece of wood. In a sawing-thong, a fibre or thong was drawn to and fro around a piece of wood to create heat through friction.

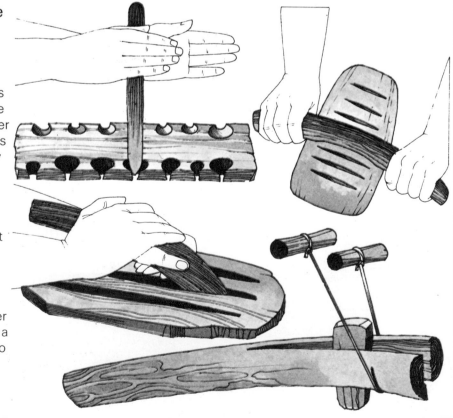

Where the heat goes

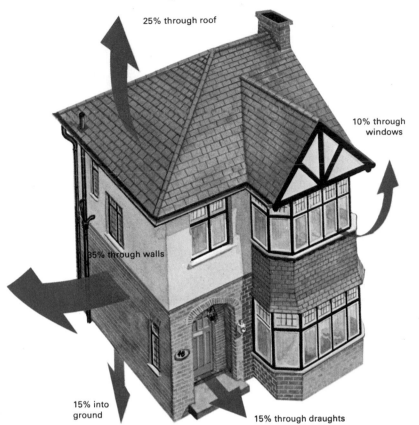

25% through roof

10% through windows

35% through walls

15% into ground

15% through draughts

An ordinary house retains only about 20 per cent of the heat produced inside it

More than 80 per cent of the heat produced inside a house is usually lost and wasted. About 20 per cent disappears through unlagged roofs; 25 per cent goes through the walls; 20 per cent vanishes through the doors and windows, and 10 per cent seeps out through the floors. The remaining five per cent finds its way out through cracks.

Left: *This drawing shows how heat commonly escapes from an ordinary house. Insulation, particularly in the attic of a house can stop 20 per cent of all heat loss and save the houseowner money in reduced fuel bills.*

Right: *Double glazing is an effective insulator. In a single window, the glass can become cold when water in the air condenses on it. This makes the glass on the inside just as cold, thus lowering room temperature. Heat in the room can escape through the glass and noise is allowed in. With double glazing there is a layer of air trapped within the two pieces of glass which acts as an insulator and stops outside noises coming into the room. Some experts claim that double glazing is the least cost-effective method of insulation as it can take the savings of thirty years of fuel bills to pay for the cost of installation, but most people, nowadays, do prefer to have their windows double glazed.*

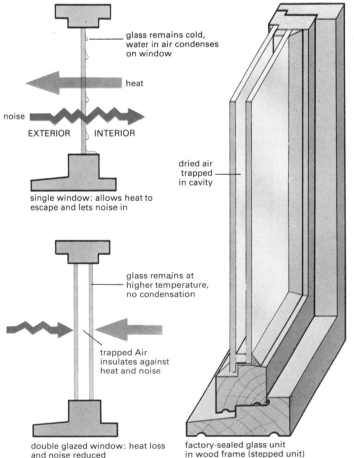

glass remains cold, water in air condenses on window

heat

noise

EXTERIOR INTERIOR

single window: allows heat to escape and lets noise in

glass remains at higher temperature, no condensation

trapped Air insulates against heat and noise

double glazed window: heat loss and noise reduced

dried air trapped in cavity

factory-sealed glass unit in wood frame (stepped unit)

Friction can cause temperatures of 1500°C (2732°F) when a returning space capsule enters the Earth's atmosphere

A returning capsule from a spacecraft enters the Earth's atmosphere at approximately 38,000 kilometres (23,612 miles) an hour and generates heat at 1500°C (2732°F). Its heat shield glows bright red and white. This heat is caused by friction with the particles in the atmosphere. In a similar way, friction creates heat when you light a match, when a rope runs through your hands, and when car tyres have been moving fast on the road.

The tide gives us electricity

The sea is one of the most important sources of many important minerals such as oil, cobalt and manganese and technology is constantly coming up with ways to help us utilise these resources. The sea is also becoming an important source of power in its own right. The constant power of the tide has been harnessed to provide electricity. This was first done in France at the estuary of the river Rance in Brittany. It was opened in November 1966 and can produce 544 million kilowatt hours an hour.

There is a limit as to how cold it can possibly be

Lord Kelvin, a Scottish scientist, invented a temperature scale based on the fact that it is impossible to get below a temperature of −273°C. This temperature is called *Absolute Zero* and is impossible to reach. No life, not even the simplest organism or bacteria, could exist below this point.

The sun's energy can be used to heat domestic water

Solar heating is now becoming increasingly common in ordinary homes, particularly in parts of America and Australia where there is a lot of sunlight. Roofs are specially adapted with a system of pipes to absorb heat from the sun's rays. Water in the pipes can be heated to more than 80°C (176°F). Unfortunately, several months of sun each year are required to make this system really worthwhile.

There is more than one kind of energy

If you carry a box of apples up a staircase you are doing work, and the amount of work that you do depends not only on the weight of the box but also on the length of the staircase. If the staircase is 20 metres long you are doing twice as much work as you would if the staircase is 10 metres long. Also, if the apples weigh 10 kilogrammes there is twice as much work involved than if the apples weighed five kilogrammes. So work done equals the amount of force used multiplied by the distance for which the force is used. If you lift a weight you have had to work to lift it and the weight is said to have energy. This energy is stored and is called potential energy. If the weight then falls it is using up the energy that it has stored and this energy is called kinetic energy. If the weight lands on something soft and makes a dent in it the kinetic energy has been used up in making the dent. Energy is never wasted but is changed from one form to the other. Another example of this is coal. Coal is a store of energy, potential energy. When the coal is burned it changes in chemical composition. These new chemicals have less energy than the coal and the extra energy is given off as heat – kinetic energy.

Different sources of power are used for producing electricity

Electricity is produced in a generator which is driven by turbines. The traditional source of power to drive a turbine is steam produced by burning coal, oil or natural gas. Hydro-electric power uses the pressure of water from dams or fast-flowing streams to drive a turbine. The wind-driven turbine uses large vanes like those of a windmill to catch the wind and provide power. Tide-driven turbines use the power of the incoming and outgoing tides in river estuaries. The power from ocean waves is also being experimented with. Nuclear power uses heat from the splitting of atoms to produce steam, which in turn drives the turbines.

Nuclear power helps man but can kill instantly

When the atom was first split at the beginning of this century, it became evident that it was possible to set off a chain of reactions which produce a powerful supply of energy. During the Second World War the Americans used this energy to devastating effect when they used the power of the atom in their atomic bomb. They dropped two, one at Hiroshima and one on Nagasaki, which killed hundreds of thousands of innocent people and brought the war with Japan to an end. But atomic or nuclear power, if peacefully harnessed, can provide an endless source of energy. In Farsta, in Sweden, the entire town is supplied with heating from one nuclear reactor. At Chinon in France as much electricity is produced from one ton of uranium as comes from 10,000 tons of coal. It is planned that nuclear power will become even more efficient. Rapid neutron reactors will, if things go according to plan, enable one ton of uranium to produce the same amount of power as 600,000 tons of coal.

Atoms may be split or joined together to produce nuclear energy

Nuclear fission is the splitting of atoms to create energy in the form of heat. This is what happens in a normal nuclear power station. Nuclear fusion is an alternative way of creating energy. Fusion is the joining of light nuclei to form heavier ones, just as in the Sun where light hydrogen nuclei fuse to form helium. Deuterium nuclei also fuse to form helium. Nuclei require great heat in order to fuse, and fusion produces less energy than fission. But there are plentiful resources of deuterium in the sea and fusion is relatively safe in comparison with nuclear fission.

In an atomic power station atoms are split to produce heat for generating electricity

An atomic power station is merely another way of producing heat, like burning coal or oil. The heat is used to create steam which drives a turbine and a generator to produce electricity. In an atomic power station the heat is produced when an atom of uranium is split by a neutron. Two smaller atoms are produced and energy is given off in the form of heat. More neutrons are also given off, which in turn split more atoms and release more energy. This is known as a chain reaction. The number of neutrons is controlled by special control rods and it is necessary that they are slowed down by a moderator. The heat generated in the nuclear reactor is taken away by water, liquid sodium or carbon dioxide gas. The heat is then applied to water, which turns to steam and drives the turbines of the generators. The reactor has to be carefully shielded by concrete, so that none of the harmful radiation escapes. There have been instances where radiation has leaked which has made the use of nuclear power very controversial.

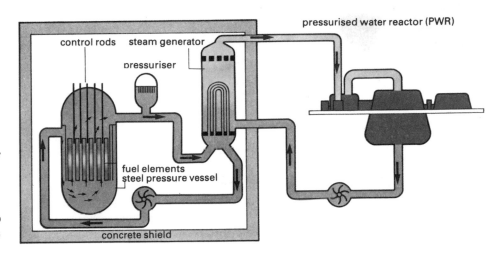

pressurised water reactor (PWR)

control rods, steam generator, pressuriser, fuel elements, steel pressure vessel, concrete shield

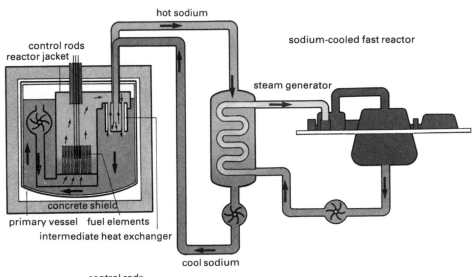

sodium-cooled fast reactor

hot sodium, control rods, reactor jacket, steam generator, concrete shield, primary vessel, fuel elements, intermediate heat exchanger, cool sodium

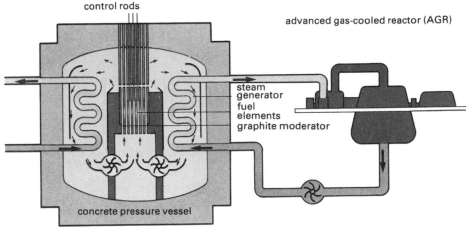

advanced gas-cooled reactor (AGR)

control rods, steam generator, fuel elements, graphite moderator, concrete pressure vessel

Above: *Regardless of what sort of atomic reactor is used, the atomic split is carried out within a concrete* 'overcoat' *to prevent radioactive leakage.*

A fast-breeder reactor produces more fuel than it burns

In an ordinary nuclear reactor the neutrons are moderated to control their activity but in a fast-breeder reactor, where enriched uranium or plutonium is used, no moderator is required. 'Spare' neutrons that are not needed to continue the chain reaction of atom-splitting are used to turn unusable uranium into usable plutonium for more splitting.

There is a great variety of greenhouses

A single market-garden greenhouse may cover 1.5 to 2 hectares (4 to 5 acres) and produce several hundred tonnes of produce each year – quite a contrast to the average small, back-garden greenhouse.
Large plastic tunnels, up to 200 metres (656 feet) long or more, are commonly used as greenhouses. These are tall enough for market-gardeners to work in.

The smallest type of greenhouse may simply cover one plant. This is often known as a 'cloche'. It may consist of two bits of glass leaning together over the plant, or a single plastic or glass container with the bottom cut off, placed over a seedling.

A cold frame is merely a box-type construction with glass over the top and filled with earth. It acts as an unheated greenhouse for young seedlings and provides some

protection against the cold in early spring.

The cheapest way to heat a cold frame is to construct the box, without a bottom, over a bed of fresh manure (a 'hot bed') with a thin layer of soil to cover the manure. The heat from the manure will be enough to bring on the seedlings in the frame much faster. Snakes and other creatures lay their eggs in manure heaps because the heat helps the eggs to hatch.

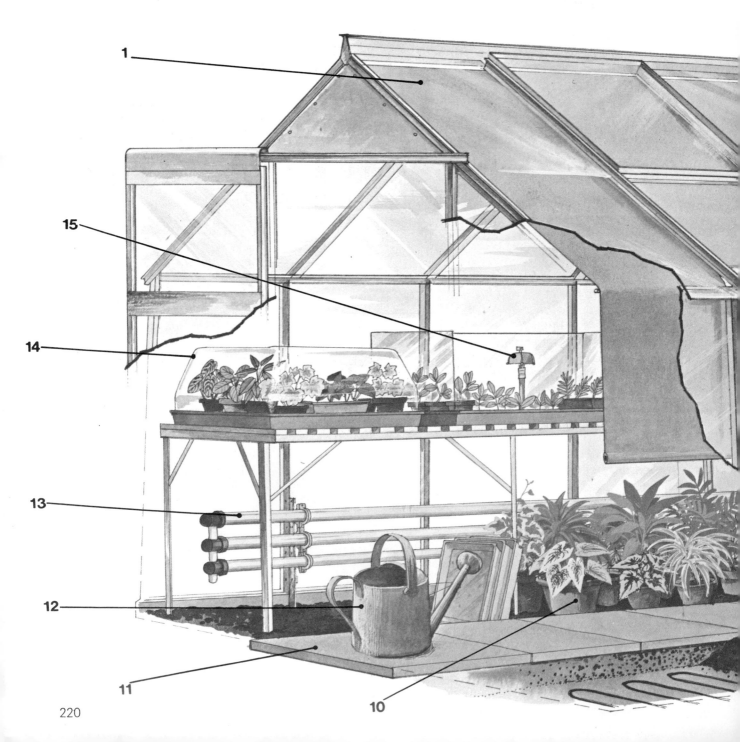

If a greenhouse is built so that one side leans against a wall, the wall should be painted black, not white. The black will absorb heat during the day and release that heat during the night, so helping to ward off frost.

The glass of a greenhouse is both an enemy and a friend. It absorbs light from the Sun and transmits this light as heat to provide energy for the plants' growth. But it also allows heat to escape easily. Even in cold countries, where there is frost every night throughout the winter, a heated greenhouse makes it possible to grow such warmth-loving fruits as grapes, peaches and nectarines.

A greenhouse (1) like the one shown here in cutaway allows its owners to grow plants, vegetables and flowers (7) that it may not otherwise be possible to cultivate wherever they live. It also allows them to grow plants ahead of season. Greenhouses require a lot of work but the results are well worth it.

They are best sited west-east (8) and should have aluminium frames (3). Heat loss is greatest through the glass (2) and (5). Roller blinds (6) protect young seedlings and ventilation (4) is essential. With glass right down to the ground, plants can be grown on the floor (10). Other essentials are seed-warming cables (9), a central path (11), tubular heaters (13) and a mister (15). In summer it is necessary to damp down three times a day (12). Plants can be propagated in a glass-covered frame (14).

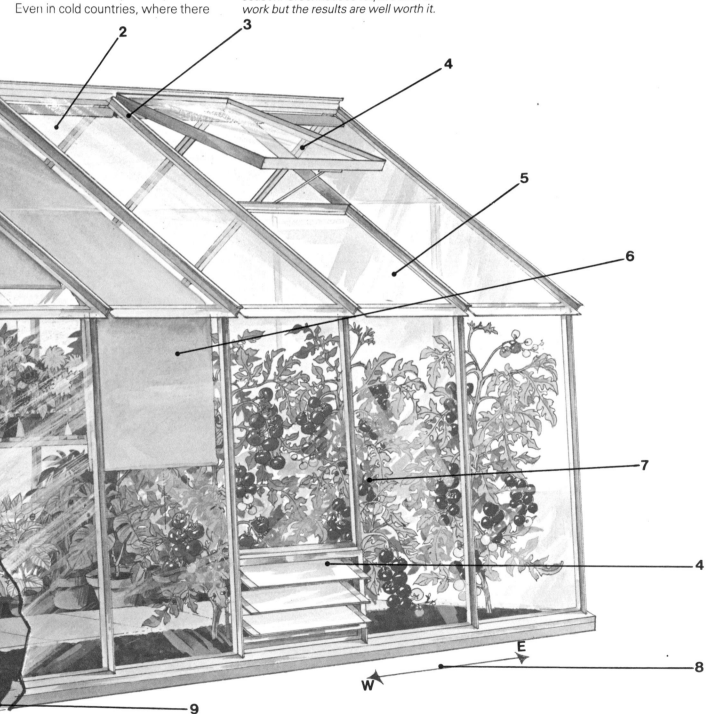

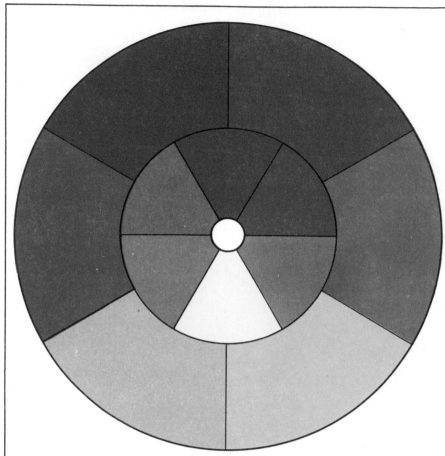

Different combinations of colours can produce harmony or contrast

Primary, secondary and tertiary colours may be arranged in a wheel pattern as shown on this page. Colours on opposite sides of the wheel are said to be complementary, or contrasting. Red and green are examples of contrasting colours. Colours that are next door to each other are said to be in harmony. For example, red and orange are in harmony. The effects of contrast and harmony are used both in decoration and painting.

Painting. Painters have realised intuitively that the right use of warm and cool colours can help create the sensation of space. We can see this from paintings as early as 350BC by Greek artists. Some painters and theorists have tried to work out the effect on us of various colours.

Three colours are known as 'secondary colours'

The three 'secondary' colours are produced by mixing together any two of the three primaries. Red and yellow produce orange, yellow and blue produce green, blue and red produce violet.

There are six 'tertiary' colours

'Tertiary' colours are produced by mixing one primary colour with one secondary colour. Thus the following pairs of colours are mixed: red and orange, orange and yellow, yellow and green, green and blue, blue and violet, violet and red. These twelve colours (three primaries, three secondaries and six tertiaries) are generally used as the basis for all colour schemes in decoration in homes, offices and public buildings.

All colours are made by mixing together the three 'primary' colours

The primary colours are red, yellow and blue. The shades of colour depend on the proportions in which you mix the primaries.

The colour of an object depends largely on what colours of the spectrum it absorbs and what colours it reflects

A black object is black because it absorbs all the colours. A white object is white because it reflects all the colours. A green object, such as grass, looks green because it absorbs all the colours except green, which it reflects. Ripe tomatoes look red to us because they reflect the red colour in the spectrum and absorb the other colours.

White light is made up of a combination of colours

By passing light through a prism, the light from the Sun can be broken down into its separate colours. The droplets of water in a rainbow act as a prism and reveal the seven colours of the spectrum: red, orange, yellow, green, blue, indigo and violet.

Pure white light does not often occur in nature

Although we think of daylight as 'white' light, it actually varies greatly in colour. For example, sunlight shining through clouds at midday will contain far more blue than direct sunlight in the early morning or late at night. White light is actually made up of green and red and blue – the three primary colours.

Colour photography began in the nineteenth century

Although colour photography for the amateur photographer became popular only in the 1930s, its history dates to the very first years of photography. The two French experimenters Niépce and Daguerre, who, with the English Fox Talbot, pioneered black and white photography, tried to reproduce colours in the 1820s. They only managed to produce colour photographs by hand-tinting their photographs, called Daguerreotypes and Calotypes. It was the discoveries of the Scots physicist Sir James Clerk Maxwell in 1861 that really enabled colour photography to progress.

Different colours have different 'wavelengths'

Every different colour has a wavelength of its own. It is for this reason that a glass prism breaks up white light into the separated colours. For instance red has the longest wavelength, violet the shortest; they are at opposite ends of the spectrum. When white light enters a prism, the light is slowed down by the denser material, and therefore it bends (or is 'refracted').

When it re-enters the air, it bends again. But since each colour has a different wavelength, it is bent at a slightly different angle from the next colour. Those with shorter wavelengths are bent more than those with longer wavelengths. So, the light is split into its separate colours inside the glass prism. Not only do the colours have different wavelengths; they also have slightly different temperatures from each other. This was first discovered in 1800 by the scientist Sir William Herschel.

Ptolemy was the first to study colour

Probably the first man to study colour seriously was the thinker Ptolemy in the second century AD. He experimented with rotating discs and discovered additive light mixtures. But it was the English physicist and eccentric Sir Isaac Newton who discovered the theory of gravitation, who began the scientific study of colour. He was the first man to break down white light into its different colours. Then in 1861 Sir James Clerk Maxwell discovered that any colour can be obtained by mixing light of the three primary colours of red, green and blue in varying proportions. He in turn was following the work of the eighteenth century English physicist Thomas Young and the German Hermann von Helmholtz. It was Young who discovered that light travels in waves.

Some colours look warm, others appear cold

A room can be made to appear smaller or larger, warmer or colder by the colours with which it is painted and decorated. 'Warm' colours such as red, orange and yellow bring the room together and make it feel cosy. 'Cold' colours such as blue and green make the room seem larger and cooler.

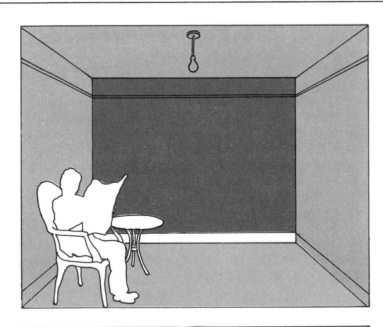

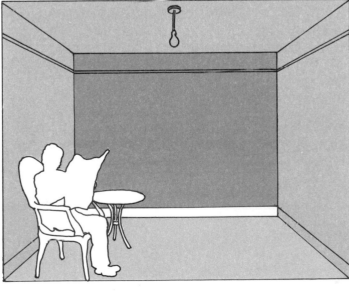

Superstitions and Myths

People have always been superstitious about cats

Since the days of ancient Egypt, cats have always been regarded as rather special. The Egyptians thought of them as sacred, largely because they were needed to keep down the rats that ate their grain. Special cats were mummified and when a temple cat or family cat died there was a general period of mourning. In certain parts of Asia, men believed that they became cats when they died. Some people even believed that if a cat reached the age of ten, it would be able to talk. In Europe, black cats were always linked with witches, but some people still think that a black cat will bring them luck.

Jonah brings misfortune

The biblical prophet Jonah has become unpopular, not because he was swallowed by a whale but because he brought bad luck to his fellow voyagers. Jonah did not want to do what God told him and so he tried to run away from God by taking a journey by ship. God sent a great storm and the ship was very nearly wrecked on the rocks, almost killing everyone on board. The crew found out that Jonah was running away from God and they threw him overboard. Immediately the storm grew calm. Jonah was swallowed by the whale and was eventually put down safely on dry land. Ever since, anyone who has brought bad luck to others has been known as a Jonah although Jonah was really very lucky!

Wedding rings are placed at the end of a sensitive vein to the heart

The wedding ring was first worn in ancient Egypt as a symbol that a marriage contract has been made. The custom of wearing wedding rings spread to Rome where iron rings were used. In Christian times the ring became a symbol of a religious agreement and gold became the metal normally used. The ring was worn on the third finger of the left hand because people believed that there was an especially sensitive nerve or vein running from this finger directly to the heart. In some countries the wedding ring is worn on the right hand instead.

The winter bear is driven off to make way for spring

Spring festivals were not only a way of rejoicing that winter was over; primitive people believed that the seasons needed a little help to make sure they came round in due turn. Many of the old customs aimed at killing off winter to make way for spring are still carried out today. One, in the Pyrenees occurs at Candlemas, on 2nd February, when a man dresses up as a bear, with a furry coat and mask. The villagers chase him with guns and sticks. They catch him, tie him up, let him escape, chase him again and finally pretend to shoot him. Then everyone in the village dances round the dead bear of winter and welcomes the coming of spring.

It was once thought unlucky to cut your nails on a Sunday

There is an old nursery rhyme that explains what will happen if you cut your nails on each of the days of the week. If you cut them on Monday, you will be healthy. If you cut them on Tuesday, you will be wealthy. On Wednesday, you will get good news. On Thursday, you will get a pair of new shoes. On Friday, you will have sorrow. On Saturday, you will see your true love on the morrow. But on Sunday you cut them for evil, 'for all the next week you'll be ruled by the devil'.

The faces of friends and foes used to be trodden beneath the soles of shoes

It is said that the ancient Greeks sometimes wore sandals with portraits of people they admired or loved painted on the undersole, so that when they walked they would leave an impression of their friend on the ground. It is also said that the ancient Egyptians painted portraits of their enemies on the soles of their shoes, so that they could stamp their faces underfoot. But there is also a widespread superstition about new shoes. If new shoes are placed on the table they will never be worn. It is widely believed that they are meant for the long march of the dead to the underworld. Sometimes this is taken instead to mean that the owner of the new shoes will lose his or her job.

A Hallowe'en pumpkin.

The spirits of dead people are supposed to reappear on Hallowe'en

The spirits of the dead are remembered in the jack o'lanterns which are lit at Hallowe'en. These lanterns are hollowed pumpkins, turnips or mangold wurzels with faces cut into them. Lighted candles are stuck inside. The dead are also remembered in the old custom of 'souling', when people went round to each other's doors begging special 'soul cakes' and 'soul bread' and ale and singing special 'souling songs' which were meant to bring comfort to the dead. This tradition is reflected in 'mischief night' when children go round knocking on doors, calling 'trick or treat'. This means that they want a treat or they will play a trick. The old idea was that if the spirits were not given food then they would cause mischief. Apples were also important at Hallowe'en as symbols of fruitfulness and apple-bobbing has always been a popular custom, even today.

Corn is thrown over the bride to make sure she has children

One typical wedding custom is to throw confetti over the couple as they come out of the church. This confetti is usually in the form of rice or coloured bits of paper. It represents the ancient custom of throwing ears of corn over the woman. Corn symbolised the fertility of the earth and was to help the bride have children.

In Britain, white heather is always lucky

Heather is always reckoned to bring good luck - especially white heather - since white was once a sacred colour in pagan times. The good luck attaching to white heather also perhaps derives from the belief that only white heather is free of the bloodstains of the Picts.

The apple tree is generally believed to be unlucky

Of fruit-bearing trees, the apple is regarded as unlucky. This is probably linked with the fruit - traditionally supposed to have been an apple - which Adam and Eve ate in the Garden of Eden. This led to their tragic ejection from the Paradise. In England, the apple's evil reputation is also linked with an ancient custom of placing an apple in the hands of a dead child.

Most businessmen avoid arranging meetings on Friday 13th

Very few meetings are organized for Friday 13th for a number of reasons. Friday itself is named after the mischievous pagan goddess Frigg. But Friday is also the day on which Adam and Eve were expelled from Eden, the day on which Christ was crucified, and the day on which condemned criminals were always executed in Europe in former centuries. Thirteen has been an unlucky number ever since thirteen people sat down to eat the Last Supper.

Bridge-builders don't like talking about their projects

Bridge-builders are particularly superstitious members of the building profession. One bridge-builder said it was unwise to talk or write about a bridge-building project, since disaster was bound to follow. He was implying that if the builder announced publicly that the job was finished he would be tempting the gods to come and knock it down. For the very same reason, superstitious builders have always been reluctant to cement the last brick of a building into its proper place.

The mythical griffin was part eagle, part lion

The griffin has the head and wings of an eagle and the body, legs and tail of a lion. It also has curiously long ears. People of ancient and mediaeval times believed that the griffin was the guardian of gold and hidden treasure, and many stories were told about it. Griffins are often shown in paintings and carvings from ancient times. They were believed to be sacred to the sun.

There were three different kinds of ancient nymph

The ancient Greeks were not the only people to believe in nymphs, the ancient spirits of the countryside. People in the Middle Ages believed in them as well. Nymphs were young girls who played outside and often lured the men of the villages to go and live with them. They symbolised all the freshness and beauty of the countryside. There were three different kinds of nymphs. Tree nymphs were known as dryads, water nymphs were known as naiads and mountain nymphs were known as oreads. Each had their own particular kind of beauty and mischief.

The Nine Muses inspired poetry and art

In ancient Greek times, the Muses were supposed to be the goddesses that inspired all kinds of poetry and art. There were believed to be nine of them. Calliope, Clio, Erato, Polyhymnia and Thalia were the muses of different kinds of poetry. Euterpe inspired flute players, Melpomene inspired the writers of tragedy, Terpsichore inspired dancers and Urania inspired astrologers. We still say that an artist who is waiting for inspiration is 'waiting for the Muse'.

The chimaera was a mythical creature made up of a lion, a goat and a serpent

The mythical beast known as the chimaera had the head of a lion at the front and a serpent for a tail at the back, with a goat's head coming out of the middle of its body. It was said to have been killed by Bellerophon in Homer's *Iliad*. Later, it was used as a description of any kind of wildly imaginative mixture of creatures. Modern scientists still use the word 'chimaera' when they talk about animals with hybrid, or mixed, characteristics.

Evil and hope sprang from Pandora's box

'Pandora's box' is a popular phrase which refers to any treasure that turns out to be more of a curse than a blessing. In classical myth, Pandora was a woman created by the gods as a punishment for the misbehaviour of the first men. Each god gave Pandora some charm that would make her more attractive to man and so more dangerous to him. Epimethus, brother of Prometheus, fell for her charms and married her. Jupiter sent her a box as a wedding present and when her curiosity made her open it, all the evils of the world flew out. Only 'hope' remained inside the box.

Santa Claus is the protector of pawnbrokers, as well as being Father Christmas to children everywhere

The name 'Santa Claus' comes from the Dutch 'Sinterklaas' or St Nicholas. Saint Nicholas lived in the 4th century AD in south-west Turkey. He was put in prison and tortured by the emperor Diocletian but was released by the emperor Constantine. It is said that he once gave three bags of gold to three girls to prevent them from having to live on the streets. The three bags have since become symbolised in the pawnbroker's three golden balls. It is also said that he once brought back to life three children who were murdered in a brine-bin, that he saved three men unjustly condemned to death and that he rescued three sailors from a wreck off the coast. He is also the protector of children, sailors, merchants, scholars, pawnbrokers and, because a fragrant plant grew on his tomb, of perfumiers.

The Sphinx used to ask riddles

Most Egyptian sphinxes have a lion's body and the head of a human but some have the head of another animal instead. The best-known sphinx is the one at Gizeh which was built in about 2600 BC. This is more than 21 metres (69 feet) tall and more than 70 metres (230 feet) long. According to ancient legend, there was a sphinx who set the people of Thebes a riddle and killed and ate anyone who could not solve it. This was the riddle: What has one voice, walks on four feet in the morning, two feet in the afternoon and three feet in the evening? Creon, the ruler of Thebes, said that he would give the kingdom to whoever could guess the riddle. Oedipus gave this answer: Man has one voice but crawls at first on four legs, then walks on two legs, then uses a stick for a third leg in old age.

The phoenix rises from the ashes of its own corpse

The phoenix was an imaginary bird from the days of ancient Egypt and Greece. It was about the size of an eagle, with brightly coloured plumage. People believed that the phoenix had no mate and laid no eggs. It lived for 500 years, then it made a nest of spices and sat on the nest and waited until the rays of the sun set fire to the nest. The phoenix was burned to ashes. From the ashes there came a worm that turned into a new phoenix which lived for another 500 years. Many people since those ancient times have used the phoenix as a symbol of rebirth.

Narcissus died of self love

'Narcissus' is not only a flower; it is also the name we give to someone who admires themselves a lot. The original Narcissus was a character in Greek mythology. One day he saw his own reflection in a pool of water. He fell in love with the reflection, thinking it was the face of another person. He was so upset that the reflection would not come out to greet him that eventually he dived into the pool and drowned.

The kraken was a monster as large as an island

Sailors of the past sometimes told stories of the kraken, a vast sea monster as big as an island, more than two kilometres (1 mile) across. Thinking it really was an island, sailors said they sometimes landed on the back of the kraken as it floated on the surface and lit fires to cook their food. They were drowned when the monster suddenly dived. Ships, too, were sucked down by the swirling waters around the kraken although the main danger of the monster was its sheer size rather than its fierceness. Stories were told about the kraken in Norwegian waters as late as the 17th and 18th centuries. If it existed at all it was probably some kind of giant cuttlefish or polyp.

The monstrous Roc was a mixture between a vulture and an eagle

In the *Arabian Nights*, Sinbad the Sailor is carried off by a monstrous bird called a Roc, which has an egg as large as the dome of a small mosque. The imaginary creature lives on an island and feeds on elepant calves, huge serpents and the carcasses of dead cattle and horses. The Roc seems to be based on the real vulture, which feeds off carcasses, and the snake-eating eagle. In the story, Sinbad finds himself thrown together with some of the carcasses and piles of precious stones. He grabs handfuls of the jewels and ties himself to one of the carcasses and waits until the Roc lifts him out to freedom. The voyages of Sinbad are only one of the stories that Scheherezade told her husband night after night to escape from being beheaded.

Pan as seen in a stone relief found at Pompeii.

The Greek god Pan was half man, half goat

Pan was the Greek god of fields and forests, flocks and herds, and wild animals. The upper part of his body was that of a man, the lower part was hairy, with hooves and a tail, like a goat. He enjoyed all the pleasures of life and played sweet music on his Pan pipes. His name in Greek means 'everything' and he symbolised the forces of nature which surround us. The word 'panic' also comes from Pan's name, because it was believed that he was responsible for all the mysterious sounds of the night that frightened people. It was also said that he had only to whisper in the ears of the cattle and they would stampede with terror.

227

Paris and Helen of Troy as seen on an Attic vase

Hercules had to carry out 12 tasks, or labours

Hercules was the strong man of the Greek myths. He accidentally killed his wife and children in a fit of rage set on him by a jealous goddess. He was condemned, as a punishment, to work for the King of Argive for 12 years. The king gave him 12 tasks, each of which seemed impossible but Hercules did them all. He slew the Nemean lion; he killed the hydra-headed monster of Lerna; he caught the stag with the golden horns and brazen hooves and captured the Erymanthian boar. He also cleaned out the Augean stables, shot the brazen clawed birds of Lake Stymphalis, seized the mad Cretan bull and put an end to the man-eating steeds of Diomedes. He stole the girdle of the Queen of the Amazons, won the cattle of the giant Geryones, took the apples of the Hesperides, and brought the dog Cerberus up from the Underworld.

The fate of one woman caused a war that lasted ten years

Queen Helen of Troy was supposed to be one of the most beautiful women of the ancient world. In around 1200 BC she married Menelaus, King of Sparta, but was taken away by Paris, Prince of Troy, who fell madly in love with her. Menelaus gathered all the Greek warriors and sailed to Troy to win her back. The war lasted for ten years. Paris was killed during the war and eventually the Greeks won the city by a trick. They sent a wooden horse as a gift to the Trojans, but they did not know it was full of hidden soldiers. Menelaus took Helen back to Sparta after the soldiers had sacked Troy.

The Fates were three old women who held everyone's destiny in their hands

The Greeks and Romans liked to give solid shape to their ideas about life, death and the unknown. They believed that mankind's fate was controlled by three old women, who were the daughters of the great god Zeus, or Jupiter. One of the women, or Fates, held a distaff on which was wound the thread of a person's life. The second spun the thread as the person went through his life. The third cut the thread when the person came to the end of his life. In some versions of the story, the first woman is young, the second is middle aged and the third is old. The idea of life as a delicate thread that can be cut at any moment has persisted in our thoughts and literature. The mythology of Rome and Greece is fascinating and is well worth reading. It is full of stories of heroes and heroines and the gods.

The brothers who founded Rome fought each other

The Romans believed that their city was founded by twin brothers, Romulus and Remus. These twins had been cast adrift in a basket on the River Tiber by their great uncle, who had overthrown their grandfather, the King of an Italian city called Alba Longa. The twins were found by a she-wolf, who suckled them. Later they were brought up by a shepherd and when they had grown up restored their grandfather to his throne. They then decided to build their own city at the spot where the she-wolf had nursed them. All went well until Romulus built a wall round the city. Remus said the wall was too small and laughingly jumped over it. Romulus was furious and killed him and ruled Rome by himself. Despite his bad-tempered action he was a good ruler and the Romans later worshipped him as the god Quirinus.

The man who built the labyrinth was the father of Icarus

One of the best-known Greek legends is that of the hero Theseus who went to Crete to see King Minos and killed the monster Minotaur that lived in the labyrinth. This was a maze, built for the king by the architect Daedalus. The king quarrelled with Daedalus after the labyrinth had been built and shut him in it together with his son Icarus. Daedalus made wings of feather and wax for himself and his son and they flew out of the maze. But Icarus became so excited that he flew too near the sun and the wax melted. He fell into the sea and drowned.

Alexander the Great had to undo a knot before he was able to build up his empire

Gordius was a peasant farmer who became king of an ancient country called Phrygia. In thanks for this, he tied up his old wagon with a deviously clever knot and dedicated it to the gods. The story spread that whoever could untie the knot would become ruler of all the land of the east. No-one succeeded until Alexander the Great heard the story when he was setting out on his march of conquest through Persia. He took out his sword and cut the knot in two and conquered as far as India.

The Lorelei rock is said to lure sailors to their deaths

The Lorelei rock stands on the bank of the River Rhine, near St Goar in Germany. It has an extraordinary echo that has given rise to a popular legend. The story relates that a beautiful girl drowned herself nearby because her lover left her for another woman. She was changed into a siren who sits on the rock singing and combing her hair, luring sailors to wreck their boats.

The bed of Procrustes fitted everyone

Theseus was a hero of ancient Greece who slew the Minotaur in the labyrinth of King Minos. He was also famous for slaying a bullying robber called Procrustes, who lured victims to his lonely castle and invited them to sleep on his bed. However tall or short they were, every visitor fitted the bed exactly. Procrustes made sure they did. If they were too long, he cut off their feet or their heads. If they were too short, he stretched them with his own hands. Theseus was warned about his nasty tricks and played the same trick on Procrustes, fitting him to his own bed by cutting off his head.

The land where people ate flowers

Odysseus the Greek warrior was never at a loss. But he needed all his wits on his voyage back from Troy. His fleet of twelve ships was carried by the current to the Land of the Lotus Eaters, whose food is flowers. Odysseus sent ashore three men to meet the inhabitants, who gave them some lotus flowers. When Odysseus' men had eaten them, all they wanted to do was stay there, eat lotus flowers and forget the sea. Odysseus had to drag them away and shut them up in his ship.

Maid Marian was Queen of the May long before the story of Robin Hood began

Robin Hood was an outlaw who lived in Sherwood Forest long ago and stole from the rich to give to the poor. Maid Marian left her family and joined Robin's band of followers. That is how the story has grown, but Maid Marian had in fact appeared in games and dances long before the time of Robin Hood. She had once been thought of as the Queen of the May.

The gorgons were mythical women with snakes in their hair

The gorgons were three terrible women from ancient Greek legend. They had wings on their backs and squat faces with fat noses and long teeth. Their tongues hung out of their mouths, like those of panting dogs, and there were snakes growing from their heads. Two of them were immortal. They could never die. But the third had once been a beautiful woman and she could die. Perseus was given the job of slaying her by cutting off her head. In order to get close enough he had to look at her reflection in his shield, because anyone who looked at the gorgons face to face was turned to stone.

Darius became king because his horse neighed

Darius became King of Persia towards the end of the 6th century BC. He and some fellow conspirators overthrew the previous ruler and then tried to decide which of them should rule instead. It was agreed that they should meet in the morning and that the one whose horse neighed first would win. To make sure of victory, Darius's groom stepped out in front of his master's stallion with a mare. The horse neighed at once and Darius became king. This may be a fanciful story but Darius himself was real. It was his army which was defeated by the Greeks at the Battle of Marathon.

Religion

The Angel Gabriel gave a sacred black stone to Abraham

Mohammed who was born in Mecca established that city as the centre of the Islamic faith. In the city there is a great mosque and in the courtyard of the mosque there is a shrine known as the Ka'aba, which literally means 'the square building'. The building is covered by a black cloth embroidered with gold letters from the Koran, the holy book of Islam. Inside the Ka'aba there is a black stone, which Moslems believe was given to Abraham by the angel Gabriel. Pilgrims to Mecca walk round the Ka'aba seven times and kiss the black stone. Every Moslem is supposed to make a pilgrimage to Mecca once in his lifetime.

The 10 Commandments of the Old Testament and the two Commandments of the New Testament are the same

Moses listed 10 Commandments given to him by God. The first four deal with the relationship between people and God. The other six deal with the relationship between people and each other. Jesus reduced these 10 Commandments to two Commandments. He said that people should love God (which covers the first four of Moses's Commandments) and that people should love each other (which covers the other six of Moses's Commandments).

Prayer beads are common to many religions

Prayer beads have for long been used as a useful way to count the number of prayers that someone has said. One bead is moved along the string for every prayer that is said. Sometimes the beads are merely knots in the string, sometimes they are precious stones or even human bones. Many religions have used them at one time or another – Hindus, Buddhists, Moslems and western monks. The number of beads differs widely according to the requirements of the particular sect or religion. In the Roman Catholic Church, prayer beads are usually called a rosary.

There was more than one King Herod

The Bible tells how Herod the Great ordered the massacre of the innocents in order to try to kill the baby Jesus before he became a threat to his power. This Herod was the first of a family of princes who ruled over the Jews in Palestine from about 40 BC to about AD 100. They were all backed by Roman power. One of Herod's sons was called Herod Antipas and was responsible for having John the Baptist beheaded. Herod Agrippa I, one of Herod's grandsons, was responsible for the death of St James and the imprisonment of St Peter. Herod Agrippa's son, Herod Agrippa II, was an enemy of St Paul and was the last of the line.

The love between David and Jonathan in the Bible is often quoted as being an example of perfect friendship

Although Jonathan was the son of King Saul and David was a simple shepherd boy, the two became close friends when David came to live at Saul's court. After David had slain the Philistine giant Goliath Saul grew jealous of him and wanted to kill him. But Jonathan warned his friend and helped him to escape. Eventually both Saul and Jonathan were killed in battle and David wept.

Five out of Christ's twelve apostles were fishermen

Christ chose twelve men from among his many disciples or followers to be his special representatives, to pass on his message. Five of these men were fishermen from the Lake of Galilee, along the shores of which Christ preached. These five were Simon Peter, James and John (nicknamed Boanerges, or Sons of Thunder), Andrew and Philip. The other seven apostles were Bartholomew (perhaps also called Nathaniel), Matthew (also called Levi), Thomas (Didymus, also Doubting Thomas), James the Less, Lebbaeus (surnamed Thaddaeus and probably the same as Jude, brother of James), Simon the Canaanite, and Judas Iscariot, who was later replaced by Matthias.

Christians and Moslems share many of the same prophets and stories

Moslems are the people who believe in Islam, the religion started by Mohammed in the 7th century AD in Arabia. There are about 600 million Moslems, mostly in Africa and Asia. They believe in one God, whom they call Allah, just as the Christians and Jews believe in only one God. The Moslems believe in many of the stories of the Old Testament, also. They have stories about Adam and Noah and the Flood, about Abraham, Moses and David. They also believe many stories about Christ but they do not think that he was the Son of God. To Moslems, Christ was a prophet and Mohammed was the most recent and the greatest of prophets. Their holy book is called the Koran and their churches are called mosques.

The story of a great flood occurs in many different religions

One of the earliest stories in the Bible is about the flood that God sent to punish the people of the Earth. Noah and his family build an ark and load it with a selection of animals. Eventually they come to rest on Mount Ararat. But the story of the flood does not belong only to Hebrew history. There is a similar story among the ancient Babylonians in their epic tale about Gilgamesh. An Indian story also tells how Manu, the hero, was warned by a fish of a coming flood and how the fish towed his boat to a mountain top for safety. Similar stories come from other parts of Asia, including China, Burma, New Guinea and the South Sea Islands, and from North and South America, too.

Passover celebrates the flight from Egypt

Pharoah at first forbade the Israelites to leave Egypt and return to their home under the leadership of Moses. God sent ten plagues to make him change his mind. The last and most terrible plague was the death of the first-born child of every Egyptian family. The Israelites put special signs on their doors so that when the plague came it 'passed over' their own homes and left them in peace. This is the origin of the feast of the 'Passover' that the Jews still celebrate today. Pharaoh was so angry that his own son, too, had died that he told the Israelites to leave at once. They had only time to eat some lamb cooked with bitter herbs and to take with them some unbaked bread before they left, traditional foods for the feast ever since.

The cross is not solely a Christian symbol

The simple cross (1) is by far the oldest of human symbols, and is not only a Christian sign. It is found all over the world. There are many different forms of cross. (2) is the most familiar Christian cross. Other crosses include the Egyptian Cross, or St Anthony's Cross (3) which St Francis of Assissi used as his signature. (4) is St Andrew's Cross, the type of cross on which the patron saint of Scotland is supposed to have been martyred. (5) is an Egyptian symbol of life, also known as the Key of the Nile. (6) is the Cross of Lorraine, and is also known as the Patriarchal Cross. The Papal Cross (7) has three cross bars to distinguish it, while the Russian Cross (8) is marked out by its slanting footrest. (9) is another familiar Christian cross, (10) the Maltese Cross. The others are Swastika (11), (12) is known as the Cross Pomée, or Pommelly, (13) the Cross Fleury (flowered), the Cross Crosslet (14) the Holy Cross, (15) the Cross patée fitchée.

Turning the wheel and thinking good thoughts is important to Buddhists

Prayer wheels are used by the Buddhists of Tibet. The wheels are usually small, ornate cylinders stuck upright on the ends of little handles and spun round and round as they are carried about. Inside the cylinders there are scrolls of paper with prayers written on them. The Buddhists believe that revolving the cylinder is as good as reciting the prayer out loud, provided that the 'wheel turner' is thinking good thoughts at the same time. And since it is considered important to recite as many prayers as possible the cylinders are kept revolving busily. Larger wheels are often placed in temples for visitors to turn and prayers are also sometimes written out on streamers that flutter in the wind with the same good effect.

A Sikh's life is governed by five 'k's

Sikhism is a form of religion that developed from Hinduism in northern India at the beginning of the 16th century. *Sikha* means a 'disciple' and the Sikhs were disciples of Nanak, who died in 1533. These pious and peaceful people became militant when they were persecuted by the Mogul emperors. They also fought two wars against the British in India in the 19th century. The five 'k's that are one of the major rules of their life are mostly symbolic left-overs of this ancient militancy. *Kes* is the uncut beard and hair that was wound like a protective turban round the head. *Kachh* was the short knee-length trousers, worn for mobility. *Kara* was the iron bangle. *Kirpan* was the sword they carried. *Khanga* was the hair comb. Most of the several million Sikhs in the world today are still in India. In the eighteenth century Sikhism became a great military power against the Mughal Empire and Islam.

There was a hermit who lived on top of pillars in the desert

In the days of the early Christian Church and throughout the Middle Ages there were many hermits. They were religious people who withdrew from everyday life to think about God. Some believed they should have no comforts and that if their bodies were made to suffer, their spirits would be more free. Many became well-known and people came to listen to them preach. One of them, called St Simeon, who lived in the 5th century AD, spent 36 years of his life on top of a pillar in the desert. The pillar was about 18 metres (59 feet) tall with a three-and-a-half metre (ten feet) square platform and balcony at the top. Simeon lowered a basket for food and preached to people from the top of the pillar.

The Greek word for 'fish' is said to symbolise Christ

The fish was used as a symbol of Christ by early Christians partly because the Greek word for 'fish', which was *ichthus*, could be made up out of the initial letters of this phrase: '*Jesous CHristos, THeou Uios, Soter*', which means 'Jesus Christ, Son of God, Saviour'. However, we do not really know whether the phrase was made up to fit the word 'ichthus' or whether the idea of the fish followed the phrase!

There are seven sins that are considered to be deadly

In the Middle Ages, the Christian Church believed that there were seven particular sins that everyone must be careful to avoid. They were known as the 'Seven Deadly Sins'. These sins, which were often portrayed in pageants by people dressed up in suitable costumes, were Pride, Wrath (or Anger), Envy, Lust, Gluttony, Avarice (or Greed) and Sloth (or Laziness).

Moses has been painted with horns on his head

Mistakes often occur when books are translated from one language to another and this even happened in the Bible. One of the best-known mistakes concerns Moses, when he came down from Mount Sinai after receiving the Commandments. The Bible says that his face 'shone' (Exodus XXXIV verses 29/30). But the 4th-century Latin version of the Bible, known as the Vulgate version, mistranslated the original Hebrew and said that his face 'had horns'. As a result, there arose a popular idea that Moses came down from the mountain with horns on his head and this idea was even put into certain paintings.

Right: *An artist's impression of Moses carrying the tablets on which were written the ten commandments. These commandments became the basic laws of the Jews and, later, the Christians. Their main message is that all who follow God should worship Him, and only Him, and that they should try to love one another and live as good lives as possible.*

The Quakers tremble in the presence of God

The Society of Friends was started by George Fox in the middle of the 17th century as a group of people who worshipped God in a simple and quiet manner, who respected all people, both rich and poor, and who did not believe in war of any kind. One of his followers, William Penn, founded the colony of Pennsylvania in the United States where many of these people settled. They are also known as 'Quakers' because when George Fox was put on trial the judge mocked him and said that he should tremble at the word of God. But the Quakers did not resent the name. They became proud to be known as the people who trembled with awe in the presence of God. And so the name has stuck.

Food and Drink

The pressure cooker was invented in the days of King Charles II

The pressure cooker is not as modern as you may think. In 1680, when King Charles II was on the throne of England, a Frenchman, Denis Papin, designed what he called a 'New Digester or Engine for Softening Bones'. He demonstrated it at a dinner given to the Royal Society in London a few years later. All the diners, including the well-known diarist, John Evelyn, were most impressed. The meal included beef, mutton, pike and pigeon, all stewed deliciously in their own juices. In a normal saucepan the steam escapes but in a pressure cooker, with the lid locked tightly on, the rising pressure of the steam inside can reduce bones to a soft pulp. The pressure in a modern cooker is about 15 lbs per square inch. In Papin's Digester, made of cast iron, the bones became soft at 35 lbs per square inch and disintegrated at about 50 lbs per square inch.

A sweet, black root is used to hide the taste of medicine

Liquorice is often used to hide the unpleasant taste of certain medicines, as well as being used for thick, black, sticky sweets. It is the concentrated extract from the root of the liquorice plant, which belongs to the same family as beans and peas. The word 'liquorice' means 'sweet root' in ancient Greek.

Moulds and bacteria help to give cheeses their special flavour

Normally, we try to stop moulds and bacteria forming on food. But many moulds and bacteria are quite harmless and it is some of these harmless ones that give certain cheeses their distinctive taste. For example, Swiss cheeses often have holes in them. The holes are caused by gases given off by bacteria that are introduced on purpose into the cheese while it is maturing. Another special mould produces the blue veins in Roquefort cheese from France. Camembert, also from France, has a greyish-white mould growing on its surface, which many consider the most delicious part of the whole cheese.

Acorns were once used instead of almonds and coffee

Acorns were an important food for man in prehistoric times and they have often continued to be so in times of famine. Today, they are generally used as food for animals. They are bitter to taste but the bitterness can be taken out of them by burying them in ash or charcoal and sprinkling them regularly with fresh water over a lengthy period, to drain the bitterness away. They can be chopped and roasted like almonds or ground up and double-roasted as a coffee substitute. They were used in this way during the Second World War, when real coffee was very scarce.

The acorn is the fruit of the oak tree, and is sometimes known as the oak apple.

Chocolate was unknown in Europe until the 16th century

Christopher Columbus introduced cocoa beans to Europe from the New World at the beginning of the 16th century, along with the idea of drinking chocolate which he had learnt from the Indians. One form of the drink, which the Aztecs enjoyed, was to crush the beans in cold water and mix in some spices and pepper. The Spaniards also drank it cold but preferred it sweetened rather than spiced. It was another 50 years before people started mixing chocolate with milk as well. Chocolate was not used for sweets until the middle of the 19th century.

Cocoa pods grow on the cocoa tree. The trees were originally found in the forests of South America and grow to an average height of ten metres (thirty feet).

Tapioca is taken from a poisonous root juice

Tapioca comes from the root of the cassava plant, which grows in Brazil, West Africa and Malaysia. The juice of the root is bitter and poisonous but when it is left to settle a starchy substance forms at the bottom of the dish. When this starch is dried, it becomes pellets of tapioca, which is used for several purposes including making milk puddings.

A juicy 'steak' may contain no meat at all

The population of the world is rising so fast that there is not enough meat for everyone. But meat is important for the protein that it provides, and many people do not want to stop eating it. The answer to this problem is an alternative source of protein that can be processed to look and taste like the real thing. Soya beans are already used for this. The soya bean can be grown easily and spun into threads like the fibres of meat, then mixed with flavouring and fats, so that no one can tell the difference. Other sources of protein are also being tried, from vegetable stalks to wood pulp.

Alcohol was tested by trying to blow it up

Alcoholic drinks are a mixture of alcohol and water and are normally measured by the strength of their spirit content. Whisky may be about 70° proof, wines may be between 10° and 20°, beer may be about 5°. But 100° proof does not mean that the drink is 100% alcohol. The actual measure varies in different countries but 100° proof is generally about 50% alcohol. Thus whisky would be 70% (70°) of 50% pure alcohol. 'Proof' was originally a very simple test of 'proving' of the alcohol. The mixture of alcohol and water was poured over some gunpowder and then ignited. If it did not burn, then the blend of water and alcohol was too weak. If it went off with a bang, then it was too strong. If it burned evenly, then the mixture was 'proved'. The mixture was then further diluted to reduce it to, for example, 70% of this 'proof'.

Sago comes from the pith of a palm tree

Sago is used in the east to make soups and cakes. In the west it is used for making a type of pudding. It is a starch that comes from the pith of a palm tree that grows in Indonesia. The tree is cut down, the bark is stripped off and the pith, or centre tissue of the tree, is pounded into a pasty flour. The grains of dough that are made from the flour become characteristically half-transparent when they are cooked.

Every part of the coconut can be used in one way or another

The trunk and leaf stems of the coconut are used for building; the leaves themselves are woven into baskets and mats; the fibres around the nut make 'coir' for doormats; the milk-juice inside the unripe nut makes a refreshing drink. As the nut ripens, the milk turns into the white flesh within the coconut and this, in turn, can be dried to make 'copra' which can be pressed to produce coconut oils for margarines and soaps, with the remnants being used for cattle feeds and fertilisers. The natives also obtain a juice from the flowers of the coconut. This can be made into a fermented drink which they call 'toddy'.

Pancake races were started to get rid of unwanted food

Shrovetide is a Christian festival that lasts for three or four days before Lent, the forty days that lead up to Easter. Lent was a time of fasting. On Shrove Tuesday, the day before Lent began, it was the custom to make pancakes to use up stocks of fat, butter and eggs that were not allowed during the fast. There were usually plenty of games as well, to get rid of people's energy before the serious religious thoughts of the next forty days. Many other religions have periods of fasting in their religious calendars, including the Moslems who fast throughout Ramadan.

Pasta comes in all shapes and sizes

Pasta is a dough made from a particular kind of wheat. The pasta is shaped into lengths called *spaghetti*, which literally means 'a small string or cord'. It is also shaped into *vermicelli*, which means 'little worms' and is a smaller, shorter version of spaghetti. It can also be shaped into *macaroni*, which is a hollow string of pasta. The same pasta is also made into certain kinds of puddings, which are usually boiled up with milk and sweetened. It is then known as semolina.

Sugar was brought to Europe by the Moors

At least until the 15th century in Europe, and for many people until much later, honey was the only way to sweeten food or drink. Keeping bees was much more common than it is today. Sugar had in fact been used in India and the East long before but it was first introduced into Europe through Spain by the Moors. The Crusaders increased the popularity of sugar by bringing back little loaves of it from the Holy Land. There are two main types of sugar, cane and beet. The cane needs the hot climates, of such countries as India, Java and the West Indies. Sugar beet can grow in much cooler climates, even in England. Although cane and beet look so different, the sugar that is refined from them tastes almost exactly the same in the end.

The first biscuits were double-cooked and had to be broken with a mallet

The original biscuits were required to be preserved, without going stale, for the use of travellers, soldiers and sailors. It was therefore baked twice over until it was several times harder than a rusk. 'Hard tack', as the sailors often called it, quite frequently had to be broken with a mallet! The word itself comes straight from the French for 'twice cooked', which is 'bis cuit'.

Peanuts grow underground

The peanut is also known as the ground nut or monkey nut. The last two names are more appropriate because the nut grows underground and monkeys like to dig it up. The nut does also look like several peas in a pod. It grows on low, bushy plants whose flowers bend down to the ground. The developing pods are forced beneath the soil and ripen under the ground.

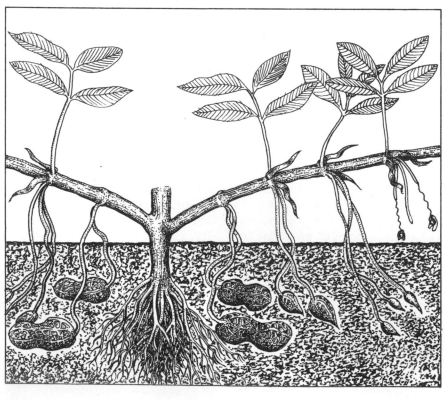

The flowers and berries from the same tree can be used to make red wine and white wine

The elder tree usually grows wild in hedgerows and woods. It produces clusters of small white flowers in the early summer and dark berries in the autumn. Country people have always used the berries as a source of food, in pies, preserves and puddings. They also use it to make one of the most pleasant of all home-made wines – elderberry wine. This has a rich taste and is deep red. The flowers, too, can be used to make wine of a completely different kind – clear, white and scented – which many people think is even more delicious. Sometimes the berries are called 'the poor man's grape'.

Elder berries.

Mead was the 'drink of the gods'

Mead is an alcoholic drink made from fermenting honey with water and herbs. It was commonly drunk in ancient times by the Egyptians, Greeks and Romans, who often called it the drink of the gods. It was also drunk in many parts of Europe during the Middle Ages. When sugar from the West Indies began to replace honey for sweetening food and drink in the 17th century, mead went out of fashion and less bees were kept for making honey. When mead is flavoured with spices it is known as methaglin.

The potato was thought of as a luxury for more than 100 years

The Indians of South America had been growing the potato for a long time before the Spaniards found it and brought it back to Europe in the 16th century. At first and throughout the 17th century it was considered something of a luxury food and crops were not commonly grown until the 18th century. It then became an important source of cheap food during the Industrial Revolution.

Potatoes were the staple food of Irish peasants, such as the girl in this drawing. When the potato crop failed in the 1840s there was mass starvation and many Irishmen emigrated to the United States.

Music

During their lifetimes, Bach and Beethoven were better known as musicians rather than as composers

Both these great composers were better known in their own lifetimes for the way they played music rather than the way they wrote it. Bach was known for his organ playing and Beethoven for his piano playing. In fact, much of Bach's work was lost after his death and his compositions were not fully appreciated until 100 years after his death. Two of Bach's 20 children were also famous composers. These were Karl Philip Emanuel Bach and Johann Christian Bach. Their father is usually known by his full name Johann Sebastian Bach.

Serenades were once sung in the evening and aubades were sung in the morning

A 'serenade' is a piece of music to be played in the evening or at night in the open air, often by a lover beneath the window of his lady. An 'aubade' is a piece of music to be played at dawn or in the early morning. The aubade once had a very practical purpose. It came from the 'alba' which, in the Middle Ages, was a song sung by the night-watchman to warn lovers that day was breaking and that they had better part before they were found out. In later times, the aubade became a piece of music to greet the arrival of important people. Aubades are still composed in the 20th century.

Mozart became a famous composer and musician early in life, yet he was buried in a pauper's grave

Wolfgang Amadeus Mozart was born in Austria and began playing the piano when he was three. He started to compose pieces of music when he was five and played in front of the Emperor of Austria when he was six. Mozart published his first music when he was seven and played before King George III of England when he was eight. He travelled throughout Europe playing to kings and queens but never earned much money and had a sad family life. Although his two great operas, *Don Giovanni* and *The Marriage of Figaro* brought him further fame, he died when he was only 35. He was buried in a communal pauper's grave, forgotten by many of the people who had once praised him.

The hurdy-gurdy is a mixture of violin, piano and barrel-organ

This odd instrument existed in France as early as the 10th century and became very popular in the following centuries. It consists of several violin strings which are sounded by a wooden wheel turned by hand at one end of the instrument. Four strings are used to play a constant drone, while the tune is played on two other strings by the use of fingers on piano-type keys. At first, the hurdy-gurdy was used for religious music and there was very often one man to turn the handle and one to play the tune. Later it became popular with the troubadours. In the 19th century it was used by street musicians. The hurdy-gurdy is often confused with the barrel-organ.

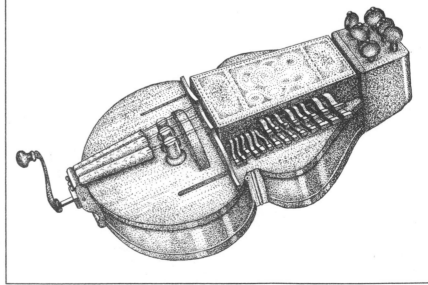

The clavichord is a keyboard instrument that you can carry around with you

The clavichord is like an oblong box, with keys like those of a piano. It is small enough to carry around. There are not many clavichords about today. They were first used in the 15th century but grew in popularity during the 17th and 18th centuries, when composers such as Bach and Mozart wrote music for the clavichord. The sound is produced by very thin tongues, or tangents, of brass that hit the metal strings. The tangents remain in contact with the strings as long as the key remains pressed down.

Some violins are still being played nearly 300 years after they were made

The greatest of all violin-makers was Antonio Stradivari, better known as Stradivarius. He was born in 1644 and lived in Cremona, Italy. He began to produce his own style of violin when he was about 40 and produced his best violins in the first quarter of the 18th century. They are known as 'Strads' and many of today's best violinists still use them. They have a beautiful orange-red, deep-coloured varnish. Stradivarius also made many violas and cellos.

The composer Schubert had to rely on the charity of friends

Despite his enormous output of lyrical songs, Franz Schubert the great Austrian composer, lived in poverty, and relied on friends and admirers for a living. Although he died as a young man of 31, he wrote 13 operas and more than 600 songs. He worked in great haste, and rarely stopped long enough to correct any of his work. A shy man, he nevertheless loved musical gatherings in the tavern or in the open-air.

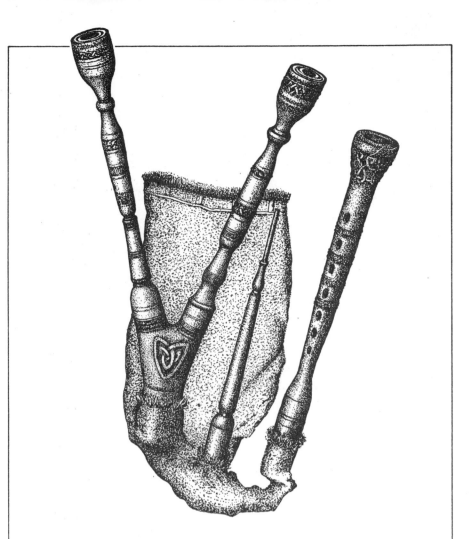

The bagpipe is more than just a Scottish instrument

Many people believe that bagpipes are purely Scottish. It is true that the Scottish form are probably now the most widely spread type of bagpipe, but bagpipers can be found in India, in regions of the CIS and in North Africa, as well as throughout east and west Europe. Primitive bagpipes used only two pipes: a drone for background sound and a pipe for notes. The bag was made out of a goatskin without the feet or head. North west Spain, France, Italy, Bulgaria and Czechoslovakia each have their own particular type.

Handel wrote *Messiah* in twenty-four days

Once he was given the libretto, the German-born composer George Frederick Handel locked himself away in his study in his London house and concentrated on writing the score. He hardly had anything to eat and lived almost solely on coffee. He became so involved with the work that he declared when he had finished writing the 'Hallelujah Chorus', 'I did think I did see all heaven before me, and the great God himself.'

Sullivan hated writing operettas

Sir Arthur Sullivan, the musical half of the immortal duo Gilbert and Sullivan, despised writing the light operas for which he is remembered. He felt he was wasting his talents writing such comic operas as HMS Pinafore, The Pirates of Penzance and The Mikado. The writing partnership was continually riven by the rivalries and conflicting aims of their writers. Sullivan, however, wrote superb classical music.

Art and Artists

An unfinished statue by Leonardo was used for archery practice

Leonardo da Vinci was born in 1452 and became one of the greatest painters of the Italian Renaissance, as well as being a brilliant inventor. At one time, he worked for 16 years in Milan. He started on a statue of Francesco Sforza, the father of his patron Ludovico Sforza. But he never completed the bronze casting of the statue. When French soldiers invaded Milan at the end of the 15th century the bowmen used the unfinished model for archery practice and destroyed it. No statue by Leonardo exists today.

Great works of art were painted on walls of wet plaster

Pictures were not always painted on canvas and framed in the way that we normally see pictures today. Artists such as Michelangelo and Raphael more often painted directly on to a wall. These paintings were called frescoes. The word fresco means 'fresh' and the paintings had to be done on fresh, wet plaster. Lime in the plaster mixed with the pigment, or colour, in the paint and bound the paint to the plaster so that it would last for centuries. Only a little bit of the painting could be done each day, and the work had to be done quickly while the plaster remained wet. A full-size cartoon, or plan, was drawn first and then traced on to the wall to guide the artists.

More than four heads were planned for Mount Rushmore

Four of America's greatest presidents have their portraits carved from solid rock in the side of Mount Rushmore, in the Black Hills of Dakota. The heads of Washington, Jefferson, Lincoln and Theodore Roosevelt are 18 metres (60 feet) tall, from their chins to the top of their hair. They are the work of Gutzon Borglum, who began the first figure in 1927 and who died in 1941 just before completing the last figure of Roosevelt. Before this project, he had already started on the head of Robert E. Lee in Stone Mountain, Georgia. This work was to have included Stonewall Jackson, Jefferson Davis and 1200 Confederate soldiers. But Borglum stopped after completing Lee and the figure was destroyed shortly afterwards.

The Gates of Paradise are in Florence

It was Michelangelo who said that the third pair of doors for the Baptistry of Florence were worthy to be called the 'Gates of Paradise'. The first pair had been built by Andrea Pisano at the beginning of the 14th century. A hundred years later, Lorenzo Ghiberti won a competition to make a second pair of doors. He took 21 years to design and cast the two bronze doors and set them up in 1424. Each door has ten scenes from the New Testament. The next year, Ghiberti was commissioned to do another pair. He completed these in 1452. In this pair (the 'Gates of Paradise'), each door has five Old Testament scenes.

Silhouette was a tight-fisted banker who produced a cheap form of art

Etienne de Silhouette was a highly skilled banker, or financier, in France during the 18th century. He raised a great deal of money for the Crown but was very mean about spending it, especially on Court salaries. When he was removed from his job as Controller-General, he made a living for himself by producing portraits of famous people. He used the simple and cheap method of drawing outlines of them, tracing their shadows thrown by a light on to a screen. These 'silhouettes' became extremely fashionable. Another fashion that bore his name was a type of coat that had no pockets. Who needed pockets when he was too mean to put any money into them, anyway?

Cartoons are not always funny or ridiculous

Most people think of cartoons as comic pictures or caricatures, used either to tell a simple story or to make fun of something. Originally, cartoons were the first sketches made by an artist or sculptor before he started a painting or statue, so that he had a good idea of what he was going to do. The cartoons of great painters such as Raphael and Leonardo da Vinci are often considered to be works of art in themselves.

There is a 'strip cartoon' that is 70 metres (229 feet) long and 900 years old

The Bayeux Tapestry is a linen strip which shows 70 scenes telling the story of the Norman invasion of England and the Battle of Hastings in 1066. It was ordered to be made by William of Normandy's half-brother, Odo, Bishop of Bayeux, and it used to hang in Bayeux Cathedral, in Normandy. There are Latin words stitched into the design describing the action. Along the top and bottom of the tapestry there are thin strips showing all manner of strange beasts and little characters.

Picasso once completed 23 major paintings in a month

Picasso, the Spanish painter whose full name was Pablo Diego Jose Francisco de Paulo Juan Nepomuceno Crispin Crispiano de la Santisima Trinidad Ruiz, was well known for the prodigious number of paintings he produced. In all he finished over 20,000 works and during one month in 1936 completed 23 major oil paintings. Always controversial, his style and media changed constantly. It is also fascinating to know that more Picassos have been stolen than paintings by any other artist.

The painter Raphael was born and died on the same day

Born 6th April 1483, the great artist Raphael, named after one of the archangels, died 6th April 1520. He was employed by Pope Julius II to decorate the Vatican, and was at work on this project at the same period as Michelangelo. The two artists did not hide their contempt for one another. Raphael was not a man to take criticism lightly. When two cardinals complained that the cheeks of St Peter and St Paul were too pink, he quickly retorted, 'They blush for shame that their church here below is ruled by such men as you.'

Gauguin was not recognized as a painter until he was dying in Tahiti

It was only at the very end of his life, when he was already dying, that the French painter Paul Gauguin received any public recognition. He was born in France, but grew up in Peru with his mother's rich family. Returning to Paris, he married and made a career as a banker. Throwing aside his security, he then devoted his life to art, and became a close friend of Vincent Van Gogh. But it was only after he had withdrawn to the south sea island of Tahiti, and was dying, that his paintings achieved any attention in Europe.

Joseph Turner's last words were 'The sun is God'

The great English painter Joseph Mallord William Turner, was a clumsy man with crooked legs and a prominent nose. He was obsessed with trying to express with paint the effects of light on the landscape. When the Houses of Parliament caught fire, he sat and made water-colour sketches of the blaze. At the age of 67 he asked to be tied to a ship's mast for four hours so that he could record a storm at sea. The resulting painting was titled 'The Snowstorm', though an unkind critic called it 'Soapsuds'.

Van Gogh was a missionary before he became an artist

Vincent Van Gogh was born in Holland in 1853. His father was a pastor. Vincent became a teacher first and then a missionary preacher among the coalminers of Belgium. Although he was very religious, he could not keep up this work and so he began to learn to paint. In 1886 he joined his brother Theo in Paris and came under the influence of people such as Toulouse Lautrec, Gauguin, Seurat and Degas. Two years later Vincent moved to Arles, where he painted some of his brightest and most moving pictures. But for the last two years of his life he suffered from serious mental disorders. He shot himself in 1890. His painting career had been tragically short.

Giotto drew a circle to prove he was an artist

Giotto was one of the earliest painters of the Italian Renaissance. He died in 1337. When the Pope wanted to find artists to work for him, he sent messengers to get specimens of work from every likely artist. In this way the Pope could judge for himself how good they were. Giotto refused to give the messengers any of his paintings. Instead he drew a perfect circle and told the messengers to take it to the Pope. The messengers were a little startled but the Pope was impressed and guessed that only an artist of great skill could have drawn so perfect a circle. Giotto got the job.

Michelangelo took four and a half years to paint the Sistine Chapel ceiling

Michelangelo Buonarroti was one of the greatest sculptors and artists of the Italian Renaissance. He lived from 1475 to 1564. One of his most marvellous achievements was the series of paintings on the roof of the Sistine Chapel, in the Vatican Palace in Rome. He was commissioned to paint this by Pope Julius II. At first Michelangelo had several assistants to help him but he was dissatisfied with their work, dismissed them and wiped out what they had done. He then spent four and a half years painting, lying mostly on his back, high up on his scaffolding. The beautiful scenes show the Creation and the story of Adam and Eve in the Garden of Eden.

The great paintings of the Impressionists were at first ridiculed

Impressionist painters at the end of the 19th century tried to capture the 'impression' that a scene made on them, instead of painting the scene exactly as people expected it to be painted. They often used bright colours to show the effects of light and shade and some of them used small dots of colour to give the impression of the light vibrating. Manet, Renoir, Pissarro, Degas and Cezanne were Impressionist painters. At first, many people did not like their work, but Impressionist paintings are now greatly valued and sell for large amounts of money at auctions.

'Miniatures' were not always small

The word 'miniature' for a certain kind of painting comes originally from the Latin word *minium*, which was a type of red-lead paint. This was used mostly for painting decorative illustrations in medieval manuscripts. It was only because these generally had to be small to fit the page that we now call all very small pictures 'miniatures'. Miniatures became very popular during the 16th and 17th centuries. Marvellous portraits were done, showing amazing details of the sitter's clothing and background.

El Greco was a famous artist from Crete

The great 16th-Century artist, El Greco, is generally associated with Spain, where he went to live in about 1570 after studying under Titan in Italy. El Greco did most of his painting in the town of Toledo. He used bold colours and elongated shapes which showed his passionate feelings about life and art. His name gives away the secret of his origins: 'El Greco' means 'the Greek'. His real name was Domenikos Theotokopoulos and he was born on the island of Crete in 1541.

Sir Joshua Reynolds painted a man with two hats

The English painter Sir Joshua Reynolds was born in 1741. He started his career as apprentice to Thomas Hudson, a man of 'little skill and less talent', as Reynolds himself later declared. Reynolds' master was in the habit of painting all his subjects in the same pose, a habit which rubbed off on Reynolds. Sir Joshua almost always painted his male sitters with their hat under the arm. One patron insisted that he be painted with his hat on his head, with the result that the finished portrait features two hats - one on the head, the other under the arm.

A ruined painting saved the artist's life

Sir James Thornhill specialised in decorating walls and ceilings in English stately homes and palaces in the eighteenth century. He was responsible for decorating the inside of the dome of Sir Christopher Wren's St Paul's Cathedral. Working high up on scaffolding, he stepped back to look at the face he was working on when his assistant saw with horror that he was about to step off the back of the platform. Without a word, he flung a pot of paint at the portrait, which made the painter rush forward in anger. 'What have you done?' he demanded. 'Saved your life,' replied the assistant. Sir James Thornhill was responsible for much of the greatest work of his time, including ceilings at Hampton Court, Kensington Palace and the Greenwich Hospital, London. For his work at St Paul's he received a mere forty shillings per yard.

Rubens was so popular that he set up a painting factory

The famous painter Sir Peter Paul Rubens was born in Westphalia in 1577. He became a painter at the court of the duke of Mantua, Italy, and later returned to his native Netherlands as both painter and diplomat. He received so many commissions for paintings, as the popular society artist of his day, that he set up a workshop of painters to fulfil them. For this reason it is very difficult to distinguish between a genuine Rubens painting, a partly-original Rubens, and a fake. He himself said that his painting 'The Last Judgement' was mostly done by an apprentice, but 'could pass for an original'.

A 17-year-old youth forged a Shakespeare play

William Henry Ireland was the son of a London book engraver. He visited Shakespeare's birthplace when he was 12 years old and was so moved that he began to forge documents about Shakespeare. He used old paper from Elizabethan books and artificially-aged ink to forge a lease with the bard's name on it. He then forged manuscripts for *Hamlet* and *King John,* and managed to fool experts that they were genuine. Encouraged by this success, Ireland counted the lines of one of Shakespeare's plays and wrote one of identical length. He called it *Vortigern and Rowena* and set it in Saxon England. He managed to convince the manager of the Drury Lane Theatre in London that it was genuine, having been given to him by an old gentleman who had had it in his family for years, along with others of Shakespeare's papers. However, the audience was not so easily fooled and the play was booed off the stage during its first, and only, performance, on April 2, 1796.

Boastful artist painted his mother

The American-born painter James McNeill Whistler made a famous portrait of his own mother - but called the painting 'Arrangement in Grey and Black Number One'. Although he used to say that he was born in St Petersburg, his actual birthplace was Lowell, Massachusetts. He was a painter who could take no criticism. His own home was a blaze of colour, with walls painted yellow, blue and white. He specialized in serving surprise Sunday breakfasts - with a menu of blue butter and pink pudding.

A nonsense verse writer regarded himself as an artist

The famous writer of limericks and nonsense verse, Englishman Edward Lear, was known in his own time as an accomplished painter and draughtsman. He was employed to give Queen Victoria drawing lessons, and made some impressive studies of the Italian landscape. He is now best known for his Book of Nonsense, which he sold outright for the small sum of £125. Edward Lear, who was born in 1812, was a very unhappy man, who suffered from epilepsy.

Sir Christopher Wren was paid only £200 per year to oversee the building of St Paul's Cathedral

The architect of St Paul's Cathedral - site of Sir Winston Churchill's funeral and Prince Charles' wedding - was treated badly for his pains. He had nothing but trouble to face during its construction, and a special clause in the contract said he could not obtain his full fee until the work was completed. For this reason he received a miserable £200 per year for his services as architect and surveyor. He died in 1723, and was buried in St. Paul's.

A painter buried his poems in his wife's coffin for seven years

Although he had an Italian name, Dante Gabriel Rossetti had never set foot in Italy. He was born in London of refugee Italian parents in 1828, and became the leader of the rebellious 'Pre-Raphaelite Brotherhood' of artists, who also included Holman Hunt. He married the beautiful Elizabeth Siddall, but was so shaken by her suicide that he buried a complete manuscript of his poems with her. He had second-thoughts seven years later, exhumed the coffin and rescued the poems.

People and Places

Cannibals do not necessarily eat human food because they like it

Perhaps, in the beginning, and in times of great hunger, cannibals ate human flesh because it was the best thing around. But often, they ate it because they believed that by eating the flesh of those enemies they killed they would gain the courage and strength of their victims. In a way, it was a kind of magic. It was for this reason that human sacrifices were eaten as well. Cannibals were most commonly found in Africa and Australia, as well as Polynesia, Fiji, New Zealand, South America and the West Indies. There may still be cannibals in the New Guinea forests and deep in the interior of South America.

Mercenaries sell their services to whoever is willing to pay

Mercenaries are soldiers whose loyalty is bought by money. They were common in ancient times and were often slaves, such as the Nubians who served the first pharoahs. In the Middle Ages, mercenaries often went to war instead of the vassals who were due service to a lord of the manor. There are still men who will enlist with whichever army will pay them enough for their services, especially in Africa where governments whose armies have had only limited experience pay for mercenaries to train their raw soldiers into an effective fighting force.

There are more than 12 million refugees in the world today

A refugee is someone who seeks refuge in another country because he fears that he will be persecuted either by the government or by the majority of other people in his, or her, own country. Often, when there is a civil war within a country whole families and tribes flee to nearby countries who look after them in refugee camps. Some refugees, like the Palestinians, have been living in refugee camps for 30 years. They have no proper home of their own. The most recent refugees are the 'boat-people' who have fled across the water from South Vietnam, and the people of the Ogaden, in the horn of Africa, who have fled from Ethiopia to refugee camps in neighbouring Somalia.

The Aborigines of the Southern Hemisphere are gradually dying out

The original inhabitants of Australia met the usual fate of widely-scattered peoples when white settlers settle and take over the land. The same thing happened to the native Indians of North America. They fall drastically in numbers. This was not a deliberate policy on the white man's part; but by a natural process probably caused by apathy and despair at seeing the white man succeed in imposing his culture in the land. In the eighteenth century there were 350,000 Aborigines. Today there are around 40,000.

The wandering gypsies were driven from their homeland

Gypsies are wandering people who exist in many European countries. They earn their living by many crafts and skills and usually live in camps of caravans. It was once believed that they came from Egypt (and so they were called 'gypsies') but they call themselves the people of 'Rom' and their language is Romany. Gypsies originally came from north-west India. They were a poor people who were pushed west by the advancing Mongols about 700 years ago. They tried to set up kingdoms in various parts of Europe but never found anywhere to settle for long. They were often persecuted and pushed onto other places. Even today they are still regarded as strangers and in many ways they like to remain independent from other people.

British convicts were once sent to Australia

After Australia was discovered by Captain Cook in the eighteenth century, the British government decided that it was an ideal place to ship convicted criminals to. Their crimes were quite insignificant but once there, they were never allowed to return to Britain. Many of them became successful farmers after they had served their terms of penal servitude. The last convicts were sent there in 1849.

Tobacco was once thought to be good for the health

When Sir Walter Raleigh returned from his journeys he brought tobacco with him and showed Englishmen how to smoke it. The Indians from the area where he found it used to attempt to cure the sick by sucking blood from them, just as English doctors used to apply leeches to let blood, and by blowing tobacco smoke into the bloodstream, as the man on the left of this picture is doing. The illustration comes from a contemporary French book on Brazil.

South Sea Islanders sailed across the Pacific in open canoes

Just when the Norsemen were crossing the North Atlantic to Labrador and Newfoundland in about AD 1000, natives of the Pacific were undertaking even more dangerous journeys from Samoa to New Zealand. They sailed more than 3000 kilometres (1875 miles) in open canoes and were the first people to colonise New Zealand. More islanders came later from Rarotonga. These were the forefathers of the Maoris who inhabited the country before the European settlers arrived.

The Japanese used to commit ritual suicide

In the twelfth century, defeated warriors who were known as samurai, used to kill themselves to wipe away the stain of defeat in battle. It was a slow, extremely painful way of committing suicide and was called hara-kiri which means belly-cutting. If a samurai was sentenced to be beheaded he was given the chance of killing himself with a short sword.

One quarter of the world's population lives in China

China is the third largest country in the world after the USSR and Canada, but it has nearly one quarter of the world's population: between 800 and 900 million people. In contrast, Canada, which is only slightly larger than China, has a mere 23 million people. The majority of the Chinese live in the low-lying eastern half of the country and work on the land, although industry has grown enormously in recent years. When the People's Republic of China was established in 1949 by Mao Tse-tung, China cut itself off from the West. Now the links are being renewed and both tourists and businessmen can travel to China to see how the Chinese live.

The Moslems established their own country

In the mid-1940s the British Government decided to grant independence to the Indian sub-continent. The original plan was to set up one country, but the Moslems of the north feared that they would be in a permanent minority, and brought pressure to bear to create their own state.

Gurkha soldiers are renowned for their toughness

Regiments of Gurkha soldiers fought for the Allies in the Second World War against the Japanese in Burma, and elsewhere in the world. They fought for the British in many wars, from the beginning of the 19th century to modern times. The Gurkhas are tough soldiers, particularly skilled in hand-to-hand fighting with broad-bladed, curved knives known as kukris. Gurkhas come from Nepal, where they are one of the main tribes.

The Jews created their own country

After the First World War, many Jews settled in Palestine and developed industry and agriculture. The Arabs living there strongly opposed their presence and there was a great deal of fighting between Jew and Arab. The persecution of the Jews during the Second World War led to even more Jews going to Palestine and in 1947 the United Nations voted to partition Palestine into two separate nations, Israel and Jordan. The Jews have created one of the world's most successful states.

St Francis of Assisi began life as a rich young merchant

St Francis of Assisi is famous for his poverty and gentleness and his simple love of birds and animals. He was born in 1181 and his father was a wealthy merchant in silks and velvets who lived in the town of Assisi in Italy. Francis lived and worked with his father until he was 20, leading the other young men of the town in fun and fashion and extravagant pleasures. But in 1202 he was imprisoned for a year during a war between Assisi and Perugia. When he returned home he was very ill and during this time he thought carefully about his life. He decided to put aside all his riches and began to help the sick and the poor. He travelled widely, teaching others what he had learnt, and he started the order of Franciscan friars. He died in 1226.

The man who sent Daniel into the lion's den was pleased when he escaped

Medes was once a nation north-west of Persia which was conquered by Cyrus the Great of Persia in the 6th century BC. The combined empire grew in strength under the Persian king Darius and became famous for its well established laws. Today we sometimes say that an unchangeable law is 'a law of the Medes and Persians'. In the Bible, the story of Daniel in the Lion's Den began with the Persian nobles being jealous about Daniel's friendship with Darius. They asked Darius to sign a law saying that for 30 days no-one shall worship any god except Darius himself. Darius was flattered and signed the law but Daniel refused to stop worshipping his own God. Because the law could not be changed, Darius ordered that Daniel should be thrown into the lion's den. He was delighted when Daniel was saved by an angel and set free.

Tutankhamun was an unimportant pharoah who ruled for only six years

The young pharoah Tutankhamun ruled Egypt in the middle of the 14th century BC. He came to the throne when he was 12 and died when he was 18 and he did nothing of any great importance during his reign. Yet his tomb contained a fabulous collection of Egyptian treasure that has told us more about him than almost any other pharaoh. Most of the other pharaoh's tombs were opened up by grave-robbers long ago but the tomb of Tutankhamun was not discovered until 1922, when the archaeologist Howard Carter first found it. We can only guess that the tombs of some of the more important pharaohs must have contained even greater treasures.

Many passengers on the Titanic didn't believe she could sink

The first lifeboat to leave the sinking Titanic had only twelve people on board, since many of the passengers refused to believe she would sink. When it became clear that the great ship was going to go down on her maiden voyage, the truth was revealed that there were only lifeboats for half those aboard. Panic followed, though some passengers retained their stoic calm. The millionaire Guggenheim gave up his place in a lifeboat, and changed into evening dress to face death as a gentleman. The captain was last seen grasping the Union Jack and pleading with people to 'Be British.'

The Jews at Masada chose mass suicide instead of defeat

The Jewish Zealots were besieged by the Roman Tenth Legion for two years, until AD 73, in their remote stronghold of Masada high on the mountaintop. When they realized they could withstand the siege no longer they agreed to die rather than submit to Roman revenge and enslavement. First the fathers slaughtered their own families, then ten chosen men killed their comrades. Of these ten, nine were killed by the tenth, who then committed suicide. When the Romans broke in the following day, they found almost all, dead.

Harun al-Rashid, Caliph of Baghdad, once sent an elephant as a gift to Charlemagne, Emperor of the Franks

It is sometimes hard to imagine that certain great people, about whom there are marvellous stories, lived at the same time and knew each other. Charlemagne and the Caliph never met but we know that they sent presents to each other. Charlemagne became king in AD 771 and his court became a great centre of learning. His reputation spread to the east and he was much admired by Harun al-Rashid. Harun is best known as the rich caliph in whose time the Arabian Nights (or Thousand and One Nights) was written. These are the stories which the girl Shahrazad told to the caliph each night to save herself from being killed and include Sinbad, Aladdin and Ali Baba. The two men exchanged gifts, one of which was an elephant.

Charlemagne's crown.

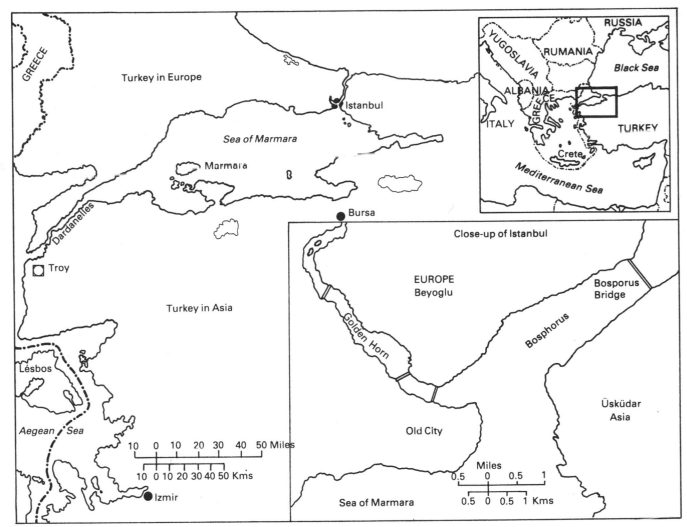

Constantinople resisted attack for more than 1000 years

Early in the 4th century AD, the Roman emperor Constantine the Great moved his capital from Rome to the ancient city of Byzantium. He renamed it Constantinople, after himself. Constantine was the first Roman emperor to allow Christians to worship in their own way without being persecuted, so, eventually, it became a Christian city and was attacked many times over the centuries by Huns, Persians, Russians, Arabs and Turks. In 1453, more than 1000 years after it was founded, the city was taken, after a tremendous siege and assault, by the young Turkish sultan Mohammed II. It was the end of 1000 years of Christianity in the city and it broke one of Europe's most important trade links with the East. It is now the city of Istanbul.

Mohammed II besieged the city for fifty days. He brought into action sixty-eight Hungarian canons - one of which was twenty-six feet long and weighed twenty tons. It was pulled along by 200 men and sixty oxen, and fired a 1,200 lb canon-ball right through the city walls. When the breach was made, 10,000 Turkish soldiers streamed through, and killed the inhabitants. The citizens of Constantinople could not flee since they had locked all the city gates.

King Solomon once ordered a baby to be cut in half

Solomon was only 20 when he succeeded his father, King David, to the throne of Israel in the first half of the 10th century BC. He became even richer than his father and won for himself a reputation for wise judgements. One example of his wisdom is told in the Bible. Two women came to him, each claiming to be the mother of the same little baby. No-one could tell which was the real mother, so Solomon ordered them to cut the baby in half and each to take one half. One woman agreed at once. The other begged Solomon not to kill the baby and said that she would rather lose it than see it die. Solomon then said that this woman should have the baby because she was obviously the real mother. It was a clever way to test who really cared for the baby itself.

Later Solomon was visited by the fabulous Queen of Sheba who came from the South to test the wisdom of this legendary king.

Maypoles once stood as tall as trees throughout the year

On May Day, in many villages around the world, people dance around the maypole. It is a short pole, three or four metres high, with ribbons dangling down, around which people dance, weaving in and out in opposite directions, each holding on to one ribbon, creating pretty patterns as they dance. The pole usually stands for one day only. But once it used to stand throughout the year and was made out of the trunk of an entire tree, 20 metres (66 feet) tall. It stood at the centre of the town until its base finally rotted away and it had to be replaced. There was one such pole in the middle of London but in the 16th and 17th centuries the powerful Puritans objected to its frivolity and poles all over the country were chopped down.

Burial customs have varied from century to century and from place to place

Ancient peoples used to bury their princes along with their possessions. Food was often included so that the dead person's spirit would not go hungry, and sometimes their wives and servants were also buried to look after the deceased's spirits. Nomadic tribes used to leave their dead by the wayside, to be cleaned away by wild animals. The Vikings set the bodies of dead chieftains afloat in burning boats. Hindus burn their dead on funeral pyres. Earth, fire and water are still the three main elements of modern burial customs. In western countries it was common for the deceased to be buried in the ground but today cremation is becoming more and more popular. Cremating means that the dead person is burned in a crematorium, which is usually next to a chapel where a religious service can be held if the deceased family wishes it.

May Day is celebrated all over the world

Countries all over Europe celebrate, in some form, the first of May, which signifies the coming of spring, fresh blossom and the lengthening days of summer. The Roman version was the festival of 'Flora'. In Celtic times, Beltane fires were lit on 1st May and the cattle were driven between two fires to purify them and drive away disease. Men jumped over the fires in symbolic gestures. In Scotland and Ireland these traditions continued into the 18th century and remnants of them can still be found today. Young people used to go 'a-maying', when they slipped out of doors before dawn and returned home at sunrise with fresh branches and buds. The young girls washed their faces in the morning dew; May queens were elected; garlands were made; maypoles were decorated and everyone danced in procession. The customs still survive around the world – and many young girls are still delighted to be voted May Queen.

Some people search for water with a forked hazel stick

Water diviners are people who find water beneath the ground without digging for it. They are also called 'dowsers' and they often find certain metals as well as water. They sometimes use a Y-shaped hazel stick, or sometimes a stick made of bone or metal. They hold the two arms of the 'Y' in their hands and point the stems of the 'Y' in front of them. The stem jerks when they pass over water. It is thought that the human body reacts to the presence of water and that it is the diviner's arm muscle movements that cause the stick to move, rather than the stick itself indicating water. There are various other ways of water divining which is a valuable skill that has been used both in ancient and modern times.

Hallowe'en is the ancient festival of autumn

Hallowe'en is a fascinating blend of pagan ritual and Christian tradition. It was once the Celtic festival of Sambain and bonfires were lit just as they were at the beginning of May when Beltane (see left) was celebrated. It marked the end of summer and the beginning of winter. At Sambain, spirits of the dead were supposed to walk about and farmers lit individual fires to cleanse the soil while their families knelt and prayed to the spirits. The Christians turned it into a celebration of the spirits of the dead saints. All Saints' Day, on 1st November, is also called All Hallows Day. Originally the feast of All Saints, or All Martyrs, was kept by the Church in May, but it was moved in the 8th century to November to coincide with the pagan festival.

The Scots 'first foot' on New Year's Eve

One of the most enjoyable festivals in Scotland is Hogmanay, or New Year's Eve. It is a time for giving presents and making sure of good luck for the coming year. Friends and neighbours go 'first footing' to each other's houses immediately after midnight strikes, to be the 'first' to place their 'foot' over the threshold in the New Year. They take presents and they are rewarded with plenty of warming drink. As you might imagine, the festivities go on late into the night and the following morning! Other customs of Hogmanay include never sweeping the house from midday on New Year's Eve until after New Year's Day, so that good luck will not be swept out of the door, and making sure the fire is well burning, so that good luck will never die out. The reason why the Scots celebrate New Year so is that when it became a Protestant country, the Scots considered that Christmas was a Catholic feast, so they took to celebrating New Year instead.

Invisible hands sometimes throw furniture around a house

Poltergeists are thought to be spirits that move furniture around the house, and knock china off shelves, throw books across rooms, rip down curtains and create strange noises and knockings in the night. The word 'poltergeist' comes from two German words, *polter* (noise) and *geist* (spirit). Although people claim to have experienced these sort of happenings in their houses, no-one has ever seen a poltergeist.

Witches were often lonely, frightened, innocent old women

During the Middle Ages and up to the 17th century, many people, all over the world, believed in the secret powers of witches. Sometimes so-called 'witches' were people who followed old pagan religions and were persecuted by the Christians who were frightened of, or disagreed with, what the 'witches' did. Often these 'witches' were simple, sometimes slightly crazy women who were quite harmless but were hunted down and blamed for any misfortunes that occurred in their village. Witches' trials were often very unfair, and they were given no chance to prove their innocence.

A 'totem' is a symbol of a close-knit family

A 'totem' is an animal or plant that is adopted by a primitive group of people as a symbol of their family unit. Every family has its own totem and no two people with the same totem are allowed to marry each other. Sometimes, individuals have totems of their own. Bears, beavers, birds and wolves have been common totems among the North American Indians. But primitive tribes in Africa, Australia, the Pacific Islands and elsewhere in the world have also used totems. Totem poles are often erected outside the family homes, showing beautifully carved designs of the totem animal. The creature is sacred to the people whose totem it is and they are only allowed to hunt it on very special occasions.

This superbly carved totem pole can be seen at the American Natural History Museum in New York. The Museum houses many artefacts of the North American Indians and is popular with all tourists, both American and visitors to that country.

Red Letter days used to be Saints' Days

A so-called 'Red Letter' day is one on which something special happens. We use it in common language now but the phrase came into being because feast days and saints' days were once marked red in the Church Calendar. The other days were marked in black. There are now so many saints that if all were marked in red, there would be very few days that there were not red letter days.

Easter is celebrated in many strange ways

Easter is one of the Christian Church's greatest festivals and a whole range of curious customs has grown up in various countries. All sorts of special foods are eaten such as chocolate hares and rabbits, pretty patterns and faces are painted on eggs and special recipes are used to make delicious cakes. There are egg-rolling competitions, egg-eating competitions, bottle-kicking competitions, marbles competitions and battles of flowers. One of the most impressive customs that has grown up in the United States, is the series of sun-rise services across the continent, as the sun on Easter day moves steadily over the land from the Atlantic to the Pacific, from Maine to Hawaii. Unlike Christmas Easter is not on the same day each year. It is fixed as the first Sunday after the full moon after the vernal equinox and can fall in March or April.

St Bernadette had visions of the Virgin Mary at Lourdes

In February, 1858, Marie-Bernarde Soubious saw a vision of a young woman in a small cave near Lourdes, in south-west France. Marie-Bernarde is better known as Bernadette. She claimed that the woman she saw was the Virgin Mary and that she saw the vision several times. The Virgin Mary showed her a place where water sprang from the ground when Bernadette touched it. Several people were miraculously cured of disease and lameness by bathing in the water. Pilgrims then began to come to Lourdes from all over the world. Bernadette died in 1879 and was made a saint in 1933.

The French port of Calais was in English hands for more than 200 years

Calais is an important port on the Channel coast of France, only 33 kilometres (20 miles) across the water from Dover. Edward III of England realised how useful Calais would be as a stepping stone into Europe and captured the town in 1347 after a year's siege. Later English kings failed to conquer the whole of France, but Calais remained in English hands and grew rich on the wool trade between Flanders and England. It was finally retaken by the French in 1558, during the reign of the English Queen Mary. Mary is said to have complained that when she died the name of Calais would be found engraved on her heart.

Oberammergau still gives thanks for being saved from the Great Plague

Oberammergau is a small village in the Bavarian Alps. Every ten years people from all over the world crowd into the village to watch a remarkable play by the villagers. It depicts the last few days of Christ and his crucifixion and is known all over the world as the

The name of a French general became a byword for discipline

The Marquis de Martinet was a French general in the 17th century, during the reign of Louis XIV. He commanded the king's regiment of infantry and was responsible for training all the young nobles who wished to command infantry regiments. These fashionable young men were put in their place by Martinet's strict discipline and military training, and his name quickly became well-known throughout the army. Even today, a 'martinet' is someone who enforces firm discipline and order.

A French doctor recommended the guillotine as a means of execution to save unnecessary pain

The guillotine is a French instrument for capital punishment. It consists of a heavy, angled blade that drops down between two upright posts and chops off the head of the person lying beneath. It was designed by a French surgeon called Antoine Louis, and was at first called a 'Louisette'. But the man who proposed that it should be more widely used was a doctor called Joseph Guillotin and so the name was changed to 'guillotine'. The instrument was used in Paris for a public execution in 1792 and was kept extremely busy during the French Revolution in the following years.

Oberammergau Passion Play. The play was first put on in 1634, the year after a dreadful plague swept through that corner of Germany. Many of the villagers were saved and they vowed to perform a play every ten years in thanksgiving. With one slight change in their dates and only three exceptions, they have kept their promise ever since. The play was last performed in 1990.

French policemen were once knights on horseback

French policemen are known as *gendarmes*. The word comes from *gens d'armes*, or 'men of arms', for these men were originally armed horsemen or knights. It was in the time of Louis XIV, in the 17th century, that they first became responsible for keeping some sort of order, still from horseback. After the French Revolution, at the end of the 18th century, they formed a special military police and now they have become the civilian police.

The Foreign Legion was a place for criminals and outcasts

The French Foreign Legion, the Légion Etrangère as it is properly called, was begun in France in 1831 by King Louis Philippe, especially for foreigners who were prepared to fight for France. No one asked any questions about those who joined and so it became the perfect escape for foreign criminals and outcasts who wanted a new life. But the new life was tough and very disciplined and the Legion soon won for itself a reputation for courage and determination. They fought not only in the deserts of North Africa but also in the Crimea, in the Second World War and in all the other wars in which France has been involved since the Legion was founded.

Marie Tussaud made death masks during the French Revolution

Marie Tussaud learnt how to make wax models from her uncle who started a popular waxworks in Paris in the 18th century. She was 'discovered' by the French royal family and worked for them until the Revolution of 1789. The Revolutionaries put her in prison and forced her to make models of the famous people whose heads had been struck off by the guillotine, among them the king

Hans Christian Andersen wanted to be an opera singer, not a story-teller

The best-known of all story-tellers was born in 1805. Hans Andersen was the son of a poor cobbler in the town of Odense, on the shores of the Baltic Sea. He left school when he was 11, after his father's death, and at 14 he travelled to Copenhagen, hoping to become a dancer and opera singer. He was turned away at his first audition. Later, Andersen went back to school and attended university. In 1829 he wrote a humorous travel book which was immediately successful. He published his first book of stories in 1835. Among his best-known stories are 'The Ugly Duckling' and 'The King's New Clothes'.

The Little Mermaid is a memorial to Andersen and sits at the entrance to Copenhagen's harbour.

and queen for whom Marie had worked! Later, she married and moved with her collection of wax models to London. 'Madame Tussaud's' is now one of London's major tourist attractions.

The great travel writer, Hakluyt, never travelled beyond London and Paris

Richard Hakluyt was an Englishman who recorded many of the explorations and adventures of the 16th century, the great age of discovery. He was a friend of men such as Francis Drake and took particular interest in explorations along the coasts of the New World. He met many sailors and wrote down what they had seen. He also learnt several foreign languages and read the reports of every expedition he could find. Hakluyt published his findings in *The Principal Navigations, Voyages and Discoveries of the English Nation* in 1589. Even though he never travelled beyond London, Bristol and Paris to meet people and look

at documents, his book was a tremendous help to explorers who wanted to know what others had already discovered.

A buccaneer became the governor-general of Jamaica

Henry Morgan was a highly successful buccaneer (Caribbean pirate). He made his fortune by seizing gold-laden ships in the Caribbean and by attacking and looting rich towns in Cuba, Maracaibo and Panama. He continued his attacks on Spanish ships even after Britain and Spain had signed a truce. Morgan was captured by the British, imprisoned for a while in Jamaica and sent to England for trial. There, he defended himself so well that he returned to Jamaica in triumph, as governor-general. He died on the island in 1688. It was believed that during his career as a buccaneer Morgan hid a great store of treasure. Most of it still remains to be discovered.

Marie Antoinette would only ever drink water

The ill-fated Marie-Antoinette was born in Austria in 1755. She was reputed to be a great beauty - but she had swollen eyes and was rather corpulent. She was, however justly noted for her complexion. She was extraordinarily modest, and wore a gown which buttoned right up to her neck even in the bath, and still insisted that a servant hold a sheet in front of her eyes when she got out of the bath. When she arrived in Paris, the first of a cavalcade of fifty carriages, she refused to eat anything except chicken. Water was the only liquid she ever allowed to pass her lips. Utterly frivolous, she said that she wanted to wash her hands in the blood of the French people when she heard that the Revolution had broken out. Her husband, King Louis XVI, was guillotined 21 January 1793 at the age of thirty-eight. Ironically, he himself had earlier suggested an improvement to the guillotine's blade.

Hunger and homelessness are the 'enemies' of the Salvation Army

The 'Christian Mission' was started by a Methodist Minister, William Booth, in the East End of London in 1865. Thirteen years later it was renamed the Salvation Army and was reorganised along military lines with Booth himself as General in command. The soldiers of the Army set about a campaign of practical help, giving the hungry and the homeless decent food and shelter in the belief that they might then be able to listen with more attention to the Christian message. The Army has continued its work ever since and has spread through many countries, providing homes, orphanages, schools, and meals in peace and war for soldiers and civilians alike.

Benjamin Franklin was a man of many talents

Benjamin Franklin was one of the greatest of all Americans. He was born in 1706 and was the youngest of 17 children. He learnt to be a printer, ran a newspaper in Philadelphia, and wrote an almanac full of clever sayings. He started a library, a fire service and a college which became the University of Pennsylvania. Franklin could speak several foreign languages, played several musical instruments and invented some useful devices including a lightning conductor. He fought against the French and Indians on the north-west frontier, signed the Declaration of Independence, and helped to work out the American Constitution after the British had been defeated.

General Custer and his men were massacred at Little Big Horn because they disobeyed orders

George Armstrong Custer made his reputation during the American Civil War as a cavalry commander. He later fought in the Indian wars and in 1876 was in command of the 7th Cavalry Brigade against Chief Sitting Bull. At that time, Custer was under the command of General Terry and was ordered by him not to attack Sitting Bull until Terry and the main force of the army had arrived to give support. Custer found Sitting Bull on the banks of the Little Big Horn River and decided to attack at once. He divided his small force of about 650 men into three groups to prepare for flanking attacks but in the end it was his own small group of just over 260 men who met the full force of Sitting Bull's Indians and were completely wiped out before help could arrive. If Custer had waited for Terry, the outcome might have been very different.

Robert E. Lee was offered command of both sides in the American Civil War

Robert E. Lee came from Virginia, in the south of the United States. He had already made his name as a brilliant soldier before the Civil War and when war began he was offered command of the northern army. He refused and instead accepted command of the army of the southern states which were under the presidency of Jefferson Davis. Early in the war he won victories at Fredericksburg and Chancellorsville and saved Richmond, the southern capital. He continued to fight valiantly against the north until he was forced to surrender to General Grant in 1865. Lee died in 1870.

The Pony Express lasted for only one and a half years

The Pony Express was a fast letter service between St Joseph, Missouri, and Sacramento, California. It began in April 1860 and ended with the opening of the transcontinental telegraph line in October 1861. In that short time it gained a reputation for the courage and determination of its riders, among whom was the famous Buffalo Bill Cody. The stagecoach firm of Russell, Majors and Waddell organised the Pony Express, which covered nearly 3000 kilometres in a minimum of 10 days. The riders changed horses regularly at the 157 stations which were about 11-32 kilometres (7-20 miles) apart. Attacks by Indians were only one of the many dangers but the mail usually got through in the end.

There has only been one president of the Confederate States of America

Jefferson Davis was born in 1809. He became an army officer and then retired to his Mississippi plantation. Later, he was elected to the United States Congress but argued strongly on behalf of the southern states who wanted to keep slavery and break away from the Union. When the Civil War began between the north and south, Jefferson Davis was elected president of the Confederate, or southern states. Abraham Lincoln became president of the Union, or northern states. The war ended in 1865, with victory for the north, and Davis was imprisoned for two years.

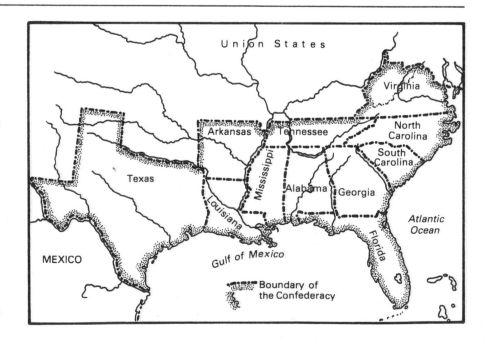

A map showing the breakaway Confederate states.

Pocahontas was a Red Indian princess who became the toast of London

Pocahontas created a sensation when, in 1616, she came to London where she was welcomed by King James I. She was the daughter of a Red Indian chief who had once saved the life of Captain John Smith, the leader of a group of Virginian settlers. Captain Smith was about to be clubbed to death by her father's braves but Pocahontas stopped them. Four years later, Pocahontas herself was taken prisoner by the settlers but was treated with kindness. She became a Christian and married John Rolfe. She helped to bring about a period of peace between the Indians and the settlers and when she and her husband and their son visited London, the people of the city were fascinated to see one of the first of the Indians about whom they had heard so much from the settlers. But Pocahontas fell ill in London, died and was buried there, far from her real home.

F. D. Roosevelt was the only man to have been elected president of the United States four times in succession

Franklin Delano Roosevelt was president of the United States longer than any other man. He was a member of the Democratic Party (as opposed to the Republican Party) and took office as president in 1933. In his first term of office, Roosevelt launched his 'New Deal' to give people jobs during the Depression. He was re-elected in 1936 and again in 1940, when America was still neutral during the Second World War. He was re-elected a fourth time in 1944. Roosevelt took part in the Yalta Conference with Stalin and Churchill in 1945. They discussed the ending of the war. Roosevelt died later that year just before the war finished.

The Statue of Liberty.

The carpetbaggers lived out of a suitcase

A 'carpetbagger' is someone who tries to gain power in local politics even though he has no real connection with the place. The phrase comes from the time, after the American Civil War of 1861-1865, when northerners went south to try to get voted into power by local southerners. Their only claim to any kind of property in the south that might make them eligible for election was the carpet-bag, or suitcase of belongings, they brought with them.

The Statue of Liberty was a gift from France to America

The Statue of Liberty stands on Liberty Island at the entrance to New York harbour. It was made by F. A. Bartholdi and was unveiled in 1886, although the idea had first been thought of at the end of the 18th century. The statue was paid for by France. It was intended as a compliment, after the French Revolution, from one country that had overthrown its king to another that had done likewise. It is one of the most popular tourist attractions in New York.

The Knights Templar were destroyed because they were too successful

At the beginning of the 12th century, in the time of the Crusades, a small group of French knights decided to devote their time to protecting pilgrims on their way to the Holy Land. They set up their first home as a religious community organised along military lines on the site of the Old Temple at Jerusalem and thus they became known as the 'Templars'. Quite soon they were joined by many vagabond knights who had abandoned their original armies. The Templars showed great courage and grew rich from gifts by grateful pilgrims including large estates in many European kingdoms. Their power aroused the jealousy of other people and the Templars were destroyed by their enemies at the beginning of the 14th century.

A royal visit gave rise to the first popular toy soldiers

Great interest was shown by the local citizens when Louis XV of France visited Strasbourg with his troops in 1744. Cashing in on public curiosity, a printer called Seyfried produced some souvenir sheets with pictures of the soldiers and sold them in the streets. Other printers soon began to copy Seyfried's idea, among them the Pellerin brothers from Epinal in the Vosges Mountains. They produced some of the best printed sheets during the Napoleonic Wars. The original printed sheets were soon developed into cardboard cut-outs which have remained popular into the 20th century. Flat metal soldiers were first produced at Nuremberg in the 17th century but they were not mass-produced cheaply until the 19th century. They were usually knows as 'flats'.

The secret burial place of Alaric the Visigoth lies beneath the bed of a river

Alaric, King of the Visigoths, fought first for the Romans but then attacked Rome itself. On his third attempt, in AD 410, he entered Rome and sacked it. This was the first time that the city had been captured for about 800 years. Alaric planned to invade Africa and seize the rich granaries of Egypt but he fell ill and died at Cosenza, in Italy. His soldiers diverted the course of a stream, the Busento, and buried him beneath its bed. Then they returned the stream to its old course. They killed all the men who knew about the burial place so that the Romans would never find the body of their leader.

The lost tomb of Attila the Hun lies somewhere in Hungary

Attila the Hun came riding from the east with his fearful horsemen and terrorised Europe in the 5th century AD. He died suddenly on the last of his many wedding nights, when he choked on his own blood from a severe nosebleed. According to legend, he was buried in a hill somewhere in Hungary but no one knows where. No one knows whether or not the burial place has ever been plundered. The legend suggests that Attila was buried with his treasure and with the bodies of those who carried him to his grave. His coffin is said to be covered with a layer of gold, a layer of silver and a layer of iron.

Treasure was hidden in various places during the Second World War

There are many stories of German treasure hidden from the Allies at the end of the Second World War in various parts of Europe but none has yet been found. Hitler and Goering were both supposed to have dropped rich valuables and money chests into Austrian mountain lakes. Rommel's treasure is believed to be even more valuable, with gold, platinum, diamonds and works of art in six great chests. The most authentic report relates that this treasure was dropped in the sea near the town of Bastia in Corsica.

The buried treasure of Cocos Island lies waiting to be found

The Island of Cocos is in the Pacific, just off the coast of Costa Rica in Central America. The story of its hidden treasure began in 1821 when William Thompson was commanding the English brigantine *Mary Deare* at anchor in Lima harbour, on the Peruvian coast. At that time the South American army of independence was driving the Spaniards from Peru. Fleeing Spaniards loaded their gold aboard the *Mary Deare*, hoping to escape, but Thompson cunningly sailed with the gold and left the Spaniards behind. According to the story, he sailed for Cocos and buried the treasure. Thompson passed his secret on to one man before he died. That man died without telling anyone the secret and no treasure hunter since has found where the gold lies hidden. Like so many other hidden treasures, it is unlikely that it will ever be found.

The bright and beautiful Catherine wheel commemorates a dreadful death

The best-known of several Saint Catherines is the one who was tortured on a spiked wheel and then beheaded because she refused to marry the emperor Maxentius in the 4th century AD. The spinning wheel to which she was tied became a popular form of torture. The legend says that before Catherine was killed fifty of the emperor's best philosophers, who failed to make her change her mind, were put to death. When Catherine was put on the wheel, it flew apart, killing several bystanders. She was put in prison, where she was fed by a dove and saw a vision of Christ. Two hundred soldiers were so impressed by her that they asked to be converted to Christianity and were at once beheaded. When Catherine herself was beheaded, milk flowed from her veins. She is the protector of young girls, students, philosophers and nurses. The firework named after her is a reminder of her torture and death.

The Ku Klux Klan began as a social club

After the end of the American Civil War, a social club of white men was started up in Tennessee. It quickly developed into a secret society that set out to terrify the newly liberated black slaves. The society came to be called the Ku Klux Klan, after the Greek word for a 'circle' – *kuklos*. It grew into a 'circle' of murderers, burners and kidnappers and was outlawed within a few years. The Klan was revived early in the 20th century and again just before the Second World War, when it increased its oppression against the weak and against minorities. Although it was officially disbanded in 1944, the Klan continues to exist and its members still meet regularly although they are not as influential as they were.

Boys were kept to be whipped instead of princes

In medieval times it was quite common for a royal palace to have a 'whipping boy'. This was a companion of about the same age as the young prince of the palace. Because it was considered to be beneath the dignity of the prince to be punished, the 'whipping boy' was 'whipped' or punished instead of the prince whenever the prince did something wrong.
This practice continued into the 16th and 17th centuries.

King Harold may not have been killed by an arrow in the eye

When Duke William of Normandy defeated the Saxon King Harold of England at the Battle of Hastings in 1066, it was believed that Harold was killed by an arrow in the eye. On the Bayeux Tapestry, which depicts the Norman Conquest, there is a man being pierced by an arrow and a Latin inscription saying that the king has now been killed. But another report of the battle indicates that Harold was probably cut down later by a Norman sword and it is possible that in the Bayeux Tapestry Harold is not the man with the arrow in his eye. The Normans did, in fact, use arrows very effectively in the battle, firing volleys of them into the air to disconcert the enemy before charging them with their swords and spears.

Davy Jones's locker is full of drowned men

The graveyard of all drowned seamen is Davy Jones's Locker, the common sailor's name for the bottom of the sea. Some say that there was once a pirate called Davy Jones, from whom the name became popular. But another possibility is that 'Jones' is an alteration of 'Jonah', the biblical prophet who was swallowed by a whale, and that 'Davy' is a form of the West Indian word 'duppy' or 'devil'. Another seaman's phrase – to be caught between the devil and the deep blue sea – mirrors the idea of Davy Jones and the Devil.

Toy soldiers were once used to protect buried warriors

The earliest known model soldiers were found in the tomb of Prince Emsah, an Egyptian warrior of about 2000 BC. They were placed there to provide a symbolic guard for his spirit after death. They consist of two groups of carefully painted wooden figures. One group is of Egyptian soldiers armed with spears, or javelins, and shields shaped like church windows. The other group is of Numidian allies, dark-skinned men with colourful loincloths and armed with bows and arrows.

Albert Schweitzer was a scholar-musician who spent more than half a lifetime in the interior of Africa

Albert Schweitzer was born in Germany in 1875. He studied theology, philosophy and music and became a brilliant organist by the age of 30. He then decided to change his life completely and to become a doctor of medicine and a missionary. In 1913 Schweitzer went with his wife to the isolated village of Lambaréné, inland from the west coast of Africa and a little south of the equator. He built a hospital and a leper colony there and devoted himself to the welfare of the Africans who lived around him. He received the Nobel Peace Prize in 1952. He died in 1965 and was buried in Lambaréné.

Everything cost five cents in the first Woolworths

F. W. Woolworth opened his first store at Utica, in New York State, in 1879. Everything was on show and everything cost five cents. Although this store was not a great success, he soon opened another in Pennsylvania where everything was priced at five or ten cents. Later he opened in England and priced his goods at three old pence and six old pence (about 1p and 2p). His stores were soon springing up all over the world and he died a very rich man.

Jeans come from Genoa and denims come from Nimes

The ever-popular blue jeans originated in the Italian port of Genoa and were much used by sailors who found the strong cotton cloth the ideal thing at sea. It is confusing to call them denim jeans, because the original denim came from the French town of Nimes: *De* means 'from' or 'of'; therefore the cloth that came *de Nimes*, came to be called denim.

The first scout camp had 20 boys

Robert Baden-Powell became a national hero during the Boer War in South Africa when he and his men held out in Mafeking for 217 days against the Boers, waiting for relief to arrive. A few years later, in 1907, Baden-Powell organised quite a different kind of thing — a camp for about 20 boys at Brownsea Island, at the mouth of the Poole harbour in England. In 1908 he published his famous 'Scouting for Boys'. This was the simple beginning of the Boy Scout Movement which today, worldwide, numbers about 11 million members. In 1910 the Girl Guides were founded. In 1920 the first international jamboree was held in London. Baden-Powell was elected Chief Scout and continued working for the scouts until he was 80. He died in 1941.

The siege of Mafeking was itself rather a ludicrous event. 8,000 Boers surrounded the outpost, which held only 1,000 British troops. Both sides observed a truce on Sundays - but when the British officers took this opportunity to play polo as relaxation, the Boer general was so shocked by the Sabbath-breaking he threatened to shell the game.

The medieval pillory was still in use in the 20th century

The pillory was a common form of punishment in the Middle Ages and for many centuries afterwards. It was an upright post with a crossbeam at head height. The beam had holes in it, through which the head and hands of a criminal could be locked, in the same way that ancient 'stocks' were used to lock the feet. Pillories were usually set up in village squares where the victim could be seen and mocked. They were abolished in France and England in the first half of the 19th century, but continued to be used in parts of the United States.

The man who invented dynamite started the Nobel prizes

Alfred Nobel was born in Sweden in 1833. In 1866, after a long study of explosives, he produced the first dynamite. Later he made other advanced explosives and detonators. These inventions made him very rich and when he died he left no family to inherit his wealth. Instead, he left a trust to establish five world-wide prizes in peace, physics, chemistry, physiology or medicine, and literature. These prizes were first given out in 1901 and in 1969 an economics prize was also awarded. The prizes are sometimes shared and occasionally not awarded at all. They are considered a great honour throughout the world and they have been received by many famous people.

Nobel himself was a rather eccentric figure. His invention, dynamite, was labelled 'Nobel's Safety Powder'. He never married, and had a long, platonic affair with his secretary. He made his will only two weeks before he died, and left nothing to his family.

Houdini was the world's greatest escape artist

Ehrich Weiss was born in 1874 and when his father died he earned money for the family by doing conjuring tricks. He changed his name to Harry Houdini and became one of the most brilliant escape artists the world has ever known. He taught himself to escape from knots, locks and handcuffs, including those of the police. He was locked in prison cells and dropped into rivers tied up with chains in a bag, but he always escaped. He was physically very fit and one of his tricks was to invite people to hit him in the stomach as hard as they liked. By tightening his stomach muscles he could resist any blow with no ill effects. On one occasion, however, he was caught by surprise and died as a result of such a blow.

The man who led the Russian Revolution was not really called Lenin

During the First World War, the people of Russia rose against the tsar and formed a Communist Government of their own. The man who led this Revolution and worked to establish the new government called himself Vladimir Ilyich Lenin but his real name was Ulyanov. He had chosen the name Lenin as a disguise when he was hiding from the authorities before the Revolution and he kept the name ever afterwards. The imperial city of St Petersburg was later called Leningrad in Lenin's honour, but it has now reverted to its original name.

Ivan the Terrible used to dress as a monk

Ivan the Terrible became Grand Duke of Muscovy when he was only three and when Muscovy was only a small state in eastern Europe. Under his rule, the state expanded and took over many neighbouring states. When he was

Karl Marx spent more than half his life in London and is buried there

Karl Marx was one of the founders of Communism. He believed that the working classes of Europe should rebel against the ruling classes and make themselves rulers of their own countries. Marx was born in Germany in 1818. He first met his friend and co-writer, Friedrich Engels, in Paris but was thrown out of both France and Germany because of his views. Marx then went to live in London, where he expanded his ideas on history and the class struggle. His most famous books are *The Communist Manifesto*, which he wrote with Engels, and *Das Kapital*. He died in 1883 and is buried in Highgate Cemetery in London.

The bust of Karl Marx at his tomb at Highgate Cemetery in London.

17, Ivan called himself 'tsar' of all Russia. He was the first to take this title. In some ways he ruled well and improved conditions for the ordinary people but he could also be very cruel, which is why he got his name 'the Terrible'. On one occasion, he even killed his eldest son in a quarrel. At the very end of his life, he regretted many of the things he had done and he dressed in the clothes of a monk. He died in 1584.

Rasputin survived assassination - but died from drowning

The evil Russian monk Rasputin was regarded as a malign influence on the Russian royal family, and Prince Felix Yussupov, with three friends, determined to do away with him. They invited him to a wild party in a cellar, and with a gramophone playing, they fed the monk cakes and wine poisoned with cyanide. Unfortunately the victim had developed an immunity to cyanide, and to the horror of the murderers he continued happily

stuffing himself. Finally the Prince shot him - but was frozen by the hypnotic eye of Rasputin. Yussupov ran off, Rasputin burst outside, was shot repeatedly, stabbed and coshed, tied up, and finally tumbled into the icy River Neva. It was afterwards discovered that his death was by drowning - not poison or bullet-wounds.

There were only six members when the Common Market began

Belgium, France, Germany, Italy, Luxembourg and the Netherlands were the original members of the Common Market in 1957. After some delays, Britain, Denmark, and Ireland joined in 1973. Norway, which had been thinking of joining, backed out at the last moment. Greece, Spain and Portugal are now members. Now known as the European Community, the Common Market is now about more than just money. The Community is influencing many other aspects of life. It is possible that East European countries may wish to join in the future.

An Arctic explorer gave his name to a special passport for refugees

Fridtjof Nansen was a Norwegian explorer and statesman. His two most famous exploits were the crossing of Greenland on skis in 1888 and the expedition of the ship *Fram* in which he tried to cross the North Pole in 1893. The *Fram* became stuck in the ice but Nansen and a friend walked over the ice to within 400 kilometres (250 miles) of the Pole. It was three years before they returned home. Later in his life, Nansen took a great interest in the problem of refugees after the First World War. He was appointed by the League of Nations to return half a million German and Austro-Hungarian prisoners of war from Russia to their own countries. A special passport, known as a Nansen Passport, was issued to people who had no country of their own. Later still, Nansen helped the Red Cross to find homes for refugees of famine in southern Russia. He was awarded the Nobel Peace Prize in 1922.

Captain Bligh sailed thousands of kilometres in an open boat and suffered more than one mutiny

On April 28, 1789, the crew of HMS Bounty, led by Fletcher Christian, mutinied against their captain, William Bligh, just off the Friendly Islands in the Pacific. Bligh and 18 others were set adrift in an open longboat and eventually reached Timor in the East Indies on June 12, 1789, after an amazing journey of about 6400 kilometres (4,000 miles). Later in his career, Bligh suffered two more mutinies. One was in 1797, when the crew of his ship the 'Director' joined the mutiny at the Nore and put him ashore. The other was in 1808 when, as Governor of New South Wales, his Deputy Governor mutinied against him and shipped back to England. Despite these setbacks, he became a vice-admiral and died in 1817.

Grace Darling hated being famous

The heroic story of Grace Darling and her father, the Longstone lighthouse keeper, is a well-known one. On September 7, 1838, the steamship *Forfarshire* was wrecked about one and a half kilometres off the Northumberland coast of England. Grace and her father rowed out in an open boat in dangerously high seas and rescued the entire crew. They were later awarded a Gold Medal for bravery and a public grant of money. But Grace found her fame tedious. Four years later, before she was 30, she was dead of tuberculosis.

Captain Scott used men instead of dogs to pull supplies

The famous English explorer Robert Falcon Scott, born in Devonport in 1868, wanted to avoid using dog-teams to pull his supplies and equipment since he believed it caused unnecessary suffering. He used men, ponies and motor tractors instead - none of which served as well. The men tired fast, the ponies could not stand the icy weather, the tractors broke down. Although he reached the South Pole, he and his four companions died soon afterwards huddled together in their shelter.

Two great explorers for different countries came from the same home town

Christopher Columbus was brought up in Genoa and in 1492 sailed across the Atlantic and reached the West Indies on behalf of the King of Spain. John Cabot was also brought up in Genoa and in 1497 sailed across the Atlantic to Newfoundland or Labrador on behalf of the King of England. The strange link between the two men shows clearly how explorers in those days, their heads full of stories of Cathay from their readings of Marco Polo's 'Travels' and other books, had to search all over Europe for wealthy kings to give them backing and encouragement for their expeditions. On Cabot's first expedition, he had only one small ship, the 'Matthew', with a crew of 18 men. On his second expedition, the following year, he had several ships and 200 men and he sailed up and down the North American coast, from Greenland to a point south of modern New York. His son, Sebastian, carried on his father's work.

Captain Cook commanded three voyages of exploration

The British explorer, Captain Cook, covered more distance around the world than any other man of his time. Having already gained a reputation for his map-making of the coast around Newfoundland, he went on the first of his three great voyages in 1768. It lasted three years and he sailed round the world by way of Cape Horn, New Zealand, Australia and the Cape of Good Hope. On his second expedition in 1772, he sailed the other way round the world and touched on the Antarctic ice. On his third, he sailed through the Bering Strait and was halted by the Arctic ice, before meeting his death in Hawaii.

The first man to the North Pole took his black servant

The American explorer Robert Peary was the first man to reach the North Pole. He took with him his black servant named Henson and four eskimos named Ootah, Egingwah, Seegloo and Ookeah. He had learned much from the Eskimos that helped ensure the success of his expedition - clothes, transport and habits were copied from them. To reach the North Pole he used 246 dogs in teams to haul supplies and equipment. Having arrived at last, he planted five flags, including a silk 'Stars and Stripes'. This looked rather dirty - he had taken it on every expedition for the last fifteen years, wrapped round his body. Peary was awarded the Royal Geographical award for all his services.

No one believed that Marco Polo had been to China

Marco Polo was a Venetian who travelled to China with his father and uncle in the 13th century to visit Kublai Khan, the great emperor. The Khan was so taken with Marco that he made him one of his officials and for 17 years Marco travelled widely throughout the land on official business for the emperor. They left in 1292 and reached Venice again in 1295, the first travellers to bring back true stories of the great power and wealth of China. No-one believed them. When Marco was taken prisoner by the Genoese three years later, he wrote a book about his adventures. This book was later read with eagerness by explorers like Christopher Columbus.

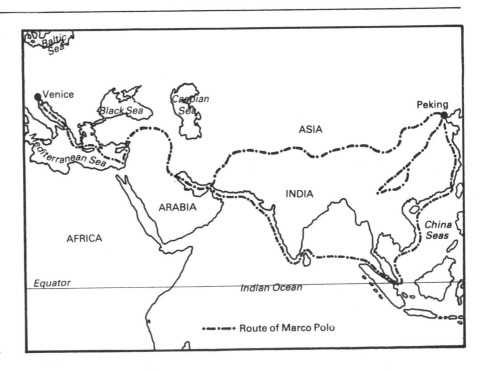

Marco Polo's route from Venice to Peking and further into China.

Amundsen, the first explorer to reach the South Pole, originally planned to go to the North Pole

Roald Amundsen was a Norwegian explorer who was born in 1872. He became the first person to sail a ship through the North-West Passage. Amundsen also planned to be the first to reach the North Pole but an American, Robert Peary, got there before him in 1909. Amundsen had by then already made his preparations for the expedition. When he set off from Norway he turned south and sailed to Antarctica, instead of heading north. In a well-planned dash with a dog sledge and four companions, he reached the South Pole in December 1911, one month before his rival, Captain Scott. In 1926, Amundsen claimed another 'first' by flying over the North Pole in the airship *Norge,* with the Italian Umberto Nobile. Two years later Amundsen disappeared when flying out to rescue Nobile from another expedition.

When Captain Scott arrived, he found the tent and the Norwegian flag of Amundsen just a mile and a half from the spot he calculated to be the South Pole. Inside the tent he discovered a letter from Amundsen which requested him to take a message to the King of Norway, King Haakon. He also discovered three reindeer bags with an assortment of contents, including old socks, and some pieces of navigational equipment. The Norwegian explorer had been helped to beat Scott to the Pole by the use of English equipment such as an English sextant and English hypsometer.

A Japanese explorer was the first man to reach the North Pole solo

Thirty-seven-year-old Naomi Uemura from Japan was the first man to reach the North Pole alone, at 4.45 Greenwich Mean Time, 1

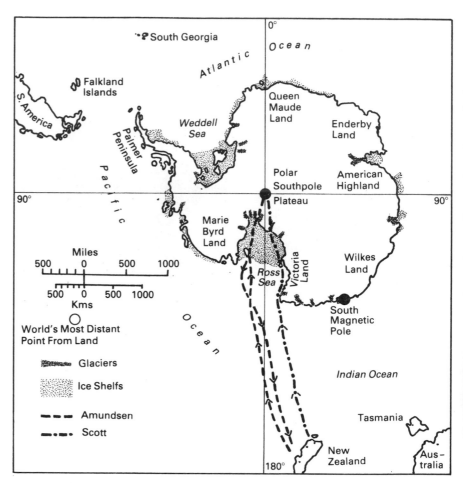

The South Pole.

May 1978. He set out from Cape Columbia, in Northern Canada almost two months earlier. On his lonely way he had been attacked by a polar bear, and one of his dogs gave birth to six puppies. But his 450-mile journey with his dog-team across the Arctic ice-cap was achieved in remarkable time. When he arrived, he informed the Smithsonian Institute in Washington USA by means of a special automatic bleeper which transmitted via a satellite. The 5'3" explorer confided when he returned that he did not like being alone.

Captain Byrd decided to go to the North Pole when he was twelve

As a boy of twelve Richard Byrd wrote in his diary that he had decided to become the first man to

get to the North Pole. So he started toughening up by wearing light underwear and no coat. However it looked as if his chances were destroyed when he broke a bone in his foot, smashed an ankle and became lame. He had to leave the navy - but learned to fly instead. He was not a good learner, and had several mishaps, including a head-on collision. He finally qualified as a pilot, but was refused work as a test-pilot because of his broken foot. He wanted to fly one of Roald Amundsen's planes, but was turned down because he was a married man. Finally he won through with persistence, and raised money privately to fly over the North Pole in 1926. In 1929 he repeated the achievement over the South Pole. When he returned to America he was made an admiral, although he had earlier retired from the navy. One of his books, *Alone,* describes his adventures.

Shackleton lived up to his motto 'By endurance, we conquer'

The English explorer Ernest Shackleton faced appalling hardships during his expeditions, but won through by endurance and application. Once he was stuck in ice in tho middlc of the frozen Weddell Sea for nine months 1,200 miles from the nearest inhabited land. He finally ordered his crew of twenty-six and one stowaway to abandon ship. Soon after having done so, they heard the ship's timbers snapping with a noise like gunfire. For the next five months the stranded sailors camped on the ice until it began to thaw and break up. Only then could they launch their small boats and row to Elephant Island. Shackleton himself with five crew members rowed through the perilous South Georgia sea, but arrived on the side furthest from the lonely whaling station he was aiming for. They had to cross a great mountain range to reach their goal. They set out gamely, but eventually reached a rocky ridge which barred their way. Putting caution to the winds, the six linked arms and slid down it together at a rate of nearly sixty miles per hour. Despite the dangers, Shackleton eventually reached safety and managed to rescue the remainder of his party. Not only was Shackleton's motto appropriately 'By endurance, we conquer'; he also named his vessel *Endurance*. Shackleton died in 1922 at the age of 48 on a journey to Enderby Land, and was honoured as one of the greatest explorers of his day. He is buried near South Georgia.

Greenland was so called so that people might believe it was a land worth living in

Greenland is the largest island in the world. Most of it is covered by a thick sheet of ice that never melts, making it a very unwelcoming-looking land. The Norse Vikings were the first Europeans to discover it, in the 10th century, and it was from here that Leif Ericsson later sailed to Vinland, or Newfoundland. At its longest, it is about 2680 kilometres (1650 miles), and at its widest about 1280 kilometres (800 miles). Eric the Red landed here in AD 982 and spent three years on the south-west coast. He returned in 986 with 25 ships which he had persuaded to join him to form a colony in the 'green' land. Only 14 arrived. The settlement lasted for about 400 years, until communications with Norway were broken off. The island was recolonised by the Danes in the 18th century and became wholly Danish in 1921.

Greenland. The shaded part in the centre is the ice cap approximately 1200 feet below sea level. The second white triangle from the top indicates the greatest known ice depth – 11,190 feet.

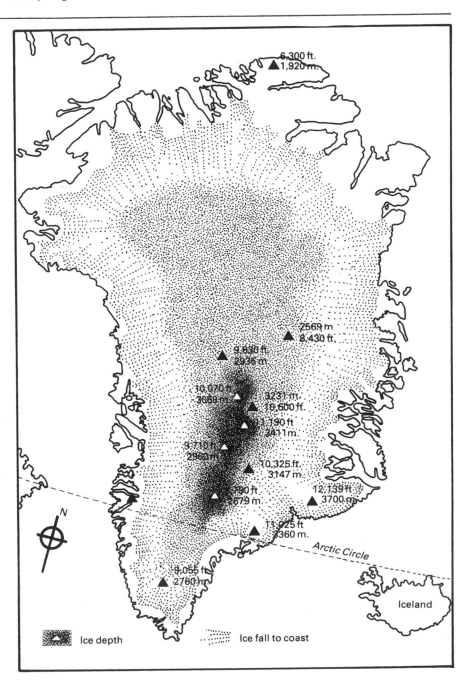

Words and Phrases

'Pearlies' are cockney barrow-boys

In Victorian London, some of the men who sold their wares off barrows used to sew thousands of buttons onto their best suits as a cheap and cheerful form of decoration. Those who wore these suits were known as the 'pearlies', because the buttons were made of 'mother of pearl'. They elected a 'Pearly King and Queen' from among their number, and the clothes were handed down from generation to generation. This tradition still exists and the 'pearlies' turn out as a tourist attraction on special occasions. Another name for the 'barrow boys' of London used to be 'costermongers', a variation on 'costardmonger'. This came from the 'costards', the type of apple that they commonly sold.

Collective nouns 'describe' other nouns

There are collective nouns for all sorts of creatures, many of which conjure up colourful and accurate pictures of those crowded gatherings: an 'exaltation' of larks describes their joyful singing; a 'murder' of crows pictures their dark looks; a 'skulk' of foxes shows them slinking through the woods; a 'sleuth' of bears, a 'leap' of leopards, a 'cast' of hawks, a 'muster' of peacocks, a 'clamour' of rooks – they all give good descriptions of the characters of animals and birds together.

Hijackers are modern highwaymen

In recent years, the hijacking of airplanes has become a common method of ensuring political pressure and publicity. A hijacker was originally a robber who seized the goods of American bootleggers – people who made and sold illegal alcohol earlier this century. The word 'hijack' may be based on the words of the robbers when they aimed their guns at their victims. They probably told them to 'stick your hands up high, Jack!'

Modern vandals are no more than ancient barbarians in disguise

Today, we think of 'vandals' as people who destroy public and private property simply because they are bored or over-excited. They get their name from an ancient German tribe of barbarians who fought against Goths, Romans, Franks, Spaniards and North Africans, creating havoc wherever they went. They eventually attacked Rome in AD 455 but spared the city in exchange for a large amount of booty. Although they were robbers and murderers, many of them did in fact settle down and follow the Roman way of life. The tribe was defeated by the Byzantine general Belisarius in AD 533.

Unmarried women were expected to spin for their living

Unmarried women were traditionally known as 'spinsters'. This comes from the days when the women of the household spent a great part of their day spinning cloth. Every young girl was expected to make her own linen in readiness for the day she got married.

'Dollar' came from a German word

The Spanish piece-of-eight had been known by the English speaking peoples in the New World as a 'dollar' for some time before the dollar was first coined in the United States at the end of the 18th century. The word came from the German silver 'thaler' that was common currency in various parts of Europe in the 16th and 17th centuries.

The first man to be boycotted was Captain Boycott himself

To 'boycott' someone is to apply pressure on them by stopping any trade or communication with them. This is usually done to persuade them to do what you want. Captain Charles Boycott was a land agent in Count Mayo, Ireland, in about 1880. He tried to increase the rents on the poor people's houses and land. The tenants resisted and refused to be thrown out of their homes if they could not pay. They made life unpleasant for Captain Boycott by refusing to sell him any supplies, and by not talking to him or co-operating with him in any way. Because of this, Boycott was forced to leave his job and the country. The success of these tactics encouraged other tenants to do the same against their landlords.

The dog days of summer are hot and lazy

The 'dog days' are the hottest days in the year. The phrase goes back to Roman times, when they talked about the *caniculares dies*. The Romans believed that Sirius, the dog star (the brightest of the stars they could see in the first weeks of July) added its own heat to that of the Sun. They also believed that Sirius was largely responsible for the fever and plague that often hit Rome at this time of year.

Flotsam and jetsam mean the same but are different!

Wreckage found at sea and along the shore is often called flotsam and jetsam. There is a difference between the two words. Flotsam covers bits and pieces of wreckage that are found floating at sea. The word comes from the Old French *floter*, to float. Jetsam covers things that have been thrown overboard, from the French *jeter*, which means to throw.

Joseph Stalin ruled the Soviet Union for nearly 30 years

Joseph Dzhugashvili is better known as Stalin, the 'Man of Steel'. His father was a shoemaker and his mother was a washerwoman. Stalin worked with Lenin to prepare for the Russian Revolution of 1917. When Lenin died in 1924 Stalin pushed out his main rival, Trotsky, and ruled the Soviet Union for nearly 30 years. He planned the industrialisation of the country and, during the 1930s, was forced to move more than 25 million people from the farms to new factories. He imprisoned, exiled or executed all those who did not do as he ordered or who threatened his power. Despite his rule of terror, Stalin led the Soviet Union to victory against Germany in the Second World War. He died in 1953 and was later denounced by Krushchev as a dictator.

Methusaleh was the oldest man of all time

If you say that someone is 'as old as Methusaleh', you mean that they are very old indeed. Methusaleh was one of the descendants of Adam and Eve. His age is given in the Bible (in Genesis 5 verse 27) as 969 years old. Several of Methusaleh's immediate ancestors apparently lived for more than 900 years. Adam himself, according to the Bible, lived for 930 years. If you think of the 'years' as months then Methusaleh would have been just over 80 years old, which seems more likely.

Paradise was once a royal orchard

In ancient Persia the royal pleasure park, with its fruitful orchards and wild beasts for hunting was called paradise. When the word was later used by Christians and Moslems to mean 'heaven', the place where humans or their spirits go to after death, many people continued to believe that 'heaven' or 'paradise' existed somewhere on Earth.

A 'fifth column' fights from within

A 'fifth column' is usually taken to mean an undercover force that is fighting inside the enemy lines. The original Spanish phrase 'quinta columna' was used in a radio address during the Spanish Civil War, in October 1936. General Emilio Mora heard that there were four columns of Franco's troops marching on the city of Madrid. He declared that Franco also had a 'fifth column' of sympathisers within the city.

The first juggernaut was not a lorry

Some of the heaviest trucks and lorries on the roads today are known as juggernauts. The meaning of the word 'juggernaut' is much more ancient than the lorries. Juggernaut, or Jagganath, is a Hindu god who is dragged on a vast wheeled vehicle from one temple to another when his festival is celebrated by his followers. Fanatical pilgrims used to throw themselves beneath the wheels of the vehicle and be crushed to death.

American soldiers have been known as 'doughboys' and 'GIs'

American soldiers during the 19th and early 20th centuries were often known as 'doughboys'. This name derived from the large brass buttons on their uniforms, which looked a bit like dough-cakes. During the Second World War, the letters 'GI' was the unofficial quartermaster's term for 'Galvanised Iron'. Later it came to stand for 'Government Issue' and was stamped on all pieces of equipment and kit issued during the Second World War. Soon, enlisted soldiers themselves became known as GIs.

'Kilroy was here' is a piece of graffiti dating from the Second World War

Words and pictures scribbled on walls are known as graffiti. Some graffiti become popular and appear everywhere for a while. One of the best-known was the phrase, 'Kilroy was here'. It first appeared during the Second World War, wherever American soldiers were to be found. James Kilroy was a shipyard inspector at Quincy, Massachusetts, who had to sign for all equipment sent over to Europe for the troops. American soldiers, finding his name on almost everything they used, started scrawling the phrase wherever they were based. Soon the joke was that, wherever they were in the world, Kilroy was there as well.

William Tell was a legendary hero of Switzerland

William Tell is a legendary Swiss hero who is said to have helped his people throw off the rule of the hated Austrians in the 15th century. The legend relates how he refused to bow down to the hat of Gessler, the Austrian bailiff, which had been set up on a pole in the market place. Gessler arrested Tell and told him that he would be freed only if he showed his skill with the bow by shooting an apple off his son's head. Tell took two arrows and hit the apple with the first one. When he told Gessler that he would have shot him with the second arrow if he had accidently killed his son with the first, Gessler arrested him again. Tell escaped from a boat on the way to prison. He shot Gessler and led the Swiss to victory against the Austrians. He is remembered by the Swiss as their liberator.

A 'tycoon' was once the commander of a Japanese army

'Tycoon' comes from two Chinese words which mean 'great' and 'prince'. The word was used to describe a shogun, or army commander, in Japan. Such a commander was virtually ruler of the country. Modern business tycoons wield the same sort of power over their companies.

Tommy Atkins is the universal British soldier

One of the most popular nicknames for the British soldier has been 'Tommy'. It has even been used by Britain's allies and enemies. It stands for 'Tommy Atkins', a soldier who never existed. The name originated at the beginning of the 19th century, when every soldier was issued with a book explaining how to draw his pay. Certain information had to be written on a form in the book, giving the soldier's name, rank, age, length of service and record. An example of the form was enclosed with each book, made out in the name of the fictitious Tommy Atkins, to show the soldier how to fill in the form correctly. The nickname 'Tommy' spread throughout the army.

A 'flash in the pan' is an old saying from the days when muskets were first used

A sudden burst of success that does not last for long, and possibly ends in failure, is often known as a 'flash in the pan'. This expression originates from the old days of early muskets, when a spark was first made to ignite a priming of gunpowder in the small pan of the gun. The priming flashed and ignited the main charge that fired the bullet. A 'flash in the pan' happened when the priming in the pan flashed but the main charge never fired, so that the bullet never left the barrel.

The Parthian shot hurts the most

The Parthians were an Iranian tribe that lived to the south-east of the Caspian Sea and became a strong nation in the 3rd and 2nd centuries BC. They were enthusiastic warriors whose strength lay in their mounted archers. It was the custom of these sturdy bowmen to pretend to flee but as they rode away they would turn in their saddles and fire at full speed with alarming accuracy at their pursuers. From this habit, there arose the idea that a 'Parthian shot' was a parting shot that caught one off-guard.

Sam Browne belts were designed for a one-armed soldier

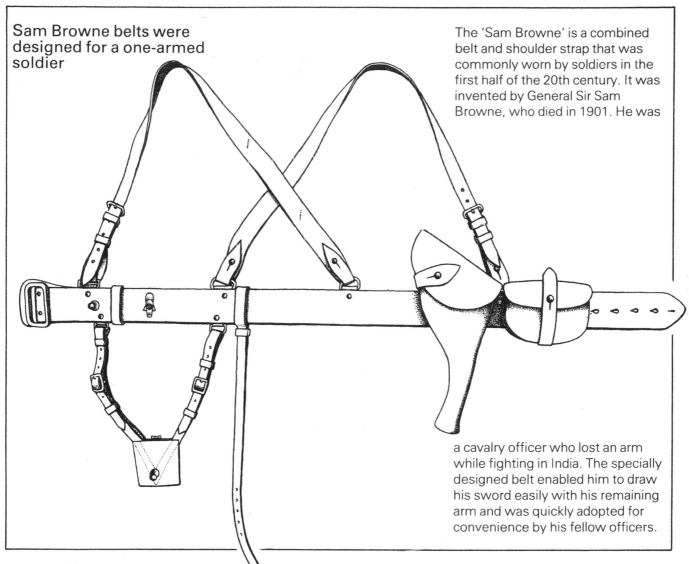

The 'Sam Browne' is a combined belt and shoulder strap that was commonly worn by soldiers in the first half of the 20th century. It was invented by General Sir Sam Browne, who died in 1901. He was a cavalry officer who lost an arm while fighting in India. The specially designed belt enabled him to draw his sword easily with his remaining arm and was quickly adopted for convenience by his fellow officers.

It is possible to discover one thing when you are looking for another thing

The adventures of the 'Three Princes of Serendip' was a fairy tale that was first translated into English in 1722. Serendip was an ancient name for Sri Lanka (formerly) Ceylon, and the three princes were famous for always making discoveries by complete accident, when they were looking for something quite different. The accidental discoveries usually brought them great good fortune. Thirty two years after the story appeared in English, the writer Horace Walpole suggested in a letter that 'Serendipity' was a good word for this kind of lucky accident and the word has been used ever since.

Dogs that gave their name to the canary

The Canary Islands lie off the coast of northwest Africa, more than 100 kilometres (62.5 miles) out into the Atlantic. They were known in Roman times and, Pliny in the 1st century AD, wrote that they were named after the wild dogs which over-ran the islands. The Latin word for 'dog' is 'canis' – hence 'Canary' Islands. Much later, when 16th century explorers visited the Islands, they brought back bright little singing birds, which they named 'canaries' after the name of the place where they had found them. Wild canaries are generally an olive-green colour and the yellow canary that we know today is the result of careful breeding.

'Mac' and 'O' mean 'son of'

Family names are handed down from generation to generation, from father to son. But some family names include the phrase 'son of' in the name itself, just to make the family connection absolutely clear. This happens particularly in Scottish and Irish clan names, such as Macdonald or O'Henry. In each case, 'Mac' and 'O' stand for 'son of', so Macdonald is really the 'son of Donald' and O'Henry is the 'son of Henry'. In fact the Donald or Henry in question is some very far-off ancestor, after whom all the succeeding generations have been named. In Old French, the word 'Fitz' meant the same, as in 'Fitzwilliam', although sometimes 'fitz' was used to mean the 'illegitimate son of'.

General Knowledge

Boiling-up animal hides, bones and fish skins produces glue

Most of the tough glues that we use today are made artificially from synthetic resins and chemical raw materials. But for many thousands of years (and in some cases, even today) glue was made by boiling up the hides and bones of animals – usually horses and cattle. These remains contain a protein called collagen, which was the basis of all adhesives. Fish skins were used in the same way. From Egyptian times until the 20th century, these natural materials were the source of most glues, although other forms of natural glue included resin from certain trees and gum from plants. The main disadvantage of many natural glues was that they dissolved easily in hot water.

The recipe for soap has hardly changed for 3,000 years

The Phoenicians, in about the 7th or 8th centuries BC, were probably among the earliest users of soap. They boiled up animal fats with wood ash and found that the mixture cleaned grease and dirt from their bodies. The important part of the wood ash was the alkali. The alkali neutralises the acids in the fat and alkali in one form or another has been an essential ingredient of soap ever since. The Romans also used animal fats and wood ash but soap of this kind remained a luxury throughout the Middle Ages and well into the 17th century. Today, vegetable and animal fats are still used, in combination with caustic soda, as the alkali.

There are 500 red corpuscles to every one white corpuscle in the blood

Red corpuscles carry oxygen through the blood. They are very small discs and there may be several million of them in a single drop of blood. They wear out quite quickly, within a few weeks, and are remade in the bone marrow. White corpuscles are much larger and rather shapeless. Their function is to fight disease in the body by crowding round bacteria and digesting them. The body makes more white corpuscles when necessary to deal with attacks by germs. The plasma itself, in which the corpuscles float, carries food and chemicals throughout the body and brings back carbon dioxide to be passed out through the lungs.

The Stone of Scone was stolen by the Scottish Nationalists

The Stone of Scone is set beneath the Coronation chair in Westminster Abbey, London. It was taken by King Edward I in 1297 from the Abbey of Scone in Scotland. In 1950, after more than 650 years, a group of Scottish Nationalists stole the stone back but it was found in Scotland the next year and replaced at Westminster. There was an old prophecy that a Scottish king should reign wherever the stone was placed. This came true in 1603, when King James VI of Scotland became King James I of England.

Light can play tricks on the eye

If you try to touch an object that is under water, you will often miss because the object appears to be in a slightly different place to where it actually is. This is because when light passes from one transparent element to another, it 'bends' or changes direction slightly because the speed of light is slower in water than it is in air. This 'bending' is called 'refraction'.

The pencil in the glass is quite straight. It is refraction that makes it look as if it is bent.

Glass fibres can bend light

No one can see round corners, unless they use a series of mirrors. But fine filaments of simple glass can now help you to do just this by means of fibre optics. The glass is spun out in to hair-like threads. A light from one end of the thread will pass down the length of the filament and shine out at the other end, however many corners it has to turn on the way. Many of these threads wound together can enable you to see round corners, too. This is particularly useful for surgeons and engineers, who need to look into awkward places to diagnose what is wrong. In the future, telephone messages may also be transmitted by light beams travelling down glass tubes, for they can carry many more conversations than ordinary wires do.

Paper can be made from anything from bamboo to old rags

Most paper is made from wood fibres, but it is also made from the fibres of bamboo, straw, esparto grass, hemp and jute. Some of the best paper is made from linen rags and cotton. Paper used to be made from papyrus, a reed found along the Nile in Egypt. The reeds were laid criss-cross until they formed a sheet thick enough to write on. Later, parchment and vellum were used. These were made from the skins of sheep, goats and calves. The Chinese were the first to use real paper, as we know it, in about 100 BC, but paper wasn't used in Europe until at least the 12th century AD.

The Bastille held only seven prisoners when the French Revolutionaries stormed it in 1789

The Bastille is probably the most famous fort in France. It was built in 1370 as a protection for Paris against English attacks. There were

The most common metal in the world has been in use for only 100 years

There is more aluminium than any other metal in the Earth's crust. In fact, nearly eight per cent of the Earth's crust is made of aluminium. However, aluminium is found only in combination with other substances in the rocks. About 100 years ago a cheap way was at last found to separate the metal from these substances by using a powerful electric current. Aluminium is extremely useful because it is strong and light (about one-third the weight of iron) and it does not rust. It is also a good conductor of heat. We use it for cooking equipment as well as aircraft and motor car engines.

Charles Hall produced the first pellets of aluminium shown here, in 1886.

eight towers, 30 metres (100 feet) high, and a 24 metre (80 feet) wide moat. The fort became a state prison and then a place of detention for important people. Even before the French Revolution of 1789 proposals had been made to demolish it but it was still standing when unrest came to a head. The people of France saw it as a symbol of royal power and oppression and decided to rescue the hundreds of poor victims of royal cruelty that they believed were imprisoned there. They stormed the Bastille on 14th July, 1789, and found only seven bewildered prisoners inside. Although they determined to destroy the fort at once, it took three years to pull it all down.

Rival firemen used to race to beat each other to the blaze

In the year after the Great Fire of London of 1666, Dr Nicholas Barbon started to insure people's houses against the risk of fire. Houses that paid insurance were marked with a lead or copper badge showing a rising Phoenix. Barbon organised teams of fire

fighters to save all the buildings that were marked in this way. Uninsured houses were left to burn. Rival companies, such as the Hand in Hand and the Sun, were established and competition was so fierce that firemen would race to any fire, hoping to impress potential clients.

The Virgin Islands are said to be named after 11,001 virgins

There is a story that Ursula was a British princess in the 4th or 5th century AD who went on a pilgrimage to Rome to avoid getting married at home. She took 11,000 virgins with her and they were all massacred by the Huns in Germany on the way back to Britain. The earliest reference to St Ursula mentions that she had 10 companions, so that there were only 11 including herself. But over the years the number became exaggerated, and most people preferred to believe in the 11,000. Christopher Columbus named the Virgin Islands in the Caribbean after St Ursula and her vast troop of followers.

Fools were once the companions of kings

The 'fool' or 'jester' is a figure of fun, with his multi-coloured clothes, his cap and bells and his toy stick. Kings and rich men once kept fools, who were usually deformed or mad, in the belief that they had powers of prophesy and could turn away evil. Some fools were, indeed, mad but others only pretended to be so. In those days, only the fool was allowed to contradict or criticise the king, and his words could be listened to or laughed at, as the king pleased. The last official French royal fool was called L'Angley. He stood behind the chair of Louis XIV (1638-1715) and made sarcastic remarks about the king's courtiers who tried to bribe him to keep quiet. There were jesters in Russia up until the 18th century.

Hydrogen is the lightest of all gases but helium is more often used in air ships and balloons

Hydrogen is 15 times lighter than air and it was used to lift the first air ships and weather balloons. But hydrogen burns very easily and there were many accidents. Now helium is used instead. Helium is non-inflammable and is therefore safer. It is twice as heavy as hydrogen, but still seven or eight times lighter than air.

The revolutionary Russians were called 'Reds'

Red had been the colour of socialism and revolution even before the French Revolution of 1789. When the Russian Revolution broke out in 1917 the socialist rebels were therefore known as the Red Army or 'Reds'. Their reactionary enemies were known as the White Army, because many of them came from the area known as White Russia or Byelorussia ('byely' means 'white').

The Great Fire of London

London had endured many great fires when, in 1666, the greatest of all broke out. It begain in a baker's house and spread quickly through the closely packed wooden houses of the city. The Lord Mayor was woken from his bed, but laughed at people's fears and went back to sleep. Within four days, however, 13,000 houses were destroyed, 89 churches were burnt down (including St Paul's) and 200,000 people were made homeless. Amazingly, only six people were killed.

St Anthony's pig is the smallest in the litter

St Anthony is the patron saint of swineherds. He is usually shown with a pig, sometimes with a small bell round its neck. As the smallest pig in the litter is often believed to follow its owner around like a pet wherever he goes, it became known as 'St Anthony's pig', or the 'Tantony' pig for short. St Anthony himself was a famous hermit who is said to have lived for more than 100 years and to have died in the middle of the 14th century.

The great city of Mohenjo-Daro was one of the first in the world

Mohenjo-Daro, in Pakistan, was a city of 20,000 people 4500 years ago. It was one of the first great cities of the Indus River civilisation, which was more advanced in many ways than the civilisation of the ancient Egyptians. Now only a few ruins remain. There is a huge ceremonial bath 12 metres (39 feet) long and nearly 2.5 metres (8 feet) deep. There are signs of a city wall nearly five kilometres (three miles) long and parts of a citadel that was five storeys high. More than 600 kilometres (373 miles) to the north lie the ruins of Harappa, another city that belonged to the same civilisation.

A wooden sailing ship was raised intact after 300 years

The 64-gun warship *Vasa* was the glory of Sweden when it was launched, but the ship sank in Stockholm harbour in 1628, before it had properly started its maiden voyage. The *Vasa* settled firmly in the mud and all attempts to raise it in the 17th century failed. No further attempts were made until 1956. In 1961 the almost intact hull was successfully brought to the surface, from a depth of 33 metres (108 feet). The *Vasa* had been protected by the harbour mud for 300 years, and is now the only complete example of a 17th century warship. More than 16,000 objects were brought up with the *Vasa*, from ornaments and coins to clothes and skeletons. The wood was immediately soaked in preservative, to stop it drying out, and now the ship rests in its own museum at Stockholm.

The Hanging Gardens of Babylon were one of the Seven Wonders of the World

Babylon was one of the most beautiful cities in the world in the time of King Nebuchadnezzar, in the 6th century BC. Its hanging gardens were later regarded as one of the Seven Wonders of the World. These gardens were built round a square-based pyramid, rising in steps up to a point. The steps, or platforms, were planted with trees and flowers, so that the building appeared to be completely covered, like an overgrown hillside full of colour and greenery. Water was drawn up from the nearby River Euphrates and stored in a tank at the top of the building, so that the plants could be kept constantly moist. It was said that the gardens were built at the request of the Queen, who was bored with the flat plains of Mesopotamia and longed for rich hills and her homeland.

Weathercocks remind us of St Peter

There are many forms of weathervane to show the direction of the wind but one of the most popular is the weathercock. The cock is a good, outdoor symbol to tell us what the weather is like, standing proudly with his tail feathers outspread. But there is another reason for his presence as a weathervane on many church steeples. In the 9th century AD, the Pope ordered that a weathercock should be set up on every church to remind people how St Peter had denied Christ three times before the cock crew.

The snake that killed Cleopatra was probably a cobra

According to legend, Cleopatra killed herself by clutching an asp to her bosom and letting it bite her. The name 'asp' was often used for various kinds of snake in ancient times. It was also the specific name for the poisonous Egyptian cobra, which was often used to kill condemned prisoners. This snake can grow up to two metres (6.5 feet) long. It has a narrower hood than the better-known Indian Cobra. The Egyptians regarded the cobra as sacred and used it as a symbol for royalty.

A 'Pyrrhic' victory is not worth winning

A so-called 'Pyrrhic' victory is a victory that is won at too great a cost. It is named after the victory of King Pyrrhus of Epirus at Asculum, against the Romans, in 279 BC. Although he won the battle, Pyrrhus lost a large proportion of his men and most of his best officers. Afterwards he said, 'One more such victory and we are lost' He was quite right. Four years later, his weakened army was defeated by the Romans at Beneventum.

The first modern circus was called an 'Amphitheatre of Arts'

The Romans had their amphitheatres, with wild animals and gladiatorial fights. The Middle Ages had travelling shows with clowns and acrobats and performing bears. But the modern circus, as we know it now, began towards the end of the 18th century, when riding experts started to put on spectacular shows of their skill. Astley's Royal Amphitheatre of Arts was one of the first of these shows and, in its time, the most famous in the world. It had acrobats, clowns, trick-riders and carefully orchestrated scenes form history, such as the story of the highwayman Dick Turpin or the Battle of Waterloo. By the end of the 19th century, circuses were travelling all over the world and becoming more and more spectacular. Barnum and Bailey's 'Greatest Show on Earth' needed more than 50 railway coaches to transport the people and animals that belonged to the circus. Buffalo Bill's 'Wild West Show' was another spectacular success.

The mummers were actors with a message of life, death and rebirth

In one form, 'mummery' has come to mean pompous or foolish or a performance that is irreligious, but the original Mediaeval mummers performed plays that were important re-enactments of the fight between good and evil. Good was represented by St George, the Christian. Evil was represented by the Turkish Knight, the Heathen. St George was always killed in these mock battles but a doctor appeared and gave him an enormous pill that cured him completely. The play was usually put on at Christmas or Easter and represented, as well as good and evil, the death of the old year and the rebirth of the new crops.

The first bicycles had no pedals

A bicycle is a vehicle with two wheels, usually one in front of the other. There are a few illustrations of bicycle-like objects from ancient times but these could not be steered and they were propelled by pushing with the feet along the ground, rather like a hobby horse. The first bicycles with front wheels that could be turned, and therefore steered, were designed by J. N. Niepce of Paris in 1816, and by Karl von Drais de Sauerbrun in 1817. These also could only be driven along by pushing with the feet on the ground but they became very popular. On the flat, a man could half-run, half-free-wheel up to 16 Km/h (10 mph). He could go a lot faster downhill but this was a little dangerous since bicycles then had no brakes The first bicycle with pedals was designed by a Scottish blacksmith, Kirkpatrick Macmillan, in 1839. There was no chain but rods connected the pedals to the rear wheels.

The people who civilised Italy before the Romans were the Etruscans

The Romans were not the first people to live a cultured and civilised life in Italy. They learnt much from the Etruscans who were there before them. Very little is known about the Etruscans. They probably came originally from the eastern end of the Mediterranean, and settled inland from the coast between the Rivers Arno and Tiber in about 1000 BC. The Etruscans were warriors and traders, and they were also brilliant sculptors and engineers.

One Norwegian encouraged Hitler to invade Norway

Vidkun Quisling was a Norwegian who encouraged Hitler and the fascists to invade Norway in 1940. He then became President of the country during the German occupation, doing whatever the Germans wanted him to do. At the end of the war, when Germany was eventually defeated, Quisling was taken prisoner and shot but his name is remembered and we use it to describe someone who betrays his country and fellow countrymen by working for the enemy who control his country.

Toy soldiers were used by generals to practise war games

Louis XIII of France owned one of the most valuable collections of toy soldiers. It was made on the orders of his mother and passed down to Louis XIV, who used it with his generals to plan his campaigns. However Louis was forced to sell the collection to pay for the wars he was planning. In the military schools of 19th century Prussia tactics were taught to young officers with the aid of model soldiers. In the Second World War, model soldiers were used for training Japanese officers.

The Danish conquest of England lasted for only 26 years

The Romans, the Angles and Saxons, the Danes and the Normans all conquered England in turn. The Romans ruled fairly thoroughly until they withdrew, leaving the island to the mercy of the Angles and Saxons, who were not very efficient. The Danish invasions which began as Viking raids at the end of the 8th century AD, met with determined resistance from men like Alfred of Wessex; and the Danes never succeeded in gaining authority over the whole country until the reign of the Danish King Canute began in 1016. Canute died in 1035 and his two sons took it in turns to rule until 1042 when the crown passed to Edward the Confessor, a member of the ancient Wessex royal family.

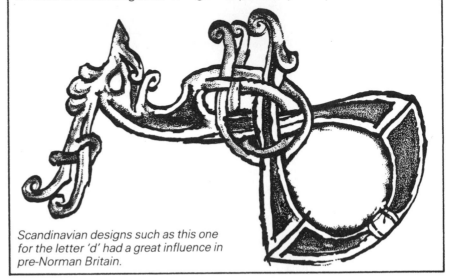

Scandinavian designs such as this one for the letter 'd' had a great influence in pre-Norman Britain.

The Star Spangled Banner was written by an Englishman

In 1814, the United States was at war with Britain. The British were shelling a fort near Baltimore and a young American, Francis Scott Key, went to the fort to ask for the release of a friend who had been taken prisoner. The commander agreed but kept both Key and his friend in custody until the bombardment was over. Eventually the British conceded defeat and Key wrote a poem about the Stars and Stripes flag that had been flying throughout the attack. Ironically, the tune that he had in mind to accompany the poem was written by an Englishman, John Stafford Smith, many years earlier. In 1931, the song became the official anthem of the United States.

The Moon's power is used to generate electricity at the River Rance

Hydro-electric power is normally generated in places where rivers have been dammed. Now it is possible to generate electricity by using the power of the rising and falling tides, which are influenced by the gravity of the Moon. At St Malo, in France, at the mouth of the River Rance, the Atlantic tides are constricted by the English Channel. This creates tides with a difference of more than 12 metres (40 feet). Now there is a 0.8 kilometre (0.5 mile) barrier across the river estuary, with 24 turbines that work both as the tide comes in and goes out. Each turbine provides enough electricity for between 10,000 and 20,000 people.

More than 3000 mature oak trees were needed to build one three-deck ship-of-the-line

It was once said that England was protected by walls of oak. These so-called 'walls' were the wooden warships, made of oak, that guarded the seas around the island. Long ago, England was covered by vast forests of oak trees. As its navy grew, these forests were swiftly cut down to provide the tough, long-lasting timber required to build the ships. An 18th-century full-rigged, three-deck ship-of-the-line with between 74 and 100 guns required the wood from about 3500 oak trees for its construction. This meant the destruction of several hundred acres of forest simply to make one ship of the line.

The emperors of China were very used to the smell of cloves

Cloves are one of the oldest known spices, along with cinnamon, pepper and ginger. They were exported from the East Indies to China long before the birth of Christ and from China they found their way through India and Arabia eventually to Europe. It was customary in ancient times that those who were granted an audience with the emperor of China placed a clove in their mouths, probably to purify the breath. 'Oil of cloves' is still used in mouthwashes and it can give some relief to toothache as well. Cloves are also used to preserve foods.

Adam's footprint can still be seen

Adam's Peak is a mountain 2245 metres (7366 feet) high in Sri Lanka (previously Ceylon). At the summit, there is a platform of about 180 square metres (1937 square feet), in the middle of which there is an indentation in the rock exactly like a human footprint, measuring about 160 x 75 centimetres (62 x 29 inches). Some say that it is the footprint of Buddha. Hindus believe it is the footprint of their god Siva. Christians believe it is that of St Thomas. Moslems say that after Adam was thrown out of the Garden of Eden, he had to stand on one foot here for 1,000 years. That is why it is called Adam's Peak.

Many of Nostradamus prophesies have come true

Michel de Nostroedame was born at the beginning of the 16th century in France. He wrote many prophecies in verse, and has become known to us today as Nostradamus. He prophesied the death of Henry II of France in a jousting accident, the Great Fire of London, the execution of Charles I of Britain, the rise and fall of Napoleon and the work of Louis Pasteur. He also foretold the rise of Adolf Hitler and the dropping of the atomic bombs on Japan in 1945. He predicts that in 1999 a great conflict will occur with war before and afterwards. He is very exact. He says it will happen in July.

The *Great Eastern* was a ship too large for its time

Isambard Kingdom Brunel designed the *Great Eastern* in 1854. It weighed more than 18,000 tons at a time when most large ships were never more than 5000 tons. The *Great Eastern* was to carry 4000 passengers and 6000 tons of cargo to India and Australia without refuelling. It was the first ship to be fitted with a cellular double bottom for safety. But the *Great Eastern* was so large 211 metres (692 feet) long that it took three months of frustrating efforts to launch it. Then the ship lay at anchor in the River Thames for two years waiting for a buyer. Eventually it was used for carrying cables across the Atlantic.

Record breaking cars are driven on salt flats

The Great Salt Lake lies in northern Utah, about 1200 metres (3,930 feet) above sea level. There is very little rainfall and most of the water that enters the lake from three small rivers evaporates, leaving the salt behind. The Lake Bonneville salt flats form a desert south-west of the Great Salt Lake, and were originally part of the same lake. Now the flats are used for attempts to break the world land speed record.

271

King Midas could turn anything to gold at a touch

Midas was the King of Phrygia who begged the gods that everything he touched might be turned to gold. They granted him his wish but he found that even his wine and food turned to gold, so he had to ask them to take his gift away again. Another legend about Midas is that he had to judge a musical competition between the god Apollo and Pan, the satyr. Midas gave the prize to Pan and Apollo was so angry that he made donkey's ears to grow on Midas's head. The king hid his ears under a turban and only his barber knew the secret. But the barber had to share the secret with someone, so he dug a whole in the ground and whispered, 'Midas has asses' ears'. Ever since then, the reeds that grew from the hole have whispered in the wind, 'Midas has asses' ears', or so the story goes!

The patron saint of England was not English

Saint George, the patron saint of England and of soldiers, was probably a soldier himself who was put to death at the beginning of the 4th century AD, at the orders of the Emperor Diocletian. He died at Lydda, in Palestine, and when his legend began to spread in the Middle Ages it somehow became associated with the Greek story of the hero Perseus who rescued Andromeda from a dragon not far from Lydda. St George was also said to have rescued a princess who had been sacrificed to a fearful dragon. George defeated the dragon, and, meekly tied by the lady's girdle, he led it to where the people were gathered. They immediately promised to be baptised into the Christian faith if he would kill it on the spot. He did so. The story was made popular in Caxton's *The Golden Legend*, one of the first great best sellers.

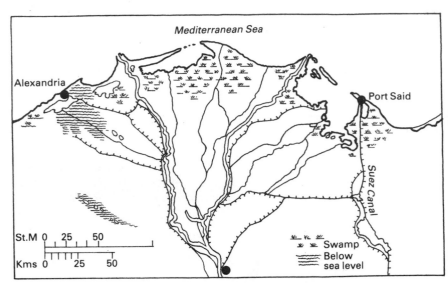

The Nile Delta. The Nile is of tremendous importance to Egypt as its waters enable basically arid land to be irrigated and hence crop producing.

Deltas are slowly spreading into the sea

The delta of a river is the area of land formed by the sediment brought by the river down to its mouth. The Greeks gave it the name of 'delta' because the shape of this kind of area often took the form of a triangle, which was the shape of the Greek letter 'delta'. The silt and sediment that builds up over the years, creates new land farther and farther out into the lake or sea. For example, the Mississippi is pushing out land into the Gulf of Mexico at the rate of about 50 metres (164 feet) a year. The Danube is pushing out even faster into the Black Sea. The Ganges in India, the Orinoco in South America and the Yellow River of China are all creating new land every year in their respective seas. The Italian city of Ravenna was once a bustling Roman port at the mouth of the River Po that could hold 250 ships. Now it is more than ten kilometres (six miles) inland.

The Apache pistol was an all-purpose weapon for an emergency

The so-called Apache pistol was quite small and could be hidden easily in a person's clothing. As well as the pistol itself, there was a bayonet-like dagger that sprung out at the front and the pistol's grip could be used as a knuckle duster. At one time it was a popular fashion to combine pistols with several other forms of defence. Pistols could be fitted into the handles of swords and even whips. Specially designed small pistols could be conveniently hidden in ladies' muffs to protect them from stagecoach highwaymen.

Ancient Britons used to paint themselves with the dye from Dyer's woad

Dyer's woad is a plant about 60 centimetres (24 inches) tall with yellow flowers and long leaves. Woad is also the name of the dye that is obtained from the crushed and fermented leaves of the plant, which has been cultivated for hundreds of years in many parts of Europe and Asia. The ancient Britons used the blue dye to paint their bodies, for decoration and to make themselves look more fierce. But it was also used for dyeing cloth blue right up until the 17th century or later until it was replaced by modern chemical dyes.

Myths, sagas and folk-tales are all different

Several different kinds of stories come down to us from the past. Myths are usually the stories made up long ago by ancient people to explain the mysteries of life and death or how the world began or whatever else they did not understand. Sagas are stories about history that have often been added to with legends of heroes who are half-real, half-imaginary, but generally with a basis of truth. Folk-tales are much lighter stories, often fanciful, that were made up to pass away the long winter evenings and to describe the hopes and fears of ordinary people. Some of these folk tales can be found in slightly different versions in many widely separated countries.

The Earl of Mercia's wife rode naked through Coventry

Lady Godiva was the wife of Leofric, the Earl of Mercia, in the 11th century AD. She begged her husband to withdraw some of the heavy taxes that he had imposed on the townsfolk of Coventry and pestered him until he agreed to do what she wanted if she would ride naked through the streets. She did so, accompanied by the Earl's soldiers! The townspeople were told to stay indoors and not look as Lady Godiva rode past, but it is said that Peeping Tom disobeyed the Earl's orders. He took a quick look from behind his curtains and was struck blind on the spot.

The Wandering Jew

There is a legend that a certain Jew refused to let Christ rest on his doorstep while carrying the cross on his way to Calvary. His punishment was to wander the world until the Second Coming of Christ. Over the centuries various people have been supposedly identified as the same man reappearing again and again.

Persian rugs may have up to 100 tufts per square centimetre

Persia, India and China have always produced some of the most beautifully worked rugs and carpets in the world, with elaborate, traditional patterns that go back hundreds of years. In some places they are still made by hand, with the tufts carefully tied in to each vertical warp before the next horizontal weft is pressed up. In the very best rugs, which come from Persia, now a region of Iran, there may be as many as 100 tufts per square centimetre. In many areas it was the tradition that girls would make rugs for their dowries.

Red hair was once used to make the best poison

People with red hair are often believed to have quick tempers and sometimes to be unreliable. These characteristics were put to good (or bad) use in the Middle Ages when superstitious people mixed curious witch's brews with the strangest of ingredients. Toads' and snakes' tongues and all kinds of weeds were used, but the best poisons were thought to need some of the hair from a red-haired person's head and even some of the fat from the dead body of such a person.

Prester John's kingdom has never been found

Prester John was believed to be a mighty Christian king who lived in about the 12th century AD. Some said that he lived in the east, beyond Persia, others that he lived in Ethiopia. All agreed that he was fabulously rich and wise. Sadly, the many stories about him are probably untrue. In about 1165, a man who signed himself Presbyter (which means priest) Joannes sent a letter to the Emperor of Byzantium in which he described his wealth and power and the peace, humility and goodness of his kingdom. The letter was intended as a mockery of the pomp and arrogance of the European rulers of the time and was a forgery by an anonymous writer.

The swastika is an ancient symbol of good fortune

The swastika is best known as the symbol of Nazi Germany during the Second World War. 'Swastika' comes from the ancient Sanskrit word, *svasti*, which means 'good fortune'. The sign was originally used as a charm to ward off evil and to symbolise the power of the Sun, lightning and the four winds. The swastika has been used in many parts of the world since very ancient times. It is also known as the 'fylfot'.

A 12th century mosaic from Turkey.

The 'Peach Melba' is named after an Australian opera-singer

The famous opera-singer Dame Nelly Melba was really called Helen Mitchell. Her father was an Australian brick-maker, but she went to Europe to study singing with Verdi and Gounod. One day, after she had finished her lunch at the Savoy in London, she gave the chef two tickets for Wagner's opera Lohengrin. He was so pleased that he immediately came up with a sugary confection of peaches, ice-cream and raspberry sauce, called the Peach Melba.

Dr Bowdler took out the naughty bits from Shakespeare

We use the verb 'Bowdlerise' to mean removing offensive passages from works of literature. We have borrowed the word from Dr Thomas Bowdler, an Englishman born in 1754. He loved the plays of Shakespeare, but thought parts of them were rude and 'unfit to be read by a gentleman in the company of ladies'. For this reason he set about cutting chunks he considered unsuitable from the playwright's works. In fact, it was his sister who did the most drastic cutting; Thomas was often responsible for putting back some of what she had cut.

Mr Biro invented the ball-point

A Hungarian proof-reader called Laszlo Biro who wearied of having to keep filling his fountain pen was the man who patented the ubiquitous ball-point - often called 'biro'. He became a fugitive from the Nazis, and fled first to Argentina, then to England, where he produced special high-altitude non-leaking 'writing-sticks' for the RAF.

The Earl of Sandwich did not invent the sandwich

It is often claimed that the Earl of Sandwich was the first man to make a sandwich. He was an all-night gambler, and in 1762, after a night's gambling, told a man-servant to bring him some beef between two slices of bread. Although the sandwich obviously gained its name from the Earl, it is known to have been eaten by Roman soldiers nearly two thousand years before.

The bayonet was invented by French soldiers

The bayonet originated from the French town of Bayonne in about 1640, when musketeers from that town charged their enemy with knives stuck in the ends of their firearms. The charge was so successful that a French officer ordered a number of round-handled swords to be made specially so that they would fit into the musket muzzles. This was the first 'plug' bayonet. With this type the musket could not be fired while the sword was in place. The 'ring' or 'socket' bayonet that fitted around the muzzle was introduced in about 1670 or 1680. The Duke of Marlborough made great use of ring bayonets in the English campaigns against the French.

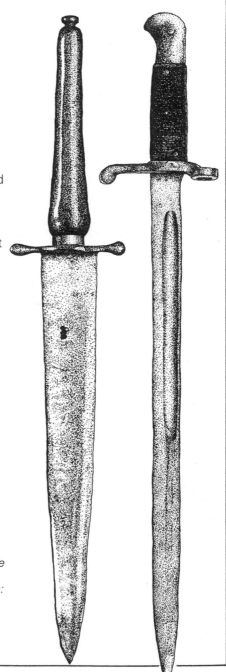

Right: *A plug bayonet of the seventeenth century. The disadvantage of this was that while it was in place, the musket could not be fired. Far right: A nineteenth-century sword bayonet, which fitted around the musket's nozzle allowing it to be fired with the bayonet in position.*

The Gatling gun was invented by a physician

R. J. Gatling was a physician in the Union Army during the American Civil War. Although his career was devoted to caring for the sick, he was the man who patented the machine-gun (or gatling). His first model could fire 350 shots per minute - almost six per second - although the US Chief of Ordinance pronounced himself unimpressed. Later the gun was improved to fire 1,200 rounds per minute.

There was a machine gun with special shot for 'good' and 'bad' enemies

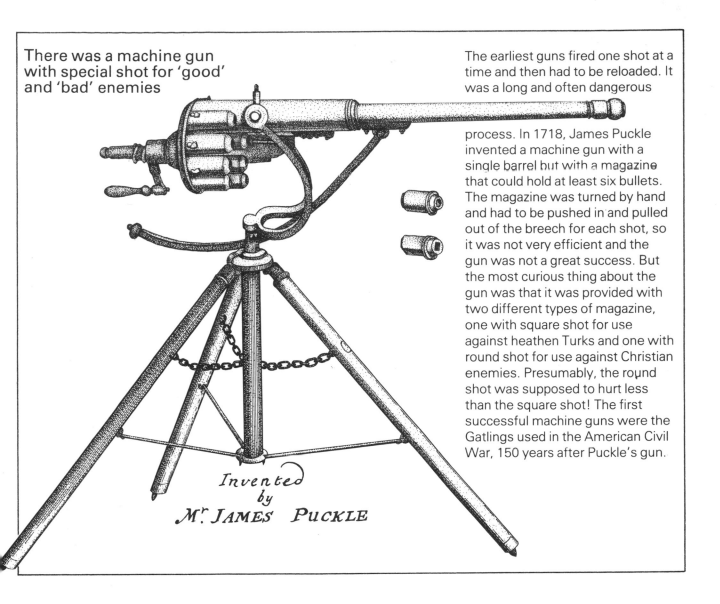

Invented by
Mʳ JAMES PUCKLE

The earliest guns fired one shot at a time and then had to be reloaded. It was a long and often dangerous process. In 1718, James Puckle invented a machine gun with a single barrel but with a magazine that could hold at least six bullets. The magazine was turned by hand and had to be pushed in and pulled out of the breech for each shot, so it was not very efficient and the gun was not a great success. But the most curious thing about the gun was that it was provided with two different types of magazine, one with square shot for use against heathen Turks and one with round shot for use against Christian enemies. Presumably, the round shot was supposed to hurt less than the square shot! The first successful machine guns were the Gatlings used in the American Civil War, 150 years after Puckle's gun.

'Teddy' bears are named after a President of the United States

Toy bears were probably popular long before the 20th century but 'teddy' bears got their name from Theodore, or 'Teddy', Roosevelt, President of the United States of America from 1901 to 1909. Roosevelt was particularly fond of bear-hunting and on one occasion returned from an expedition with a live baby bear. The newspapers picked up the story and for ever afterwards children's toy bears were called 'Teddy' bears. Roosevelt was a very popular president who did a great deal to make America an international power during his term of office.

A frustrated king gave his name to a locked-up drinks cabinet

A modern 'tantalus' is a special case for decanters of whisky, port, sherry or some other alcoholic drink. The case is locked in such a way that you can see the decanters but cannot get at them. It is named after King Tantalus who was a king of Lydia in Greek mythology. He was punished for revealing the secrets of the gods to mankind and was forced to stand in a river. There was a bunch of grapes hanging from a tree above his head. He could never quite reach the grapes when he was hungry and every time he wanted a drink the water sank away. It was a very 'tantalising' torture.

'Big Ben' is not the name of a clock but the name of the bell inside

One of the most famous clocks in the world is the Great Westminster Clock, in London, better known as Big Ben. The clock itself was designed by E. B. Denison, later Lord Grimthorpe, and erected in 1859. It has four faces, each six metres (twenty feet) across, and a pendulum more than four metres (thirteen feet) long with a two second beat. The clock is accurate to within one-fifth of a second in every 24 hours. It is, in fact, the 13-ton bell that is properly called 'Big Ben', after the man who was Commissioner of Works at the time, Sir Benjamin Hall.

275

Fish that are mounted in cases on the wall are usually only plaster casts

When small animals are mounted by taxidermists in museums, their skins are usually filled with artificial materials to keep the original shape. It is difficult to do the same with the skin, or scales, of the fish. For one thing, the original colours fade as soon as the fish is taken out of the water. Therefore a plaster cast is often taken of the body of the fish. This is then carefully painted and the original head and tail are sometimes attached to it. Plaster casts are often used for snakes as well.

What is rude in one country, may be polite in another

Most of us shake hands when we meet someone but in India people place the tips of their own fingers together and touch them to their own foreheads as a sign of greeting. Some of us kiss people we know well, on the cheek or lips, but the eskimoes and Polynesians rub noses instead of kissing. The Polynesians sit down rather than stand up when an important visitor arrives and in Burma people take off their shoes rather than their hat when they go into a church or someone's house.

British stamps do not bear the name of their country

The first postage stamps in the world were introduced by Rowland Hill in Britain in 1840. They were a one penny black and a two penny blue, each with the head of Queen Victoria shown on them but no mention of the country. Since they were the only stamps in existence, they had no need to mention the country. When other countries also began to introduce stamps, they put their names on the design but British stamps continued to leave their name off.

Mickey Mouse is more than 60 years old

Walt Disney created his first great cartoon character, Mickey Mouse, in the cartoon film *Steamboat Willie*, in 1928. He went on to make full-length cartoon films, the first of which was *Snow White and the Seven Dwarfs*, in 1938. He created many other famous cartoon films, including *Bambi, Pinnochio, One Hundred and One Dalmatians* and the musical *Fantasia*. He also made real life films about animals in the wild, such as *The Vanishing Prairie* and *The Living Desert*. When Walt Disney died in 1966 Mickey Mouse was still his favourite character. Another of his most famous creations was Disneyland in Los Angeles, which is probably the most successful amusement park in the world.

Punch and Judy shows have been performed for 400 years

The Punch and Judy puppet show has been popular since the character of Punch as a mischief-maker was established in 16th century Italian plays. From Italy, they moved on to France and England in the 17th century. According to the story. Punch

Troubadours often invented songs as they went along

Troubadours were originally wealthy young men from the south of France, at some time between the 11th and 14th centuries. The word comes from the Provençal or southern word *trobar*, which meant 'to invent' or 'to find', for the troubadours often made up their own songs as they went along. Sometimes they were songs of love and sometimes of knights and war. Similar poets in the north and centre of France were known as trouvères, from the northern word *trouver*, which also means 'to find'. Many of the songs that the troubadour sang were handed down from generation to generation and have now become familiar folk-songs, popular around the world.

strangles his child out of jealousy and is beaten by his wife Judy. He then beats her to death as well. He is arrested, put in prison and escapes. After many other adventures he goes free (although in some versions he is eventually slain). Although he is a bully, he usually gets the better of life and his sense of humour and fun generally make people forgive him despite all his faults.

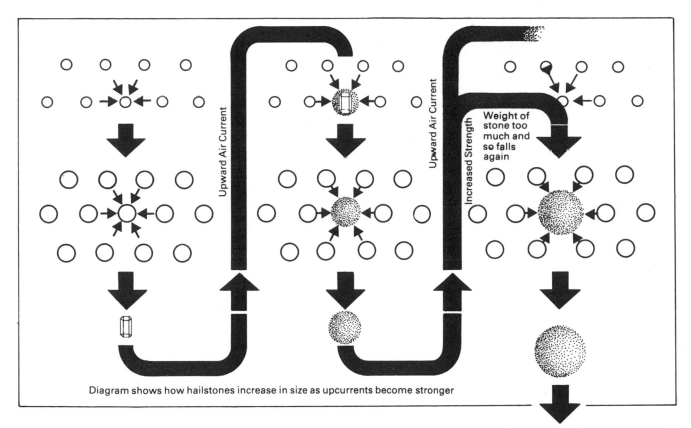

Upward Air Current

Upward Air Current

Increased Strength

Weight of stone too much and so falls again

Diagram shows how hailstones increase in size as upcurrents become stronger

Hailstones begin small and end up large

The diagram above shows how a hailstone is formed. A small frozen particle of water falls through the cold atmosphere. As it falls it attracts other particles until a crystal is formed. The crystal acts as a nucleus and is swept back upwards into the colder atmosphere where more frozen particles are attracted to it. The size of the eventual hailstone depends on how many times it is swept upwards. The more this happens, the larger will the hailstone be.

Cicadas sleep for 17 years and wake for only 5 weeks of their life

Cicadas are the insects you may have heard in the evening, clicking and shrilling when everything else is quiet. The male cicadas make this noise by vibrating pairs of membranes underneath their bodies. There are about 2000 species of cicada. One of them is very strange. When born, it burrows into the ground and sucks away at the root of a tree, virtually asleep, for 17 years. This is the 'nymph' stage of its life. Then it wakes up, climbs the tree and appears as a fully-grown, winged cicada to enjoy just five weeks of real life. Another type spends 13 years underground. The ancient Greeks used to eat cicadas, and in many countries they have also been kept as pets.

Dry rot is not necessarily dry

Many old houses suffer from what is known as 'dry rot'. This is a fungus that feeds on timber, making it so weak and brittle that eventually it falls down. It will inevitably occur in a damp house but it will also grow on what appears to be dry wood hence its name. The fungus can do this because it produces its own moisture once it has got started, and once started it can spread very quickly.

There is a language that can be understood and spoken between all nations

Sign language is one way of communicating between people of different countries but it can often lead to misunderstandings and it is not very satisfactory for complex transactions. In 1889, Ludovic Zamenhof published an entirely new 'International Language' under the pseudonym, Dr Esperanto, which means 'someone who hopes'. Esperanto, as the language came to be known, borrowed words from many different languages and it is thought to take far less time to learn than any other single language. An Esperanto Organisation was formed with its headquarters in Rotterdam and about 50 nations formed local organisations. However, despite the several million people who have learnt to speak the language and the praise that was given to Zamenhof for his work. Esperanto has not yet become the accepted international language he planned it to be, probably because people are proud of their own language and prefer to use it.

A		B		C		D	
1		2		3		4	
E		F		G		H	
5		6		7		8	
I		J		K		L	
9		10					
M		N		O		P	
Q		R		S		T	
U		V		W		X	
Y		Z		TH			

Above: The dots of the Braille system and what they mean.

The Braille system was inspired by an army night-reading system

Louis Braille was born in 1809. His name has become famous for the system of raised dots that enables blind people to read and write. He himself was blinded at the age of three when playing with tools on his father's workbench and he went to a school for blind children. The only system of reading was by a cumbersome series of raised capital letters. In 1819, Charles Barbier, an officer in the artillery, invented a system of night-reading, using a combination of twelve raised dots that could be felt by soldiers and written by using a small punch. Braille knew of this and worked out an even more simple six-dot system, which was at first rejected by the organisers of the blind schools. They did not adopt Braille's system until 1854, two years after he died.

In ancient times, people used parts of the body to measure length

The Egyptians had a standard length from the elbow to the middle fingertip, a distance of about 45-50cm (17.6-19.7in), which they called a cubit. The width of the hand, or four fingers, was called a palm, or hand, and was about 9-10cm (3.5-3.9in). We still use 'hands' for measuring horses. The ancient 'fathom' was the distance between the outstretched arms and is still used for measuring depth at sea. It is about 1.8 metres (6 feet). The 'foot' may have come from an ancient Babylonian brick measurement but in fact it works out at the approximate length of a man's foot, about 30cm (12in). The 'finger' became an inch, which the Romans made into one-twelfth of a foot. In medieval England, three barleycorns laid end to end added up to one inch (2.54in). These and many other measurements were not standardised for a very long time.

A metre is one ten-millionth of one quarter of the circumference of the Earth

The French introduced the metric system after the French Revolution, at the end of the 18th century, when they were anxious to throw out all the old and inefficient ways. They wanted a universal and accurate form of measurement. Twelve scientists were appointed to organise such a system. They chose the 'metre' after the Greek word for measure, 'metron' and, for simplicity of multiplying and dividing, they decided to base it on the number 'ten'. One metre was to be one ten-millionth of one quarter of the circumference of the Earth measured from the Pole to the Equator. The old weights were also abandoned and grammes were introduced. Similarly, litres were introduced to replace the old liquid measures. At first people were reluctant to adopt the new measures but in 1840 they were made law and there were punishments for those who refused to use the metric system.

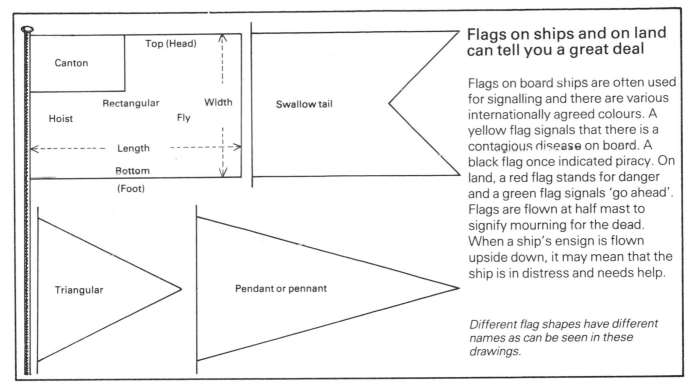

Flags on board ships are often used for signalling and there are various internationally agreed colours. A yellow flag signals that there is a contagious disease on board. A black flag once indicated piracy. On land, a red flag stands for danger and a green flag signals 'go ahead'. Flags are flown at half mast to signify mourning for the dead. When a ship's ensign is flown upside down, it may mean that the ship is in distress and needs help.

Different flag shapes have different names as can be seen in these drawings.

Barbers once did the work of surgeons and dentists

The traditional barber's pole, with its red and white spiral pattern, represented the patients' blood and the surgeon's bandage. Blood-letting, to let out 'bad' blood, used to be a common cure for many illnesses. This was always the job of the barber-surgeon. Many barbers were also the local dentist. A special Company of Barber Surgeons was founded in 1461 in England by King Edward IV. Barbers and surgeons were not properly separated into their special duties until the middle of the 18th Century, when surgery became a little more scientific.

Artificial limbs were in use a long time ago

Amputation, or cutting off a limb, is one of the oldest surgical operations. The earliest references to artificial limbs are in Hindu writings of about 1500 BC. One of the oldest artificial limbs in existence is a Roman leg made of bronze strips fitted to a central wooden stick. Peg legs were common in the Middle Ages but hinged legs were not developed until quite recently. Electronics is now used to transmit signals from surviving muscles to artificial hands, feet, arms and legs.

King Harold may not have been killed by an arrow in the eye

When Duke William of Normandy defeated the Saxon King Harold of England at the Battle of Hastings in 1066, it was believed that Harold was killed by an arrow in the eye. On the Bayeux Tapestry, which depicts the Norman Conquest, there is a man being pierced by an arrow and a Latin inscription saying that the king has now been killed. But another report of the battle indicates that Harold was probably cut down later by a Norman sword and it is possible that in the Bayeux Tapestry Harold is not the man with the arrow in his eye. The Normans did, in fact, use arrows very effectively in the battle, firing volleys of them into the air to disconcert the enemy before charging them with their swords and spears. It was in this charge that Harold was probably killed.

Animals helped win a battle

In 1814 a small band of Chilean patriots had been struggling for four years to free their country from Spanish rule. They were led by a certain Bernardo O'Higgins. The Spanish poured men and arms into Chile, and it seemed that the patriots were fighting a lost cause, especially when O'Higgins was wounded by a Spanish bullet. However, he ordered his men to round up as many animals as they could find. The herd of animals – sheep, mules, goats and dogs – were scared out of their wits by the Chileans and charged off towards the Spanish. The Spanish had to rush aside and let the Chileans escape behind the charging herd, into the mountains where they could continue their campaign. There, they reorganised their forces and enlisted new recruits to their cause. Three years later, the Spanish were finally defeated by O'Higgins' army and he became the first ruler of the independent Chile.

The iron maiden killed people

An 'iron maiden' was an agonising instrument of torture used in the Middle Ages. It was an upright box with a hinged door. Sometimes the box was shaped like the case for an Egyptian mummy. Sharp spikes projected into the inside of the box from all sides and from the door as well, so that when the door was closed the spikes pressed into the victim who had been put in the box. He was usually left to die inside the iron maiden, for the spikes were carefully placed to press into the most painful parts of his body.

The dunce who was a brilliant scholar

A 'dunce' is someone who is stupid. There was a time in schools when a stupid child had to sit or stand in a corner and wear a long, pointed dunce's hat. But the name comes from a brilliant scholar of the 13th century. This was Duns Scotus, named after his birthplace in Dunse, Scotland. He challenged some of the Church's ideas and his followers were called Dunsers or Scotists. His ideas were rejected after his death by other scholars. They condemned his teaching as stupid, thus changing the meaning of 'dunce'.

Berserk was a mythological character

Berserk was a character out of Scandinavian mythology, who fought with savage ferocity but who never wore any armour. All he wore was a bear-coat or 'bear-sark', from which he probably got his name. Viking and Norse warriors copied his way of fighting, and used to gain their courage by eating certain plants which put them into a kind of trance. A warrior who had 'gone berserk' terrified the enemy as he fought with such ferocity and was in such a state of excitement that he would scarcely feel any wounds.

'Manna' kept the Jews alive in the Wilderness

In the Old Testament of the Bible, it says that the Israelites ate 'manna' when they were wandering in the Wilderness of Sinai after Moses led them out of Egypt. This 'manna' tasted like honey-flavoured wafers and lay on the ground in the morning like a sprinkling of frost. They could gather as much as they needed. 'Manna' may have been one of two things. It could have been the white sap of the tamarisk tree which drips to the ground or a particular type of lichen that grows in certain parts of the desert.

The name 'tweed' for cloth was a mistake

Tweed is a strong, fairly rough cloth, which usually has at least two colours in the same yarn. It is generally made in Scotland, where the original word for it was 'twill', which meant 'double threaded' and was a cloth woven in diagonal lines. 'Twill' gradually came to be pronounced 'tweel' in Scottish and it is said that 'tweel' was misread as 'tweed' by a London merchant. Since the cloth was made near the River Tweed, in any case, the name stuck. Tweed is also made on the islands of the Hebrides in Scotland.

A 'white elephant' was originally a present

The King of Siam had a very clever way of getting rid of courtiers who were bothering him. He gave them a gift of a white elephant. These white, or albino, elephants were rare in Siam and it was the law that they should be treated with great respect and fed only the very best of everything. This was, of course, very expensive and the courtier often preferred to leave the court in a hurry rather than accept such a gift. As a result of this trick, the phrase 'a white elephant' has come to mean a splendid but useless gift.

The myrrh and frankincense that the three wise men brought with their gold to Bethlemen, were types of resin

When the three wise men came from the east to visit Jesus as soon as he was born, they brought gifts of gold and frankincense and myrrh. Frankincense literally means 'pure' incense. It was a gum from certain trees that grew in Southern Arabia and Somalia and it was used in ceremonies by many ancient civilisations. Myrrh was also a type of resin that was used in perfumes and incense. Both frankincense and myrrh were considered to be extremely valuable gifts, almost as costly as gold itself.

The Gospels were written shortly after the death of Christ

The four Gospels in the New Testament of the Bible were written by Matthew, Mark, Luke and John, who are sometimes called the four evangelists, or preachers. The word 'gospel' means 'good news' and the evangelists wrote down the good news of Christ's life for later Christians to hear. Each Gospel is a little different in style and character. St Mark's was the first to be written, about 30 years after Christ's death, to encourage the Christians during the Roman persecutions. Matthew and Luke wrote their Gospels about 10 or 20 years later and took several of their stories from Matthew's Gospel. St John wrote his Gospel in about AD 90 or 100.

Hitch-hikers used to travel by horse

Hitch-hiking is a popular way for young people to travel long distances. They walk along the roadside and catch lifts from passing cars and trucks. Sometimes they simply stand with a sign saying where they are going and hope that passing motorists going in the same direction will stop and give them a lift. But hitch-hiking used to be the way in which two people could ride with one horse in 19th century America. One man would ride ahead an agreed distance and then hitch his horse to a tree and walk, or hike, on from there. Meanwhile his fellow, who had started on foot, walked until he reached the horse and then rode on, past his companion, until he himself was some way ahead. Then he, too, hitched the horse and started walking again. Thus they passed each other at regular intervals and each got turns at riding – unless someone else stole the horse in the middle!

Cynics were said to be 'dog-like'

It is very easy to be cynical, to criticise other people's good intentions and to find fault with everything they do or think. A little bit of cynicism, not to accept things too readily, may be good but too much can be unpleasant. The word comes from the Latin for 'dog-like', a variation on the Latin word 'canis', which means a 'dog'. It was used to describe the Greek philosopher Diogenes, who tried to live as simple a life as possible to show how much he criticised the standards and ways of life of the people of his time. The people were annoyed and said that the kind of life he lived was no better than a dog's. But Diogenes laughed at this and replied that, if he was a dog, then he was the watchdog of public morality.

Monks stay in and Friars go out!

Monks are religious men who live together in a monastery, working and praying and obeying a set of very strict rules, cut off from the rest of the world. The word 'monk' comes from the Greek word for 'alone'. One of the most famous

monks was St Benedict who was born in about AD 480 and founded the Benedictine Order of monks. The Benedictines have strict rules, but the Cistercians have even stricter rules of behaviour. In contrast to the isolation of monks, friars go out into the world to help others, teaching and preaching and helping the sick. The name 'friar' really means 'brother'. The Franciscan friars were started by St Francis of Assisi at the beginning of the 13th century, shortly before St Dominic founded the Dominicans.

Freemasons were originally stonemasons

There are groups of freemasons in many countries. Each group is known as a 'lodge'. The masons raise money for the poor and the aged, for schools for orphans and to help the widows of members who have died. The idea began with the guilds, or groups, of stonemasons in the Middle Ages. As they moved about to different places of work, they formed new groups to pass on and keep secret their methods of working and their traditions. In time, they opened their groups to others who were not originally stonemasons but the traditions of secrecy and helping each other continued.

The third president of the United States was known as 'The moonshine philosopher'

Thomas Jefferson, the third president of the United States, was always busy. He designed his own house at Monticello, Virginia, and filled it with gadgets he had dreamed up, including self-opening doors, a fridge, a perpetual clock and a device for measuring how far he had walked. He founded the University of Virginia, and was the author of the Declaration of Independence.

Abraham Lincoln received eighty death threats before he was shot

After the assassination of United States president Abraham Lincoln, eighty letters threatening his life were discovered in his desk. It is reported that the very morning of his death he said 'I believe there are men who want to take my life. And I have no doubt they will do it.' He asked the Secretary of War for a special bodyguard, but the incompetent guard he was given was having a drink when the assassin John Wilkes Booth shot him in his box at Ford's Theatre, Washington.

A record-breaking pilot crashed in mysterious circumstances

Amy Johnson, the British pilot who once flew solo to Australia without a radio, crashed in the Thames Estuary in ordinary weather. Although she was a skilled pilot, and had taken off alone, she crashed 100 miles off her course, and was seen to have a passenger on board when she landed in the icy River Thames.

The 'Father of Clowns' had his head cut off before burial

The famous clown Giuseppe Grimaldi was also a dentist, ballet-master and renowned acrobat. He was known for his morbid personality, which explains his name 'Old Grim'. 'The Father of Clowns' was so frightened of being buried alive that he demanded that his head be cut off before he was buried. Before he died, Grimaldi once faked his death to see what his family would do. One son warily went into mourning, but another incautiously danced round the corpse joyfully. The one was left money, the other was not!!

The Marseillaise was written in return for a bottle of wine

Claude Rouget de Lisle, a captain of sappers stationed near Strasbourg, was asked by the mayor to write a patriotic hymn and offered a bottle of wine as payment. De Lisle came up with words and music which were called 'The War Song of the Army on the Rhine', aimed defiantly at the advancing armies of Austria and Prussia. Later, as a volunteer citizen army was on the march from Marseilles to Paris, they picked up his song, giving it its popular title. Three years on from that the French revolutionaries adopted the Marseillaise officially as their national anthem. Ironically, Rouget de Lisle was himself a Royalist who narrowly missed being guillotined.

Joan of Arc was burnt for wearing men's clothes

Born of a wealthy farming family - not peasant-stock - in Lorraine, Joan of Arc claimed to have had visions of the Archangel Michael, St Catherine and St Margaret since the age of thirteen. In 1429 she said they told her she must save the people of France from the wicked English and from Burgundy. Dubious at first, she finally took up arms and led the French troops to the re-capture of Orleans. She then had the weak dauphin crowned King Charles VII of France at Rouen, and proceeded to try to capture Paris. Her voices had warned she would be captured - and she was. The troops of Burgundy took her prisoner, and sold her to the English for 10,000 golden pounds. The English then tried her in a church court, accusing her of heresy and witchcraft. They forced her into making a confession, and sentenced her to life imprisonment.
She had to promise to stop wearing men's clothing. However, her captors had confiscated all her women's clothes, so they had an excuse to burn her at the stake, at Rouen in 1431.

Vidocq was the world's first private detective

Ex-actor and thief, Francois Eugene Vidocq, who was born in Arras, France in 1775, became the world's first private detective. The police first called on his services as an informer. He later used his extensive knowledge of the criminal underworld when he formed the famous French Sûreté, along with four other ex-criminals. They then set about pioneering methods of detection which included finger-printing, handwriting analysis (or graphology) and scientific investigation of firearms (ballistics). In 1832 he formed a private detective agency, but the Sûreté, which he himself had helped create in 1792, closed it down because it was too successful. They imagined he was planning crimes simply to embarrass them.

Talleyrand always knew when to change sides

Charles de Talleyrand-Périgord was born in 1754. He was lame, witty, cunning and immoral. King Louis XVI made him Bishop of Autun, and he was luckily away in England on a diplomatic mission when the French Revolution broke out in 1789. He went briefly to the United States, but then returned to France, made his peace with the new government, and became Foreign Minister under the Directory. He kept a foot in both camps during the coup which made Napoleon First Consul, and when the Corsican made himself Emperor, Talleyrand was appointed Grand Chamberlain. When he realised Napoleon was on the way out, Talleyrand began building bridges with the Bourbon royal house, and helped make their path back to the throne a smooth one. In this way he ensured that he retained office.

The wheatear has a white rear

A wheatear's name has nothing to do with wheat or ear. It is a small bird that travels between Africa, where it spends the winter, and Greenland and Arctic North America, where it breeds in summer. The 3200 kilometre (2000 mile) long return flight from Greenland to Portugal (where it first stops) takes it about 48 hours, during which the bird loses as much as half its body weight. The male has a grey back and a black strip on either side of its head. The female is light brown, but the little bird is primarily distinguished by its white belly, rump and upper tail, from which it gets its name – white rear. This eventually became shortened to Wheatear.

The largest steam engines were used in the USA

United States' steam engines were the largest because their routes were the longest and they needed a great deal of fuel and water. Some had 14-wheel tenders with 28 tonnes of coal and 95,000 litres (20,897.5 gallons) of water. In the very largest, the engines were articulated, or jointed, with two separate engines to make it easier to go round bends. The Union Pacific's 'Big Boy' was the largest articulated engine ever built. It was used for freight in mountainous areas and weighed about 600 tonnes (590 tons).

Superstitions about cats

To sailors, a black cat is a sure sign of foul weather ahead but tortoiseshell cats are considered lucky.

My Own Fascinating Facts

My Own Fascinating Facts

My Own Fascinating Facts

My Own Fascinating Facts

My Own Fascinating Facts

My Own Fascinating Facts

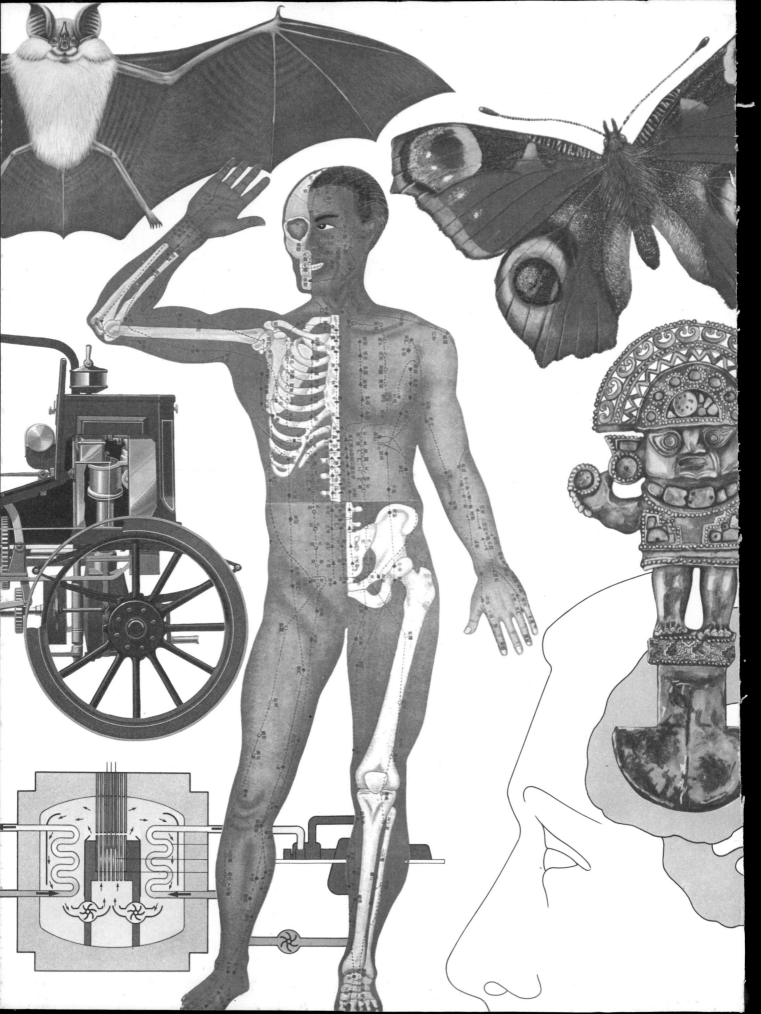